Nick Kraeer

A DEPLORABLE CAD

The Worst Of Men Chasing The Best Of Women

SIGMA WOLF

A DEPLORABLE CAD

THE WORST OF MEN CHASING
THE BEST OF WOMEN

NICK KRAUSER

A Deplorable Cad, Volume 2 of the Nick Krauser memoir, First Edition.

www.krauserpua.com

ACKNOWLEDGEMENTS

I greatly underestimated how much blood, sweat, and tears would go into writing a four-volume memoir of my sexual escapades. Back when I began, in early 2014, I thought I could whip them out fast. Oh how wrong I was! Now that three volumes are completed (and the fourth is a completed early draft) I can appreciate just how invaluable the help of others has been. For this volume, A Deplorable Cad, I'd like to specifically thank the following people.

My dozens of Skype conversations with Roy really helped tease out the stories and themes, and his final turn-in was a good manuscript that greatly sped up the process. When I embarked on my extensive chapter-by-chapter rewrite, Brian was a great help in reading each chapter as I completed it, feeding back in real time. Sarah and Casey came to my rewritten manuscript and their extensive editorial input helped polish it further. As a final exercise I sent the manuscript to this book's main supporting character, Jimmy, who provided me with an insider's feedback on the events described and was also gracious enough to tolerate those sections where I present him unfavourably.

I also extend thanks to Cristian and Alexey for their artwork and layout design respectively, and to Davorin for his cover design.

This book has consumed the greater part of a year to write and it's been great fun to do so. I take great satisfaction from recording for posterity the greatest period of my life so far. Hopefully the 165,000 words that follow have done justice to the good friends, good girls, and good times I encountered along the way. As ever I appreciate feedback on my writing at my blog krauserpua.com. I still have one volume left to write and I'd like to make it as good as I'm able.

INTRODUCTION

I n the spring of 2011 I was thirty-six years old and life was good. I was living in a huge house in the nicest part of North London with ten of my best friends. Every day I'd sleep in till late, wander down into the communal areas and 'shoot the shit' (as Americans would say) without any job, commitment, or entanglement interfering with my day. When the weather was nice we'd lie on hammocks in the tree-lined back garden, soaking up the sun, and reading pulp fiction. Sometimes we'd take the Number 13 bus into Central London and hit on girls.

We were "daygamers." Pick-up artists. Each of us had developed an obsession with chasing skirt, treating it as a skill to be learned, honed, and eventually mastered. We'd moved into our Hampstead mansion to create the best possible environment to focus on this goal. There were the old hands who'd been rattling new girls for years – Tony and Jimmy – and also the new kids who were still flush with excitement at the endless potential our quest seemed to offer. Together we called ourselves *Rock Solid Game* and made money on the side teaching other men what we'd learned so far.

Two years earlier I'd been a completely different man; socially awkward, bitter, and lonely. My wife had left me after a nine-year relationship, and I'd turned to the underground art of "game" to try to find a new girlfriend. Volume One of this memoir, *Balls Deep*, charts my path in those first two years. It's mostly a story of misery and desperate hope. Judging from book reviews, readers liked the sheer bleakness of it all.

By 2011, after multiple mental breakdowns and an ungodly amount of time on the streets approaching pretty women, I'd had a year of consistent success. I was a long way from banging supermodels, but I'd been laid with a pretty new girl every month for almost a year and had just slotted a bona fide Russian catwalk model who was now angling to become my girlfriend. My life was changing. I felt like I was on the cusp of a new chapter – I no longer merely fantasised about becoming a "player." The fantasy had taken shape and was now a realistic goal.

This volume is the story of the next two years. It's the story of ten men with nothing better to do than chase skirt, each with his own personality quirks and with different demons chasing him away from the normal life of office, wife, and mortgage. You'll see the beginnings of "daygame" as a way of life soon to be practiced by hundreds of other men not dissimilar from yourself. You'll read of close friendships and unexpected betrayals as each man tried to balance his moral code against his own personal quest, all the time struggling under the immense emotional pressure exerted by the "players journey."

We moved into "Château RSG" because we'd become tired of reading adventure stories. We wanted *our own* adventures. We wanted to travel the world, drink the bars dry, and bang the hottest girls we could get in front of.

This is how I became an International Man Of Mystery. This is how I came to *Live The Dream*. It's rather more squalid than you may expect. I hope you like it because there's plenty more where this came from!

Nick Krauser
Moscow, September 2016

Living the dream

Rock Solid Game

ROCK SOLID GAME

Jimmy Jambone thumped the long dining room table and said, with an air of finality, "We will call it Château RSG." As if defying anyone else to disagree, he crossed his long, gangly legs at the ankles and leant so far back in his chair he was almost horizontal.

We liked the name. It was grandiose, mythological, and it spoke to an inherent style. Everything we did was designed to make ourselves larger than life, both to others and in our own minds. Thus we'd hit on a name for our rickety, old house in Hampstead, London, a cavernous former residential care home that had leaking pipes, a collapsing roof and which frequently flooded during heavy rain.

"RSG" came from abbreviating the name of the pick-up coaching company Jimmy had created: *Rock Solid Game*. Back in 2008 Richard LaRuina's *PUA Training* company was the market leader in London and Jimmy had gone along as a student to check it out. He'd been thoroughly unimpressed and considered his own game tighter than every coach bar Rob Beckster. In his typically self-congratulatory style he'd decided, "I can do better than them."

So Jimmy hunted around the local PUA forums and arranged meet-ups with fellow aspiring pick-up artists until he'd hand-picked the founding members of *Sarge School;* Tony T, Diamond, Ace, Tomas, and himself. The new group soon built an underground reputation for doing free boot-camps every other month, and by the time I encountered them in the summer of 2009 they were still only charging £99 for two days of coaching. Sarge School would expand to bring in Johnny Wisdom, Mick, Fernando, Lee, and eventually myself. By late 2010 we'd re-branded as Rock Solid Game and presented ourselves as a hybrid of a dating company and a group of rock stars.

Diamond had dropped out, and Ace left for university in his native Poland. The rest of us were now in a house meeting, sitting around a long table in the lounge listening to Jimmy. It was September 2010, and we'd all moved into the big London house a fortnight earlier.

Chateau RSG as drawn by Julia

House meetings were as common as a sighting of Lord Lucan, but there'd been a big house party the night before, and we'd all felt the reluctant call of duty to clean up. As the clock ticked on to twelve and normal productive members of society took lunch breaks from their office jobs, the reprobates of RSG emerged one by one from the deep, dark recesses of the house. I suspect several of us lay awake in bed all morning rather than go downstairs and confront the task of cleaning up the mess. It was an entirely different way of life to my previous corporate existence.

Lee was sifting through some lecture notes for an accounting degree he'd started, while Mick picked at his toenails. Tony was at the head of the table, taking slow deep breaths and responding to everything in slow motion as he was wont to do. I was in the kitchen fiddling with the coffee machine and swearing loudly after stepping barefoot onto some mouldy lettuce that had been knocked off the bench where Lee had left it three days earlier.

We all sat around the table and agreed to Jimmy's suggestion: We'd call our home Château RSG.

The grand-daddy of the PUA industry is Erik Von Markovich, better known as Mystery. Although not the first man to systematise and teach seduction (Ross Jeffries and R. Don Steele were first to market), it was Mystery who shaped the industry into the form we all recognise today. His first book *Mystery Method* is a coherent, balanced, and beautifully presented total package that draws heavily upon cold-calling sales theory and, oddly, dog training manuals. It displays a degree of rigour and comprehensiveness that earlier writers couldn't match. He was also the first to move pick-up coaching out of the seminar room and into the live environment of cafes, bars and nightclubs. Mystery invented the "boot camp" weekend in which students are taught early-evening in a seminar room and then taken in-field to watch coaches approach women in bars, then experiment themselves.

However, the main reason Mystery established himself as the premier pick-up artist of the 2000-2008 era was due to him befriending Neil Strauss, a *Rolling Stone* writer who would write the seminal *The Game* memoir where he featured Mystery as his mentor and main supporting character. That book was a *New York Times* bestseller, thrusting Mystery's persona into the mainstream.

If there's one thing Erik Von Markovich is absolutely excellent at, it's gaming other men to fuel his own rise. He even managed to get a VH1 reality TV show called *The Pickup Artist* that ran two seasons.

Neil Strauss's book retold the story of his entering the then underground world of pick-up artists in Los Angeles. Mystery spotted

Neil's utility as a talented writer with good connections and quickly brought him into his world. They'd then feed off each other. Neil would learn Mystery's game while Mystery leveraged Neil's LA connections to get into better parties and find richer students. It's a great book, and I thoroughly recommend it. Prior to the advent of YouTube as a platform for small PUA businesses to market to prospective clients, *The Game* was every PUA's gateway drug into the community.

The centrepiece of *The Game* is when Neil and Erik decide to rent a huge mansion in Beverly Hills where a dozen PUAs would live together and hit on girls en masse. They dubbed it "Project Hollywood" and the legend was born. It's a habit in the seduction community to invent grandiloquent narratives for occasions when normal people would use everyday words. Project Hollywood was really just a flophouse for male virgins, but Neil's writing had immortalised it. I mean, who *wouldn't* want to live in a Beverly Hills mansion with a load of other guys, all of whom were going out to hit on women? Compare that to sitting alone on your sofa in a shit-box studio apartment watching *The Sopranos* on DVD.

I'd watched the show and read the book back in early 2009 when I was a nervous office drone first toying with the idea of becoming a pick-up artist. For me Project Hollywood was living the dream; a gang of expert seducers and hot bitches every night. Later, RSG felt like a rat pack when we all met up on the weekend to teach boot-camps. We'd lounge in a big private room in the East Rooms or Milk & Honey drinking beer, joking around, waiting for the students to show. It was the camaraderie I'd missed since starting my finance career in London and brought into sharp relief just how uncool my pre-game friends were (and of course, myself too).

The idea of doing a similar project sounded cool; get a big house in London, give it a great name, and move in a bunch of guys. Not only would it be fantastic motivation to build and refine our own Game, it would also bring the rat pack together on a daily basis. We figured we could do Project London better than the original Hollywood version.

The dream came true in September 2010.

Jimmy and Tony were clearly the leaders of RSG and not just because they were the founding members. Both had amassed immense experience picking up girls. Jimmy had rattled over a hundred girls since going to university. A phenomenal number for late-90s and early-00s England that simply didn't have the "hook-up culture" of modern USA universities and metropolitan bar scenes. He also had high standards, which really depresses a man's lay count.

Jimmy was a smart methodical man in all areas of social dynamics, and he'd work a bar with the same precision as Mystery advised. At university his creativity and strength of character had established him

Mick and Jimmy looking for sets

as leader of his small pack of bad lads, then he'd take them out drinking, causing a ruckus, then see which girls gave him the eye. In many respects, RSG was just a more grown-up version of his bad lads gang.

Tony was a sniper with women and deeply immersed in romantic fiction. He worked out, was an excellent salsa dancer, and dressed like a modern-day Valentino. He'd shaped himself into the smouldering masculine archetype women fantasise about while reading novels. He didn't like cold approach but had learned how to ease into sets in bars or on the dance floor. Often, the women came to him. By the time I met him he'd rattled three hundred women and kept copious notes on each seduction.

The penny wouldn't drop until much, much later, but the innovation of RSG's coaching was our ability to blend the mechanical systematic style of Mystery Method (via Jimmy) with the masculine polarity and seductive vibe of romance fiction (via Tony). The West Coast PUA movement that had inspired us was almost entirely the former, and it felt unbalanced and hollow.

RSG would grow and evolve. Ace brought in his love for the douchebag game of Hank Moody in *Californication*. I took a one-one-one with him in Jewel bar in early 2010 and was amazed with his playful arrogance. Midway through the evening, I brought over a pair of Chinese English girls who told me they worked in city law firms. Ace sat in a chair, legs wide open, a whiskey glass dangling precariously from his hand as I approached him.

"Who are these bitches?" he asked.

Both girls cracked up laughing and couldn't keep their hands off him the rest of the night. He never fucked them but it felt like watching a glitch in the matrix; he was so rude and they lapped it up. Later that night as we stood outside in the smoking area I said to him, "if there was anyone in RSG whose game I want to emulate, it's yours."

I'd learn incredible things from being surrounded 24/7 by talented seducers. "Project London" would be a pivotal period in my life and this is its story.

"We'll each have an en-suite room," Jimmy enthused over the phone, one month prior. "The location is amazing. It's probably a third of the market rate, with all utilities included." Standing in the tiny backyard of my grotty south London flat, I can't say I wasn't tempted.

"It's £300 a month."

"How?" I replied, "How is that possible?"

There had to be a catch. I lived in a ground floor one-bedroom flat in an old Victorian building, a thirty-minute walk from my office at St Paul's on the river. I had a lounge, bedroom, small dining room, kitchen, and tiny enclosed yard. It was £900 a month rent, and another £200 to pay off the council tax and bills.

This sounds OK, right? A decent-sized flat in a central area.

No. I lived in Kennington, which is next to Elephant & Castle. The price is low (for London) because it's a majority black and Muslim area and thus, absolutely disgusting. South London is like a suburb of Monrovia or Mogadishu. Every time I went outside I was reminded that my country was under foreign occupation, and I was being taxed to feed, cloth, house, and educate the invaders. It wasn't good for my vibe.

"Well, it's not exactly a typical renter's agreement," he responded. "We have to keep the gypsies and squatters out."

I don't like gypsies, their travelling parasitical lifestyle being very much at odds with the host culture in Britain. Vlad Dracul had the right idea when he invited them all to a feast then barred the door and torched the place with them still inside.

"You've got an hour to decide. The letting agency said they'll hold it for us until 4pm, and after that they are calling their waiting list. Really, you don't want to miss this."

I looked around my pokey little flat with its chipped paint, rising damp, and bad memories. It was where my ex-wife and I had first moved in together after the wedding and where things had all fallen apart three years later. Every room held memories that scaled the full range of emotion. There was the kitchen that she'd once lovingly kitted out with red pots, pans, and other assorted utensils, and which she'd used to cook me a different meal every evening, always delicious. Now it was bare and unused as I tended to get takeaways on my way home from work. Then there was the dining room with the walnut-shaped table around which my old friends would gather every second Thursday for a poker night, until they all quietly disassociated themselves from me after my divorce. I barely saw my old friends now. Rock Solid Game was my new social circle.

I visualized my walking home every evening from the investment bank where I worked, just across the Thames; a brisk half hour's walk ending at my 1930s-era apartment block, where I stepped in off the street and knocked on my door with an expectant smile. My wife would always be waiting for me, wearing her make-up and a beaming smile, and then stand on tiptoes to welcome me with a kiss before ushering me through to the dining room, where dinner was on the table. That felt great every single time.

But I also remembered making the same walk home in February 2009, after we'd separated, to find she'd come by in the afternoon to strip the apartment of every single one of her possessions, including all the cute accoutrements that had added life to it. She'd left £400 in an envelope with a note that it should cover the shared property she'd taken.

My flat now seemed like a dilapidated old prison. In spite of that, since becoming a player, I'd managed to fuck a bunch of new girls on the same bed (and couch, floor, and walnut-shaped table).

However, the apartment was part of my old life. I needed a clean break, so the decision wasn't hard to make. I tipped all my bank statements into a bag, grabbed my chequebook and passport then took a tube to the agency's offices in Islington. I was taking the room sight-unseen.

When I finally moved out a week later, as I closed the door for the final time, it felt like a grand symbolic gesture. I didn't so much feel that I was finishing a chapter of my life, more that I was opening a brand new book.

The Château RSG experiment owes its genesis to a side of Tony's character that always aggravated me. He's a cheapskate. In all the time I've known him, he's never had a real job. Every time we had team meals, he'd insist on a happy hour or a restaurant accepting the Taste London discount card. It jarred with me because I'd spent the last few years in a $100K office job and couldn't fully appreciate the minimalist lifestyle Tony adopted.

Like most things I'd learn about game and life, I resisted it in the beginning. Watching Tony live, I'd gradually pick up on his soft, easy-going vibe, his unwillingness to be rushed or buffeted, his deep passion for the emotional pay-off of seduction, and his continuous effort to challenge and suppress his own ego. Looking back I can appreciate the profound impact he had on my eventual success. But at the time I thought he was a sanctimonious cunt and we frequently clashed.

He's one of those guys who has always managed to get by on whatever crazy idea he's had, sometimes much better than merely getting by. He was a competitive salsa performer and milked his salsa classes as an "ecosystem" to score girls. Being a good-looking man who kept himself in shape at the gym helped, but he still had to be able to dance and make the whole thing work... which he did with great success.

Tony's a masculine guy and very much a hustler. He stretches each idea until it stops paying him or it starts to feel like work and then he finds something else. After the salsa became humdrum, he started selling himself to medical experiments – drug trials specifically. Those paid well, but it was feast or famine. We always knew he'd been at a trial because there'd suddenly be a plush leather recliner in his room, a new flat screen TV, and M&S food on his fridge shelf. Then he'd be back to scrutinising itemized bills at restaurants and clipping Asda coupons from newspapers to stock up on value-brand beans. Easy come, easy go. Tony very much lived for today.

At the time, I thought it was dissolution. Madness, even. I was brought up as a saver, not a spender. Later, as I continued to extricate myself from the rat race, I came to empathize with his laid-back attitude to money. Why wait for retirement before enjoying it?

I suppose the best way of summing up Tony is to say that he'll always look for the edge in any situation. If there's a dodge, he'll take it. He'll do virtually anything to make money, except getting a job. That mindset led him to hit upon the idea of property guardianship.

At any given time there are thousands of properties sitting empty in London. Perhaps the tenant has moved out and his replacement is delayed, perhaps the building is to be re-purposed and remains empty in the interim, or perhaps it's to be rebuilt but the developers need planning permission. Amazingly, for a country with so many vacant properties, England's legal system is very much biased *against* landlords. This has created an entire class of predatorial rent-seekers, be they gypsies or anarchists, who move in and steal the place.

There are all manner of sections, sub-sections, clauses and sub-clauses in English common law dating from hundreds of years ago which give squatters (i.e. Occupy Wall Street-type characters) legal rights that you wouldn't really expect. Often, there isn't much a landlord can do to kick him out. That makes it very easy for hustlers to move illegally into an empty property against the owner's permission, and as long as they don't cause any damage that can be construed as the criminal offence of "breaking and entering" the police can't evict them. The law deems it a civil not criminal matter, thus the landlord is on his own and a squatter's downside risk is capped at simply leaving the house and trying it on again elsewhere. Within the eviction process there are also all sorts of odd time limits and human rights laws that further complicate matters. In fact, in some cases, squatters who manage to stay put for ten years are awarded legal title to the property as "adverse possession" under the 2002 Land Registration Act.

The scammers in England, mostly Irish or Romanian gypsies, took this as a green light to break into empty properties, scam the legal system to get title to the property, sell it, make money and move on to the next score. Continental Europe's solution to the gypsy squatter problem has, historically, been murder and mass expulsion. Being fair play, cricket-loving English, we came up with a rather less extreme solution. It's called property guardianship.

Anyhow, I digress. There are specialist letting agencies who deal in vacant properties. They promise the owner that they'll take over management and then introduce tenants ("guardians") to live there. These tenants have agreed to restricted rights, including exclusions from all those laws that squatters take advantage of. An occupied building keeps the squatters out, both as a deterrent and also because if squatters enter, it's a clear case of criminal entry and thus the police can be involved.

The only downside for guardians is the lack of choice over where you stay. Many properties are shitholes and the plum properties go to those the agency know and trust. Tony and Jimmy were in that boat when they signed on with one of the two main agencies in London. They first moved in to a massive residential care home way out east. I visited Jimmy one evening and felt it was Project Auschwitz. It was good forty-five-minute ride on the Underground just to get a sniff of civilization from a Starbucks or Pret-A-Manger. Not only that, the place was horrible. It may have been massive, with about a hundred rooms in the whole place, but only a tiny part of it was habitable. The ceiling had fallen in and there was rubbish strewn all around.

I'm not joking when I tell you it reminded me of a Vice documentary I'd seen about Liberia – that tiny West African rat-infested toilet engaged in civil war. Part of the documentary visited the old Hilton Hotel of Monrovia. During European colonial times, it had had a top-quality restaurant, a glittering swimming pool and a roaring tourist trade, but since being handed back to the Africans it had become a crack den, not safe to walk through without armed guards. And that's exactly how Tony and Jimmy's first guardian property looked.

But that wasn't the worst aspect. Already in residence were six horrendous women. They were a mix of English, American, and Dutch girls, ranging in age from their mid- to late-twenties. They didn't like the idea of new tenants moving in to share their place, having nurtured the idea that it was *their place*. Rather than make the best of it with the new tenants, they wanted to drive Tony and Jimmy out. They started blanking them, locking doors on them, complaining all the time, and even hiding shower gel. It was *Mean Girls* in Zone Six.

Unfortunately for the girls, Jimmy and Tony are strong, resourceful characters, and they certainly weren't about to be pushed around by a pack of soap-stealing hags. The script was soon flipped. The boys stood their ground with cocky smirks, knowing this would prompt the girls to double down on their annoying antics to no avail.

It couldn't go on.

Everything came to a head when two of the girls brought their new boyfriends into the house; a pair of young black guys who dressed hip-hop. Had they met Tony and Jimmy randomly in a bar they'd probably all have had a couple of drinks together and shared a few stories. However, the girls set them up to fight by playing victim and asking their boyfriends to stand up for them.

Tony and Jimmy sussed immediately that the boyfriends weren't violent men. They were just full of bravado and ghetto talk, accompanied by a little bit of pushing and shoving. It was clear that that was as far as it was going to go. Tony would've probably de-escalated a confrontation but it was catnip for Jimmy. He loves provoking others and isn't averse to kicking off either, especially when drunk. So when the girls goaded their boyfriends into action, it didn't go as planned.

"You should leave this place. You're not wanted here."

"Sorry pal, I'm just not scared of you. You couldn't knock the skin off a rice pudding."

As the repartee flowed, the two boyfriends got so worked up they started shouting threats, informing Tony and Jimmy in vague terms about the many kinds of doom that would befall them if they didn't cease their taunting forthwith, retire to their rooms, and lock the doors. It was at that point that Tony got his mobile phone out and started recording the scene on video.

"Can you say that again? What did you say?" he inquired. The angry boyfriends told him in explicit terms that they intended to do him in.

"Perfect. And how would you do that exactly?" Tony asked, gaining a few more valuable seconds of angry footage. The impassioned threats went on for a while longer until the boyfriends could see that nothing positive was going to come out of the confrontation, and they slinked off.

The next day, Tony and Jimmy went back to the agency.

They sat down and, in grave tones, Jimmy said, "Look, we've had death threats from the boyfriends of the tenants."

"Yes," Tony added, "we feel unsafe there." As he showed the agent the video, Jimmy put his head in his hands as he tried to keep a straight face. "So you can see why we're upset. We fear our lives are in danger."

Jimmy looked up at the agent with a sigh, and then with just the right hint of desperation in his voice, asked, "Do you have any other property?"

Visions of litigation danced in front of the agent's eyes. In its desire to avoid a lawsuit, the agency was ready to propel Tony and Jimmy all the way to the top of the queue for a prime property. Their response was immediate. "Well, actually, next week we have this really good place coming up in Hampstead. Why don't you guys have a look at that?"

Tony and Jimmy looked at each other, and then back at the agent. "Yes. That could work," they conceded.

They drove out to the property that same day. It was a stunning twenty-five room building in a leafy suburb. As they looked around, Jimmy and Tony could hardly stop laughing.

"Fuck me, this is absolutely incredible. We have to jump on this!"

They then began to negotiate with the agent, saying, "Look, given our bad experience of sharing with people we don't know, we no longer feel safe with strangers. Could we perhaps fill this place with our friends?"

Agencies view properties as problems to be solved, and whether they are filled with guardians or friends of guardians didn't matter as long as the buildings were filled and the paperwork filed. Nobody wants a lawsuit.

"This is really quite irregular," he moaned, straightening his Next polyester tie and shuffling his papers unhappily. "We can hold the property back until the close of business today and no later."

Which is how I came to receive a phone call from Jimmy while standing in the tiny backyard of my flat, eating a Curly Wurly I'd bought from the corner shop. I was renting my flat from a friend's wife on a verbal agreement that I could leave with just a month's notice. There were no contractual issues to moving out quickly.

"Look, we've got this amazing place. The location is perfect. It's massive. It's cheap. And if any gypsies *do* come around, you can take first crack at them. But you've got to sign up today if you want it. Are you in?"

"Of course I am," I said. We all were.

Sitting in the office in Islington, my pen poised over the contract, I was given a rundown of our tenancy terms: we would be on two weeks' notice and could be thrown out at any time, real estate agents could come through with prospective buyers, and we were expected to keep the property clean. I signed contracts, exchanged keys, and walked out into the office lobby where the rest of the RSG gang was sitting shoulder-to-shoulder on rickety chairs each clutching their own signed contract and pair of house keys.

"To Hampstead!" announced Jimmy then strolled out the door like Captain Cook leading his explorers up a mountain trail. The great adventure at Château RSG was about to begin.

*Exploring
with
Dovile*

*Trafalgar
Square*

*Team
Hampstead
supporting
Lee at his
boxing debut*

Cads and Bounders

LONDON

CADS AND BOUNDERS

Welcome to the House of Shite."
    I set my bag down in our new home and took it all
    in. My new French girlfriend Adele pressed up against
me for security, her big startled eyes roaming around the hallway
taking in the paisley wallpaper and chipped paint. I felt deflated by
the decor.

"What's that smell?" she asked.

"Old Jews."

I explained that a company called Jewish Care owned the building
and that until very recently it had boasted full occupation of elderly
Jews. The entire Golders Green area from the tube station ten
minutes down the hill right on up past our house was heavily Jewish.
Retirement homes line the entirety of Finchley Road, sterile semi-
hospital places that make visiting your grandmother in her gaff seem
like an absolute delight in comparison. This house was no exception.

People had left in a hurry, as if they'd gotten wind an SS battalion
was approaching.

Apparently, Jewish Care had needed to move out all of their
residents after the government enacted a new regulation setting
a minimum size for rooms in retirement homes. Château RSG's room
sizes had been deemed of insufficient dimensions, so all the coffin-

dodger patients had been moved out pronto. It was now against the law for them to live in the place.

(That's pretty awful really because when you move old people, some of them die. What's the betting that this new regulation killed more old Jews than any minor Nazi Party functionary had achieved?)

I walked Adele up to my room and unlocked it. We stepped in with some trepidation considering the squalor of the ground floor. The carpet was worn and dirty. The curtains were a garish orange and beige. I opened the sliding door of the wardrobe to find it filled with women's clothes, and when I pulled open the creaking door to my en-suite bathroom, a pair of false teeth glistened atop the sink.

"This place is strange," said Adele.

I looked at her slim nineteen year old legs and her flimsy t-shirt. I wanted to fuck her right away. The footsteps of my friends were audible on the ground floor so to be on the safe side I dragged her into an office on the top floor and fucked her over a desk. Then we went back to our exploration.

Jewish bric-a-brac littered the building: Stars of David everywhere, countless books on Jewish history and culture, and menorahs on every dresser. I say "building" singular but a communicating corridor joined it to next door, which boasted a further fifty rooms and only served to make the whole place feel like a ghost town.

I imagine this is how the Allies felt liberating Buchenwald. I wondered if these kitchen ovens were also still warm to the touch.

Even without all the old people stuff lying about, we'd have guessed its previous use because the smell of piss was overwhelming. It smelled like the Post Office queue on pension day. It seemed to permeate every nook and cranny.

I wondered if there was a pile of gas masks stashed in the cellar for staff use.

"So where do we start?" I asked Jimmy as we regrouped in the back garden.

The agency said we'd probably only have six months before the new owners took possession. That made us reluctant to invest too much time and effort into sprucing it up. We started with cleaning and painting, and as we became increasingly confident of staying we implemented more and more ideas.

The ground floor was blessed with two massive lounges fronted by floor-to-ceiling windows looking over the garden. I bought some used sofas from Gum Tree and had them delivered. Well, Tony scoured the site for a bargain, and then I paid all the money and did all the work, he was in a cheapskate phase right then. We had seats for twelve people and that quickly became the default room everyone hung out in. We set up an Xbox360 in the other lounge and made use of some pre-installed sliding partition doors to cut the room in half. The back half had only a small window so it perfectly suited our plan for a home cinema. Hayley was one of two girls in the house (Tomas's girlfriend, Isabella, the other), and as a trainee psychotherapist she was thrilled to hang out with a gang of PUAs. She loaned us her projector for the cinema room. Jimmy and I put up a big screen and three rows of sofas. Opening night was a showing of Robert Rodriguez's *Machete*.

Tony claimed the best room on the ground floor. There were another three bedrooms and a small office on the same floor but the letting agency had locked them all up. We felt like the kids from an Enid Blyton story as we searched the house for keys. Mick found a lock-box and waved a set of keys triumphantly. As the weeks progressed and we realised the agency was lax in its inspections, we decided to open up and re-purpose the off-limits rooms. Mick moved into the larger bedroom, Hayley claimed the office for her fledging psychological consulting business, and we redecorated the smallest room as a guest bedroom for friends to stay over in. There was one room left on the ground floor, and I claimed it.

Lee, Fernando, and Jimmy all liked fight stuff so I roped them into making it our own boxing gym. It was tucked away in the far corner of the house with a fully-matted floor, a full-length mirror, and a punch bag. I hung a large portrait of Sagat from Street Fighter 2 on one wall and promotional posters from two Japanese MMA shows on the other. It felt great. That was my little project, and for the next three years there'd be a metronomic thud emanating from within as I did my regular kick-boxing bag-work.

In the end, the place scrubbed up really well. It still had that tatty air from having never been refurbished and the ceiling sometimes collapsed in the rain, but it was clean, repainted, and filled with our own furniture.

We wanted a Rat Pack vibe. We'd live together, hang out together, and would all teach pick-up boot camps together every six weeks or so. Before moving in, we'd tried hanging out with each other as much as we could. However, living in different parts of London complicated things. Now life was easy. Very easy.

I'd already quit my job so it was a period of pure sloth.

As I sit writing this memoir in 2016, my mind fills with nostalgia at all the fun we had in that house; ten friends constantly around each other. Instead of the usual ball-ache of meeting up one Friday night per month, suddenly we were all sitting down for breakfast together, or playing the Xbox in the lounge, or sunning ourselves out in the garden when the weather was nice. The accessibility was incredible. If I wanted to go out, I'd knock on Johnny or Fernando's door and say, "Hey, I'm thinking of doing some daygame today. Do you want to come out?" It was *that* easy. From being atomized, spread across London, and just meeting up once every now and again, we were together the whole time. It was very exciting and I didn't miss my former corporate life for a moment.

Readers of *Balls Deep* (volume one of my memoir) will know that I'd been quite a reclusive introvert. Most of my life occurred in my head – be it reading, writing, video gaming, or watching movies. Now I was living with the "cool kids" and loving it, like a hippo rolling around a muddy African riverbank.

Naturally, Tony and Jimmy took the best two rooms – large, bay-windowed and wood-panelled lavish affairs – on the ground and first floor respectively. They'd been the movers and shakers behind our new home, and we looked up to them as leaders, so it seemed fair. I was on the first floor next door to Jimmy, winding around the corridor came Johnny next, then Hayley, then Lee. Finally at the end of the line was Tomas in a shared room with his girlfriend Isabella, a sometime catwalk model. Tomas never did any Game outside of demo sets on boot camps, but I guess he was happy with the routine of knobbing the same fairly hot leggy girl every few days. Up on the top floor, there were a few locked rooms and Fernando, my best friend at the time, who hails from a small town near Sao Paulo in Brazil.

We'd jumped in at the deep end. Goodbye to the grind of work-rent-tax-pub-Sainsburys and "hello" to adventure. The last time I'd lived in a shared house was at university twelve years earlier. As it turns out, I'm quite difficult to live with. That's another lesson I'd learn about my past – my tendency to live alone wasn't entirely my choice.

After six months in Château RSG I'd completely settled into my new life and could barely comprehend how I'd lived just one year earlier. The spring of 2011 was around the corner, and I'd knocked off a couple of hot girls on the trot. I was dating a Russian catwalk model called Zaria (see volume one). I was getting fairly good at game and was past the beginner's self-doubt, epitomized by such questions as "Can I do it?" and "Should I do it?"

Life as an apprentice player was good, very good indeed. I was still failing with the vast majority of girls, and I still struggled, but I was over "the hump." I'd fucked a new girl every calendar month for the past eleven months, and they were getting hotter. If I could just close out a new girl in April, I'd have a major milestone.

I wanted the identity of a "player," to be congruent with the mindset and lifestyle, which meant I must break the chains. No longer was I to be a normal office drone working fifty hours a week and handing over half of the proceeds to the thieves in government. The downside was that I broke contact with most of my old friends. It wasn't a deliberate or conscious severing of ties, more a drifting apart. They were still living their regulated lives, with their grotty girlfriends, sex on Saturdays, a blow job every other Sunday, dinner parties, weekends at Ikea, and baby christenings, things which were very alien to me at that point.

I'd changed. My expectations of life, sex, and girls had changed.

Up until my marriage, almost every girl I'd ever slept with had been "age appropriate" (that is to say, within a few years of my own age) and only a couple of them had been genuinely hot. My wife was one year younger and the hottest girl I'd ever slept with. This meant I didn't have reference experiences of sleeping with girls younger and better-looking than me. I was twenty-five when I'd last had sex with a teenager, an eighteen-year old Japanese scally in Okinawa who gave me my only ever STD – something fungal and itchy that didn't clear up until a month later when a doctor in Malta gave me some pills while I was on a scuba diving trip. That's just a seven-year age difference and hardly impressive – although picking her up in a nightclub and fucking her in a children's play area at midnight was quite a good story. In contrast, my *average* age difference for 2016 up until the moment I write these words was twenty years.

Yes, in 2016 I was forty-one years old and banging girls with an average age of twenty-one. Stay along for the ride, and you'll learn how I made that situation my regular sex life. You'll have ample opportunity to disapprove too.

By the end of *Balls Deep* and the beginning of this volume, I'd slept with only sixteen girls from "the game," all younger and hotter than me. That's not a huge number, and I knew I had a long road ahead of me. I was getting laid reasonably well and learning my craft but I was still clumsy and frequently clueless. There was a lot of room to grow into.

I had to work very hard for my lays. I was daygaming several times a week, often racking up fifty sets or more. There were interminable instant dates (taking a girl on a date immediately after first meeting on the street) and first dates that went nowhere. Many girls would string me along a few dates and then smoothly drop out of my life unfucked. Every lay felt like a major achievement, and I wasn't to be discouraged, but I wished it wasn't so difficult. I didn't want to take the easy way out by scaling back my ambitions. I'd started in the Game with dreams of banging top quality women so that's what I'd aim for.

Slowly but surely, I was getting better.

LONDON

CHAPTER THREE

My Own Master

MY OWN MASTER

I have some embarrassing memories from my teenage years. Not to put too fine a point on it, I was a bit of a pussy. Here's an example.

At fresher's week at my new university I was wandering around the Student Union hall checking out the stalls of the various activity clubs. There was Ramblers Society which hired minibuses to drive members out into the hills for hiking trips. Cocktail Society was the most popular – a society that hired out entire nightclubs once a month and put on buckets of cheap cocktails. Turning up to their events in my second year would get me two same-night lays despite being a fresh-faced nineteen-year-old chump.

Tucked into the corner next to the public toilets was the stall for the small club I was really interested in – Ninja Society. They were an athletic club who taught ninjutsu twice a week at the sports centre. Yes, I wanted to be a ninja.

It was a classic gamma desire. After loving the 1980s ninja craze with all those Sho Kosugi straight-to-VHS movies and also reading the original *Teenage Mutant Ninja Turtles* comics, I was well up for it. Two of my favourite games of the 1980s were *The Last Ninja* and *Saboteur*. As I became interested in karate while studying my A-levels, I'd begun reading the UK's monthly martial arts magazines in the popular magazine shop WH Smiths. Bear in mind this was pre-UFC. The first Ultimate Fighting Championship wouldn't be held until October 1993, coincidently about the same week I was signing up to become the sort of ninja who Royce Gracie clowned in Denver that month.

The martial arts scene in 1990s Britain was a sickening gaggle of gamma males trying to one-up each other on who had the deadliest system, like each fancied himself a character from *Mortal Kombat*. None of them ever proving themselves in real competitive fights. Each promised a secret system that could make any pussy into a hard-case.

I was a pussy who wanted to be a hard-case, so I was intrigued.

It's often said in the seduction community that Game is 90% mindset and 10% technique. That rather underestimates the importance of good technique, but the point is good. Girls can sniff out insecurity and low self-esteem like dogs, so if your inner game is wobbly you will struggle to get a girl all the way to the bedroom.

Most of our inner game comes from our parents. Since late 2010 I'd started therapy sessions with the elder statesman of the London PUA community, Colin Skeletor. By early 2011 we'd uncovered just how many of my assumptions and natural reactions could be traced directly to my childhood. In particular, my problems stemmed mostly from the inverse polarity in my parents' marriage. My mother was the head of household, with some narcissistic traits, who treated many family interactions (whether she was involved or not) as a source of attention. Thus she'd make all the decisions, elbow her way into every conversation, and twist everything to be about her and her feelings. My father took the co-dependent role, passively allowing her to run riot and avoiding conflict. I was lucky in that I instinctively rebelled against this polarity rather than accepting it as normal. However, the damage was done. I modelled a lot of my mother's self-absorbed behaviours, and my ability to consider the thoughts and reactions of others never really developed. I would treat any social environment as a china shop to bulldoze through and by age sixteen I was rather dominant.

Thoughtful readers will have observed that narcissism, self-absorption, and social dominance are all very powerful traits in seducing women. As my Game journey progressed, I'd learn to harness these in-built strengths and to smooth off the rough edges. However, as a teenager and well into my twenties, these characteristics severely limited my ability to build and maintain social circles. For most people, I was too difficult to be around.

In contrast to my wild, overbearing, intellectual and social style, I was physically underwhelming. My physique was average, and I didn't like sports unless I could win easily. My parents were always disparaging about athletic competition; my mother hadn't raised a sweat in her life, and my dad had a brief flirtation with long-distance running in high school and then never exercised again. When I tried to watch football on TV my mother would witter on about how silly and pointless it was while my dad would just grumble with a never-ending stream of negativity over the competence of the players, the manager, and the referees.

"Fifty grand a week and they can't even kick the ball straight!" he'd shout.

This was a toxic environment for any boy wishing to play sports and become a man. When I'd once persuaded them to let me learn judo as a ten-year-old, they quickly withdrew me from class the first time my nose bled. By the time I left school at sixteen I was a total faggot. My ego had reframed my lack of athleticism, so now I overrated the importance of intellect and book-learning – because that's what I was good at and was encouraged in.

I joined the local 'anti-fascist' group in Newcastle when I was sixteen. I use scare quotes because like Churchill said, "the fascists of the future will call themselves anti-fascists" it's just we were too naïve to realise how we were being played by the older revolutionaries. I'd drifted into anarchism via the punk rock music I was listening to at the time. My interest was idealistic. I genuinely believed anarchism was the answer to all the horrible things I was learning about the world as I read widely. I'd later leave in disgust as I realised that for every conscientious teenager who wished to fight for justice, there were another five who were a mix of drunks, degenerates, drug addicts, welfare scroungers, or evil Marxists. The reason I relate the story is this: The stereotypes are true. Left-wing men have no upper body strength and can't fight for shit. This is how a typical 'Antifa' action went down in 1992 Newcastle:

"Nick. There's a demo in Durham on Saturday. Are you coming?" says a fellow.

"What's it about?"

"There's a Skrewdriver gig on. The redirection point is the Bears Head on Old Durham square. We're going to crash it."

Skrewdriver was a punk band who sang about protecting English culture from foreign invasion. They had skinheads and may have been more approving of Adolf Hitler than the UK average.

Saturday lunchtime we met at the train station and every one of us was dressed in a black hoodie, black combat pants, and black Doc Marten boots. I was pleased to note my eighteen-lacers were the tallest boots. As our gang of fifteen walked down to the square I noticed Johnny, the singer of my punk band *Rigor Tortoise,* had a plastic shopping bag with a tin of beans in it. So did Geeky, our lunatic Scottish drummer.

"What's that about?" I asked.

"It's great, mate. We can swing it like a cosh, but it's totally legal if the rozzers stop us."

OK. We arrived at the square and wasted the first hour following random bald-headed men around town who were just looking for a pub showing the football match. Twice we almost attacked some in a back alley.

"I'm telling you, he's a Nazi," whispered Graeme, as we stalked them behind British Home Stores.

"I dunno, man. He's wearing a Sunderland shirt. They are playing Wimbledon today, and it's on telly."

"Well, Sunderland fans are nearly as bad as Nazis," he grumbled, itching for an unprovoked attack on any fellow Englishman minding his own business on a sunny afternoon.

After an hour we were bored. Shoppers were chatting amiably in the street, a few grannies were feeding the pigeons, and some children whooped and hollered as they chased each other with water pistols. This was intolerable. We wanted to ambush some Nazis.

Finally Graeme spotted a target who, if you squinted your eyes enough, looked like they just may have once said something vaguely patriotic.

"Those three. Shaved heads, and going into the Bears Head. They have to be Nazis."

Close enough. We closed in on them and then just before they reached the door, Geeky ran up and punched one in the back of the head. The trio spun around in surprise, and then Johnny piled in swinging his bean-tin cosh and caught another man on the shoulder. The men scrambled inside.

We didn't really know what to do next. Should we follow them inside? That felt a bit scary because the cramped space might force us to fight one-on-one. I wasn't convinced they were Nazis.

Behind me, a child dropped his ice cream and began to cry.

We stood outside the pub and chanted some kind of "Nazi punks fuck off" admonition for a minute or two then somebody said the cops were coming so we ran off. Huffing and puffing under a tree by the river, Johnny upended his plastic bag and was thrilled to see a dent in the bean tin.

"Got the bastard!" he crowed.

Back home later that night, I lay in bed and stared at the ceiling. The adrenalin had worn off, and I was frightened. There was a nagging feeling that we were just cowardly thugs attacking outnumbered strangers – which was true but wasn't what really bothered me. There was something far deeper; what if those men had fought back? What if it had been me at the front and not the thickly-muscled Geeky? I didn't know how to throw a punch, or dodge one. My instinct when confronted with imminent violent confrontation was to back down.

I had no idea how to fight. What kind of man can't protect himself and his people?

I raised the issue at the next Anti-Fascist Action meeting that was in a small function room above the office of the local miner's union in Newcastle. The group leader knew someone who knew someone who's dad was a karate black belt and also a Marxist. As teenagers we didn't grasp the irony of a Marxist teaching Anti-Fascists, as we'd yet to comprehend the duplicitous Fascist nature of the Left.

He'd teach us once a week for a couple of quid each. So I started to learn karate.

It was shit, but learning anything at all felt more powerful than just flailing my arms in a fight. After six months, I had the brash overconfidence of a paper tiger and was packing my bags for university and a week after that I attended my first ninjutsu class at the sports centre on campus.

Contrary to the popular stereotype, our ninjutsu coach was not an awkward, egotistical gamma. Richard was a mid-twenties guy who had a ripped gym body, extremely friendly manner, and had represented Wales in amateur boxing. He was good-looking, too. It's one of my regrets in life that I acted like such a faggot in his class. Whereas he was a believer in nutrition, gym, and hard training, I was still a believer in secret systems. I wanted the *Kung Fu Panda* path to martial arts mastery.

All martial arts classes have a guy who acts as crash test dummy for the teacher to demonstrate technique on, called the "uke." Richard's uke was a small Lancashire kid called Matt. He was in shape, keen, and never seemed fazed at being thrown around for two hours twice a week. I should've learned from his attitude but didn't. Sometimes Richard would give Matt a rest and demonstrate on the regular students. Each time he picked me we both regretted it.

It fills me with embarrassment to write these words.

If you've watched martial arts seminar videos from the 1980s (before the UFC burst their bubble) you'll have noticed a particular dynamic. Students approach the teacher in an orderly manner with weak, scripted attacks and invite the teacher to destroy them. If the martial art is particularly shit (such as Aikido) the students will actively propel themselves through the air to make the techniques look more effective. There are entire YouTube playlists of sycophantic students somersaulting backwards from the slightest shove or dropping dead from gentle touches. Steven Seagal has some especially comical videos.

So it was a "thing" in martial arts to co-operate with your teacher to make the techniques look deadly. Everybody in the room gained an ego-hit from the charade. Add into the mix that ninjutsu moves can be very painful. Getting your wrist twisted to breaking point, or a stiff thumb jabbed into your lower ribs is unpleasant. And remember I was a pussy.

Richard called me to demonstrate a technique where I had to throw a slow motion left-right combo at him. Twenty students formed a ring around us to watch. I let the first punch go, and he whipped his clenched fist outwards so the knuckles rapped against the inside of my wrist, flinging my hand up and away. It hurt like hell and the momentum rocked me off balance. So what did I do?

I fell to the ground like I'd been shot. Like in the videos.

Richard stood looking down at me, hiding his dissatisfaction. He was a polite friendly chap, after all. Rather than finish my part so he could demonstrate a technique, I'd collapsed theatrically to the mat. To my credit I learned my lesson immediately, but I was deeply troubled – I wanted to learn ninjutsu, but I hated being in class. I wanted to be tough, but I was too pussy to endure the punishment. Eighteen years of being a faggot was catching up to me.

Just as learning daygame required me to grit my teeth and will myself through a year of Beginners Hell, learning to fight came with its own challenge of mentally overriding my extreme aversion to the process. Years later I'd become a competent boxer, wrestler, and Brazilian Ju Jitsu practitioner. I'd never be the gym star, but I'd muck in, get my hands dirty, and spar hard with well-trained opponents. I even had five full-contact kick-boxing matches in Tokyo. It took a long time to kill the inner pussy, but by my mid-twenties I'd done it. It would be a strong foundation for when I started hunting down the outer pussy, on the streets.

A pet theory of mine, that I first read about on the *Anonymous Conservative* blog, is that most of our behaviour is conditioned by a part of the brain called the amygdala. This is what identifies threats and feels irritation when the world doesn't go our way, stimulating action. Challenge and danger in the world will develop our amygdala like a muscle whereas soft-living and staying in our comfort zones will retard its development until it atrophies. Movies such as *Fight Club* are telling the story of men with atrophied amygdala finding ways to toughen up and become more manly, hence the famous quote: "After a night at fight club, everything in the real world gets the volume turned down. Nothing can piss you off, your word is law, and if other people break the law or question you, even that doesn't piss you off."

I'd challenged myself academically throughout childhood to build my intellectual fortitude, but it was only when I turned to boxing that I found a route to develop my amygdala to oppose physical threats too. Daygame would be another step outside my comfort zone, encountering extreme social challenge, and I was fortunate to have these earlier combative experiences to have prepared me. I'd need all of my tenacity for what lay ahead.

The emotional journey to becoming a competent fighter had been triggered by my deeper insecurities of being a weak-necked pussy. I didn't want to live in fear, as a man who couldn't look after himself or his loved ones. Any man who has overcome such a challenge is immediately imbued with confidence, and usually also with a love of whatever skill-set he used to drag himself away from the abyss. For me, it was boxing.

I'd ditch ninjutsu and take up boxing in a gym a short walk from my house in Newcastle. The coach, a local doorman called Bernard, was a fantastic trainer and lots of fun. He had us jogging outside and then lined up on the mats doing push-ups, crunches, and stretches. As we struggled against fatigue he'd shout his one-liners at us:

"It's mind over matter. I don't mind, and you don't matter."

"This one trains your biceps. If you don't have any, there's spares in the cupboard."

"Don't say anything bad about slags. You never know when you may need one."

"This exercise will work your neck muscles and help you take a punch. You might fail a brain scan, but you'll be able to take the punch."

He gave us expert technical advice and years later, after training in Tokyo's kick-boxing gyms with Lumpinee Muay Thai champions and top coaches, I'd still be impressed at the solid fundamentals Bernard gave us. Like discovering Johnny Wisdom's street game in summer 2009, boxing was my first real step forwards after a year of floundering. I'd hit upon a path which would lead me to my goals if only I had the courage to walk it.

I couldn't get enough of boxing. I threw myself into it both in classes and in absorbing everything I could outside the gym. I'd buy the big PPV fights on VHS tape through classifieds in the back of *Boxing Monthly* magazine. I subscribed to the big US monthlies (*The Ring*, *KO*, *World Boxing*) and the weekly *UK Boxing News*. Before long I was steeped in the history and tradition of the sport.

Sitting in the Château RSG garden with Jimmy, Fernando, and Mick, we'd been discussing a big fight. The conversation soon hit a tangent on boxing's concept of the linear champion, the-man-who-beat-the-man.

"Yeah, that's right," said Lee, walking out from the patio with a cup of tea. "It's like its own championship belt. You have to take it off the former owner, and then you've got the bragging rights as The Champ."

There was something in this, we thought.

The RSG spirit was one of ribaldry, support, and trolling each other hard. Surely we could leverage boxing tradition to give us our own tradition that would inspire more friendly rivalry and add some texture to our slapdash race for notches?

Biology dictates that men chase and women receive advances. It's men who must make things happen, to have a plan. Waiting around for a girl to jump you may work for the average man in the world of *American Pie* movies but not in real life. If you don't approach, you are condemned to scraping the barrel with women several points below your own Sexual Market Value ("SMV").

Hot girls don't need to initiate because they hold the bargaining chips.

Men must have a plan, and this bakes outcome dependence into the seduction cake. There's no way around it. Pick-up artists will fudge the issue with concepts such as "flip the script" or "make her chase," but the simple reality is that you must make getting laid your goal and this will entail a large amount of "cold calling" to generate leads (to use sales terminology).

Girls can take-it-or-leave-it for sex with a new man, certainly in the beginning until the man gets a strong hook in. A young, hot girl has a line of potential suitors that is close enough to infinite. She could stand in the street holding a sign saying, "I want sex. Who's up for it?" and watch the queue form. We know how well that strategy would work for us.

A woman's default reaction to seduction is to dismiss and disqualify the suitor. If the current man fails to catch her, another will be along soon enough. If she accidentally deletes his number, no big deal; she can get as many numbers as she wants. The younger and hotter the girl, the more lackadaisical her attitude to new leads. Men occupy the opposite role in which we are often lackadaisical about committing to relationships. Up until sex happens, we must make things happen and nurture each lead to its conclusion. Corralling a hot, young girl into bed is like pushing a supermarket trolley with dodgy wheels in a straight line. She'll careen off in random directions on a whim because she just doesn't care. She's hard-wired to not make it easy.

Imagine two rival castles facing each other down on opposite hills, across a wide plain. Castle Man and Castle Woman.

I'll tell you what *never* happens in this fictional war-torn fiefdom: the female army sallies out onto the battlefield to engage with the male army. Rather, the female army always stays within the safety of its fortified walls, forcing Castle Man to cross open plains to besiege Castle Woman. Women always begin the seduction dance from a fortified position. Bringing that metaphor to the street, men chase women and try it on, on her home ground, playing by her rules. She is in a lofty position, leaning over the balustrade of the gallery, saying, "No, no, try harder."

A new daygamer may find this desperately unfair and a daunting task. We seem to be crashing headlong into old-school social anthropologist Robert Briffault's law of sexual dynamics: "The female, not the male, determines all the conditions of the animal family. Where the female can derive no benefit from association with the male, no such association takes place."

There is a way around it, which I teach my students. A woman's frame is never as strong as it first appears. She's just sitting at the top tower in her castle while you're trying to climb up with your ladder. It doesn't mean she's strong or confident. It just means that your respective situations are unequal. She is starting from a position of mild interest and outcome independence. She wants you to reach the top of the ladder, but she won't help you until you distinguish yourself from every other invader.

Often girls say "no" due to a *lack* of confidence. Saying "yes" requires them to let down their guard, and they worry about their ability to handle what comes next. They know what happens when they let go. They are no longer in control.

Let me give you an example. A couple of days ago (in 2016) , I approached a stunningly beautiful catwalk model. I was rather apprehensive at first, but she smiled, I hooked her, and chatted amiably. She refused to give her number.

"Why not? I like you. You like me."

"Yes, but I'm frightened of you. You are too confident."

I lightened the moment suggesting, "Let's meet in a cafe next to a police station. You'll be safe there."

She laughed and gave up her number. The average man would assume a top-tier girl would be in full control of herself and brimming with confidence, but that's hardly ever the case. It was clear from our ten minute conversation that she was a balanced and thoughtful girl, but that doesn't matter to her when dealing with men. She knows full well that if she came to like me, her rational brain would surrender control, and who knows what may happen then. Some girls will nip it in the bud before stepping onto the slippery slope.

Aspiring players need to dispense with the idea that every hot girl is ultra-confident with loads of rich guys chasing her, and *no way* someone with such an interesting and exotic lifestyle would be interested in *them*. But that's looking at it from the wrong angle. Every morning when she gets out of the shower, like all women, she'll look at herself and worry.

"Do I look fat?"

"Am I pretty?"

"Do I have lines under my eyes?"

She may whip out her smart phone to check Facebook and Instagram for new likes. Women have their insecurities, too. Men worry they are turning into their father and women worry they are turning into their mother.

The point is this: Men's role in the courtship ritual requires them to be intrinsically outcome- dependent from an earlier stage than the woman. The ten of us in RSG wanted to put some distance between that unavoidable aspect of the Game, and we'd come up with an idea: *Let's have our own championship belt.*

We wanted a way to transfer our outcome dependence from the girl onto something else. We wouldn't be fucking her *for her.* We wanted to *win the title.* This might create a gap between us and our outcome dependence, injecting more fun into the process. Hopefully it would send off subtly different signals to the girls, interfering with their poise.

Our second trip to Lithuania in September 2010 would be the inauguration. Think of us as fighting for the vacant championship. Fernando came home one night having banged the first new girl of the trip. One of his RSG nicknames at the time as "F-Town" (Jimmy would add random words to the first letter of our names. I was "K-Bone" back then).

"F-Town got his F-close," shouted Fernando as he slammed the front door shut and kicked his boots off in the hallway.

Jimmy and I looked at each other, the spark of inspiration kindled.

"That's it! That's the championship. It's called F-Town!"

We quickly drew up the rules: F-Town is won when any RSG player closes a new girl outside of his country of residence. A literal championship belt was too unwieldy, so I went on eBay and had a ring engraved with "F-Town" and sent through. We gave Fernando an elaborate presentation in the garden of Château RSG when we got home.

It didn't matter where any of us met the girl, so long as the first fuck was not in the UK, which was where we all lived. Fernando and Mick also had Brazil and Australia ruled out because those were the respective countries that they'd been born and raised in. Jimmy, Mick and myself all kept public blogs charting our adventures so we each kept a list on the blogs for the lineage of F-Town, updating it as it switched hands, sometimes on the same day.

There were few greater pleasures in 2011 than walking up to the F-Town incumbent and taking the ring from his finger, usually accompanied by trash talk in front of an audience. It was in the rules that he had to stand there and let you take it. He wasn't allowed to just hand it over on his own terms. The rules were bigger than any one of us.

This Is The Rhythm Of The Night

THIS IS THE RHYTHM
OF THE NIGHT

H ave you got another rotter coming round, then Mick?"
I asked.
"Fuck off."
"Which is it this time, a fatty or a whore?"

Mick tutted and waved me away, trying to concentrate on a YouTube video of a snowboarder outrunning an avalanche. He was flopped into a hammock he'd strung diagonally along his room. Mick was getting laid more than me, but he'd been struggling with quality so it amused me to bait him about it.

"Hmm, I see what's happening here," he replied, reaching down to pick up his fruit juice from the floor. "Are you still salty about me getting laid last night? I'm sorry, buddy, but she just couldn't keep herself from screaming. I hope it didn't distract you from your reading. Alone."

"You're a fat Aussie bastard," I said.

"A big fat Aussie bastard" came Jimmy's shout from the hallway. He'd been walking by in his dressing gown, coming down for his lunchtime shower.

Mick and I became good friends, but back in early 2011 we still didn't get on very well. Jimmy had brought him into RSG the same time as me and an awkward friendship developed. It was mostly a personality clash. He considered me an objectionable, abrasive character. For my part, I found him woppy and snidey. I'd guess a good part of ruffling each other up was because he was far more effective at closing girls whereas I still tended to lose them somewhere between the date and sex. Living in a competitive household magnified my frustration, and I sometimes projected it onto Mick. He'd react so our banter sometimes had a hard edge and spilled over into bitchiness.

Mick had received an email through his blog from a hardcore daygame junkie we all called Angry Mark. He was so named because he was on the streets every evening for hours on end, spam approaching the poor girls of London. He was a fanatical Yad fan and never deviated from his same, robotic script (which ironically is the opposite of how the free-wheeling Yad talks). He must've opened thousands of girls but still wasn't getting laid, and he'd passed the point of no return – he was now bitterly angry that the girls weren't rewarding his hard work with sex. You can imagine how that negative spiral looks.

Angry Mark was conducting an odd solo research project in which he decided to test out all the London daygamers and had already done a one-on-one with me. Now it was Mick's turn.

While coaching him in Covent Garden, Mick's demo set was a hot, black prostitute called Herone. He didn't find out the prostitute angle until they were on a date, but if anything it just made him more excitable. It was Mick's dream to "shore" a whore – i.e. to have sex with her for free. He'd been reading some player blogs about South East Asia, and in some cities prostitution is so endemic that shoring is literally the only way to bang a pretty, young girl for free. There are no non-whores there pretty enough to fuck. Mick loved his squalor so he talked Herone into visiting Château RSG sometime in the near future.

A few days passed, and Herone messaged to say she'd come over. Mick was also working through the Plenty Of Fish internet dating site with a new system he was trialling with Jimmy. They were getting lots of messages, but it's an inherently flaky world. Mick had taken to double-booking girls under the assumption one or both would flake at late notice. So this particular Wednesday evening Mick had lined up Herone, another girl he'd kissed on a date but considered a tenuous lead, and also a Plenty Of Fish mystery first date. Mick liked such complexity in his dating life. What could possibly go wrong?

He lay on the floor in Jimmy's room watching him play Skyrim while I pottered away typing a blog post on Jimmy's bed. We waited to see what would transpire. The internet girl cancelled so the options whittled down to two. Soon after his phone buzzed.

"Date girl is on her way," trumped Mick and shuffled off to change out of his surf shorts and t-shirt.

Half an hour later I followed the smell of pizza down the corridor to the kitchen where Mick and his girl were cooking.

"Homemade pizza. Delicious," said Mick.

It was his latest wheeze for closing on dates. You have an excuse to make the girl invest by giving her a list of ingredients to shop for, then an excuse to have her in your house, and finally an excuse to order her around the kitchen so she falls into your frame. Like most of Mick's game, it was smart and imaginative, his version of a gambit used by many generations of old-time players. No matter how the date goes, you get fed.

The girl was a giggly, mid-twenties seven. Not bad. I saw his phone light up, and it buzzed. Mick wiped his dough-smeared hands on his trousers and swiped the screen. He turned his back on his date and gave me the "oh fuck!" face.

Herone was outside Château RSG.

I walked the long way around to a window so I could spy outside without her seeing me. Hmmmm, she was quite hot. Maybe as good as an eight. Long black legs and a straight weave. Mick hadn't expected her to come, and I had no idea how he'd handle it.

"Sorry, I'm busy now," he replied over WhatsApp.

I got back to my perch at the window just as she read the message. I saw a moment of disbelief and then anger. She typed something in and banged the door. I rushed back to the kitchen. It felt like watching tennis, my head going back and forward with each shot.

The pizza was loaded up onto plates, then they went into the lounge. Mick was fretting now because our side-door had two big glass panes that gave full view of the hallway Mick had to cross to get to his room. The same hallway had a toilet and was the main thoroughfare between the amenities and each housemate's room.

- If his girl went to the toilet, they'd see each other.
- If any housemate came downstairs, he'd naturally let the girl in, not realising the situation.
- If Mick wanted to pull his date into the bedroom, the girls would see each other.

I felt like watching MacGyver trapped in a barn with just a plank of wood and a sprocket wrench. How was Mick going to get himself out of this and bang the girl? She was fluttering her eyelashes at him over her pizza slice, clearly ready for action. Unfortunately I was becoming a spare wheel so I gave Mick space to work by retiring to my room.

"What happened, mate?" I asked him he next morning. "Didn't you have enough money for the whore?"

"Fuck off."

"No, really, I want to know. Couldn't you pay off your whore? And what about the other one? Which website did you use to find her, Admiral Escorts?"

The quality on sites such as Plenty of Fish and OK Cupid is abysmal, at least compared to daygame, so I liked to needle him about that, saying he only got sixes and fatties. It wasn't true but so long as Jimmy and I acted like we believed it we succeeded in riling him.

"Oh, fuck off you Geordie cunt," he said before breaking into a laugh. "At least I can get laid. How many girls did you close this week? Zero?"

He had me, and he knew he did.

"The world is right, mate," he said. "It's only right that I should have two, and you should have none. The world is fair and just."

I was in the midst of a dry spell that had lasted almost a month. I'd closed the Russian catwalk model Zaria in mid-March 2011, but now it was almost the end of April, and I hadn't had so much as a sniff of anything new back to the house. Mick knew I was a soft target for it.

"Fucking Aussie cunt," I muttered. "What happened last night?"

"We sat in the lounge with a bottle of wine until I was absolutely sure Miranda was ready to fuck, then it was the moment of truth. Herone was still hanging around outside and blowing up my phone. So I texted that I'd meet her at the front door. As soon as she said OK and walked around the corner, Miranda and I nonchalantly strolled down the hallway into my room."

"Plus one," he added, our code for adding a new notch to the figurative bedpost.

Evidently he'd learned from watching me play *Metal Gear Solid*. Throw the rock in one direction to distract the guard, then crouch-run the other way to your waypoint.

I was determined to come out on top, at least for long enough to troll Mick some more. It was just a question of biding my time and waiting for my luck to change. If I could rattle a girl of higher quality than Mick usually managed, I could then reframe the rivalry so that his greater quantity wouldn't matter anymore; I had a list of insults ready and waiting to be unleashed as soon as I had solid ground from which to hurl them.

The Game Gods were about to smile down on me.

Late April 2011 had a run of good sunshine. It was glorious outside and a wonderful day to be English. The future King of England was about to marry, and the entire country was engrossed in love and voyeurism. Better still, I was in Piccadilly doing a short one-on-one with a local Asian student when I bumped into the hottest girl I knew, Soraya from Brazil. We were crossing the road by Burger King when I spotted her from ten yards away, so I waved, caught her eye, and said hello. Later the student actually thought it was a cold approach and that I was just that good at daygame. I disabused him of the notion immediately.

An extremely awkward conversation ensued between Soraya and I as I realised she wasn't at all pleased to see me. We hadn't met since late the prior year, and I'd completely forgotten about her. Just another hot girl that seemed "on" then infuriatingly dropped off the hook. It was happening a lot around those times. Towards the five-minute mark I completely lost the frame and cut things short saying, "Give me a text sometime and we'll go out." As her tight, Brazilian ass disappeared into the crowd, the student looked at me like I was out of my mind and said, "What happened? How could you let her walk away?"

But the truth was that I'd already let her walk away on about eight previous occasions.

I'd first met Soraya in September 2010, about three weeks after she'd arrived in London from Sao Paulo for the first time. She'd made a habit of resurfacing, showing interest, and then disappearing again before I could gear up to take any action. I guess it was the daygame equivalent of whack-a-mole. I was torn. Half of me said, "She's fucked in the head. Nix her," while the other half said, "Look at her! She's the hottest girl you know."

Back in September I was out with my best buddy Fernando, combing the streets for girls. While walking past Trochadero at Piccadilly, a very elegant and poised brunette strode past on the other side of the road. I couldn't help but be impressed by her athletic grace and coordination. She had long leather boots on like a fashion version of horse-riding gear, and a thin wool figure-hugging coat. I went in.

Perhaps this is a good time to digress into how I met Fernando.

In September 2009 the streets of Covent Garden were my hunting grounds. I was still a terrible day-gamer but trying hard to improve. Walking down the pedestrianised cobbled Neal Street early one Saturday afternoon, I saw an absolutely stunning Estonian girl glide past. She looked like a catwalk model. It was around lunchtime, and I was thinking about grabbing a bite to eat, but all thoughts of food quickly disappeared as I moved in to take a crack.

To my surprise, she lit up a cigarette and stopped for a chat: I'd been expecting such a hot and fast-walking girl to just blow me out and keep on walking. I leaned up against a pavement bollard and tried to pull her. It was going well by my standards at the time and while I was talking to her, I noticed two guys looking at us from the other side of the street. One of them was a thirty-year-old skinhead and the other ten years his senior. Both watched intently. The girl also noticed.

"Are they your friends?" she asked.

"Nope, never seen them before. To be honest, I think it's *me* they are checking out."

She laughed, and we spoke a little more before she gave me her number and went on her way. She never replied to my texts, but I would eventually bang a young Estonian catwalk model in Prague in 2016, so I consider this set practice.

Anyway, the two guys had seen me note down her number and came sauntering over to introduce themselves.

"I'm Fernando," said the skinhead. He was Brazilian.

"I'm Chris," said his silver-haired friend.

They'd just started daygaming two weeks earlier, having been to a *PUA Training* boot camp, but they didn't really know what they were doing. Seeing me approach and hook the Estonian they assumed I was doing well, so they'd stopped to watch and were impressed when they saw her give me her number. I suggested we daygame together, which we did for a couple of hours.

I got on better with Fernando than I did with Chris and that led to the two of us hanging out together as wings. We quickly became friends, and he became my first real daygame wingman. He'd left Brazil in his early twenties and worked several years in the USA before arriving in England. He'd been in the country a couple of years doing manual work, and he'd heard about Game and just decided to give it a go. As I got gradually pulled further into RSG by Jimmy and Johnny, I pulled Fernando in with me.

He eventually became one of the main coaches, but in late 2011, he started feeling homesick and returned home to Brazil.

"You look like a horse-rider who's lost her horse," I started telling Soraya on that Piccadilly street.

She laughed, hooked, and told me she was a fresh-off-the-boat Brazilian. Perfect. Ten minutes later I took her number and trousered my phone, walking back to Fernando who was gazing at the Ripley's Believe It Or Not display across the road. Light text game ensued, and we met for drink a week later.

"A date with a nine!" I crowed to Fernando. "Fucking *stunner*."

That rather overrated her as I was wont to do, but it's long been my saying: *Every girl gains a point if you're the one fucking her*.

Soraya the day after doing the dirty

My high hopes were quickly dashed when she showed up and said she was between appointments and had only twenty minutes to spare. Add her then-stilted English language skills to the equation, and I got a sinking feeling. We had a half pint of beer outside The Lamb And Flag in Covent Garden then I walked away, mentally crossing her off my list as a no-hoper.

We exchanged a few texts and surprisingly she agreed to a proper date, again around Covent Garden. I kissed her in The Cross Keys during the second drink, and it seemed to be progressing. A few days later I finger-fucked her while standing against the upstairs bar in the John Snow pub in Soho. It was a bright busy bar so she absolutely loved the danger of it, but wouldn't go home with me. A few weeks after that I met her at Golders Green station, and she'd come as far as a pub a ten-minute walk from my house but no further.

Something had to be going on in the background. Her communication pattern was hit-and-miss and though she clearly fancied me, she wouldn't move past her line in the sand. I could only assume her reluctance must be due to a boyfriend back in Brazil. Any time we were face-to-face she melted into me, then in texting she'd be hard to get. I gave it up.

Several weeks later, in mid-November, I was walking past the second-hand bookshops along Charing Cross Road holding hands with my Thai girlfriend, Tasanee, when I bumped into Soraya again. Soraya didn't like that at all, looking down at our handhold, then gave Tasanee the once-over. This feeling was confirmed by her subsequent radio silence. It seemed dead. I'd already agreed with Tasanee that she was my non-exclusive girlfriend so unlike Soraya she was quite entertained by the chance meeting rather than shocked.

A week later I got a late-night call from Fernando. He was out working late-evening "gutter game" on Oxford Street with Lee. Gutter game is a London community term for fast-paced highly sexual street game done at night when girls are wandering around late. They'd seen Soraya, and Fernando had thought, "Fuck me, she's hot. My set!" and jumped in. At this point Soraya had never met my friends so it was just a wild coincidence. After defaulting to their shared language of Portuguese, Fernando soon realized she was the same girl he'd seen from a distance that September day in Piccadilly. Like the good mate and solid wing he is, he back-pedalled his intent and started DHVing me to her instead. His phone call was a heads-up about that, and just over an hour later, I received a gushing text from Soraya, telling me how fate had struck.

It was back on, and we dated a few more times but the pattern was always the same. The only time she came into Château RSG was for a big birthday party, and she left early to go clubbing. Eventually, she went back to Brazil to care for a dying relative. Well, that was the story she gave me, but who knows? She texted quite regularly over the New Year, but I'd had enough of her playing coy and couldn't be bothered to invest in what appeared to be a no-hoper lead. I replied but didn't care when her messages dried up.

I would never put up with her kind of behaviour now, but back then, I was far more indulgent with girls wasting my time. It's not that she was a bitch; it's just there was clearly something else going on in the background that I couldn't impact, so it wasn't worth sinking any more time into her.

To be honest getting the attention of a girl as hot as Soraya was still a novel experience to me back then. At that time, she would have been the hottest girl I'd ever slept with; her youth tipped the balance to make her even hotter than Zaria. However, my patience ran out, and by the time she bumped into me with my student I'd ruled her out.

The very next day after our chance meeting, she messaged to say how glad she was that we'd talked again. She complained of working crazy hours with little free time but that she'd love to see me again. However, she finished the message with these words:

"I like you a lot but as a friend... and I don't know if it is OK for you... xxx."

Seeing as I'd already given up on ever fucking her, I was quite happy to accept the "Let's Just Be Friends" and see if I could somehow pawn her off in a bar some time in the future. I responded, "That's fine. I'm not single anymore."

My curt reply and subsequent roll-off must have touched a nerve because a week later, she hit me up on Friday morning, asking if I was free that night. I had nothing lined up, and this struck me as an opportunity to perhaps put one over on Mick somehow. So I agreed to an 8 pm meeting in Camden. True to form, she texted fifteen minutes before: "I'm late. Can we meet at half past?"

Here we go again. I said okay and changed the location to another pub down the road. Incredibly, she was on time, and not only that, she had clearly put extreme care into her appearance with tight clothes, jewellery, and careful make-up. Still, I'd come to do the LJBF thing, and that's exactly what I did. For three hours, I showed zero sexual interest in her, just leaning back, using solid non-verbals, and doing zero chasing or escalation.

My self-control was so good I could've worn speedos at a Victoria Secret swimming gala and no-one would know what was in my mind. And wouldn't you just know it, she started chasing me... hard! She leant inwards, touched my arms and shoulders, brought up sexual topics, and couldn't stop complimenting me.

My first thought was, "she's setting a trap," carefully laying out bait to see if I'd jump forward with my tail wagging like a little puppy and give her the validation of knowing I was still on her hook. So I played it cool and did nothing. I was Pontious Krauser. I could see the confusion setting in on her face. Then it struck me that she'd been burning a flame for me the whole time, and all that LJBF talk was bullshit. The past months, I'd assumed she was friend-zoning me because I'd *failed* to meet her attraction threshold, but the realization dawned that it was the opposite. She was trying to LJBF me because she *was* attracted to me and knew because I was a player, she shouldn't get involved. Whatever back-up option she had was more serious than what I was giving her, even though her intense energy while with me suggested she probably considered me more attractive in a simple sexual sense.

Suddenly everything was clear and I had a read on her. She didn't want to give up her primary option (whoever that was), nor did she want to give up the excitement of being with me. I've since seen this dissonance play out in dozens and dozens of girls. It was game on after all. A window of opportunity was opening, so I reviewed my strategic and tactical options. I decided it was of primary importance to let her continue chasing but give her enough encouragement that she wouldn't lose heart and give up. I'd try to outplay the player.

I continued the friend-zone treatment but threw her a bone every now and then. For example: "Well, physically, you're my type. And you're sweet. I'd date you, but, to be honest, you're too random and flaky."

"Well, what kind of girl do you date then?" she replied, asking to see pictures of my last girlfriend and the one before her. I enjoyed showing off Zaria and Dovile. It was solid pre-selection.

There was no doubt that it was on. We were increasingly drunk and retired to The Hawley Arms (the one Amy Winehouse loved passing out in). Some local chumps tried to hit on her, but as she didn't get out of her seat and rise to their comments, they just stood in front of her losing value. I ignored it and opened a couple of Italian girls who were sitting next to me. Meanwhile, the chumps continued probing.

"You seem tall."

"Oh, thanks."

"How tall are you?"

"Five foot nine."

"Hmmm, you seem a bit shorter."

"Oh."

Once I was sure Soraya had seen me with the giggly Italians, I stepped in. "He's trying to make you stand up to show him. On your feet, girl!"

Soraya stood up, and I took over the conversation for a minute until we dismissed them by sitting back down and turning our backs. I'd just made her think I was trying to palm her off on other guys and she started throwing me more indicators of interest. "*I like you so much. You're such a nice guy. You're the only guy I can rely on*" she cooed.

We finished our drinks and moved on to another pub, but by then we were both trashed.

"I feel unwell," she bleated, and sat outside on the pavement for some fresh air. I carried on drinking.

She hadn't returned after ten minutes; I went out to check on her, only to find her slumped on the ground, up against the wall, with another two chump white knights trying to "rescue" her. She was mostly ignoring them, so I went back to my pint. I'd been through so many on-off moments with Soraya that by now I really wasn't fussed if she was stolen from me. I was drunk and beyond caring. Even so, I gave it another ten minutes, then went and fetched her, pulling her up and helping her along to my table. She kept leaning on me, so I had to prop her up on the seats before I could go to the toilet. The world was a blur.

I returned to find one of the chumps in my seat, next to my beer, hitting on her. Unlike them squatting outside talking to her earlier, this was a more blatant territorial play from them so I couldn't let it stand. I chucked him out, and he slunk away.

It was getting on to midnight now, and we were in a blurry, drunken lust bubble.

"Let's go back to Hampstead," I said.

"Do you have any weed? I want to smoke," she said.

I'd never bought weed in my life, had trouble inhaling it, and never used it with girls. Still, the player's journey is about trying something new. I walked her up to Primrose Hill so we could sober up a bit under the night sky. We lay down on the grass and looked at the stars. After a decent interval, I kissed her for the first time in three months. She liked it, but it was getting cold, so we walked back to the main road and scored some dope from a shifty-looking black guy who sat under the railway bridge like a troll, before catching a bus home. Never let it be said that Krauser doesn't do things in style.

As Soraya sobered up, she started getting arsey as the pre-emptive Last Minute Resistance surfaced. I ignored her ramblings and gave her a quick tour of the house before we repaired to my room. On the way upstairs, we passed Mick coming down with a plate of half-eaten tacos. His reaction on seeing Soraya was priceless.

Yes! Back of the net!

That wasn't childish or egotistical *at all*, so don't say.

She rolled a joint while I lay on the bed organising the music on my laptop. That loosened her up enough for us to make out, although now she was giving the "we won't have sex" talk. Every time I got close to her breasts, she'd bat my hands away and stand up to smoke. Then she'd come back onto the bed. Now it was 3am, and we were both under the duvet, Soraya in her underwear and me in my boxer shorts.

Finally, I decided that she wasn't going to put out and the more I tried the more control I handed her. It was time to lie back and sleep. She'd been setting hoops and traps for me for several months and those were yet more. I heard the clock tick. It was now the early hours of April 30th, and my monthly new-notch streak was about to snap on the twelfth month. I shut my eyes and felt Soraya shuffle into a comfortable sleeping position next to me.

My eyes snapped back open five minutes later, and I stared at the ceiling.

No! Fuck this! I'm not taking it anymore! Bitch comes into my bed, bitch is gonna get fucked!

Relaxing on Hampstead Heath

I rolled onto her and went after it with renewed intent. She said, "No," and I said, "Yes." Then she moaned and gurgled, "Aahhhhh," squirming with pleasure and letting me know that she was getting turned on when I breathed in her ear and licked her lobe. More gentle caressing of body parts followed, culminating in me forcing my hand between her legs so I could rub her up and break through her token resistance. I fingered her hard and she grabbed me tight, moaning and reaching for my cock.

The moment had finally arrived. For the first time since meeting, I was convinced that I was definitely going to fuck her. I pulled away slightly and moved my cock towards her face while continuing to frig her hard.

"No," she said, in a rather half-hearted manner. "We're not... ahhh... having... ahhh... sex. We... ahhh... just friends."

As her mouth was open and I didn't want to hear any more shit from her at that stage, I pushed my cock into it. She sucked it a couple of times, turned away, and said the magic words.

"Do you have a condom?"

I rolled over to my bedside cupboard to fish one out of the drawer, and when I turned back, she'd ripped off her panties.

I squashed her into the mattress for the next half hour. Her fantastically firm gym body enthused me, and it's no exaggeration to say that up until that moment she was the hottest girl I'd ever rattled. All twenty-four years of her. Four thoughts crossed my mind in the small hours of that last day of April as a hot Brazilian bounced on the end of my dick.

I had a new notch, which meant I'd fucked a new girl every calendar month for a full year, with the twelfth-month fuck coming just before the final whistle was about to blow.

Three of my last four lays were full-on eights.

Poor old Prince William was consummating his enormously expensive marriage to an unremarkable twenty-nine-year-old trout at the same time I was consummating my new notch that had cost me five beers and a bag of dope.

And best of all, Mick was sleeping alone next door, no doubt hearing the whole affair and crying tears of ineptitude. The world had shown it was fair and just after all.

I was once more reminded of an important rule of sales – you never burn a bridge or a potential client. You never know when things will swing back into your favour.

Chateaux gym

Sparring Lee

Holiday to Barcelona

CHAPTER
FIVE

Aphrodite

CHAPTER
FIVE

APHRODITE

The PUA industry is an unregulated market that frequently resembles the Wild West. Every week a clutch of new websites pop up with lame domain names like *alphaman101.com* or *sexsecretsseductionnow.com*. Any man fool enough to click on them will see a page of cookie-cutter "me-too" posts about the "How To Start A Harem" or "Five Tricks To Make Her Wet And Chase You."

If it's a daygame blog, chances are the owner just chose a page from *Daygame Mastery* and re-phrased my content.

There are no barriers to entry in my business, and that cuts both ways. The upside is any talented player can set up a site and draw regular readers through providing consistently good content. There is no cartel to protect incumbents from competition, and thus everyone must stay on their toes. Back in the mid-noughties there was in fact a PUA Cartel in which the big-name internet marketers, bullshitters such as David DeAngelo, Vin DiCarlo, and Carlos Xuma, would cross-promote each other's seduction products and share email lists. It was little different to the fat loss or penis enlargement industries. None of those men had even proven their bona-fides by picking up women on camera or live infield.

In fact if you google David DeAngelo's wife, you'd demand an instant refund on his products. The man has elite class *anti*-game.

Thankfully, with the rise of blogging, YouTube, boot-camp coaching, and lightly-moderated forums it means that the internet marketers only ever get one chance to dip their hands into a newbie's pocket before he sees through the scam and moves on to the real material.

The downside of an unregulated market is the sheer volume of spam from fakers, cranks, and charlatans. There's a lot of noise to filter out, and it might take a while for an aspiring player to differentiate between the legit players and the keyboard warriors. Even now, a few of the biggest names in the industry are men who have never proven their ability to pick up women.

One such man goes by the nom de plume *Sixty Years of Challenge*, and yet his material is fantastic. He released a four-part e-book in 2010 that was quickly passed around the London seduction community, and we immediately began testing his ideas. Key to his system was strong eye contact, hand-holding, and then rapid escalation. *Sixty* believed seduction to be almost entirely non-verbal and that moving fast and decisively was in itself attractive. Until him, PUA orthodoxy held that attraction is an *emotion* felt by the girl whereas escalation is a *process* to move past milestones on the route towards sex – they are different categories. *Sixty* upended the orthodoxy to claim that fast escalation doesn't just rely on attraction to fuel it, but it actually *amplifies* that attraction.

That idea intrigued me. Mystery Method split the seduction dance into three stages – attraction, comfort, seduction – and each of these into a further three sub-stages. He advised opening (A1) and then "running attraction material" (A2) until the girl gives you indicators of interest. You can then make the girl run her attraction material on you (A3) until you both have mutually confirmed attraction. At that point you move into Comfort, which is where you get to know each other better as real people. It's not until A3 that the player should make an overt indication that he is sexually attracted to the girl. Until then his intent is hidden (or at least nebulous).

Sixty disagreed. He suggested making your intent obvious from the opening seconds and then rapidly escalating. You cannot create attraction out of nothing, but you can amplify and kindle whatever small flame is already there. So *Sixty* suggested filtering hard in the opening seconds, as this would both eliminate girls who are not at all interested in you (saving you time and emotional investment in dead leads) while also amplifying attraction in the girls who do like you. The very boldness of your escalation would heat up pre-existing attraction and create strong momentum. This is analogous to a salesman qualifying his cold call leads.

It sounds obvious written like this, especially as a similar method developed by an Electrolux salesman in New York has been taught since the 1920s, but for the seduction community it was revolutionary. It would be awhile until the concept was neatly embedded into the London Daygame Model, but through much of 2011 we were trying all manner of retarded escalations.

Sixty wasn't just about technical advice. He also wrote the first manual for players managing girls they've already slept with, called *Relationship Roulette*. It was an eye-opening read, and I was initially resistant to his frame because his major two themes were:

- All women are dirty whores.
- You can never keep a girl for long unless moving towards children and long-term co-habitation.

His e-book read like a systematic dismantling of Disney romance. He posited that women have a *body agenda* imbued by nature which drives them to attract and pair up with the right man. During the early phases of courtship – be it walking hand-in-hand along a beach or smashing her in a nightclub toilet stall – she will be in "acquisition mode" and presenting her best front. She'll be initially agreeable, submissive, and enthusiastic. The problems arise after the honeymoon sex wears off. Then she'll begin slotting you into a pre-defined space in her life – are you the casual lover, or a serious babies-and-ring prospect? If she decides you're a cad, the clock starts ticking down, and you'll lose her soon enough. This is because after passing her initial filter between sexworthy/non-sexworthy to get your notch, her body agenda will put you through a second filter – are you worth investing in with the bloom of her youth, or should she discard you and find a stronger prospect? If you find your fuck buddy getting cranky after a couple of months, it's likely she's pegged you for a cad and is checking out of the relationship. Her acquisition phase has ended, and she'll have little trouble moving on when a stronger prospect enters her life.

Over the next few years my experience would prove *Sixty* correct. You can't keep a girl hanging longer than two years, and to get that far she needs lots of affection. Usually they drop off much sooner. It's not due to any lack of attraction or relationship mismanagement on your part. It's simply the harsh reality of the female life-cycle: she's only young and pretty for a short time, and she must cash in her casino chips before she hits The Wall – typically around her early thirties.

It's disappointing to learn that there's a hard time limit on how long a womanizer can have consequence-free sex with any one woman. A man must revise his expectations downwards and adapt to the reality, meaning:

- The grind never ends. Girls will always drop off the hook so you must constantly work new leads.
- Running a "harem" is ultimately a fool's errand. After the initial ego trip and excitement wears thin, it becomes a lot of ball-ache.
- It's best to pick women who are at the right stage of their lives: either young enough to feel no rush to settle down, or girls wanting one last fling before marrying a chump.

You probably didn't pay attention to the last few paragraphs because you're still hung up on the "all women are dirty whores," aren't you? Well, allow me to explain.

Sixty coined the term *purity fantasy* for men's tendency to think women are either a Madonna or a whore. Contrary to their own chest-pounding bravado, men desire female affection more than they do sex. The problem is we can't accept affection from "bad girls" and thus we must make ourselves believe any object of affection (whether giving it or receiving it) is a "good girl."

This binary categorisation was created by men who aren't experienced with women. A good girl is just a bad girl who hasn't been caught, and the latter is simply more overt in pursuing her body agenda. It's a continuum rather than binary categories and, depending on the girl's ability to control her lust for you, you either get fast sex or slow sex. Some girls don't mind publicly signalling that they prefer faster sex (through fashion and body language) and this visible tip of the "bad girl" iceberg gives a misleading impression to the inexperienced man.

I still had a purity fantasy in 2011. Like most men, I wanted to date good girls and steer clear of dirty bar skanks. Now I'm inclined to believe the "bar skank" is up there with the "natural alpha" as a mythological creature (mainly because I've never met either, though I'm willing to concede that others may have). Maybe there's a waterfront dive bar where the bar skank and natural alpha are having a drink together as I type, at the next table to prime Mike Tyson and the Easter Bunny.

The bar skank concept is needed as a foil for the angelic good girl. The former provides the contrast that shines the pedestal of the latter. It's human nature to define our enemies as the blackest of black-hearted rogues so that our heroes appear more saintly by comparison. For the man struggling to get laid, 'bar skank' is convenient sour grapes shorthand to pre-emptively dismiss any hot girl who wouldn't ever fuck him, without him feeling the sting of real rejection he'd get if he actually tried it on.

Given the tortuous lengths men will go to deceive themselves, the obvious question is: why?

Why do men carve the female population into good girls and bad girls, then pedestalise the former?

The root cause is cuckoldry. Men fear it like women fear rape because, genetically, it's the same outcome – a member of the opposite sex completely derailing your reproductive strategy by force or guile. A women suffering rape would be (in the pre-modern times that hard-wired her psychology) exposed to many risks: sexually transmitted disease, mortality in child-birth, ruined marriage prospects, and of course a pregnancy that forces her to raise a child who carries a genetic code that is fifty percent garbage. In the raw economic calculus of the sexual marketplace, rape is equivalent to grand larceny. Sex for a man has no such dire consequences, but investing his productive efforts into raising a child can – a woman who persuades or cheats a man into raising another man's child is perpetrating grand larceny upon him. That's why we have such instinctive contempt for cuckolds – they are surrendering the hard fought gains of their entire genetic ancestry.

A woman always knows a baby is hers but the man never does. Men must take an awful lot on trust regarding their woman's fidelity. This simple division between the sexes (and the biological potential for women to cheat a man out of twenty years of protection and resources) explains the entire history of what feminists like to call the "evil patriarchy."

- Why were medieval women fitted with chastity belts when their husbands went off on crusades?
- Why don't men believe it when the woman's family all coo that the newborn "has her father's eyes"?
- Why do men's rights organisations push for DNA paternity testing while feminist groups resist such testing with more vigour than they resist immigrant rape gangs?
- Why aren't women allowed out alone in Arab countries without a male family member as chaperone?

The answer is the same in every case: "Bitch, you can't be trusted."

Men will go to extraordinary lengths to create paternity-certainty, and women will resist them every step of the way. When a woman is in the acquisition phase she'll take great pains to present herself as a good girl to her prospect and thus worthy of his investment. She'll tell him how all those other women are just whores, and that she's only had two boyfriends before. Oh, and did she say he's the best sex she ever had? There's just something *special* about him. She actually *enjoys* the sex with him. Those previous two boyfriends? Barely had sex with them. Didn't raise a sweat. Honest!

You know all that bullshit you whisper into a girl's ear to get her into bed? Don't think it's one-way traffic. She's got her own plans for you.

There are all kinds of real-world things a man can do to reduce his odds of being cuckolded, but those odds never drop to zero.

You just need to pop out for a newspaper at the wrong time, and if you don't return early for your forgotten umbrella, you'll never catch her in bed with the milkman. The odds of cuckoldry are always higher than zero, and that means there will also be cuckold-related anxiety. Such high stakes are why we say *all is fair in love and war.*

Cuckold-related anxiety is the wellspring for the purity fantasy. The fantasy helps a man to suppress and displace this anxiety. The worse he is with women, the stronger the anxiety and thus stronger the fantasy.

Of course, this isn't a conscious thought process. Unwittingly, a man deals with the cuckoldry problem by convincing himself only bad girls like casual sex. Good girls don't like sex and have to be cajoled into it over a lengthy courtship process. If our hero can just find such a unicorn, he will be safe from raising another man's bastard. Furthermore, his ego basks in the validation that it was only due to his super seduction powers that he persuaded his angel to end her vow of celibacy against her better judgement.

The seduction was so long, so involved, and he's so special that there's *no way* this good girl can be stolen by a charming cad. No way!

I'd suggest this man demurs from reading volume four of this memoir, *Adventure Sex*. His girl is probably in it.

Some girls really wouldn't dream of cheating. I've tried to fuck a whole bunch of girls who clearly fancied me, were clearly horny, but they had sufficient self-control to prioritise their self-image as a Good Girl above the stirring of their loins. I'll talk about the r/K spectrum later, which offers men some hope that their girl isn't just one flat tire and one hot recovery mechanic away from her next pregnancy.

That said, given the right man and a fortuitous (for her) chain of events even those 'good girls' probably could be enticed into adventure sex, at least once.

I was drawn to daygame because I wanted to meet Good Girls. Everyone knows only Bad Girls hang out in clubs and bars. I didn't concern myself with pulling girls quickly because surely that just confirms the lucky lady is a Bad Girl, right? I told myself it's smart to take several dates and intermittent Long Game to catch my prey.

I'm sure there's a small number of truly bad girls out there – their number likely growing as our civilisation collapses further. I'm equally sure that by focusing on low-class bars and status-whore nightclubs, PUAs are experiencing an adverse selection feedback loop that goes as follows:

- PUA theory says all girls are sluts, that we should act like jerks, and pick-up is best done in bars and clubs.
- PUA goes to where sluts congregate, acts like a jerk.
- Normal girls recognise him as a jerk and blow him out. Those sets last a few minutes each, tops.
- Sluts recognise him as a jerk and like it. Those sets last a long time and sometimes end in sex.
- PUA doesn't spot the difference, thinking the normal girls were just a statistically-predictable attrition.
- PUA writes lay report that confirms all girls are sluts, it's best to act like a jerk, and that pick-up is best done in bars and clubs.

This is akin to an inexperienced salesman trying to pre-qualify his leads and mistakenly filtering out his best potential customers and referrals. It doesn't make sense to base your 'sales strategy' on sluts and bad girls ('strong leads' to the inexperienced PUA) because there just aren't very many of them around, and they are usually grotty. It's more relevant to delineate the continuum and learn to place any given girl (all leads) on it to know how to deal with her.

It takes quite awhile to learn the signals a Bad Girl gives off because they are not like the TV stereotype – The stereotype is based on only the visible tip of the iceberg. A player is keenly observing everything about her; body language, her instinctive reactions, her eye contact, and how she moves. The TV show stereotype of dyed hair, piercings, short skirts, visible tattoos, and so on are second-order associated characteristics, not primary. The Bad Girls are statistically more likely to show those traits, but it's just a shorthand filtering guide – what a player needs to place the girl are her first-order traits. It works the other side of the spectrum, too.

My naïve pursuit of Good Girls led me to prefer the younger and less-experienced – virgins or near-virgins – and over time I've gotten much better at reading their signs. And yes, I explain these signs in more detail later.

Have I confused you, poor reader? Which is it, that good girl/bad girl is a fake dichotomy fuelled by a low-SMV man's purity fantasy, or there really is a good girl/bad girl spectrum and a savvy player can learn to read it? Read on, grasshopper. That's a core theme of the book.

By 2013, I'd made the switch from being the guy who girls might cheat *on* to being the guy that girls cheat *with*. Most guys fall into the first category and, as a result, they attempt to manage the risk by increasing their "relationship equity." This means they pour more time, attention, emotion, and money into their relationship so that the girls will feel grateful. Unfortunately, this has zero impact on a girl's primeval attraction and instead encourages her to make logical, rational decisions about him, pushing him further out of the "hot guy" box. Girls may know rationally that a man is a *great guy* but if he's not *attractive* she'll be emotionally flat to him even as she chastises herself for being unable to fancy the man she knows is good for her. This internal struggle in female dual mating strategy becomes especially troublesome for her as she approaches The Wall and time forces her hand to choose a man and settle down with him.

Player-hate is a natural outgrowth of cuckold anxiety. A chump's awareness and fear of cads forces him to confront the possibility his angel may cheat on him. As the chump's relationship investment increases, he stands to lose bigger should it all come crashing down. He's quite aware of the high price he's paying for access to his girl's vagina and resents the cads who pay far less for the same thing. It's not much different to buying your new car at list price and then watching the salesman offer the very next customer an 80% discount before you've left the lot, just because he's cooler than you.

Cuckoldry doesn't impact a player with the same emotional resonance as it does a normal chump. It took me a long time to make the switch myself, and for the period covered by this volume I still found it very difficult to accept that some of my girls would also have boyfriends. The root cause is a man's natural inclination to reject affection from a girl he knows is sleeping with another man. He doesn't wish to get pulled into an emotional attachment with a pre-existing cuckold risk (i.e. if she's already sleeping with another man, half of the conditions for cuckoldry are already present). Throughout this volume you'll notice I vacillate between seeking and avoiding emotional connection with girls as I struggled with this issue.

If I slept with a girl in another country who also had a local man there, it would bother me a little knowing he was rattling her in my absence. *Sixty* advised that women do sleep around, and you'd better get used to it because the purity fantasy denies reality and the fantasy is eventually even more harmful. *Sixty's* attitude is a gateway into the 'Secret Society': the shared understanding between *all* women and a *tiny minority* of men about how casual sex really works, which leads that minority of men to get most of that sex. Girls can sense in your sub-communications when you 'get it', and it takes all the sleaziness out of a sexualised approach.

As I became better with women, I increasingly adopted the abundance mentality, knowing that should any given girl cause me problems I'd just go out and find another. It might take a little time but there was no doubt I'd eventually get an equal or better replacement. This is the foundation of a player's freedom. The chump Nick Krauser of 2009 never had that option, which is why my divorce hit so hard. Aside from the predictable emotional turmoil of rejection, abandonment, and frustrated love, there was an additional rather more pragmatic emotion: fear that I'd blown my last chance with pretty girls.

Take away that fear and cuckolding isn't such a salient risk. So what if one of my regulars decided she liked her new man more than me and extricated herself from my sweaty grasp? I could just hit the streets and replace her. So what if she got knocked up by a brown man on her summer holiday to Turkey? – I wasn't ever going to marry her anyway. Remove the consequences, and you remove the anxiety. As the risks associated with cheating diminished, I was quite surprised to find my ability to get morally indignant diminished in equal portion. When first reading manosphere horror stories about, for example, a US Marine returning from a combat tour of Iraq to find his girlfriend had starred in amateur porn in his absence, I'd be incensed.

Kill the bitch!

Now I think, "dumb-ass."

I doubt this is a weakening of my moral resolve. More likely it's confirmation of my theory on the true foundation of moral law, namely:

- Half of human morality is a codification of "I scratch your back, you scratch mine" cooperation into simple principles and prohibitions.
- The other half is malignant sophistry that scumbags infect you with so that you'll act in their interests rather than your own.

Try applying those two axioms to any one of your cherished moral principles. You'll probably find you believe that principle simply because it benefits you. If it ceases to work in your favour, you'll likely find your moral principles changing. A male prohibition on female cheating clearly works in the favour of low-SMV men by rigging the market against a woman's freedom to choose and also against the high-SMV men they'd prefer. So the chumps of the world will unite against cads and moralise on the evils of cheating, attempting to bullshit the women and cads from acting in their own best interests. It's like socialists uniting to keep entrepreneurs and their employees down.

I just triggered you, didn't I?

There's a good case to be made that a prohibition on cheating is integral to civilisation because it reassures normal men that they really can trust women, and thus it's wise for them to go to work and create the wealth that gives us all housing, running water, and sanitation. I'll admit, there's a point in there. However, if you want to sleep with many hot, young women, you'd best dispel your illusions and learn to see the human world as it really is: it's a complex ecosystem where everyone has competing interests, and alliances between different demographics are necessarily fragile.

What we call civilisation is very fragile, and it's riddled with loopholes. There are groups of people who are actively working against your interests, and if you are too blind to see, they'll probably succeed. Perhaps you don't care; perhaps you believe your child really does have your eyes.

Adopting the player role isn't entirely an upside in comparison to the chump life. Sure, we get plenty of sex without all the emotional damage a woman can cause us, but we lose out on the warm, fuzzy feelings that dating women can provide. *Sixty* believed men desire female affection more than they do sex itself – and I agree. The problem is affection leads to connection which leads to risk. I was attempting to square the circle by seeking out inexperienced young women for sex because then I'd feel more comfortable giving and receiving affection in a casual-sex relationship.

And of course younger women are way hotter than old hags. Once you're pushing your age-range up to 28-years-old, you might just want to shoot yourself.

There was a more pragmatic reason to seek out the stable, slightly-introverted, thoughtful young women; seducing them played to my strengths better. I'd already tried gaming bars and nightclubs. It was hard. Every style of pick-up benefits men of different types. For example, Tinder is all about the profile photo and your (declared) age. There's simply no other way to distinguish yourself until after the match. Confidence means nothing, nor your banter, nor your calibration: unless you can somehow convey it through the photo. Even height is irrelevant as it cannot be accurately determined in a couple of cherry-picked photo-shopped photos. Nightclubs are frequently too loud to talk, too stimulus-laden to display body language subtleties, and due to the vast quantities of Dutch courage sold at the bar, even the confidence to cold approach isn't much required. Instead nightclubs play to the strengths of men who are tall, good-looking, well-dressed, in a well-connected group, and of a boisterous extroverted manner.

Basically, not me. I understood my strengths and weaknesses.

Nightclubs force you to move very fast in order to counteract a drunk party girl's natural flakiness. For fast pulls to succeed the girl must be feeling both high attraction and sexual arousal. There's no opportunity for a slow build, as she'll soon be distracted by her friends, the music, another man, or she'll just get too drunk and forget she gave her number.

I was gradually refining my daygame style to best take advantage of my strengths while compensating for the weaknesses of being a thirty-six-year-old man of average height, average looks, with a bald head and introverted demeanour.

Daygame with good girls let me take it slower and enjoy the process more. They're willing to sit around in cafés talking, giving me a chance to reel them in. I can get into their heads through long game and enjoy the emotional connection. In the closing chapters of this memoir, you'll see it in practice with my Serbian girls, who each fitted slap-bang into the sweet spot of the purity fantasy plus slow steady seduction.

After all this hunger-inducing talk about good girls and virgins and why I prefer to fuck them, you'd probably like a few for yourself. Here's a few pointers for how to spot them. Several years of chasing these girls has honed my radar, and now I've developed a mental check box that I can tick off as I talk to them.

So what to look for? Let's begin with signals apparent from just looking at her before you've opened.

She needs to be young, as every passing year increases the odds of a dick finding her vagina, and any kind of rebel or outcast look increases the odds that she's both inexperienced with sex and – incongruently –

more likely to have sex quickly with *you*. Ask yourself if she appears to stand apart from the crowd. Does she conform to the dress code of other girls her age, in this town, in this season? For example, I just returned from a trip to Warsaw where the spring fashion was blue jeans with multiple rips in the knees and thighs. As a rule of thumb, more rips meant more of a fashion junkie and thus both more mainstream and more likely to prioritise social status over psychology – a bad sign for a daygamer. Of course, that can only be a rough guide, but it's a good starting point. In the Belgrade and Zagreb summers of 2012 the fashion was denim shorts, single-colour thin-strapped vest, and Converse All-Star shoes. Girls dressed differently than this are more likely to be outsiders and thus better daygame fodder.

A girl walking confidently down the street like she's on the promenade is clearly comfortable showing herself to the world and wishes everyone to notice the results of her fashion and gym regime. This tends to suggest she is outgoing, externally referenced, and likes to be "in the mix." Each trait slightly increases the odds that she's been fucked by several men, is active in a wide social network, judges people primarily on their social status rather than personality, and is juggling multiple orbiting suitors. It's not an exact science, but pick-up requires a player to stack the deck every chance he gets. I prefer to choose girls who look confident but a little modest, the type who think promenading around is gauche and vulgar. This indicates they are likely to be introverted and hostile to displays of social status, and thus more likely to value my proposition.

You do need to talk to the girl, and it's at this point you'll tick the most boxes to determine her type. Look for introverted speech patterns, particularly an ability to stick to one topic without distraction. Is she educated and intelligent? Shy or timid? If she has little or no sexual experience she'll still have plenty of pent-up sexual energy, so even a timid girl's eyes will flash with some fire if she fancies you. Don't think timid girls are weak – they just don't feel comfortable with the early stages of making friends. Their line in the sand will be as strongly enforced as the queen diva in a nightclub.

Does she have interests that seem unusual for her age, such as strange musical tastes, writing poetry, or involvement with an alternative sub-culture? Girls are herd animals so the mainstream girls will all like the same predictable things. If your girl likes 1970s British rock, or *Doctor Who*, or is reading Chaucer, then she's independently-minded and has a foot outside the herd – that means she's far more likely to choose a coffee date with you over a party night with her university friends.

How is her sense of humour? Is it quirky or she names unexpected sources (for example, the typical Russian girl will not know Monty Python)? You're looking for any information that suggests she is disengaged from her peers. That doesn't mean she's unpopular, because a girl can go to all the right parties and hang out with the cool crowd, but in her mind she has a secret existence. Such girls live in their heads and are usually dissatisfied with their "small town" existence. Life has primed them to seek out "the other" which is very often a dominant older man from another country.

Dating Turkish girls in London

As you engage her in conversation, steer the conversation onto topics that let you probe for such information, then tick the boxes. If she fulfils the criteria, you have yourself a live prospect. Often she'll make an effort to overtly disqualify your usual competition to indicate the field is open for you. For example, she might say "Polish men are so boring. They only like football and drinking."

A large proportion of these girls do not go to nightclubs because they rarely drink alcohol, they don't like pretty boys, they don't date boys their own age, they don't use social media in the way you'd expect, and they have clunky old mobile phones.

Assuming you have established she's the right type, it's time to whip up the romance for her *"Fifty Shades"* moment. Be prepared to play the long game. Same Day Lays ("SDLs") do happen, but that requires a whole raft of other chance factors to be present and in your favour. The battle is won or lost at the mental level so you must get them sufficiently intrigued that they'll give you time to showcase your intellectual mastery.

The preceding guidelines are just that – guidelines. Each girl is different and represents a unique challenge, necessitating you to think on your feet. When a player begins his journey he must learn rules and concepts to direct him and they'll rarely fit a situation exactly. As his journey continues he'll increasingly free himself of such strictures and learn to calibrate specifically to each girl. However, so long as you follow the template as laid out, you'll nudge your percentages upwards. There's no magic.

April's showers bring forth May's flowers, apparently. Early May would certainly give me an opportunity for a de-flowering.

In late 2010 RSG had taught a custom boot camp for a group of eight men who'd formed their own rat pack. One guy, a thirty-year-old musician with a PUA moniker of Whitewolf, did lots of daygame, so I'd tried him out as a wing. We got on fairly well, and on Saturday afternoon he brought two of the others with him to Camden Town for a walkabout. Bright sunshine had brought stacks of girls out, all eager to shake off their winter blues and prance about in their spring finery. I did a few unremarkable warm-ups, just getting into my stride, and then on my fourth set I saw a tall, dusky girl walking under the railway bridge towards the market. She wore a yellow and black woolly cardigan.

"You look like a clumsy bumblebee," I said.

She laughed and after five minutes let me walk her off to a market café tucked in a corner by the canal lock. That's how I met Alexandria, a twenty-year-old student from Greece. She was on a week's trip to London from her university in Brighton.

I directed her to a table by the window so we could sip our drinks looking out over the high water of the canal. After ten minutes or so, I noticed her unconsciously fiddling with her empty bottle of orange juice. This suggested an element of emotional involvement and – in particular – a moment of decision. This was a good sign because it hinted she now considered me a stronger prospect for frollicks and now was mulling over just what such frollicks would entail. And the more we talked, the more she twisted and pulled on it. Attraction was handled so I pushed on into rapport.

"I'm in the UK on a university exchange for a few months. I'm studying fine art, but my real passion is ballet."

Promising. She was situationally ripe to seek holiday adventure away from the prying eyes of her family and social circle.

"I came to London for a ballet workshop. Today we finished early so I came to the market."

That told me my window of opportunity was good but time-limited. She was alone in a strange town, didn't know anyone, and looking for adventure. Perfect. It was a case of pressing ahead and hoping her line in the sand was somewhere *after* getting naked on my bed.

"I'll show you a nice park around the corner. It's called Primrose Hill. We can sit on the grass and look out at a stunning view across all of London," I suggested.

"Ooooh, let's do that!" she cooed.

We climbed the hill and sat down, chatting away like any other of the dozen couples nearby. I pulled her towards me to rest her head on my belly as she gazed up at the blue sky. Still we kept talking until, with her face near mine, we went quiet, and I held her gaze. It was an achingly obvious kiss-close moment, so I pulled the trigger... and she turned her head away!

"No" she said.

She didn't move, so I tried again.

We kissed a few seconds then I pulled away, looking up through the trees. I wanted her to feel I wasn't too thirsty while simultaneously making her pulse race and letting her process the moment. Girls usually have a stronger physiological reaction to kissing than men.

Though careful not to take anything for granted, I started thinking the three magic words – Same Day Lay. I helped her up off the grass, and we walked hand-in-hand to the nearest pub to get some alcohol down her neck. I was still in the habit of taking numbers rather than pushing forwards, so I had to steady my resolve and decide to push for the bounce-back. I thought back to my prior Saturday afternoon in Camden where I'd instant-dated and kissed an Italian girl under exactly the same circumstances (and even picked her up just ten meters further down the same street). That had fizzled out on me because I lacked the stones to bounce-back when the opportunity had arisen. No way I was going to let that happen again.

We touched some more, I qualified her hard, and before too long she agreed to come back to Château RSG to eat some noodles. So far, so good.

After the noodles, I gave her the house tour, eliciting a giggle when I stopped her at the door to my room and told her she wasn't allowed in unless she took her shoes off. I escalated her on the bed, slowly and steadily. It was all plain sailing until I reached the zipper on her strides.

"No."

It's always worth battling the Last Minute Resistance, but this fight stretched to two hours, and I was never going to win. When I finally rolled off she pouted, looking at me wide-eyed as if she was expecting me to be angry and disappointed. I'd already accepted what was and came to terms with it.

"I'm a virgin."

Ah!

I tried to reframe her, saying I'd take responsibility for making a woman out of her. She relaxed a little, but the little voice inside was telling her to resist. Whatever her innermost thoughts, the impact on my sexual ambition was clear – she'd reached her line in the sand and sex wasn't going to happen. I took her to the Underground station half an hour later, and we kissed goodbye.

I was still fumbling and inexperienced with the more difficult girls. But no matter, another virgin, a hot nineteen-year-old Lithuanian called Auguste wandered out of "long game" and into my kill-zone right on cue the same day.

We met in Vilnius, back in January, when I'd gone there to close Dovile. She'd been walking down Gedminos shopping street with a spring in her step when I introduced myself and took her on an instant date. As usual in early 2011, I messed up the i-date by talking way too much about myself and not keeping sufficient detail hidden to create intrigue. To make matters worse, when I took her on a date the next evening, I'd already arranged another date at the same place afterwards. The girls met each other as Auguste vacated her chair and Laura arrived.

In truth it probably didn't matter. I think both girls had an initial interest in me, and then as the date progressed the spark died. They were hot, young eights, and I just wasn't cool enough to get girls like that unless I was very lucky. It would take time to develop sufficient self-belief to keep a girl like that attracted.

After some failed long game on Facebook, Auguste had dropped off the radar. However, she texted me the same day I met Alexandria to say she was in the UK with a friend, attending a university on the south coast. She was visiting London for a few days so I invited her to Château RSG for a BBQ we'd decided to put on.

Auguste was sexually unresponsive from the beginning. Nowadays I'd either ditch her pronto or, if social propriety made it awkward, aggressively friend-zone her. However, back then my inexperience carried me forwards to accept her LJBF texts and try to "beat" them. I was searching for the good girl and believing I could turn her around when she hadn't ever given off any real signs of sexual interest.

I learnt that if a good girl isn't giving you the flash of attraction in her eyes on your initial meeting, then sex isn't going to happen, and you're wasting your time. Had I been of a more outgoing inclination I'd have recognised her as a potential "referral" for her friends but that kind of networking has always tired me.

Two days after Auguste, I persuaded Alexandria to come out again on her last night in London. We downed a few beers in a Soho pub, and she rebuffed my kiss attempt with a "not here." I pulled back completely, taking the hint.

"Let's buy a bottle of vodka and make White Russians," I enthused.

She merrily followed me home, and we rolled around on the bed some more. She was resolute in not having sex, but at least I contented myself helping her achieve a few personal firsts: blow-job, face-fuck, and some fingering. I think Alexandria was never going to let me fuck her, preferring to just fool around on the right side of her line. Okay, *fool around it is* I thought, and had her wank me off at the bus stop while we waited for the number 13 back to Trafalgar Square.

I'm classy like that.

I sought out Tony so he could debrief the set with Alexandria. He asked me about the timing and details of the escalation until he noticed something curious.

"She wouldn't allow herself to orgasm," he said.

Several times she'd come right to the edge, grinding and writhing, pushing into me with tension and then suddenly pushed me away and cooled down. That had confused me.

"Girls know their limits. They know the point at which they lose control, and if they don't want to have sex they'll stop you before they reach it. For most girls, it's skin-on-skin contact with their pussy but it varies."

There's a chance another date would've resulted in sex, but it's more likely she'd decided how far she was ever willing to go while fiddling with her orange juice bottle in the first cafe in Camden Market. She went back to Brighton, and I never saw her again.

Estonian Cherry

ESTONIAN CHERRY

he now-familiar *Euro Jaunt* model, in which a few daygamers will buy budget flights out to a European capital and spend a week living in cheap Airbnb apartments and chasing girls, didn't really exist in early 2010 until Jimmy and I invented it. That's not to say no man had ever gotten the idea to travel and fuck local girls – I believe Genghis Khan, Marco Polo, and Alexander of Macedonia may have been the first big name Euro-Jaunters – but I certainly hadn't heard about anyone making a thing of it.

And in my world, if I don't know about something then it probably never happened.

Rock Solid Game had first flown out to Lithuania in July 2009 to teach a boot camp in Vilnius with a local organiser. That had opened our eyes to the talent in Eastern Europe. Jimmy, Fernando, and I had taken further trips to Poland, Croatia, and Latvia. We'd hit upon something exciting and wanted more. We just needed someone else to pay for it. Taking students along to pay our bills struck us as being a good wheeze, and we started to wonder if it was a sustainable business model. After all, you only need one or two guys to make it work. We had a growing reputation so we decided to put it to the test.

In early May 2011, Mick received an email via his blog from a Russian guy in St. Petersburg. He owned a sex toy company, was loaded, and wanted daygame coaching. The same week I received an email from an Indian guy who worked in the Swiss finance industry, asking much of the same thing. I already had flags from Lithuania and Latvia, and now I wanted the "Baltic Triple Crown." We offered them a shared residential in Tallinn, Estonia.

The lure of another free holiday more than overcame Mick's and my reluctance to spend a week together. We booked ourselves for ten days in all, giving us some time to ourselves to pursue our own nefarious ends after the students went home. Mick was still in full-time employment as a financial technician in Central London so it took some conniving for him to arrange the time off.

May weather in Tallinn is perfect. Although it's a small town with high social pressure, it felt like hot girls were everywhere, spilling out onto the streets like migrants from a ferry. It felt like we were constantly in set, chatting up girls. Though Mick and I were initially awkward with each other, the shared mission helped. As the days ticked by, we warmed to the task of coaching and started to rub along better. At the end of the ten days we were getting on like normal friends.

In subsequent years we were to discover that, as with all Baltic countries, it's really easy to burn the place down by doing too many cold approaches. Even now, every few months I hear a horror story or two:

"My regular in Tallinn told me there's an Italian guy running around the Old Town trying to pick up every girl he sees. He's been out every day for a month and the girls all talk about him."

Still, in May 2011 the town was untouched by daygame cockroaches, and we had the run of the place. Mick in particular came on leaps and bounds because he discovered how to get his intent out early. Let me explain.

Game literature frequently distinguishes between *direct* and *indirect* approaching. Opening direct means you display your sexual interest in the girl quickly and obviously, such as saying, "I wanted to talk to you because you look pretty." In contrast, opening indirect means hiding your true intention until you find it judicious to reveal it, usually after she's given you some IOIs. The latter is classic Mystery Method: male-to-female interest (A3) comes after the inverse (A2) .

I'd started out direct from the very beginning of my daygame journey because that's how Johnny Wisdom had taught me on that first boot camp in summer 2009. Later that year I'd fall under the influence of Yad and Andy Yosha's material, which toned down the directness and instead offered an awkward middle-ground – you'd compliment the girl on looking nice but she never really knew you were hitting on her until much later. That's all very Disney, removing the sexual element from daygame and relying on chat and banter as if it's a boyfriend interview designed to convince the girl that she's making a new best friend. To the uninitiated, the "nice guy" opening gives the impression that it's direct because the conversation starts with something almost-sexual ("I think you look nice") but then quickly neutralises itself and becomes so-so generic chat.

A seasoned "nice guy" daygamer can collect lots of numbers from really hot girls, as I can testify from my own and other's experience trying it, but the numbers turn out to be worthless. You *must* hit on the girl. Otherwise she walks away thinking "that was a nice chat" and puts you out of her mind.

This should be obvious. When you're upfront about your pitch, those that aren't interested drop out quickly, and you don't need waste your time on them. If you disguise the product as something else – a bait 'n' switch – girls don't understand your real motive. When they find out, not only do they drop off the radar, they may get angry with you for misleading them. Since the inception of the PUA industry, players have experimented with every possible permutation of how and when to reveal your intent – it's the Philosopher's Stone. The balancing act must address these contradictory features of seduction:

- The longer a girl gets to know you, the better you can demonstrate traits that will increase her attraction to you.
- The longer you avoiding hitting on a girl, the less you can demonstrate to her the attractive masculine traits of confidence, decisiveness, and entitlement.

That puts every player in a bind. Walking up to her to say, "hey bitch, come get some," will earn you points for cockiness but forces her into a Yes/No decision before you've had a chance to reel her in – I call them 'Ultimatum Openers'. At the opposite end of the spectrum, telling her she looks nice and chatting for ten minutes lets her walk away thinking you're pleasant but a bit of a pussy for not pressing your advantage. The latter style gained traction in the daygame community because it appears more successful to the untrained eye on YouTube and in the field. Students liked it because they could avoid the harsh rejection that often follows a declaration of intent by an uncalibrated noob.

My fellow cad in Tallinn

That said, there's a good time and place for the indirect method. If the social situation determines that a meandering non-sexual chat is appropriate, such as sitting on a park bench next to a strange girl on your lunch break, you can start running Mystery Method. Open casually and off-handed, hide your intent, and start dropping Demonstrations of Higher Value ("DHVs'). When she perks up and IOIs you, begin qualifying her and then declare some intent. That's a different world to chasing a girl down and stopping her in a shopping mall.

Before we went to Estonia, Mick had been going out every day for months during his lunch break, chatting up girls in the park where office workers eat their sandwiches. He'd crank the handle of the daygame sausage machine to get a few sets in each time, stacking them up as the weeks and months passed. Unlike me, he's naturally sociable. He enjoys chatting to strangers for the sake of it, whereas I hate it. He'll start up conversations no matter where he is – to a supermarket cashier, a barber, his car mechanic. In contrast, I'll say the minimum necessary to be polite. That's how his style developed, and it makes him excellent at bar game because he doesn't view all of this chat as work.

When he took the same indirect style into his street daygame it led to a predictable flake problem, what works in one social situation can seem odd in another. It's simply weird to chase a girl down, stop her, and then hide your intent. She's obviously wondering, "why did he stop me to say this?"

There are only two ways she can answer that question: either you *aren't* sexually interested in her, in which case she's got no reason to see you again (a flake), or you *are* interested but are hiding it, in which case you must be a bit of a pussy (a flake). You can't win that unless she just likes you so much in spite of it that she'll override such objections. We'd soon find a third way in which you sub-communicate your interest through nuance and innuendo without stating it overtly and forcing an ultimatum upon her – this is "plausibly deniable direct game," but in 2011 we weren't yet so sophisticated. This latter type of game is powerful precisely because you are surfing the edges of nuance and thus able to demonstrate high social intelligence. It's also much harder to get right.

Once our feet touched down in Estonia, Mick experimented with a more direct style, making his sexual intent obvious. I could see the change in his face, that look of liberation we all get when no longer suffering the incongruence of shackling ourselves. Direct game is always the more congruent approach – it feels *right* and a big weight is taken off your shoulders. It also avoids getting trapped in long no-hoper sets because it lets you quickly pre-qualify girls.

Mick and I ran around like two excitable puppies approaching all those lovely Estonian girls in the parks, malls, and streets. They responded well. We became progressively bolder and decided to spend one day just propositioning girls outright. After a minute's chat we'd say, "You're kind of hot and I just want to get laid. Would you like to come home with me?" The girls said no, but usually laughed out loud because they thought it was bold. We didn't care that it was a no-hoper opener because the social experiment was so much fun. We were pushing our boundaries of what we could say on the street.

On that third day we agreed to push hard for bounce-backs with an overt and flagrant sexual proposition. We were pumped. On the way to a bar to meet a date that Mick had fixed up, we saw a slutty-looking two-set stroll by: a young blonde and an age-matched redhead. Their curvy figures were barely concealed by their ripped-up punky clothes. Mick and I exchanged glances. They weren't especially hot – maybe sixes- but they had a looking-for-trouble vibe we hadn't seen much of in the city.

Estonia with Mick

"Let's blatantly hit on them for sex," I said, and we were off. I opened.

"Hey girls. My friend and I were just over there when you walked by. We're on holiday and about to go drinking, but we're feeling a bit tense, so we thought that if we could find a couple of girls, take them home right now, and fuck them… then we'd be able to relax and have a better night."

As the words tumbled out of my mouth I couldn't quite believe I'd said it. I finished my piece, and then we stood looking at them, waiting for a reaction.

The girls were dumbfounded, their legs visibly wobbling as a huge adrenalin spike hit. They'd gone from ambling down the street with a general air of promenading in front of men to suddenly facing an actual decision on whether to get fucked. It's one thing to show skin intending to draw stares but quite another to get called on it. To a girl's physiology it's like being confronted by a mugger, or a millionaire handing out free money. The dial of life suddenly gets turned to maximum, and an immediate decision is needed.

Amazingly, they didn't just auto-reject us and walk off. Instead, they hooked strong like deer-in-the-headlights. We kept ploughing on, and they quickly realized we weren't about to back down, and we did actually intend to bounce them the fifty metres down the road to our apartment.

"Really. We live there, at the blue door by the lamppost. We have some beers."

Their curiosity grew.

"We'll walk over there, sit inside, and put on some music. I'll crack open the beers and we'll drink a little, getting to know each other. Then we'll pair up. There'll be some touching. I'll help you out of those clothes and run my rude hands all over your delightful body."

The sun was still shining, and tourists milled around us with cameras and souvenir bags. I could tell the little redhead was in high sexual state and up for doing it right then – she kept staring at me, blushing, and her body swayed slightly. Unfortunately her blonde friend was showing more resistance. After a few minutes she started pulling on her friend's sleeve to leave. I decided to let them chew it over in their minds.

"We're going drinking now. We'll swap numbers and then later if you get horny and fancy some great rough sex, just let me know."

The redhead gave me her number and we said our goodbyes. I'd never asked her name so I said I'd call her Cherry, as her new 'stripper name'.

We reached the shisha bar, where Mick's date, a stunning 21-year-old nine he'd picked up in the souvenir shop where she worked, and her friend were waiting. The plan was to have a couple of drinks before moving on to a good club that had been recommended to us.

One of my leads from the previous night was waiting for me to show up, but as we entered the club and ordered our first bottle of beer, the redhead texted me.

"Hi, it's Cherry. We are in Hell Hunt. How are you?"

Hell Hunt was an old-style bierhaus popular with students and backpackers. It was also right next to our apartment.

It was decision time. We'd only been in the club for five minutes, chatting to Mick's date's friend while helping Mick raise his state and remain independent of his target. The 19-year-old-old virgin I'd kissed the night before was somewhere in a club, waiting for me, but it was packed, and I hadn't seen her. Cherry, who seemed well up for it, was fifteen minutes away but replying well on texting. Should I stay in the club to help Mick while also trying to work the virgin? Should we both leave to join the two ratbags in Hell Hunt?

"Mate, my girl here is much hotter than the blonde ratbag. And anyway, I don't think the ratbag is up for it. She'll cock-block us all if we go to Hell Hunt. Only the redhead is on, and that's your set."

It was a classic bird-in-the-hand/two-in-the-bush scenario. I messaged Cherry to probe where she stood.

"I'm in Club Prive with Mick. We're a bit busy. Why don't you come join us?"

"My friend doesn't want to come," she replied.

"That's okay. Just come by yourself."

She didn't respond for fifteen minutes. I'd tried to reel her in too fast, and the fishing line had snapped under the tension. Not surprising really – she was an eighteen-year-old girl who knew almost nothing about me and the entirety of our five-minute chat has been me suggesting we fuck right away. It was Saturday night, and she was out with her best friend partying.

Then my phone beeped. Mick was propped up at the bar in what we called the *Jimmy position*, leaning back, surveying the club, with the two girls huddled around him.

"I'm outside Club Prive. Can you come out?" typed Cherry.

It was a no-brainer. I said goodbye to Mick and headed down the stairs.

Cherry was by herself and looked at me with wide eyes. My initial plan had been to bring her into the club for a couple of drinks to get her comfortable and horny. I ditched that idea and started walking her back to my place. The whole time I was thinking *comfort, comfort, comfort* while engaging her logical mind. She was brave, and I didn't want to overload that courage.

"Take your shoes off," I said as we stepped into the apartment. "The wooden floor has just been cleaned."

We went straight through to the bedroom to watch YouTube videos. She lay down on the bed next to me, shaking with combined fear and excitement. My heart was thumping with anticipation, as I'd walked up to an eighteen-year-old girl and propositioned her for sex right in front of her friend, and now she was actually here in my bed three hours later. As unreal as it seemed for me, at least I was a trainee-seducer, had come on holiday precisely to get laid, and had approached her with that plan. She was just a young girl walking to a pub – it was even more dramatic for her.

I rolled over and closed her.

There was some predictable token LMR but nothing that a little intent (and some fingering) couldn't defeat. I subjected her to some dirty talk and then midway through sex I took her anal virginity. Evidently she was in full adventure mode.

Mick arrived home a few hours later. He'd kissed the girl but nothing more came of it. Our shared bedroom was off-limits because of Cherry so he went to sleep on the couch.

"What is your sexual fantasy?" I asked her, while doing her in the ass a second time.

"I think I'd like to be picked up by a long-distance truck driver – you know, as a hitch-hiker – then he'd come on to me and rape me in the back of his truck."

Interesting.

"Have you let many guys fuck you?"

"You're the second," she said, then moaned a little. "I don't know why I'm here, but it feels good."

"My friend Mick fucks lots of girls. I don't know how he does it but they all like him. There must be some magic to it, I think. His girlfriend in London is a catwalk model."

That catwalk model thing was a lie but a player should DHV his friends, and I had a plan.

"He's cool," she said.

"I want you to go into the lounge and fuck him."

"I don't know. I like him, but this is maybe too much. I just met you and you already put your dick in my ass. I think another man is too much. I'm not so wild, you know."

She considered it for a while, as I kept trying to DHV Mick while I reframed her. I heard some suspicious movements from the lounge as Mick could obviously hear me and was wondering how it would turn out. Ultimately, she said no.

A few days later, I booty-called her.

"Come here, Cherry. I want to fuck you."

"I don't know. I'm at the other side of town. I'm at a party."

"I don't care. I want to fuck you. Come here."

"Okay. It will take me an hour to get there."

When she finally showed up I took her into my room, and we did the dirty. Afterwards, lying in bed together she still seemed quite confused.

"This is weird. I was really enjoying myself at the birthday party and then I just walked out without telling my friends. I walked five miles through the worst part of town, in my heels, and ignored my friend's calls. I don't understand it. It's like my feet moved automatically, bringing me here."

CHAPTER
SEVEN

The Daygame Carnival

THE DAYGAME CARNIVAL

The Rock Solid Game guys were not the only wannabe players running around London chasing girls. Something was building, a still-amorphous fog through which shady daygamers moved. In 2010 it was still rather vague. A few people here, a few there. No real daygame community existed, and we didn't have the group self-awareness we have now.

Pretty much anyone reading this book will have heard about Tom Torero – if not, prepare to be introduced to another fascinating personality in the London daygame world. From 2011 through 2014 we'd spend a lot of time hanging out or otherwise thinking about each other. I'll end the suspense now: we never bummed each other. I once slapped his arse while he was banging a Romanian tart, but that's as close as it got.

He started in daygame around the same time as I did, although the precise date changes according to who he's telling. He's an intelligent guy with an obsessive-compulsive streak; two traits shared by almost every good daygamer. He'd been plagued with poor social skills and a nerdy demeanour as a child so that led to him being bullied at secondary school and withdrawing into a world of books and academic study. He did some rather bizarre things, such as getting married in his early twenties (that's odd for the UK), getting divorced, training to be a monk in a Corsican hilltop village, travelling into the wilds, studying under Richard Dawkins, and finally settling down as a primary school teacher in London. I may have garbled those details a little, but he's talked about them on his YouTube channel.

By his late twenties he was at a very low ebb in life. Divorced, socially inhibited, and had only had sex with a couple of girls in his whole life. He read Neil Strauss' book *The Game* and half-arsed the advice on a doe-eyed exchange teacher from France working in his primary school. He fucked her, dated her for a little while, then the shrikes in his teacher's common room gave him a ton of shit for it. He drifted into more half-arsed bar game using Mystery Method, rattled a couple of girls, and then took a new job opportunity as a chance to move to London.

Much like I'd had my "this cannot stand" moment while playing Battlefield Bad Company in early 2009, he'd had his own moment of decisive action. His came from watching YouTube videos of Alex Coulson, one of the daygame pioneers and also a confirmed fraud (unfortunately most of them were).

Coulson rambled around Sydney approaching girls out walking their dogs or sitting in patio cafes. He'd open indirect and slide into chats, then make a weaselly grab for their number. It was pretty shit, and when he finally released an "in-field kiss close" video, some PUA sleuths outed him as a fake – he'd called an ex-girlfriend to act the role of being picked up. The sleuths had managed to find her on Facebook and have her admit on a screen-capped chat that they'd dated a year before thevideo was shot.. That's Alex, by the way. Tom himself would get caught faking his kiss close video in 2012. There are rather a lot of fake in-field videos out there.

Back in 2009 wide-eyed naïve Tom didn't know about the fakery and was instead inspired by the seeming ease of daygame. Like myself and numerous other introverts, he'd found nightgame PUA advice jarring. Rather than run around an awful bar high-fiving staff and wrangling large groups of girls, he'd been intrigued by the low-key nature of chit-chat with solo girls mid-afternoon.

"I can do that," he thought.

Thus he hung around Trafalgar Square on weekends and after work, chatting up tourists and other solo girls. He could indeed "do that," and within a couple of weeks he started rattling some grotty girls. That was in late 2009, as I was discovering the *London Seduction Society* ("LSS") forum and dipping my toes into the local scene.

I first heard about Tom from his lay reports posted up on the LSS. Flush with success, he was putting up a new report every month or so, maybe even more often, I forget. The nerdy virgins of the LSS absolutely hated success so he was quickly flamed and after a few months just stopped posting. By then he was offering free coaching so a bunch of local aspiring (maybe also asping, to use a colloquialism derived from Asperger's Syndrome) daygamers had met him. While out on Shaftesbury Avenue, I saw him walking across the road from Forbidden Planet. My wing at the time, I forget who, pointed him out.

"That's Tom Torero," he said.

We still never met. While sitting on the Trafalgar Square steps plying his trade, he'd begun to notice another guy doing the same thing, a Syrian-born and Lebanese-raised swarthy dude called Ramy. After a few weeks sizing each other up with peripheral vision they'd introduced themselves. Ramy too had been a shut-in finding his way to daygame through Alex Coulson's videos. They'd started within days of each other and soon became fast friends.

Both were even more obsessive about Game than I was. They went out every single day of the week, often four or five hours at a time after work. Success came. I was happy trundling along with the RSG gang, and our paths never crossed.

Midway through 2010 Tom contacted another LSS poster, a young German called Antony. Daygaming solo is very tough on the soul and beginners constantly fret over whether they are doing it right. Thus every new daygamer has the experience of experimenting with new wings found on forums, and you must usually wade through a handful of soul-killing meet-ups with vile freaks before chancing upon a genuinely decent wing. Antony was twenty-seven, fiercely intelligent, and though average height, he was rather good-looking in a brawny, masculine manner. He'd been the cool, bad boy in school and dated the hot girl in his class. In fact, he'd dated her for ten years, including the whole time he was learning game and clacking ratbags – and I never did find out if she knew about it. Antony had exactly the personality you'd expect from an intelligent German; analytical, harsh, and only ever one careless word away from invading Poland.

Tom and Antony became tight, although Antony was more into nightgame. With his good looks, muscular frame and confidence built up from having always been the cool kid, he was very good in bars. When attempting the transition to daygame, his problem was being too sexually aggressive. He'd pull too hard, freaking out the girls he chatted up. So, in a way they complimented each other, and they were able to learn from each other. They played off each other somewhat like Fernando and I, only more obsessive.

In February 2011, I booted up my laptop to find this email:

> *"Hi Krauser,*
>
> *Just as a quick introduction: I work with Beckster and will help Yad on some boot-camps soon. So, I am not an LSS stalker ;-) I enjoy following your journey in this Game and your web page is very strong!*
>
> *I don't want to demand your time, but I would love to hear what you think about some of my approaches. I gave you access. Please don't forward them or the alike. I can't go public with my infield material for various reasons.*
>
> *It is great seeing that there are some smart guys out there with real insights. If we bump into each other in central, we will go for a coffee. Great stuff!!!*
>
> *Antony"*

I watched the three infield videos he sent me through Google Docs; I was impressed. He had a cocky arrogance and flair with girls paired with German obsessiveness that made him good at learning technique as well. I was excited to meet him because I was enthusiastic about Game in general; my own daygame was getting better, which thrilled me greatly, and now here was another guy with a similar mindset. I replied, and he said he knew Tom so how about all three of us meet in Piccadilly?

We did some sets together and cautiously eyed each other up, trying to assess our relative abilities. Blow-outs and rejections are part of Game so we were all greatly relieved to see each other get them. We'd confirmed that, as yet, there is no secret sauce and we were all encountering a similar reality on the streets. Every daygamer wants to know whether his success rate at each stage is normal or below average. PUA marketing would have you believe cold approach is rejection-free, which created the wrong idea among students. I'd been able to measure myself against people like Mick and Fernando, so I knew I was normal, but I had to see whether Tom and Antony had similar experiences. As it turned out, they did, so that was one more anxiety to cross off the list.

We were soon hanging out every week or so. I was impressed by their all-consuming obsession for daygame. Tom told me that at he'd gone out every single day for a whole year, with no let up, and in between number farming, he had dates to fulfil as well. He and Antony were relentless in their pursuit. Every player should leverage that early-game obsession phase as that's where you rapidly accumulate the in-field experience and have the most enthusiasm for both the drudge work of reviewing your methods and also the heart-pounding drama of trying new things that might fuck up badly.

It soon emerged that both guys were getting laid more than me. I was still stuck on about one girl per month whereas Tom and Antony, who'd started the same time as me, seemed to be doubling and occasionally tripling that. I'd asked Tom about it while we wandered Trafalgar Square mid-afternoon. A brunette flitted by, and I gave her a good look and demurred. Tom liked her and sped off, taking her number a few minutes later.

"I have to go home now, but let's get a coffee tomorrow and talk about it," he said.

The next afternoon I waited for him in a Starbucks next to *Abercrombie and Fitch* behind Regent Street. He waltzed in with the same brunette in tow, an Australian. She wasn't too shabby at all, a solid seven. I'd let her pass without opening the previous day because she hadn't seemed hot but evidently I'd gotten that wrong. I thought nothing of it at the time, but with the benefit of several year's hindsight, this was the first instance of Tom's impression management with me. Every time he rattled a pretty girl he'd be sure to parade her in front of me, either through a +1 Facebook photo on WhatsApp or preferably in person. Still, she was a good score.

She was acting weird and then stormed off.

"Banged her last night," Tom gloated once she was out of earshot. "Same day lay."

He brought a cappuccino back from the counter then we got stuck into our statistical analysis. After I outlined my data on opens, numbers, dates, and lays, he reclined back, put his feet on the low table, and declared his opinion.

"This is simple, mate. You don't open enough."

I pressed him on details.

"Look mate, you do what – thirty or forty sets a week, tops? I'm doing sometimes five times that. I get just as flaky numbers as you, and just as many shitty dates. I get more lays because I'm working a lot harder."

This pleased me. I don't mind anyone getting laid more than me. I do mind people doing exactly the same work as me but getting better results because that means I'm doing something wrong. Remember, at this stage there was almost no solid material or stats on daygame. The only reason there is now is because Tom and I wrote it all.

"A few days ago I had three dates in one day. I had a coffee with an English bird who works in an architect office. Not much happened – maybe it goes somewhere maybe it doesn't. Then I had a time-waster date in Notting Hill that I literally walked out of halfway through the second drink. Then later on I had a second date with a dappy French tourist. I got her to my front door, making out with her on the steps. I tried to drag her in but she fought back and ran away."

He leant over to sip his coffee.

"Literally ran away. You need to be more ruthless, mate. It's a tough sport."

I winged with Tom and Antony about once a week in early 2011. The three of us were very exuberant, as we were still in the "honeymoon" stage of daygame where everything was new and exciting, and besides approaching, we spent quite a bit of time discussing techniques and what worked and didn't work and how to improve it.

We were like the three blind men touching different parts of an elephant and each getting a completely different and equally inadequate conception of the whole animal. There was no book or video laying it all out the correct way, no model showing the correct shape of a good daygame set. Different philosophies abounded and we tried each, trying to get abreast of it all and drill down to the centre of things to discover the core method that worked. On the plane back from Lithuania in January, I'd scribbled down the bare bones of my emerging model that was subsequently expanded into my first book; *Daygame Nitro*.

Antony proved to be particularly helpful in analysing my game and feeding back. He'd frequently send me emails such as this one, from March 2011.

Hey Nick,

After having watched you and spoken (to) you for a few times, I will give you my honest and straight forward feedback in bullet points. I can already say that you are amongst the best daygamers I have seen so far. Yet, it is about improvement and thus I will tell you what I think. I am not implying that I am better. That's simply what I would value the most as a feedback. This feedback serves me the purpose of avoiding making similar mistakes. Nobody is perfect and I have other deficits.

1) I don't think that more theory will help you. Your theoretical knowledge is very deep and strong. I think theory destroys your vibe at times. There are too many exogenous factors that you can't take into account (husband, got raped, just broke up that day); many times you will end with wrong conclusions. The trick is to be happy (later more). Theory only gets you in your head and that's the last thing you want because it destroys your vibe. I tended to be like that three months ago (it is my nature as an academic) and when I simply let go of the desire to find the perfect game model I got better again.

2) I can feel that there are still internal issues. I know that you are an honest and straight forward person and I know that you are not afraid of situations; I highly value this because I know you would fight for me if the situation came up. I still feel that you are coming from a place of negativity (sometimes or in some respects) as if you have to prove something to yourself. Even if you don't have to externally validate yourself, sometimes you may have to prove something to yourself. That is the wrong mindset and it comes from internal issues. I think the aim should be to be very positive, to be happy with yourself and to exude this energy. At the end, if you are happy with yourself, nothing and nobody can affect you. That's very attractive.

3) This is related to 2). I think that you get hung up on the idea of being 'alpha'. Alpha is just a label for something undefined. So the label alpha is firstly allusive and secondly another concept that people get obsessed with. If you can let go of the idea of becoming 'alpha' you will a) be more in the moment and b) actually become closer to the person you want to be. A desire to become a certain person (alpha) implies that you are missing a value that you want to obtain; i.e. you are not (yet) happy with who you are. People feel when you are not happy with yourself and it is not attractive.

Again, don't get me wrong: you are very good. To master the above it probably takes time and it is very advanced but fundamental. I know that you will sort all this out very soon because you won't give up.

In summary:

A) Let the theory be theory for a bit. You know more than enough now

B) Enjoy the moment and don't actively look for flaws or improvements all the time; instead, everyday you get up tell yourself *the great things you have achieved and how much you have to offer. I look at it this way and it is actually a feeling: I offer others the opportunity to get to know me, and I value them according to how they act and what they say, but I have no problem walking out on them because I know that I am happy with myself.*

I don't need to tell you what things you are good at since you already know that!

That's me being as honest as I can be!

I think this email nicely conveys not just the depth and breadth of our self-analysis but also the systematic and sometimes harsh manner in which we approached the subject of daygame. It was a slap in the face to read such clinical criticism about something I was so ego-invested in. I let the moment pass and my logical brain reasserted itself, grateful for the analysis. I replied to Antony the next day thanking him for his analysis and mostly agreeing with it.

He was right that I tended to debrief my work while still on the streets and this is anathema to maintaining a carefree vibe. Like Yad before him, he'd seen my vibe still needed work so I explained how I was working on this with Colin. I also appreciated that he could see I was still trying to adopt the behaviour patterns of 'alpha' without having yet internalised the mindset. We'd have several such email exchanges and many long discussions over coffee. We were obsessed with 'active learning', assessing and reassessing our process of learning as much as we did the subject being learned.

It was really the beginning of London daygame, or, at least, the time when it started to become codified into a recognizable model. The same week that I printed my first sales copies of *Daygame Nitro*, Andy and Yad did the filming of their *Daygame Blueprint*.

Andy was expanding his daygame.com business and running a lot of boot camps, many of which used Tom as a coach. That wasn't enough for someone of Andy's vision, so he concocted a grandiose plan to do the be-all-end-all daygame product, something that would chisel his name into PUA history.

To understand how he went about it, you need to understand how Andy conceives of running a business. Imagine a teenage boy sitting in his room listening to rock music, sticking Kiss and Rolling Stones posters onto his wall and playing air guitar.

"I want to be a rock star," he declares aloud.

Unlike most young boys, he's serious. So he starts reading rock star biographies, the metal press, and newspaper clippings. Each time he learns something new about rock stars, he jots it down on a scrap of paper. Pretty soon he has a bullet point list of "How To Be A Rock Star:"

- Trash hotel rooms
- Snort cocaine
- Get tattoos
- Fuck groupies

You can see the problem, no?

Looking at the things rock stars *do,* that is, the superficial trappings of their lifestyle, is not the same as understanding *why* they are rock stars. The essence of being a rock star is to write and perform catchy rock anthems that inspire fans to buy your records and attend your gigs. That's it. That's the base and without that none of the other trappings mean a damn thing.

When Andy set up daygame.com the first thing he did was rent an office in Marble Arch, an expensive part of London. Yes, he rented an office to run a business which requires only a laptop and a bunch of coaches. Later he paid thousands of pounds to set up a hi-tech video podcast studio including new leather sofas, coffee table, and elaborate interior design; to create something anyone with a laptop and mobile phone could do equally as well. Andy wasn't a friend so I doubted he would've taken business criticism from me had I offered it.

Production of the Daygame Blueprint was beset by the same fundamental problem of pissing away money on superficial nonsense while neglecting the core drivers of value.

To start with, he hired out the main function hall of the famous Charing Cross Hotel, located in prime real estate by Trafalgar

Square. He flew in a camera crew from the USA at a cost of about £20,000, and, apparently still running below his max credit line at the bank, he had several giant cardboard cut-outs made, like the life-size Tom Cruise and Jason Statham displays you see in the foyer of a cinema. This all to record video of two men standing still on a stage.

He sent out an offer to his mailing list that all attendees get in free and receive complimentary copies of the finished video product. Probably a hundred guys showed up, and when I chatted with them, many told me they'd come from around Europe. Andy had it in his head that he needed a big crowd to match the visual style of David De Angelo and Real Social Dynamics videos.

A dozen local daygame notables were drafted in to approach coach, including myself. At the time I felt quite flattered when I got the call from Yad.

The whole affair was to last four days, each involving a lunchtime in-field session to split up the morning and afternoon lectures. The content was to walk through the entire model from beginning to end. We were all excited because it was the first time Andy and Yad were going to take everybody through their model. At the time Yad was considered the grandfather of London daygame.

Tom, Antony and I were no exceptions. Avid theory junkies that we were, we looked forward to gleaning whatever tips and insights were offered over the next four days.

On the first morning I laced up my boots, donned my best leather jacket, and then knocked on Jimmy's door on my way out.

"I'm off to watch the Blueprint. Are you coming?" I shouted.

"No thanks mate, I'm gonna play through Bioshock 2 again. Save file got corrupted."

As we filed into the main hall to take our seats I noticed they were running late. Andy was hunched over his laptop tapping away to finalise his slides for the presentation he was due to give. Typically, he'd spent big on the peripherals and neglected what really mattered. As a result, the Daygame Blueprint turned out to be an unfocused waffling mess. Andy and Yad ate up the long runtime by meandering around their subjects and never getting to the point. It was painful.

In fairness, an astute observer could find some gold sprinkled in amongst the mud, and I finished the event with several pages of notes. Although ultimately a disappointment, it was still an exciting occasion, the first major daygame event ever. Tom gave a talk on leading and on the second day, I received my first hardback copy of *Daygame Nitro* back from the printers and took it along with me. That created a buzz amongst all the coaches. While Andy and Yad were on stage, we all went outside so they could pore over it and make comments.

Strangely, the most interesting part of the whole week happened when I was actually on the bus to the Blueprint. Let's wind the clock back a little for context...

A few weeks earlier, I'd been recognized and stopped by a daygamer in Camden. He introduced me to a friend of his who played bit-part roles in TV and movies. During the course of our conversation, he told me his birthday was coming up, and he wanted to organize a party for his actor and actress friends but didn't have a house large enough to host it. I ran the idea past the RSG gang, and we offered him use of Château Hampstead. As it turned out, the party was a bust and hardly anybody turned up, but that was mainly because the actor was full of shit.

Our regular cleaner came in on Fridays, but the party was booked in for the Saturday. We figured the place might become a little worse for wear, but he was already busy on Sunday so we needed a new pinch-cleaner. I checked out the jobs-wanted cards in the window of a local newsagent and took down about five numbers. One card really caught my eye. It read: Romanian girl, 26, good cleaner, great English.

I thought it a bit odd that a cleaner would also advertise her age. I called, and she said she was busy that day but would send her mother around instead. Great. She came around, did a good job, and I paid her. As far as I was concerned that was the end of it but the next week, as I was sitting on the bus on my way to the Daygame Blueprint, my phone rang. It was the Romanian girl. The conversation started off with the usual pleasantries and soon turned weird:

"My mother says you've got a nice big house. I kind of wish I'd been able to clean it."

I wondered if cleaners dream of the Big Score, too.

"Do you need a regular cleaner?"

I demurred, explaining it was a one-off deal brought on by the party.

"That's a shame. I'd like to be your cleaner. Is there anything else you need, like ironing shirts or washing?"

"No, thanks. I don't have an office job, so I don't need any shirts ironing, and my washing's taken care of."

"Is there anything else?"

"No."

"Because I do a lot of things."

At this point my spider sense was tingling, but I was caught off guard. I asked what kind of things. I suddenly felt dirty. It seemed the other passengers on the bus were looking at me.

"Well, I can't really say on the phone."

The penny dropped, but I remained coy. A fat black woman sitting opposite me shuffled uncomfortably then hoisted her grocery bags onto the space beside her. She seemed to be staring at me. I told the Romanian I didn't understand her point.

"Well, I'm a pretty girl, I've got big breasts... I do a lot of other things."

"How do you mean?"

"Blow jobs and sex, you know."

I covered my mouth and tried to keep my voice quiet as I explained that I don't pay for sex because I'm good at picking up women and was actually on my way to teach some other guys how to do the same.

Mick's voice seemed to call out to me, echoing in my head: "Shore the whore, Nick! Shore the whore!"

Okay this was my chance to tick that box. I flipped the script and started gaming her. By the time I got off the bus at Trafalgar Square, she'd agreed to come to Château RSG that night for a drink. I reiterated that I didn't pay for sex.

"That's fine. You can fuck me and pay me what you think it's worth."

That night, Jimmy and I sat on my bed playing *Call of Duty Black Ops* when she called me to say she'd be late because she'd only just finished her last job. She sounded nervous, as if worrying I wouldn't really be waiting at home to meet her.

"Fair enough," I said, not really that bothered whether she turned up or not. "See you when you get here."

She called again half an hour later to say her bus was late. Again, her voice crackled with nerves.

"I can only stay an hour because my husband is expecting me home."

I really do wonder about Romanians. Her mother had pimped her out after spotting we lived in a big house, and now her husband was letting her come to fuck me.

A third call told me she was outside the house, so I looked from the window, not knowing what to expect. I saw a blonde girl of average height and enormous breasts. Unfortunately, her ass and stomach were also rather big. She was a five. Pretty but chunky. Suddenly the story didn't feel so compelling. Jimmy sniggered.

You might as well see it through, I thought to myself as I stepped into my monster feet fluffy slippers and walked downstairs. She was waiting at the fire door at the side dressed in light blue jeans and a tight white sweater.

She blurted out a nervous hello then stepped inside. I just couldn't understand why she looked so anxious, like it was an important job interview. Then it occurred to me, as far as she was concerned, it *was* a big opportunity. She was completely cowed and under my thrall. Why, I didn't know, because I hadn't promised her anything, but there it was. It was as if she felt really lucky to be there.

I took her upstairs, and she shuffled behind me eagerly. I picked up an Xbox controller and retook my seat on the bed, leaning into the corner walls. She sat on the edge of the bed and tried to make conversation. We'd look in her direction to make a comment or answer a question and then turn back to the game. That only made her try even harder, and she started showing us her holiday photos and telling us stories.

The whole time Jimmy was subtly reframing her to find out where she was at sexually. He asked leading questions and made apparently off-hand sexual comments then gauged her reaction. We could see she was absolutely gagging for it, but I didn't want to fuck her. Not even for another notch and to beat Mick in his own goal to shore a whore.

"What's the most men you had sex with," asked Jimmy, as he camped out atop a Russian army barracks and picked off a few bots with the sniper rifle.

"Ooooooh, let me think," she gushed, thinking it as a chance to impress. "I did nine guys in Greece, with another girl."

"All at once?" I asked, my eyes intently watching the progress bar as I picked up a Care Package that contained a Hellfire missile.

"Yes, it was an orgy," she said. "Brown men."

That extinguished what little interest still remained in my fucking her. She then boasted about how she was amazing at blow jobs.

So Jimmy said, "Prove it!"

She looked up at me with puppy dog eyes, and I nodded my assent. I kept hold of the Xbox controller and ran my kill-streak up to fifteen to get the attack dogs perk. Meanwhile, the Romanian whore unzipped my jeans and took out my dick with the utmost care and reverence. Jimmy managed to ignore her completely while she went down on me.

I'll admit that her boasting was entirely well-founded. She was absolutely brilliant and remains to this day the most skilled blow job I've ever had. My focus was still on *Call of Duty* so she kept asking if it was good and was she doing it to my satisfaction. I got a little shy with Jimmy being there, so I took her around the corner to my en-suite toilet and then came on her face. She kneeled in front of me, head tilted up with a big smile, completely spattered. She seemed so pleased with herself.

"Thanks!" she gushed as she came back out a minute later after freshening up. "Would you like a blow job?" she asked Jimmy.

"No."

She continued to thank me as I showed her the door. We made some small talk, and I cracked a couple of jokes.

"If you ever want to fuck, call me. It's free," she said, then skipped away.

It had all been perfectly friendly right from the beginning, and she hadn't asked for money once.

A few days later, she messaged me to ask if I'd changed my mind and would I like her to come around and suck me off again. I declined. And that was that – one of the oddest things that can crop up in the Game, and certainly one of my strangest experiences.

On the third day of the Daygame Blueprint, there was a break in proceedings when the cameramen had to make some technical adjustments to their equipment. Andy was faced with a packed auditorium and an hour to fill. He asked Jon Matrix and I if we'd keep the crowd entertained by talking about text game. Fine by me. I didn't know Jon at all, but he'd been winging with Yad the past six months and built up a reputation as a solid daygamer.

We sat on the stage and took questions from the audience, reading out texts from our phones to illustrate our points, and it was going well until Jon accidentally backhanded the pitcher of water next to my phone and knocked it over. My phone whirred a little then switched off. Not only did it contain all the text chats I was going to read out during our talk, but it had all my daygame leads as well. I wasn't happy.

We fumbled our way through the next half hour, and afterwards Jon suggested I place my phone in a plastic Tupperware tub of rice for twenty-four hours to dehydrate it. It worked, because the rice sucked all the water out of it. To his credit, Jon also said that if it didn't work, he'd buy me a new phone.

I never did become friends with Jon. His reclusiveness makes him a difficult man to get close to. He spends most of his time indoors playing poker and only pops out for a few hours to daygame. He's a classic example of how it's possible to get laid despite having no social life.

Another Game legend that I met around that time was Beckster, or to give him his proper name, Robert Beck. He is the archetypal daft-lad-in-the-club and England's first successful PUA. He read Mystery's forum posts back before Neil Strauss had even written his book and decided to learn game himself. He'd read the old Alt-Seduction forum then go out in-field to nightclubs to try it out. After two years of what were, by his own admission, "hard work and brutal lack of success," he cracked it and became a good player.

His major ruse was to set himself up as a club promoter and then go out in the street, handing out cards to hot girls and getting their numbers. He'd tell them he'd keep them in the loop regarding club promotions and offers. Club management were happy for him to bring girls to the club, and he was happy to get VIP table service and treated like a big shot. Those tables gave him an opportunity to work a social status game while guaranteeing the girls' presence at least until the free drinks ran out. As the legend of Beckster grew, he began persuading flunkies to do the legwork on the streets for him. Tom and Antony did it for awhile until they sussed out how he was milking them.

Having gathered a whole stack of numbers, Rob would mass text the girls to invite them to such-and-such a club for a big party on a particular night, telling them to arrive before a certain time and to mention his name on the door. Management would pay him between £5 and £15 for every hot girl on his guest list who showed up. Girls came because they'd get free entry, be escorted to a VIP table (his), and given a couple of free drinks.

The girls would experience Rob as the king of the club who knew everybody and was treated with respect by staff (as he was a revenue generator). He'd sit at the head of the table, organize the drinks and be surrounded by ten or so hot girls, looking every inch the stereotypical player.

But that was just his launching pad. What comes next is truly advanced, and I'd not spot it myself until tipped off by Antony (and would subsequently confirm over the years with other former friends of Rob's).

A nightclub's economy runs on two things: money and hot girls. Of those, the hot girls are more important because without them no men will come to spend the money. Promoters are valuable to a club because they go out into the world to catch the girls who are used to bait the line for the real money-spenders: chumps. Rob had the foresight to use the promoter system to bring girls into his orbit on favourable terms to game them (as opposed to the classic nightgame method of cold-approaching as just another guy in the club). That's smart.

Smarter still is bullshitting a group of wannabe players that you'll coach them and let them in on your "social circle" if only they'll go out and do the legwork on the streets for you. Rob was now getting his VIP table stacked (and his pockets filled) without even doing the work himself. It was the nightgame version of a pyramid scheme.

Any player would look at this set-up and think it smart. I did. However, Rob put yet another layer on top of that which not only made his pulling easier but also greatly enhanced the perception of his cold-approach pick-up skills in front of the students who'd paid him a fortune in coaching fees. This is how it worked.

Everyone else in the nightclub would see Rob at the head of his table making a grand performance with the girls. The men would look up and think, "lucky bastard, surrounded by lots of girls," and the women would also notice. Just being at the table surrounded by girls elevated him above every other man in the club. Having established this image in the eyes of all the other club patrons, Rob would start surreptitiously looking around at the other girls, on the dance floor, at the bar, standing by the VIP rope, fishing for IOIs. It was a fair bet *some* girls would throw one out. Whenever he got one, he'd go over to the girl, open her, and pull her into his party.

The girls from his guest list were seeing him reasonably favourably, but their perception of him was throttled somewhat because he was still *free-stuff-promoter-guy* to them. They were there primarily for what they could get out of him as a transaction. The girls Rob pulled in from the public club areas were different, they initially encountered him as the *cool-guy-having-fun-with-lots-of-girls* and that's a much better identity. Not only that, but by fishing for IOIs, he was selecting hotter prospects who were genuinely intrigued and inserting them into a social environment (the VIP table) that he controlled. Rob would then use the social dynamics to get the girls to play off against one another. A bit like classic

Mystery Method bar game where they all compete against each other to vie for his attention. It's a potent combination, and it got Rob laid a lot.

Even better, the oblivious students would be blind to the whole apparatus and just think "that Beckster guy is amazing at the nightclub cold approach." His reputation grew.

This is known as Entourage Game, and Beckster invented the modern version of it. It's pretty much the opposite of what I do. He builds an elaborate structure based on many moving parts that elevates him to a position of situational high status in an environment where party girls go to party. I roam solo on city streets picking off girls who know nothing except what I convey in one-to-one conversation.

I met Rob by chance a fortnight before the Daygame Blueprint event. I'd had an advance copy of *Daygame Nitro* printed and wanted Antony to take a look through it and provide feedback. We arranged to meet at *The Porcupine* pub in Leicester Square. Jimmy came along, and while supping our first pint Antony got a call from Rob. He was in the area and wanted to ask Antony a few things.

Although I'd never met him before, he'd been the coach at a boot camp Jimmy had attended a couple of years previously, and Jimmy had great respect for him. That was good enough for me, so I awaited his arrival with curiosity.

Rob barnstormed into the pub and immediately tried his game on us. He wanted to set himself up as the leader of our table. There were no girls to witness it, but he just couldn't switch off whether there were girls present or not.

"Phew, what a day! I'm knackered mate. Late night, I'll tell you about the threesome sometime. So, what are you guys talking about...."

"Open loop," Antony mouthed at us soto-voice and rolled his eyes.

Rob tried a few more open loops to pull us into his frame but neither Jimmy nor I were too impressed.

"I think Burnley have a good shot for winning the Championship this year," Jimmy said. "There's two good kids coming through from the youth team."

"Newcastle aren't doing so well," I added.

Rob realized his ploy wasn't working and shut it off immediately. Not the most auspicious of introductions, but at least we were then able to have a normal conversation. This was a period when I was getting to meet all the 'name' PUAs in London and while they all had something I could learn from, I was struck by how strange they all were. It was like a little boy's club. Our house of cads in Hampstead looked sane in comparison.

Speaking at the Blueprint with Jon Matrix

CHAPTER
EIGHT

Bathroom Break

BATHROOM BREAK

I t was late afternoon on Oxford Street, and a light drizzle greyed out the sky as shoppers considered whether to unfurl their umbrellas or brave the run between shops. Jimmy lolled along beside me, hands deep in his pockets. We were about to call time on the daygame session so I could pop into River Island to buy a t-shirt. Just as I walked in, a cute brunette walked out and flashed me a look, holding eye contact for what felt like several seconds.

I was still unaware of the importance of scanning girls for indicators of interest. Like many inexperienced daygamers I treated the streets like a blank canvas and simply opened any girl who was solo and who I liked the look of. I hadn't learned how to be sensitive to IOIs much less force them, but there was no doubt about this one.

Alla had big chubby hamster cheeks, wide hips, massive tits, and long thick brown hair cascading down to her waist. She was slim by UK standards but a bit overweight for a Russian. She was exactly my type.

"Hey, wait! Let me say hello. I'm Nick."

She smashed wide open, grinning ear-to-ear. She was so happy to be in London, exerting a vibrancy and exuberance about her person that was infectious. She was visiting from Moscow and had a couple of days left. She was nineteen.

"This rain is getting heavy," I said and gestured for us to move under the awning outside M&S.

After ten minutes or so, I walked her across the road to The Marlborough Head pub to get some alcohol into her. She trotted along pleasantly, gaping at the long bar's brown wooden panelling and prints of fox hunting scenes on the walls.

Only a handful of customers were inside, dotted around at the bar and a couple of tables. We took our pints and sat down at a table directly opposite the bar. I noted the disabled toilets off to the right, the doorway sufficiently hidden from the barman's line of sight that we could slip in unnoticed.

"I'm here for a two-week language exchange," said my new hamster friend. "I go home in three days."

Logistics dictated I must push hard and fast even though she was the type of girl ripe for dating. I nodded and made listening noises, my eyes darting first to the toilet door and then to the other punters.

During our first drink, I rushed through the simple get-to-know-you stuff and moved into deep rapport quickly. She was obviously really into me, eyes sparkling and grinning constantly, but when I moved to kiss her, she refused and gave me a monologue stacked with the whole checklist of "bullshit things girls say to men". Highlights were:

"I don't kiss on a first date. I'm not that kind of girl."

"I have my principles, and they won't be bent."

"We'll never have sex. It's not like that."

"I only have sex with my boyfriend."

Hearing her say such things in a logical order should've been off-putting, but her imminent departure meant I had to throw myself all-in on a fast escalation. I eased off temporarily, engaged her again on some deep topics, then tried again to heat her up.

"I like your long hair. It's very sexy how it flows over your breasts and down to your hips. Let me play with it."

I reached across and twirled it around my fingers, a look of fascination crossing my face.

"You're really very pretty. I'd like to grab a handful and pull hard. Then I want to slap your ass."

Her pupils dilated and a sheen sparkled over her eyes. This was my moment so I moved in, cupped her chin and kissed her. She liked it, moaning softly.

"I must go. My classmates have invited me to a formal dinner this evening."

"What time must you leave?"

"In forty-five minutes."

No time to lose! I waited until nobody was looking then dragged her into the disabled toilets. She half-heartedly resisted but when I shut the door behind us I saw her cheeks were flushed. I pressed her up against the wall and squeezed her tits. She gasped and writhed in pleasure so I reached down and pulled them both out.

Good lord, what an *amazing* pair!

Firm, natural, and very, very large. I put them in my mouth, and she was well into it.

"Oh, that's nice. Wait, this is too fast. Oh god!"

I tried to get my dick out to fuck her there and then, but she suddenly snapped back to reality.

"No! I must go," she whimpered and rearranged her modesty. I took her number and walked her to the station.

We met at 9pm the next evening outside Camden Town station. She'd dressed up nice but complained of a slight cold. I teased her a little and pushed her around to spike up the energy as we walked across the road to the World's End pub. Sitting down with our drinks I soon pulled her back into the deep introverted conversation she liked, asking her about philosophy and arts. Then I asked her what she liked in men. At first she said I'm not her type but ten minutes later she'd changed her mind.

"You know, you are a beautiful man for me. You have beautiful face," she cooed.

For my part, I played on her love for England and everything English, laying it on thick. I'd learned that Russian girls treat England as if it's a hobby rather than a real country, but many of them don't get to meet actual English people because they are in London for only short periods and frequently ghettoised with other language learners.

I'd guessed correctly with Alla. She spent all day with a rabble of Italians and Spaniards, making her English teacher and her host family her only contact with native English.

I kept my hands to myself, figuring that getting her tits out the previous afternoon was sufficient confirmation of mutual attraction.

The first drink went down smoothly, so I bounced her to the next pub, the Hawley Arms. She knew exactly where the night was heading, and her forebrain was kicking in with some resistance. Her eyes darted around like a startled animal and she occasionally dragged her feet en route. Such signs express discomfort so the answer is to ease up on the escalation and replace it with soothing words.

"Nothing will happen except what you are comfortable with," I said as we pushed open the pub doors and stepped into a cacophony of noise from a live indie band playing in the beer garden.

We took the drinks upstairs and started making out.

She became overly enthusiastic, flinging her arm wide and spilling her wine all down her dress. My heart sank as I thought this would completely pop the lust bubble. Fortunately a quick dab with tissues, and she was throwing herself at me again.

"We won't have sex," she said, then reached under the table to grab my dick.

Time to go.

There was a minicab office next door, but she refused to enter on the grounds that she was going clubbing later on and had to go home first to change. Incredibly, it's only now as I write these words five years later that I've connected the dots and realise that the only reason she needed to change was because of the spilled wine. At the time, my mind was too focused on alternative solutions to the taxi home.

"Fair enough," I said, being nothing if not gallant and walked her towards the bus stop. "It's a nice walk through this park," I said, taking the scenic route.

I pushed her up against a series of walls, trees, and parked cars to make out until we finally entered Primrose Hill park and set walking upwards. Halfway up the hill, we sat down under a tree. The rising moon outlined the silhouettes of a dozen drunken teenagers having a party at the crest, so I took it as a cue to get our own party under way with another make-out.

Alla lay back on the grass and moaned as I pulled her tits out again. "We can't have sex here," she moaned.

A rogue hand slid down inside her jeans until I'd fingered her into a heavy state.

"Do you have a condom?" she asked.

Another notch and very pleasant it was, too, outside on the grass in the cool night air. We didn't go at it very long but it was memorable. Afterwards we walked to her bus stop and that was the last I saw of her, although she did text me the following day:

:) it was brilliant :) i forget about my cold and my dream was wonderful :) thanks for that :) :) wish you all the best for today :)

I did try to get her over to my place before she returned to Russia, but she had her moment of magic.

Taking London Real infield

*First attempt at
a daygame book*

A street interview before the studio

CHAPTER
NINE

Game On

GAME ON

G ame is a journey of self-discovery. It is impossible to make progress without turning your focus within and understanding who you really are and how you think. Inner game-work is slow but rewarding. I'd begun by reading through pop psychology books and found the Myers-Briggs test particularly useful in classifying myself as an INTJ : introverted intuitive thinker judger.

My biggest shock, as I relate in *Balls Deep* (volume one), was discovering I wasn't anything like the man I thought I was. I'd grown up thinking my life completely normal, my childhood close to idyllic, and my social skills normal. I'd been so successful as a student that I considered myself an academic star. I'd even convinced myself that I was cool and charismatic.

It was hugely delusional, and deep down I knew it. It was fascinating to investigate my mental blind spots and learn why I'd been able to successfully delude myself for so long. It was an arduous process, fighting my ego every step of the way, but ultimately my study of the male socio-sexual hierarchy provided the answer with highest explanatory power.

Game literature is ever evolving. I had assimilated and integrated both the mass market psychological advice and the standard Mystery-era Game advice. At around this time I discovered Vox Day's popular AlphaGamePlan blog, and he'd only recently written an interesting post outlining a version of the male socio-sexual hierarchy that offered more nuance than the binary alpha-beta offered by Château Heartiste. In particular, I was fascinated by two particular ranks.

"Gamma: The introspective, the unusual, the unattractive, and all too often the bitter. Gammas are often intelligent, usually unsuccessful with women, and not uncommonly all but invisible to them, the gamma alternates between placing women on pedestals and hating the entire sex. This mostly depends upon whether an attractive woman happened to notice his existence or not that day.... In the unlikely event they are at the party, they are probably in the corner muttering darkly about the behaviour of everyone else there... However, they are sexual rejects, not social rejects."

It was chilling to read. Gamma males live inside a carefully crafted Delusion Bubble through which all real-world data is filtered to ensure it doesn't disturb his own grandiose self-image. The gamma considers himself the Secret King, a man of great ability and importance but as yet not recognised by the world.

The gamma male is hugely delusional, and deep down he knows it.

"Sigma: The outsider who doesn't play the social game and manages to win at it anyhow. The sigma is hated by alphas because sigmas are the only men who don't accept or at least acknowledge, however grudgingly, their social dominance. Everyone else is vaguely confused by them. In a social situation, the sigma is the man who stops in briefly to say hello to a few friends accompanied by a Tier 1 girl that no one has ever seen before. Sigmas like women, but tend to be contemptuous of them. They are usually considered to be strange. Gammas often like to think they are sigmas, failing to understand that sigmas are not social rejects, they are at the top of the social hierarchy despite their refusal to play by its rules."

I'd very much liked to consider myself precisely the kind of cool lone wolf which I'd just learned was labelled sigma. It seemed to explain why I didn't have many friends, didn't socialise much, but still considered myself to be hot shit.

Game had already taught me that I was much further down the pecking order than I preferred to believe. Few things splash cold water into your face than doing a thousand daygame approaches without getting laid. However, by early 2011, I'd made great progress and was clearly and unequivocally rattling some fairly hot young women. I certainly wasn't a loser, but I was still aware that something wasn't right about me.

Vox had put his finger on it. I was a gamma-sigma hybrid, with too much of the former and not enough of the latter. It explained why I was able to kick beyond my coverage with girls but still had some pretty loathsome traits that needed to be dealt with.

I was now in the realm of frontier Game theory. Bloggers and players were outlining new psychological theories informed by the Red Pill – an analogy to Morpheus offering to show Neo the truth of the Matrix in the famous movie of that name. In that scene Morpheus presents Neo with a choice of two pills, telling him, "This is your last chance. After this, there is no turning back. You take the blue pill – the story ends, you wake up in your bed and believe whatever you want to believe. You take the red pill – you stay in Wonderland and I show you how deep the rabbit-hole goes."

I was deep down the rabbit-hole, scouring the internet for anything that would explain the world around me. Just like my fellow daygamers were engaging in frontier street techniques, I was applying the same principles to my inner game.

It had to be Red Pill. There was little point going to a legitimately credentialed psychologist and saying, "Can you straighten out my inner Game so that I can better rattle large numbers of hot women?" I don't think that's free on the National Health Service. I'd already seen that feminine-primary social programming infested the entirety of modern social sciences. If I submitted myself to mainstream psychological advice, I'd be letting the Blue Pill back into my brain. I'd be letting the Matrix undo all the hard work of the previous two years.

Curiously, I've found that a number of gamma traits that were bad for my social life and social standing as a teenager have since stood me in good stead in the Game.

After a psychologically balanced childhood, I began to lose my calibration in adolescence. I was always extremely dominant, both intellectually and socially, but before puberty it didn't really matter. Children weren't yet sorting themselves into sexual hierarchies and without the raging hormones of a teenager, my character wasn't too abrasive.

From the age of about six until I was thirteen, I was popular. My best friend Neil was the most popular kid in the school, and I was almost equally well-liked. Unfortunately, he and his parents moved away to a small town far away, and he changed schools. This left me at a loose end at precisely the time when everyone was hitting puberty and was sensitive to any slight weirdness. I became slightly weird.

After Neil left, my social status declined. Between the ages of fourteen and sixteen, I had a bad time socially. I was subject to social exclusion by the cool kids I'd previously hung out with. It happened gradually but I started to feel it. For example, I used to call in on my friend Paul on my way to school, and we'd walk down together every morning. One day I knocked on his door and his mother said he'd already gone. That happened a few times before I twigged what was going on. I also used to have one or two of the prettier girls asking to be my girlfriend, but those offers dried up, too.

One friend, Derrick, stayed firm with me, and we'd sit together in most classes right up to the school-leaving exams. He also had odd habits and communication style but was more likeable than me. We'd hang out, but when the cool kids invited him to activities he had to ditch me.

I drifted downwards socially and ended up hanging out with boys in the mid-tier. At the time I was aware of the drift but didn't know why and didn't see its importance. I'd learned from my mother to just be completely oblivious to the social dynamics around me – it was both a contributor to the problem and something that softened the blow.

I wasn't much interested in girls then despite having had a couple of girlfriends in the past when my social capital was higher. My last few years in school were dominated by my interest in thrash metal and later anarcho punk. I'd spend my Friday nights drinking in Newcastle city centre with the older metalheads, and every Sunday we'd go to Images club in South Shields by the coast for the weekly metal night. The metal scene wasn't bad, and it was by no means just a dumping ground for outcasts. There were quite a few cool guys and pretty girls there. I fucked a few of them just because I was a teenager and that kind of thing just happens when you're that age. At first, I got attention from the girls and briefly dated some who even now I'd rate as sevens or even eights. However, my weirdness would always show through, and after about six months I was drifting to mid-table in the metal scene too.

Fuck my luck.

By now I was studying for my A-level exams at a local college, preparing for university entrance. Gateshead College was utter shit. Bad teachers, bad administration, and half-arsed recruitment. I wondered where all the cool kids had gone because my social science classes were full of goths, emo kids, and fat losers. It was nothing like the college life displayed in commercials and on MTV. I completely switched off socially at college, not bothering to make new friends as there was nobody I wanted to hang out with. Instead I did all my socialising in the local punk and anarchist scenes.

Anarchist punks are not popular with the cool kids.

At the time, I was quite happy and unaware consciously of the processes that were taking place. I was oblivious to social dynamics and sexual hierarchies. My mind was on whatever intellectual or creative passions enthralled me and my friends. I was as happy as a pig in shit. I actually made out with quite a few girls in bars and parties through cold approach, although I never seemed to have much interest or ability in moving them towards sex. Several friends asked me how I was "so good with women" because I would often cold approach a student girl in our regular pubs like The Barley Mow or The Egypt Cottage and make out with them soon after. The irony was I rarely tried to take them home or set up dates. I just didn't much care to get involved with girls.

This period of social decline is most relevant to my Game journey because apart from the brief period aged 16-17 when my overall happiness and focus on a mission gave me a good vibe, I'd lost my ability to be good with women.

University gave me a chance to build upon my resurging vibe and make a fresh start, but I blew it immediately. The university was Top Ten and full of students from good grammar, private, and public schools. It was as mainstream as an Enid Blyton novel and while many kids were into music and style subcultures, nobody took it too seriously. I turned up as a skinny vegan punk with long hair and stupid strident anarchist politics. I hadn't yet developed any interest in sports or working out. I also had an abrasive northern chip on my shoulder.

In a hall of residence of three hundred teenagers all looking to make friends, I should have been onto a winner. I was on friendly terms with nearly everyone and frequently involved with parties and nights out. However, I could sense that the cool kids were keeping their distance. This was brought home to me at the end of the first year when everyone was making plans to rent private housing for the second year. None of my cooler "friends" included me in their plans, and I ended up sharing a house with a couple of other pleasant but low-ranking men who were into the emerging Brit Pop scene.

I dare say this was far from disastrous. I had lots of fun at university and up until I lived in Japan, I considered it the best three years of my life. It's just looking back now, knowing what I do about Game and physical fitness, that I see it as a squandered opportunity.

I got lucky with girls a few times in my freshman year. Despite a skinny-fat body, awful fashion, and anti-Game skills, the fact was I was a teenage boy surrounded by horny teenage girls. Things happen. Occasionally one of them chose me. One became an infrequent fuck buddy throughout all three years. One chatted me up in the queue outside a nightclub, and I Same Night Laid ("SNLd") her five minutes after entering the club. I even picked up a local hot girl from the dance floor in Rock City and fucked her ten minutes later.

This is why I pay no attention to university-age men talking about their game. I was absolutely hopeless and still banged a few respectable girls in record time. It's called "being at university."

My sex life nose-dived midway through my second year. I was drinking four times a week and eating takeaway pizzas on the way home from nightclubs. My weight ballooned up to over twelve stone (without any extra muscle added to the nine -stone frame I brought to university). The clubbing was mostly just getting shit-faced with friends and ignoring women. On the rare occasions I tried chatting them up, it went surprisingly well and I got a few more SNLs. I really do wonder why I didn't do it more often.

My vibe became toxic. I'd become ever more politically-minded and fuck-the-system. That leaked into my social life and made me a little angry and selfish. I was very difficult to be around, and these views created rifts between me and the people I had in my life. I became very literal in the way I related to people and used blunt logical arguments when I spoke to them rather than behaving as normal people do in a more give-and-take manner. I was also into philosophy and read all the great thinkers, forming my beliefs using logic and rational argument rather than sentiment (at least, so I thought), and while that was good for my intellect, it was a disaster for my social life. I was increasingly aspy, and it led to me committing many social *faux pas*.

I went through a period of browbeating people into submission during the usual drunken student-bar debates. It entertained the crowd but didn't win any friends. It seemed few people would take me to one side and explain where this was leading me, and I doubt I'd have listened anyway. I was steadily building up a combative attitude, a super-strong frame, and a disregard for social disapproval.

This is poison for a close-knit university social circle but absolute gold for a travelling daygamer.

Imagine an average-looking forty-year-old guy (i.e., me) trying to hook a hot Russian 'greyhound' girl who's got hundreds of admirers and can pick and choose whoever she wants to date. Imagine stopping her on the street as she's on her way to meet friends and trying to fuck her. Being normal won't cut it. Being sensitive to your rightful place in the sexual hierarchy won't cut it.

However, having a delusionally strong frame and considering yourself a Secret King *might* just cut it. When every little piece of feedback she gives you is twisted and reframed so as to feed your delusions of grandeur, she might begin to fall into your frame. "Who is this guy, and why does he have such a high opinion of himself?" she may think.

Of course, most won't buy into it, but the success rate of a delusionally self-confident frame is far better than rational defeatism ever can be. Nowadays it's good for me because I've introduced calibration and social dynamics, and I've done considerable inner game work to try to blunt many of my more unpleasant personality traits. Back at university, I was nowhere near; hence the social purgatory I frequently found myself in.

University as a whole was quite dry with regards to sex, particularly in my final year when I only fucked one new girl. In fact, I only laid six girls the whole time I was there. On the plus side, I started light fitness and jogging, bringing my weight back down to ten stone.

I graduated top of my faculty and went on to do a Masters degree at another university where I graduated top there too. I drew considerable self-worth from my academic progression so I studied very hard. Brace yourself for another major gamma "tell."

One of the ten students on my one-year course was a thirty-year-old Japanese woman called Reiko (I was twenty-one). She had held down a high-powered TV job but remained single and binned it all to change the direction of her life. She was hopelessly out of her depth on the course because she spoke poor English on a highly verbal course. The only reason she was admitted was fee-greed on the university's side.

I'd help her out and explain the lectures, and one night we ended up getting drunk and making out. Apart from my undergraduate fuck buddy, I hadn't had sex for ages, so fucking Reiko felt like winning the lottery. I'd rate her a six now but she was slim, sported thick long black hair, and was nice to me.

We dated for the whole academic year, and it was the first time in my life that I'd ever had regular sex. Up until then I hadn't even cared much about regular sex. I really enjoyed it, and I developed my sexual technique while I was with her. When the course finished, I went down to London to work, and she went back to Japan a month later.

Before arriving in London, I'd only ever spent extended periods of time in Newcastle and away at university. My horizons were limited. I became interested in Japan, considering it the most outlandishly foreign country imaginable. I played Japanese video games, watched some anime, and even dabbled in ninjutsu at university. Now I'd fucked one of their pre-Wall women.

I found it stressful to adjust to London life. I was now working hard and studying for professional exams in my spare time. I quickly struck lucky in a little Japanese takeaway in Chinatown where I used to go a couple of times a week to buy ready-to-eat sushi. I'd practice my crappy Japanese ordering, which probably amused the pretty counter staff to no end. Over the course of a couple of weeks, I started chatting about Japan with the prettiest one, amongst other things. One day, I asked her if she'd like to go out with me, and she said yes.

She came out dressed to fuck – careful make-up, tight clothes, and an overall alluring vibe. I ended up taking her home the same night and fucking her on my lounge floor and again in my bed. Hiroko was pushing thirty, too, but had a fantastic stripper-like body and firm big tits. I figured I'd gotten myself a new girlfriend, but that was as good as it was going to get because Reiko came to visit, got wind of Hiroko, and went to the restaurant to tell her to lay off. Despite that, I met Hiroko for a second date, but by now the stresses of my financial apprenticeship had crushed my vibe, and I was negative and whiny. She ditched me. A very disappointing end to a promising prospect, but it did mean that I'd fucked two Japanese girls in a row, which gave me a taste for the country that would result in me living there four years and marrying a native.

Unlike university life which always puts pretty young women in front of you, living as a working stiff is far more isolating. There were no natural mechanisms with which to meet girls.

I soon hit upon a weasel scheme.

There were loads of Japanese girls in London, all there to learn English. I was a native speaker so I carried value for language exchange. I put up a card on *The Japan Centre* notice board, a bookshop-cum-Japanese supermarket in Piccadilly. I was flooded with twelve phone calls that night, eleven of which were from girls, generating so much interest that I had to take the card down the following day because I simply didn't have time to meet everyone who expressed an interest.

I met all the girls over the course of three evenings in the same Caffè Nero on Brewer Street. The staff were totally bemused to see me with so many different Japanese girls and they had to wonder what I was doing. It was similar to the reactions I'd get later on in my daygame career when I would have multiple dates with girls in the same establishments on the same day or during the same week in places like Minsk, Belgrade, and Prague.

I filtered the girls down to five, based on who I fancied most, seemed to be the most interested in me, and didn't mention a boyfriend. I'd end up fucking two of the five. I'd blundered my way into a primitive form of eco-system game but I just didn't much care about accumulating notches. By the time I'd finished a hard week of stressful work, I was satisfied with just boning the same regular girl.

I'd go on to date two more Japanese girls until I met my Japanese wife, who was the hottest of the bunch. I think we can all agree my pre-game sexual history placed me slap-bang into the middle of Gamma territory.

LONDON

Two
For One

TEN

TWO FOR ONE

The summer of 2011 saw me quite embedded in a range of interpersonal relationships, and I felt my life was resembling a TV soap drama. Nowadays I'll be rootless in my nomadic adventures in Europe and then reclusive while resting back in Newcastle. In 2011 I had a lot of ties to other people's lives, and it created more drama than I'd like.

Dovile the Lithuanian was a shy twenty-year-old student when I first met her in Vilnius the previous autumn (see *Balls Deep*). She'd be the first girl I deliberately deep-converted, a powerful way of making a girl fall for you. What began as a series of tentative late night chats on Facebook became a paternal sexual relationship. I rattled her in January during a trip to Vilnius with Jimmy and then arranged for her to visit London for a three-month internship on the Erasmus study program. She'd fallen in love with me and was completely in my thrall.

I'd fuck her a couple of times a week then go out and do my daygame with Jimmy, Mick, and Fernando. Dovile wasn't very happy about that but I wasn't to be diverted from my path.

Now that I was increasingly comfortable that I'd always be getting sex with decent birds, I had a platform from which to experiment. I'd been reading up on threesomes, pimp game, and other oddities outside the norm of simple one-on-one seduction. I wanted to push my boundaries. I'd been too square for too long.

If only I knew some degenerates with similar ideas...

Tom was knee-deep in a seedy obsessive spell, going out with Antony most nights after street game then getting drunk and occasionally doing cocaine. They had a head-start with sleaziness. Antony would eventually end up in fetish parties and dogging meet-ups, but I get ahead of myself. There's a compelling logic to the PUA lifestyle in which we are always tempted to want more. I'd already shifted the goalposts several times:

- Get a half-decent girlfriend, became...
- Rattle a pretty girl every month, became....
- Get hot girls, became....
- Totally dominate and lead the life of a young girl, became....
- Have the sleazy, degenerate sex I'd previously only read about with distaste.

It's no joke when people call pick-up a slippery slope to depravity. I like to compare it to "cognitive capture" in the finance world. Allow me to explain.

The financial crisis of 2008 was *not* a "black swan event," it was not unpredictable, and it was an outrageous lie for bank CEOs and government officials to state "nobody saw it coming." As the recent movie *The Big Short* makes clear, many people saw it coming, but they were shouted down and harassed.

I was working with banking clients right when the financial system collapsed, and I, too, saw it coming. It was pretty obvious if you read independent financial blogs and knew how to read quarterly reports and financial statements critically. I even predicted to my work colleagues (four months in advance) that Lehman Brothers would be the next big bankruptcy. It was written clearly in the notes to their financial statements for anyone with a brain to see.

One interesting concept to emerge in the crisis was written about on the blog *Naked Capitalism*, which alongside *Mish's Global Economic Analysis* and *Calculated Risk* were my daily reads at the office. The writer, Yves Smith, talked about "cognitive capture." It means this:

There is a revolving door between Wall Street banks, business schools, regulatory authorities, and political appointees. For example, the Federal Reserve Bank funds almost half of all economics doctorate degrees, meaning that if you disagree with the reigning neo-Keynesianism economic theory adopted by the Fed, your academic career goes nowhere. The outcome is all Western economics departments are stuffed with apologists for Fed policy. It's a subtle machination on a par with communist control of Soviet academia or mass Saudi funding of Islamist students in European universities. Whoever pays the checks determines the thought.

"It is difficult to get a man to understand something, when his salary depends upon his not understanding it!" *Upton Sinclair*

Particularly corrupt was/is the relationship between the Securities Exchange Commission tasked to regulate Wall Street and the actual firms they regulate. The revolving door was simple – a banker will be hired by Wall Street in his twenties, spend a few years on sabbatical working for the SEC or a Rating Agency, then go back to Wall Street for a big pay raise. There is no practical separation between the sheepdogs from the wolves they are meant to guard against.

This leads to *cognitive capture* in which the interests of nominally-opposed parties are so closely aligned that they share the same mindset and values. They conceive of the world the same way. We see a similar phenomenon in Western politics as nominally-opposed political parties are filled with staff and politicians drawn from the same social class, same universities, and same interning background. It's a charade.

You have been cognitively captured when your thought is driven by the reigning cross-party orthodoxy more than it is by the principles required by your job or your own character. The PUA world cognitively captures its greatest talents. It's not hard to see why. The path into PUA breaks down your frame and rebuilds it with the PUA frame. It's a form of self-brainwashing. Here are some typically-encountered facets of the PUA hive-mind:

- You can never fuck enough women;
- Relationships are for chumps;
- A man's worth is determined by his notch-count;
- You need to keep pushing to "the next level."

That summarises my goals in 2011, too. I should probably add that being cognitively captured by the PUA community is considerably more fun than being a chump. I don't regret it for a moment.

I was living in a PUA house with fellow reprobates, scouring the blogs and forums for PUA wisdom, and now hanging out with a pair of sleazy PUA reprobates in Antony and Tom. My life was 24/7 PUA. Even communist re-education centres struggle to match this level of immersion.

Tom had recently met a 21-year-old Romanian girl, a student at Cambridge University, called Manuela. As usually happened when he found a pretty girl, Tom was very keen to parade her in front of me. She had a deceptively natural English accent, good-girl body language, and I'd rate her a solid 7.

She most definitely *wasn't* a good girl. She was literally a nymphomaniac. I don't mean in the "oh god, my bird likes sex, she's such a nymph" manner. I mean she was clinical, to the point where it was the bane of her life. Naturally Tom hadn't twigged to this during his initial street stop on Oxford Street, but she told him later that when he'd started talking to her, she'd wished that he would take her home and fuck her right there and then.

"When I'm on the Underground, I just stare at men's crotches and imagine them all fucking me," she said.

Having fucked her and discovered her secret, Tom lent some thought as to how to leverage the situation, which was how one night, when I was at home playing *Call of Duty*, he called me up.

"Mate, what are you doing?" he said.

"Just lolling on the Xbox."

"Do you want to fuck my Romanian bird? She's here now, gagging for it. I asked her if she wants another dick and she said yeah."

It was almost midnight, and a taxi to Earls Court would cost £25. Mere trifles.

"Is it properly on?" I asked. "She hasn't even met me."

"Trust me mate, she's gagging for it."

Half an hour later I was knocking on Tom's thick wooden front door in a nice part of town. An old man walked his dog on the other side of the road, and it sniffed flowers as he walked it into the large graveyard opposite. Tom came to the door in his dressing gown, a haggard defeated man.

"I'm all-in, mate," he croaked. "I've been fucking her for two hours, and even the Viagra can't keep me going."

He'd fucked himself to a standstill.

"Come in, and I'll put the kettle on," he said and ushered me inside.

We went through the kitchen and up the stairs to his squalid little room. There were no posters on the wall, no family photographs. It looked like a bedsit for transients. Just a double bed, a flimsy cupboard, and cheap Ikea lamps. The first time I'd been there, a few months earlier, I'd been surprised at the total lack of personalisation. There was no colour, no warmth, no ornaments or knick-knacks, no rug on the floor, and yet he'd lived there for over a year.

It was a typical PUA's room. Only notches matter. Everything else is a distraction.

Manuela sat on the bed wearing one of Tom's work-shirts, and she and I were introduced. It was a rather odd situation. She was certainly pretty enough to inspire the will to fuck but how to negotiate the task? I'd come to fuck, and she'd agreed in principle but even the most obvious sure things can be torpedoed by social faux pas. Tom had told me he'd already done a couple of threesomes with Antony recently but he seemed rudderless here. I guess Antony had led the other ones, and Tom had followed his guide.

I figured the best bet was to lounge on the bed, be cool, and see what happened. We made small talk until Tom came back in with cups of tea. Manuela took a few sips, perked up and said to Tom, "I like him."

That was it.

Tom left the room, and Manuela jumped me the moment the door clicked shut. She just leapt across the bed and landed on me. Without any preamble I started mashing her tits, and she was sucking me off within seconds. She was a good fuck, holding nothing back. About twenty minutes in, Tom came up with a fresh brew and left the cup on the night stand. That kind of thing no longer struck me as odd.

"Do you want to join in?" I asked. It seemed only fair.

"No thanks, I'm still knackered."

So I carried on fucking Manuela until it was time to shower off. I stepped back into my jeans, laced up my boots, then left Manuela half asleep on the bed to join Tom in the kitchen. A solitary lampshade above the dining table cast a soft low-wattage glow over the scene, shadows shrouding everything.

"I have to be up in five hours for work tomorrow," he said.

"No worries," I said, shook his hand, and stepped into the chill night air to find a bus home.

Sitting on the upper deck of the night bus as it chugged on up Finchley Road, I thought about how weird the whole situation had been. Tom had just handed me a pretty girl on half an hour's notice. No legwork. No catch. Nothing. Unbelievable! On reflection, sex with Manuela hadn't been noticeably different to my other girls. It was good but deep down I'd always assumed sex with a nymphomaniac must be qualitatively different than with normal girls. It wasn't. It was just a notch.

The mystery of why Tom had called me instead of Antony was cleared up two days later when he admitted the cheerful German psychopath had been out on a date. Not that I'm complaining. I now owed Tom a girl and events would conspire such that I couldn't repay the debt until late 2014 when he was in Moscow, and I was able to set him up with a local girl I'd already banged (see later).

"Have you ever kissed a girl?" I asked Dovile, the next day. She was naked underneath me.

"Yes. I think I told you already on Facebook. I was really drunk at a party at Christmas and kissed my friend."

"Have you thought about sex with another girl?" I pressed.

Two days later Dovile overtly agreed, in principle, to a threesome with another girl. She'd been a good girl her whole life up until we'd met in Vilnius. Five years of vanilla sex with a nice-but-boring local chump had failed to satisfy her thirst for adventure. Then I came along and enticed her into my world.

She was now on a three-month London adventure and becoming more sexually open was a big part of it. I should have already had a threesome a month earlier with her and her best friend Gita. I'd had them both lying on either side of me on my bed at night, drunk, while I kissed them both. A strange sense of etiquette prevented me from pushing harder because we'd recently had an argument and it felt a little ungentlemanly to push at that time – that she agreed easily to have a threesome when I suggested it made my previous fuck-up even more galling.

On holiday with Dovile

I found a *How To Have A Threesome* e-book on the internet, and the advice seemed solid.

It recommended first agreeing with your girlfriend / fuck buddy that you want a threesome. Getting laid involves a delicate interplay of subtly and intent inside a lust bubble that can pop at any moment – getting prior agreement from your girl defuses half of the potential landmines. The only remaining chaotic element is the other girl you're trying to rope in.

Walk in to a lesbian/gay bar together, sit in a visible spot, and kiss your girl during the first drink. Every girl in the room now knows you are together and sexually-minded. Next, send your girl on to the dance floor to gyrate provocatively and let her eyes wander to the other girls. Female eye-coding should do the rest because any curious girl will start dancing with her until they decide if they like each other. Your girl walks off back to you with the new girl (who knows she's with you), and you get to know each other. Don't be too sexual or run too much attraction because at this point the sale is almost complete. You all know what's going on anyway so comfort is paramount. Finish your drinks, suggest an after-party, then get a taxi home together.

It seems so simple when written out like that. If only.

I read the e-book and assessed it against my knowledge of social dynamics. It sounded foolproof – the only important variable was whether the bar would have any pretty girls who liked the idea. Everything else was easy and fully within our control.

"Let's go to G.A.Y. tomorrow evening," I suggested, and Dovile agreed. I called Tom the next morning and told him my plan.

"Sounds great," he enthused. "I think I'll try to do the same thing with Manuela."

So the next evening the four of us sat in a swanky bar round the corner from Old Compton Street, the gay area of London. Well, *all* of London is gayer than two Turks having anal sex, but this was the *officially* gay area. We introduced the two girls and intuitively knew not to mention I'd already fucked Manuela a few days earlier. What was openly acknowledged was that we were all there to seek out two separate threesomes.

It turned out there was another unexpectedly confounding variable in the plan – the quality of women at G.A.Y. There wasn't a single hot girl in the club. Instead it was 90% loathsome faggots and 10% lesbians. Not the hot lesbians from porno movies, mind. No, no, no. This was the fat, short-haired, angry-faced butch lesbianism of the real world. Gross.

We all sat around a table with dejected expressions, watching the decline of Western Civilisation paraded in front of us in all its HIV-ridden glory. Our plan was unravelling before the first drink was ordered. We gutted it out but after an hour in and a few drinks each, we'd lost hope.

"Let's just have a bit of fun and let the girls dance," I said. "Maybe a couple of hotties walk in eventually."

Dovile and Manuela danced together while Tom and I stood by watching them and chatting. All of a sudden, the penny dropped. I looked at Tom, and he looked at me.

"I think we ignored the obvious answer," I said.

It was clear both girls fancied each other. Manuela, a self-confessed bi-sexual and nympho, was seducing Dovile right there on the dance floor, and my little Lithuanian was loving every moment of it. There was one spanner in the works: Dovile was my 'girlfriend' in the sense we met regularly and shared a deep affective bond, so I couldn't let another man fuck her. Tom and I put our heads together and struck a deal. We agreed on the foursome but with the ground rules that he wasn't allowed to put his dick inside Dovile. Anything else was fine.

"Girls, come here!" I called. "Let's ditch this place and get a taxi back to Château Hampstead. I've got a big bottle of gin with our names on it."

The girls were already bumping and grinding each other, cheeks flushed with booze and passion, so they readily agreed. It was all laughs and giggles in the taxi, but as we drew nearer to the house a black cloud of silence descended. The reality of what we were about to do had dawned and shit was getting real. Surprisingly Manuela wobbled most, showing reticence and verbalising objections. Dovile was so totally in my thrall and in a mood for adventure that she remained solid. In contrast, Tom and Manuela were fuck buddies and thus he didn't have much control over her. We managed to calm her down, then I led the way into the house and up to my room.

Dovile poured generous measures of gin while I put on seductive music. The atmosphere soon became carefree again, like we were exaggeratedly making light of the situation so we wouldn't all freak out. Tom and I encouraged Manuela and Dovile to start making out on the bed, and now the Romanian was in her comfort zone and showed enthusiasm and poise in leading my girl. I told Dovile about the restrictions on sexual acts with Tom, and she looked relieved. She'd only ever agreed to another girl.

Given that I'd fucked Manuela already, Dovile was my deeply-converted girlfriend, and it was taking place in my room – I was the king of all things. I'll not go into too much detail, but trust me it was an exceptionally memorable experience to fuck two hot 21-year-old girls at the same time.

How Dovile felt afterwards

Tom sat on the sidelines at first pouring and handing over drinks, then got involved after a quarter hour. Since that night, I've had foursomes involving Jimmy and Mick, and they too suffered from the same temporary loss of libido early on. It's never bothered me to have someone else in the room. As an aside, when I was twenty-eight and living in Japan. I appeared briefly in three porn movies and had absolutely no problems fucking to order in a room full of people and cameras. Porno wasn't much fun, and the money was lousy. Still, it was one for the scrapbook.

The foursome session lasted three hours, and we tried all kinds of combinations (none involving Tom and myself touching, before you ask), some being more memorable than others. That evening I learned threesomes/foursomes are not very sexy. The sensuous eroticism of couple sex is missing. That's not to say I didn't enjoy it, because I did. It was fucking brilliant, although at times it resembled playing Twister, one of the things that contributes to making threesomes/foursomes more *funny* than sexy.

As the night wound down I showed Tom and Manuela to their guest room downstairs then went back up to fuck Dovile properly.

"How to do you feel?" I asked her.

"Great! My hero has returned to me," she gushed.

Tom tried to make it a regular thing with Manuela and other girls, but it just never happened. In my experience, threesomes rarely happen with consistency. There are too many factors mitigating against them. I think the only men who get them on a regular basis (apart from super-celebrities or men paying hookers) are those involved in fetish clubs and swinging. To reliably get threesomes otherwise, you need to be seriously dating a ratbag girl, which can't be fun.

Balling it

*When
I could do
emotional
connection*

Barcelona holiday

LONDON

Slag Heap

SLAG HEAD

've never done well with wops – that is to say, with the girls from the Mediterranean side of Europe. I've lusted over Salma Hayek and Penelope Cruz as much as the next man, but actually getting wops to fancy me and come out on dates… It just didn't happen much.

I suspect a large part of that is the inability of wops to organise anything at all, not just with me. I'd usually encounter large groups of them standing at the bottom of escalators or in the middle of shop doorways just jabbering on in their stupid pseudo-language, waving their hands in the air. The few times I visited wop countries on holiday, I was struck by their drivers' inability to follow the rules of the road and the never-ending vistas of inactive construction sites with never-to-be-completed hotel complexes.

There's something seriously wrong with the DNA in that part of the world – I guess they took in too much Mohammedan blood before the Reconquista and Crusades – but so long as we don't give them any higher positions of responsibility than "trainee barista, Caffe Nero," I'm sure London will survive.

Let me tell you about two wops who *did* like me, and the woppery that ensued.

I was daygaming in Covent Garden late 2010 with Fernando when I stopped a Spanish girl with her curly hair dyed dark red. She was flighty at first, but soon settled in to a chat, and I bounced her down the road to a nearby Starbucks for an instant date. Her name was Isabella, and her English was weak, having only been in the UK a few weeks. She wasn't especially pretty, but I took her number anyway.

She flaked a couple of date invites then came out at the third time of asking.

We sat across a low table in the Cross Keys pub in Covent Garden, a picturesque ye Olde English establishment swamped by colourful flower baskets on the outside and heavy farming tools hanging threateningly from the ceiling inside. We chatted fine, but she wasn't having any of the escalation.

"I have a boyfriend in Spain," she said.

That appeared the end of that. We exchanged Facebook details but after a couple of brief chats confirmed her resolve, I let it drop and soon flew to Poland on a jaunt (see *Balls Deep*).

Many months later I was juggling a few Facebook chats while sitting at home, and I saw Isabella was online. She'd gotten herself a job as a hotel receptionist and lived on Edgeware Road. I'd find out she often worked the late shift killing time on social media, which gave her incentive to reply to my speculative message. I figured it was a waste of time trying to get her on another date, but if I could draw her into dirty talk online something might shake out.

"The party girl is partying" I opened, the message time stamp being almost 2am.

"haha noo i'm just in the sofa" she replied.

"I'm getting ready for bed, shall I tell you a secret?" I wrote.

"OK…tell me…"

"I'm naked :O except for my boxer shorts and dressing gown"

"haha"

"and slippers"

It was just a feeler, like a long shot from the half-way line while the referee is checking his watch. She kept it going a little longer and it is from such literary heights that this seduction flowed. So far she was just a bored girl idling in front of the internet, so I didn't get too excited. It doesn't take much to get a girl playing along if all she has to do is coo and giggle from the other side of a keyboard. It requires rather more to put your dick in her arse.

I still didn't have much aptitude for Facebook game. I'd been trialling different strategies since late 2010 but it was all rather hit-and-miss. I didn't have the patience to spend every evening exploring Isabella's hopes and dreams, and she didn't seem to be the introspective type anyway. So we had brief chats every few days that went something like this.

Her: i'm bored
Me: masturbate
Her: :/ is what u do when u are bored?
Me: depends if I have a new video game
Her: haha
Me: lock your door put some music on pull your skirt up and rub one out you'll be fine
Her: ...
Me: then make a coffee
Her: hahaha i dnt have coffee
Me: but the rest is fine I know
Her: hah OK...i'll do that then
Me: ;) send me a photo
Her: no i'll send u a video
Me: good girl

A bit later she started yapping on again, clearly bored at the reception desk so I ask about her uniform. Apparently it was similar to an air hostess so I accused her of being a pervert, to which she accused me of trying to pervert her.

This childish drivel continued over several chats, and all I really cared about was getting her to talk about sex. I didn't care if she resisted it or threw herself into it so long as she didn't try to shut me down. That's the key thing – a girl can continually rebuff you, but as long as she's responding and allowing you to lech, there's possibly something in it.

Me: Spanish girls are not good at sex
Her: did u try?
Me: yes, quite disappointing, even though she was beautiful
[this was a lie because I still didn't have the Spanish flag]

Her: but i'm catalan, much better
Me: Haha, catalans are the WORST !!!
Her: no, we are the best, we are more frustrated, that's why we are better in sex
Me: so you are all screamers and biters, then?
Her: at least
Me: I'm totally not impressed

By the next night we were joking that I'd fuck her but only if she made me a quality cup of tea afterwards. Again it was all me pushing it onto her, but she continued to sit at her hotel reception desk typing replies. She was giving amber lights – *I won't help you out, but I'm not blocking you.*

Reading back on these chat transcripts it's clearly a pretty crude and try-hard version of PUA reframing, positioning myself as the prize. Of course she was completely wise to it so the fact she played along was a good sign. She agreed in principle to a booty call so now I was trying to set it up. Again, she was evasive.

Me: Get a taxi now text me when you are inside it I'll expect you around 9pm
Her: i'm not gonna take a taxi now hahaha i'm working tomo again
Me: I'll send you home at 11pm
Her: noo not todayy
Me: I'm quite busy this week. Can't guarantee Sunday I'm free tonight. Take the opportunity
Her: monday?

We agreed I'd come round Monday afternoon to rattle her. She said her flatmates might be in so she might have to put some music on.

Her: hahahaha i dnt need to be noisy to be great
Me: I'll be the judge of that, young lady
Her: hahaha

It all seemed rather odd that by throwing enough shit at the wall some of it had stuck. She decided to come visit me on Monday instead, and that was an odd day.

Zaria, the Russian catwalk model, had stayed overnight on the Sunday and I woke up with Monday morning wood, so I banged her while she was still half asleep. Slotted in mid-afternoon was the chance to slot Isabella. Dovile was due to fly into London later that evening with her friend Rita to live in our guest room for a week or so until they found a room-share deal elsewhere.

Isabella was both my first Spaniard and also the first girl to escalate from friend-zone to DTF entirely by Facebook. She messaged to say her bus had arrived, so I went out to the bus stop to collect her. She'd made a real effort with careful make-up, a nice cocktail dress, and sexy underwear. I wasn't overly enamoured by her unseemly fat ass, but everything else was fine.

It was so obviously *on* that Game was unnecessary. I did the decent thing of pouring her a drink and showing her around the house, and then after a ten-minute chat, I pulled her in. There was no LMR, just wild, intense, unconstrained fuck buddy-like sex, with her obediently submitting to my every whim. I did her in the arse then came on her face.

The moment I finished I wanted rid of her.

It felt rude to just throw her out, so I poured us another glass of wine and asked her to show me her prior boyfriends on Facebook. There was a striking pattern: every one of them was a black-haired Australian. *If Mick had a good-looking brother he'd be just like that,* I thought. A germ of an idea formed, but then I had to send her on her way. A couple of hours later Dovile and Gita showed up. Around midnight Dovile came up to my room, and I rattled her.

Three girls in one day. I was drained. It was nice to tick the checklist but I was underwhelmed.

A couple of days later Isabella was back on Facebook chat, angling to come around to get fucked again. I wasn't much enthusiastic because now Dovile was here.

"You like Aussies, right?" I asked.

"Yes. Have you got one for me hahahahaa"

"Actually, yes"

It was easy. I showed Mick a few photos, and he gave the thumbs up, and Isabella did likewise to his photos, so I sent a friends suggestion through Facebook to let them communicate directly. Within two days, she was in his bedroom with her tits out.

"Ass-to-mouth," Mick messaged me at midnight.

A day or so later, we chatted again on Facebook, and I asked her how it had been. "It was great! He's cooler than you," she gushed.

"I'm glad to hear it, darling. You realise this means you now owe me a girl?"

Surprisingly, she agreed. "I'll think about which of my friends might like you," she said.

I still held limiting beliefs about women and their orientation towards sex. Somehow I thought they don't discuss it so mechanically, like horse traders. I was resistant to the idea that Isabella was a ratbag slut, even though the evidence was overwhelming. I just didn't like to think of girls that way.

Mick also agreed he owed me a girl but never came through on it. About two weeks later, Isabella contacted me to ask if I'd like to go out and meet her two flatmates. She was explicit that it was about trying to set us up so I'm sure she was equally explicit with her friends. Jimmy and Mick were curious too so they came along to see how the flatmates looked. Mick was interested in the sex angle and had Isabella as a regular by now, but Jimmy went along more for the laugh.

Isabella sent sample photos the day before, which warned us the girls were in the 6-7 range.

Early Sunday evening we all sat on an A-frame wooden table bench outside a Baker Street pub. The girls had already been there about an hour by the time we rolled up, and as they were all sitting down one side of the table, we sat down on the opposite side. It was all a bit strange because everyone knew what was going on, but no one wanted to specifically reference it, so we just chatted and cracked a few jokes.

Jimmy and Mick left the play up to me. The Italian flatmate Chiara had a pretty face that her photo hadn't done justice. Had she stood up so I'd been able to see her arse perhaps I'd have been less enthusiastic. She was like two different women stuck together from a female body chop shop – a slim pretty face and torso perched atop a waddling arse. The Chinese flatmate also seemed to fancy me, but being a low-6 she was below my attraction threshold.

We were all getting along rather nicely when Zaria called.

"Nick, I'm back in London. I want to see you."

She was back to try pulling me in to a relationship. I was happy to have her as a fuck buddy, but I'd resolved that I wasn't ready for exclusive dating. I'd been sorely tempted after first knobbing her, but after discussing it at length with Colin in a therapy session, it became clear that I had unfinished business with women. I'd never rest until I'd rattled a lot more girls.

"I'm at Baker Street drinking. Come and join us," I said to Zaria.

Given my ambivalence about Zaria, I figured it was worth throwing her into the mix just to see what happened. If it all burned to the ground, so be it. I was firmly in the try-anything stage of my PUA career.

Zaria strolled up with her well-trained catwalk strut and the gulf in class between her and the trio of ratbags was obvious even to a blind man. It was like putting a Cruft's winning Afghan Hound into a dog pound of assorted strays and mongrels.

Zaria sat down on the edge of the bench with a barely-suppressed *what the fuck is going on here* expression. She immediately had these three girls' number. She remained quiet as the group chat ensured, but at the same time, I could see the three ratbags shrivel up inside. They knew they'd been over-matched. Real competition had arrived, and they had lost their winning card of being the only girls at the table. It was weird for me because there was no way I could carry on flirting with the girls in front of Zaria, and it occurred to me that I'd blown any chance of taking Chiara home.

I liked the squalor of the situation. It was all senseless. I went back to Zaria's flat and banged her. We lay around in bed chatting, slept, and then walked around Covent Garden market the next afternoon like a normal couple. Back home in the evening I logged into Facebook to find waiting messages from Isabella.

"They both like you. So, who do you like?"

"Chiara. I'll fuck her" I said.

"Okay!"

She sent a friends suggestion, and that night Chiara and I chatted. As you'd expect, having been virtually pre-arranged, the chat was easy, and we agreed to meet a couple of days later in Camden. That was when I finally got to see her arse, but I told myself to keep my eyes on her face and think about getting the Italian flag. We went to a couple of pubs, ending up in the Hawley Arms where we made out, and she gave me the talk, which went like this:

"OK, I'll be honest. I want to have sex with you. Not tonight because I've been going to the hospital and I can't for a week or two, but I will soon. It'll just be casual, and if we both like it then great, we can become fuck buddies. If not, that's okay too."

The bit about the hospital amused me. She danced around the subject, but I think she was telling me that she was recovering from an STD. Okay, I agreed but inwardly I was thinking, *could this get any worse?*

We left the Hawley Arms drunk and horny, so I walked her to Primrose Hill, and I swear Alla's shape was still imprinted on the grass under the same tree. We made out, and I stuck my cock in her mouth until she sucked me off, and I came all over her face.

I lay on my back looking at the stars and pondering my life choices while Chiara fumbled around in her handbag for some tissues to wipe herself clean. Even in the poor light, I could see she'd missed some spots but I declined to mention it.

"I shouldn't have done that," she grumbled. "I could catch something again."

I dread to think what went on in that shared house of theirs. When she was good to go, I put her on her bus, and we went our separate ways.

A week later, Chiara messaged me.

"Hey. I'm healthy again. When should I come around?"

We had a house party coming up that weekend so I invited her, and she dolled herself up and came over. Looking around at the other girls there, I found myself in the ignominious position of having the least attractive one in the room, a position I was not used to. I felt like Mick.

Oh, the shame!

I hustled her up to my room, being careful not to look at her arse, gave her another drink, and escalated really fast. I just wanted to get it over and done with so I could claim the notch, the flag, and draw a line under the whole sordid episode.

Clothes flew off and Chiara got really into it, screaming loud and clawing at the pillows. If she'd been a stone and a half lighter, I'd have enjoyed it one hell of a lot more, but as it was, it was fine. As we were fucking, I kept thinking about the notch. Because she'd been thrown at me, there was no sense of achievement, and she wasn't much of a catch because of her weight and general sluttiness. I knew there was no way I'd ever fuck her again.

She didn't mind at all when I eased her out of the house and my life.

I showered, poured myself a triple measure of whiskey and spent some minutes wondering what I was doing with my life. Chiara, Isabella, and Cherry meant I'd been scraping the barrel of quality for three of my last four notches. Such girls make for good stories and a notch is a notch, but it's not why I was in the game. I was spiralling towards depraved sex with ratbags when what I really wanted was classy birds with long legs, tight asses, and chaste behaviours.

Bottom-feeding was easy and might become a nasty habit, but it wasn't what I was in the Game for. I believe alcoholics would interpret my night with Chiara as finally hitting "rock bottom." Something triggered in my subconscious. I wanted to clean up my act and pursue quality.

"This can't go on," I said to no one in particular.

Intermission at The Mousetrap

The Hemingway Suite

LONDON

Two Puppies Fighting In A Sack

CHAPTER
TWELVE

TWO PUPPIES FIGHTING IN A SACK

Mick and Isabella were both into dirty, squalid sex, so they soon settled into being regular fuck buddies. Once a week when I'd walk down to the shared kitchen, I'd have to go past his bedroom door and she'd be there. There'd be a squeaking of bed springs and girl's sighs, then Isabella would emerge sweaty and dishevelled, wandering into the kitchen like she lived in Château RSG.

Sharing a good holiday together in Estonia and now sharing the same Spanish slut had brought Mick and I closer together. He didn't think I was so selfish now, and the cattiness between us was greatly reduced. We were daygaming together in London, and we helped get each other a couple of lays. Harmony reigned. Jimmy was mightily pleased.

"This is great," he waxed. "There's nothing I want more in this world than for the fat Aussie cunt and the bald Geordie bastard to be friends."

It wasn't just us three. The whole house was calm with everybody getting on with everybody else. Life was good and about to get better.

168

Towards the end of a midweek daygame session I had little to show for my afternoon's work except some inconsequential i-dates. My stomach grumbled and a tofu curry from Wasabi looked just the ticket. I crossed over Oxford Street by Selfridges to take a break and recharge my batteries at the Japanese fast food store. Ten minutes later and a few pounds heavier, I stepped back onto the busy shopping street and almost bumped into a curvy, Polish-looking chick clad in a tight black, figure-hugging dress.

She was striking. The first things I noticed were her massive, fake tits, a DD set she'd tell me later. She had a slutty feline look about her though she turned out to be meek and sexually restrained.

"Oops sorry!" I said with exaggerated politeness. "I wouldn't want to spill tofu curry on that lovely dress."

She hooked easily, and it turned out my cold read was completely wrong. Rather than being a slutty Polish stripper, she was called Angelina from Canada and had come to England six months ago to work on the perfume counters in a very high-end store. She'd just passed their image test which has strict criteria for looks, posture, manners, and voice, etc. However, given the immense size of her knockers, I wasn't surprised to find that she had extremely low self-esteem. She'd have her lips Botoxed and her breasts enlarged even bigger within the year. She was also a gym rat. These are tell-tale symptoms of a low-esteem girl who compensates for it by making herself look like a sex doll.

It's a neurosis I welcome because she looked great. But, back to the street...

She looked so dirty that I couldn't help getting sexual with her right away. I'd been experimenting with sexual daygame, and she seemed an ideal subject. A couple of minutes in I asked her, "Have you seen any girls today with a better rack than you?"

She smiled and said no, so we stood side-by-side, checking out other girls on the street to see if anyone fit the bill. I pointed to a couple of girls and asked, "How about that one?"

"No, mine are better."

Not a single serious contender walked by in over a minute, so I told her she must have the best tits on Oxford Street and pretended to pin a gold star to her chest. She loved that and laughed in a soft, low-energy, sultry manner which reminded me of a cat that's just woken up. My initial opinion of her was as a dirty stripper type who'd be quite easy with a guy she liked and that my best route to success would be through being overtly sexual. That turned out to be a rookie error.

Rather than work the set patiently, I took her on an instant date to the nearest pub I could think of, a gay bar across the road, and started escalating. We walked in off the street around four o'clock and the place was almost empty. I steered her over to a corner by the toilets because I knew from a previous instant date with another girl that the doors leading into the male and female toilets were side-by-side and shielded from the rest of the bar by a wooden screen. Nobody in the pub could tell which toilet you were going into. Additionally, because it was a gay bar, the women's toilets wouldn't be very busy, leaving it empty should the opportunity present itself.

For the uninitiated, that might sound a bit sordid but it's on such small details that a daygamer's reputation and success rate can depend. All good daygamers know of at least six pub or hotel toilets in London where they can rattle a girl.

I bought our drinks and we sat down in a booth. Angelina was quiet and timid, looking down in a demure way, but when she did speak it was in a soft voice that smouldered with sexual energy. I verbally escalated hard by telling stories of fucking and showing her dirty text message exchanges. She cooed and giggled, and soon her hand was on my cock. It was looking good.

"I'm married," she said and waved her wedding ring under my nose.

"I don't believe you," I retorted.

She'd already said she was only twenty-two years old. Something just didn't sit well with me. Girls who fashion themselves after live sex dolls don't marry that young, and young married girls don't act let themselves get swept up so easily when a strange man talks to them. She stuck to her story.

I pressed ahead, and we made out a little. Once I was pretty sure she was horny, I tried dragging her into the toilets.

"No!" she said, and remained with her big, firm ass rooted to the booth cushion. "I want to go home now."

She'd given me her number so we soon chatted over Skype messenger that evening, and I kept verbally escalating. I knew this was probably overdoing it, but she was playing along and even sent me a picture of her tits. Looking back, I definitely miscalibrated

Sitting at the top of Primrose Hill with Angelina

by pulling too hard and over-sexualizing where I should've been giving comfort. Charging hard with sexuality was all quite new to me, and I had it in the back of my mind that I wasn't good enough for centrefold-type girls like her. Surely she'd have plenty of other options, and I somehow had to make up for it. Her beauty acted like a force-field that prevented me really registering all of the subtle signs of low self-esteem that she threw off.

We met in Camden Market a few days later for coffee, walked along the canal, and went up to Primrose Hill where we lay down on the grass, and I tried to kiss her again.

"That's so inappropriate," she said and squirmed away. Nonetheless she stayed with me in the park a couple of hours and we chatted amiably. I felt it was on but that she wanted to move slowly. Our second date was in a couple of bars by Goodge Street station but a migraine came over her midway through.

"I get these several times a week," she moaned. "It's a nightmare." We barely exchanged a word for an hour as she sat with her head in her hands, groaning. I got her water and suggested ordering her a taxi home, but she wanted to gut it out. Finally she relented and went home. I wondered if her migraine had been real, but I'd find out a few years later it was a persistent problem for her.

More Skype followed, and it was slow progress. She sent me more pictures of her tits in a new bra. She also came clean about her wedding ring, admitting that she wasn't married but wore it as a ploy to ward off the creepy rich Arabs in Harrod's who offered to take her back to Saudi Arabia as a concubine. I was becoming exasperated and doubting I'd ever fuck her. Momentum had stalled.

I met Tom for a lunchtime drink in Trafalgar Square and bemoaned my lack of progress with Angelina. We'd set up a third date in Regent's Park for later that afternoon. It was a gloriously sunny day.

"What would you do, Tom?" I asked.

"Pull, pull, pull! You *have* to go for it. Fuck her today or die trying."

I agreed. It was time to go in all guns blazing and damn the consequences. That's fine in theory but easier said than done with Angelina because she was so hot, and I didn't want to take such a risk with such a rare and valuable lead. It was a dilemma that often crops up when you're working at the hotter end of your reach. There's a temptation to treat the hotties like unicorns.

Isabella she wasn't. I thanked Tom for his advice and went off up to Baker Street station to meet her. It was then that I got an eye-opening window into a strikingly hot girl's life.

Angelina came walking towards me with a fifty-year-old black guy, one of the tour bus operators, following alongside obviously trying to pick her up. He clearly had no more chance of fucking her than I had of knocking out Evander Holyfield, but her insanely curvy body had short-circuited his brain. Eventually he saw me and shuffled off.

"What was that about?" I asked.

"He was selling bus tickets when I walked past. He just started following telling me I'm beautiful, and he wants to have sex with me."

"That's weird."

"Not really. It happens a lot," she mused.

She hung onto my arm, and we walked up to Regent's Park. In the three hundred or so meters between the station and the park entrance, at least thirty men checked her out. It wasn't so much that she was classically beautiful – I'd call her a solid eight but no more, yet her proportions and slinky walk just oozed sexuality.

As we walked through the park even fathers pushing prams were turning around to ogle at her. She was a head-turning bundle of sex. She noticed me observing male reactions. "It's like this every single day," she said. I couldn't tell if she was boasting or lamenting the fact.

I enjoyed having every man wanting to fuck the girl I was with. Walking around with Zaria a couple of days earlier had created a similar effect, though with a nuance of admiration for her beauty and poise rather than the raw lust Angelina inspired. I wasn't used to trophy girls on my arm, and it gave me a tremendous ego boost.

We circumnavigated the park then lay down on the grass by the lake. I could feel my legs trembling because I'd decided in advance this was where I'd go for it. I was ready to burn the set if necessary, so my anxiety at possible failure was nerve-wracking. Angelina wouldn't put herself in a position to be smoothly kissed so I jumped on top of her and pressed my lips onto hers. She turned her head away again.

"That's so inappropriate," she said.

"I don't care, I'm an inappropriate kind of man."

I grabbed hold of her chin and held her head in place so I could kiss her. She protested a few seconds then went floppy, disappearing into the kiss. Some girls get a thrill from being taken, as if they are the heroine in their own romance novel. We made out for a short while, with her pushing me off and then allowing me back on, and my thoughts turned to the extraction.

"There's a wine bar by the park entrance. Let's get a glass of wine there," I suggested. The bar was close to a taxi rank and only one street away from the bus stop for the number 13 to my house.

"You're never going to fuck me," she said ten minutes later, sipping her white wine. "We are just friends."

"Whatever. No worries. I'm fine with that, but I would like to show you the house I live in. It's very unusual, and this weather is perfect for sitting out in the garden."

"I'll come, but we're not having sex. Okay?"

Yeah, sure. Okay. It never crossed my mind that she might be nervous or insecure. I just saw those massive knockers and nothing else mattered to me except hatching a plan to get my hands on them.

The outcome balanced on a knife edge, and I knew a single false move could startle her into rushing home. She'd been flighty since the moment we'd met. The taxi rank was empty, and the walk to the bus stop seemed to have trebled in distance since I'd done it the week earlier. The bus arrived soon enough, but those five minutes felt like half an hour because I could see that she was jittery and constantly weighing up whether to bail on me.

I barraged her with inconsequential nonsense to take her mind off things. The bus ride took thirty agonizing minutes through occasional heavy traffic, but we got to Hampstead, and I walked her into the house with some relief.

I gave her a tour of the house to settle her nerves and made her a cup of tea. It was then that I made a mistake that could have scuppered the whole deal. I knew that Mick was in, so I wanted to knock on his door to introduce him to Angelina. That was dumb enough in itself as it removed the Secret Society anonymity she'd enjoyed up to that point, but even worse than that, she might have seen it for what it really was – me wanting to parade a really hot girl in front of my friends. If she had sussed that, she might have taken umbrage and walked out.

Fortunately she didn't. She was docile and followed me around without a peep of protest.

I knocked on Mick's door, and Isabella opened it. She looked at me, at Angelina, then back at me. Her face dropped visibly because Angelina was such an obvious and massive upgrade on her – maybe three points hotter. It ruffled her feathers more than I knew then, as we'll see soon. For now, I got away with it. Mick said hello to us both then I took Angelina upstairs to my bedroom.

My legs were trembling again. I felt like a *Dark Souls* player carrying sixty thousand souls after a boss battle but unable to find a bonfire to rest at to bank them all. I'd come so far but that final leap could still end in disaster. I poured us both a vodka and mixed in orange juice. Then Angelina snapped out of her trance and began resisting me.

I kissed her while standing then she backed off and looked out the window at passing traffic on Finchley Road. I stood behind her with my hand around her waist so after a minute of that, she stepped away to peruse my bookshelf. She let me push her onto the bed but soon sprang up again. This chase-me routine went on for ten minutes, two steps forward one step back, until I just held her down on the mattress and made out strongly.

"No! This is so inappropriate," she complained.

I was a little rattled. I wasn't used to combative escalations. I certainly didn't want to rape the girl, but I could see that a gentlemanly acceptance of her protests would disappoint her. What to do? I racked my mind and my subconscious rewarded me by popping a visual image of a work Health & Safety seminar into my mind.

"All fire exists must have a clear and unobstructed route to them," the presenter had admonished us while clicking through her PowerPoint presentation. That's it! I should leave Angelina with a clear path to de-escalate and see what she did with it.

I stood up and sipped my drink with a look of calm resignation, like a retired British Army commander sitting on a Brighton beach deck chair watching homosexuals play in the sea. Then I walked into the en-suite bathroom to clean my teeth. Angelina could now leave if she so wished. Would she? My legs were trembling again.

Another office seminar memory floated up from my subconscious: "To retain workers, you must train them so they can leave you."

I counted off two minutes on my watch then went back into the bedroom. Angelina was still sitting on the bed. I jumped her again, this time pulling off her shirt and trousers until she was in just her underwear and socks. She kissed me then started pushing me away.

"This is really inappropriate," she said.

I noted that she never said the key words *stop* or *no*. It was always weasel words like *inappropriate* or *ungentlemanly*. Even so I felt like I was right on the borderline of how hard I was willing to push. I got up again.

"I need some more orange juice. I'll be back in a minute."

I counted off another two minutes before I returned from the kitchen with a litre of Sainsbury's own brand of freshly squeezed juice. She was sitting up on the edge of my bed but hadn't put on any of her clothes. She was enjoying the fight, being able to push me away and then watch my expression of desire in coming back and trying again.

I held eye contract with her as I pulled off my t-shirt and jeans.

"I can't believe you are undressing. Put those clothes back on," she squawked, while staring at me with sparkling eyes.

I sat next to her and reached around to unhook her bra. Those glorious tits spilled out, and I finally got a mouthful of them. It was perhaps the happiest moment of my life so far, like touching perfection. She let me push her back onto the mattress and pull her panties off.

I looked down at her gorgeous body, ripped off my underwear and put on a condom. I was kneeling between her splayed legs.

"Really, this is highly inappriate," she bleated.

She just lay there. I wasn't touching her, and she wasn't moving.

"We aren't going to have sex," she said, a moment before I pushed my dick into her.

She gasped, pulled me in, and I started fucking her. It seemed too good to be true, and sure enough it was. After about one minute, she suddenly released her grip on me and went stiff. I raised my posture so I could look down on her amazing tits and body, thinking it must be like fucking one of the world's hottest porno stars.

"I can't. I just can't," she said. "I want to but I can't."

Then she wriggled away up the bed, and I was no longer fucking her. What could I do? I just said it was okay, and she put her clothes back on again.

"You're just going to fuck me and not call me again," she said, looking out onto the streets with a sad face. "I can't go through that again."

That was her low self-esteem talking. I absolutely intended on fucking her as many times as humanly possible, but she just didn't believe me. I guess my hard-charging escalation in the first gay bar had set the wrong tone about who I was and what I wanted.

She soon calmed down and was smiling by the time she asked to call a taxi but the moment was gone. She kissed me goodbye at my front door and skipped off. Later that evening, she Skyped me.

"I can't believe you put your dick inside me," she said, in much the same way as she may recall not believing she'd found a tooth in a McDonald's Happy Meal.

I just smiled and told her I'd enjoyed it. We continued to Skype for a few more days, but I couldn't get her to come out again. She added me to Facebook, and we had the occasional short chat over the next year, and then she told me she was leaving the country.

About a year later, she started modelling and posted up some of her shoots. I left a few teasing comments, just to test the waters, but although she liked what I said it never went any further. Then she moved to Dubai, and I forgot about her.

One day in 2015 she posted a link on her Facebook page to a marketing video someone had done for her. It was clearly a PR campaign intended to go viral on clickbait sites, the hook being that she looked too much like a certain famous singer and that was intimidating men so much they dared not approach her.

"I'm too hot to get a boyfriend," basically.

A minute's Google-fu showed me her story was all over the internet – in The Huffington Post, the Daily Mail, and so on. The most surprising thing about the story is that the factual elements were all true – where she came from, her low self-esteem, working in Harrod's, her migraines. Only the headline about being unable to find a man was fake and even then her Facebook rarely showed any photos of men. And this was her real Facebook, not a modelling highlight reel page.

Angelina was a (mostly) honest girl. However, the articles revealed one thing she'd kept quiet about while dating me: she'd been in a relationship from arriving in England right up until the time she went to Dubai when it had broken up. That was the missing piece explaining her hot and cold behaviour with me. She'd been cheating on her boyfriend with our little adventure and never quite became comfortable with it. Putting my dick in her had forced her to pull back from the brink.

Over the years I've had many additional data points to confirm this pattern. Any time you get a girl who is clearly hot for you but who keeps locking up at the hottest points of escalation, it's a fair bet there's a boyfriend in the background, and her guilty conscience is holding her back. Fair enough, girls have their own game to run.

I received a friend request on Facebook from an Italian girl called Giulia. I couldn't remember giving her my details so I messaged her asking how she knew me. She replied we'd met at a party. That was suspicious for no other reason than I never go to parties. It was obvious that she'd mistaken me for some other man.

However I clicked through her photos and determined she was a solid eight, so I decided to accept the add and run with it, having already started to chat to her online. Perhaps I could turn the situation around and test my game on her. She responded well, albeit somewhat coy. She didn't have many pictures up, and she wouldn't commit to anything, which was a little strange, but I put that down to the fact that she knew I was trying to chat her up online, and she'd realised it was mistaken identity.

We chatted every few days for the next three to four weeks, and she became a bit more open. Her craziest sexual story was fucking the boss of the company where she worked, in his office. She also sent me photos of her sister, who was even hotter.

I couldn't get her to agree to a date but she seemed interested. It was a low investment game, to ping her while I had all my other Facebook chats going on.

A few weeks later I received another friend request from a girl I'd never met, this one a Spaniard.

"Hey, I don't think I know you," I messaged.

"Sorry, you don't. But we have a mutual friend, Isabella."

Now I was suspicious. The Spanish girl went on to explain she and Isabella were friends from back in their Catalan hometown, and Isabella was trying to mess with the mind of some guy there. It wasn't clear if the Spanish girl was dating the guy or competing for him but she suspected that Isabella had set up a fake Facebook account under the name of Giulia and was using it to stir trouble.

I'd have liked to have forgotten Isabella, but she hadn't forgotten me.

"Giulia sent him text messages from a UK number. Can you tell me Isabella's UK number?" asked the new Spaniard.

"No," I replied. "I can confirm if it's the same number you have, but no more."

She gave me the number, and yes, it was indeed Isabella's. I confirmed it. She thanked me and logged off. While this was happening, Giulia was flirting with me on another chat window. I felt odd, having busted her ruse but she didn't yet know it.

The next day, the Spaniard came back online and wrapped up the story. Giulia was Isabella. She'd been using the account to stir up all kinds of trouble with multiple people for unrelated purposes. She added that she'd confronted Isabella, who'd naturally denied all knowledge of Giulia, but the shifty way she'd tried to avoid the accusation and change the subject had been suspicious.

"I'm going to destroy her reputation in our town," she said.

"That sounds rather harsh. Can't you just slap her wrists?"

"No. This bitch deserves everything she's got coming to her."

For my part, I put both Isabella and Giulia on restricted access to my FB, as I wanted to keep communication open to give Isabella a chance to tell me her side of the story if she so desired, but I heard absolutely nothing from her or Giulia ever again. Isabella also stopped seeing Mick, which taken with her radio silence, was as good as an admission that she'd been caught out.

I suspect Isabella had started her Giulia shenanigans without any thought about me but after getting her pride pricked by Angelina's presence she'd decided to mess with me too.

What a ratbag.

CHAPTER

THIRTEEN

Daywalker

THIRTEEN

DAYWALKER

Romania is a major exporter of human capital throughout Europe. They have cornered the market in gypsies, pickpockets, squatters, and whores, and it's only recently that Muslims have muscled into their market for ripping off the welfare state. For all this, the country has somewhat redeemed itself by its other chief export: pretty girls who are up for fucking British men. My first "Game" girlfriend Luminita was Romanian, as was my first free blow-job from a whore and my first foursome with Manuela. Flavia was the next Romanian brunette to pass along the same conveyor belt of sex.

Following the Daygame Blueprint filming, Andy had asked me to help out as an *ad hoc* instructor for his weekend boot camps. It was an unpaid trial run for the first two weeks. I wasn't at all interested in splitting off from Rock Solid Game, but I figured hanging out with Yad a little might help my daygame so I accepted. They liked my work those first two boot camps, so I was taken on at £400 per boot camp, though I only did one more before tiring of it and knocking it on the head.

On the second boot camp Yad went off to eat, and I took the four students down to Piccadilly. A tall, slim brunette walked past so I chose her for my demo set. She hooked well and laughed at my racist jokes about Romanians, vampires, and gypsies. After ten minutes I took her number and sent her on her way.

As usually happens with strong leads, Flavia was enthusiastic and compliant throughout the text messages, accepting my first date invitation for the following Friday. I was experimenting with a new closing gambit during the street stop and following it up with the texting invite: "Do you think you could be an English lady and drink proper tea from proper china cups? I know a great teashop…" Flavia liked the role-play and assured me she could indeed put on the necessary airs and graces.

Autumn 2011 was the time we were constructing our dating model, trying to get that as finely-tuned as the street segment was. There was so much contradictory advice in the PUA world. New York player Paul Janka had released a *Get Laid In NYC* book, recommending meeting girls in a bar directly next to your apartment and then bouncing them upstairs after one or two drinks. Janka was a tall guy with male-model looks and operating in the sluttiest city in the Western hemisphere. He was just filtering mediocre girls to see who was down to fuck. Naturally, that didn't work for us normal men in London trying to bang quality totty.

Mystery and Style were recommending the "seven-hour rule" where you hang out with girls and ladle on the comfort until enough time has passed – seven hours in total adding up all dates – for her to feel comfortable.

"The game is played in comfort," said Mystery.

We tried that too, but it was too hard to get girls through seven hours in one date – there was too much going on in London, so dates were a lot shorter. They'd frequently come on the first date, return home unfucked, then simply not come out again. That approach was too slow, too boring, and too timid.

Mick had been experimenting with "adventure dates:" he'd rent bicycles and take girls around the park. He'd found a bench in Regents Park where, if you stand atop it on tip toes, you can see the monkey and penguin enclosures of London Zoo without paying. He'd knobbed a few girls by whirling them around like this and filling them with ice cream. Tom would later codify his version of this in a video product called *The Girlfriend Sequence* for Andy's business. It was all rather over-wrought and interminably time-consuming.

I thought Jimmy had the best idea. Just turn up, go to a bar, and be cool. So long as you DHV and smoothly escalate, you don't need any external support and you can still convert the Maybe Girls who'd run away from a Janka-style "are you going to fuck or not?" ultimatum date. Jimmy's problem was that he just couldn't articulate the details of his dating system. I had to settle for observing him on a few dates and then reading between the lines of his comments afterwards.

My personality ushered me towards low-energy simple dates. Running around pretending to be extroverted grated on me. I sat down with Antony in the Argyll Arms just by Oxford Circus station one evening, and we discussed dating.

"It's about the venues," he said. "So long as you progress the girl smoothly from each location, it'll go well."

His pet theory was that three venues is sufficient so long as they each change in character to become progressively more seductive:

- Venue one: brightly lit, no alcohol.
- Venue two: brightly lit, alcohol.
- Venue three: dark, alcohol.

He then expounded on the need to suck a girl into the Lust Bubble early. For the first venue you mostly keep your hands to yourself and instead probe her mind and encourage her to open up about her hopes and dreams. The player's role is mostly as an active listener so the girl is not just doing most of the talking, but she's also talking mostly about what matters to her. By the end of the first drink she'll be deeply invested in the conversation and comfortable in your presence. Antony had a number of go-to topics and questions to nudge her along this route.

Her jitters gone, she'll be more likely to progress to alcohol in the second venue, and this starts her on the slippery slope towards "it just happened." Now that she's relaxed and drinking, you can start spiking her up with teases, innuendo, and touching. After that, you turn your mind towards preparing the extraction. This requires the creation of a seductive sexual mood, and that requires a quiet corner in a dark bar.

Antony came at it from the opposite angle to Jimmy. He was all about making the girl invest and getting her to open up – comfort first because enough attraction had been done on the street. Jimmy preferred to DHV at length, weaving a web around the girl and enticing her to try to solve the enigma.

"Get her to ask you questions, then reward her by letting her in a little," he'd say. She had to earn her own comfort by probing you.

Antony relied upon the situation to carry the weight of escalation – just keep moving her to progressively more seductive locations and supporting the vibe with alcohol. Jimmy was entirely about the talking. He'd happily spend the entire date sitting in the sunshine outside a cafe because the engine of his seduction was what happened inside the girl's mind rather than where her feet took her.

Naturally, I felt like some combination of the two would be most powerful. I didn't like Mick or Tom's way of outsourcing the date progression to a shared adventure activity. I wanted the date to be about pulling the girl into my world – I wanted to capture her mind. So I adapted Antony's venue progression with Jimmy's verbals.

Flavia was waiting for me outside Top Shop with nice leather boots, a tight skirt of modest length, and a fitted shirt. She looked respectable and pretty. I was pleased with her.

"Let's walk down to Camelia's tea shop," I suggested. "It's in a pretty arcade down this way and the tea is great."

We sat face-to-face over a rickety circular table and got to know each other better. I paid great attention to resting my forearm on the table at the correct angle because I was wearing a watch that housed a spy cam. I wanted to capture the date on video and analyse it later.

I alternated between probing her to open up and dropping DHVs. She told me about how different England felt to Romania and her attitudes on life. The eye contact was good, and she was easing her way into it. She liked me.

We drained a second cup of tea each, and the pot was empty.

"There's a classic English style pub a few streets over. I want to show you" I said. I rarely *asked* a girl if she wanted to move to the next venue. It's better to make it a statement.

We walked down to the *Sir John Snow*, a Samuel Smith's pub in their old-time style, no music, real ales, English styling. The downstairs rooms were full of media types from the surrounding Soho offices having a snifter after work. They spilled out onto the sunny streets, smoking and chatting. I took Flavia upstairs.

I came back from the bar with two pints of bitter then slid in alongside her in the corner booth. There was still a space between us, but it had narrowed, and I now had the opportunity to test some light incidental touching. The latest theory I was testing was that girls will maintain a specific comfortable distance from you, and this will gradually close as she becomes increasingly amenable to sex. Each time I reached towards her or pulled away, I monitored her reaction in maintaining that distance.

My date game was still pretty raw, so I looked for every scrap of information that would tell me where I stood. I'd observe her eyes, her language, her energy, and her posture. Talking to Antony made me realise how similar our attitude towards the game was – girls throw out a ton of data, and a savvy man can learn to filter it all.

Flavia was a highly educated girl with excellent English so I felt able to run my verbal game at the limit of my intelligence. I let myself flow on high falutin' theories of life, trying the intellectual mastery. Capturing a girl's mind is powerful but runs the risk of sexually de-escalating because it's easy to turn a seductive conversation into a dry and logical debate. She was giving long pauses after I stopped talking, as her mind scrambled to unpack my words. She seemed flat. Perhaps I'd overdone the logical angle?

Over a couple of minutes her eyes brightened appreciably. It was sinking in. I'd spent an hour carefully marshalling my resources, showing her different sides to me. At one moment I'd be truculent and boorish, making a crude comment about her legs, and the next I'd expound upon a point of political philosophy. I wanted to present myself as a study in contrasts, an enigma. This Jimmy-style game was woven in with the Antony-influenced probing into her personality. It took awhile, but the pieces fell into place, and the physical distance between us closed.

We finished our drinks and went to the dark and secluded venue across the road – Milk & Honey member's bar. The "Red Room" on the first floor has dark, leather sofas and mellow jazz tunes. It's subtly lit so each table feels like its own cocoon in a sea of darkness. Unfortunately the waiter showed us to a table with two sofa chairs rather than one shared sofa. I wasn't expecting it, and it upset my plan to kiss her there. The distance had widened again as we sat with a table between us. What to do?

I started dropping my lifestyle DHVs.

I led with my favourite – the "financial and geographical freedom" spiel about unplugging from the matrix and travelling the world with my friends. Jimmy, Mick, and I had spent many evenings sitting in the Hemingway Suite at Château Hampstead puffing ourselves up over how cool we were. We'd come to believe it so I could drop the DHV congruently, absolutely believing my own bullshit. Most girls find freedom and independence seductive both for themselves and in men. Flavia ate it up, her own mind spinning off to what she'd do with all that free time. I always enjoyed the topic.

Dealt a bad hand by the seating arrangements, I wanted to get this drink over with and move on. I told a few stories about my nephews and my time living in Tokyo then hustled her on to the next bar, *Bradley's Spanish Bar* tucked behind Tottenham Court Road station. At this time of night patrons would still be at the street level bar, spilling into the back alley, and the dark basement bar would probably have free seating.

We walked up Poland Street, and it was there I went for a kiss. I stopped her, gently turned her to face me, then went for it.

"No," she said, turning her head away.

Importantly her feet didn't move, her hands didn't push me off, and she stayed pressed up close. Okay, later. We walked on.

Bradley's was perfect. There was a lively buzz on the way in, and as we walked down the rickety stairs into the basement, the sounds of The Clash reverberated up from the jukebox. A small after-work crowd was chatting excitedly, feelings of merriment filling the bar. It felt good. Dark, dingy, and good. Flavia bought a round and brought it over to a small booth tucked under the staircase.

We were right up against each other now.

MICK KRAUSER

"This is how you make me feel," I said, then took her hand and put it on my boner. Her eyes widened, she smiled, and then squeezed.

I owed that move to former RSG coach Ace. A year earlier in the Crazy Bear member's bar, he'd given a presentation on Douchebag Game. That was a signature escalation move of his, and I've used it dozens of times since. He told me, "When in doubt, get your cock out. It can change a 'no' into a 'yes.'"

Flavia kept her hand on my dick and started rubbing. It was the "it's on" moment. I wasted no time in pulling her outside and bundling her into a waiting taxi.

"Where are we going?" she asked.

"Disneyland," came the reply.

We arrived at Château RSG fifteen minutes later, and the place appeared empty. However, two crumpled ten pound notes were on the table just inside the entrance where Mick left them after I'd texted him en route to warn him I'd run out of cash to pay off the taxi driver. I walked Flavia through the lounge and into the garden. The air was still and quiet, almost spooky under the black sky. We walked upstairs and heard hooting and hollering down the corridor towards my room. We rounded the corner to see Jimmy's door open and half the gang getting shitfaced on imported vodka his new girlfriend Kesia had brought back from Poland the week before.

Having learned from the Angelina experience, I didn't want my housemates to see Flavia until after we'd done the dirty, but it was impossible to walk past the open door unseen. So, taking a deep breath, I walked her into Jimmy's room.

"Boys, this is Flavia. Flavia, this is Jimmy, Mick, Fernando, Lee, and Johnny."

Mick held up a sheet of white A4 paper with a "7" scrawled on it in marker pen. The other four quickly scribbled down scores and held them up, like they were judging Olympic ice skating. It was a line of sevens.

Yes, lads. Very funny. I'm sure Flavia caught the joke, but she certainly didn't seem to mind.

The party vibe was infectious, but I didn't want to tarry lest Flavia's buying temperature drop. She'd been grabbing my dick in the pub, come home in a taxi, and was walking to my bedroom. It was as on as it ever could be, so I didn't want any diversions. We walked next door to my room and took our shoes off.

She messed around on my laptop for five minutes choosing music then I pounced. Zero LMR. She was a good lay.

We got dressed afterwards then joined the party in Jimmy's room. I tried to subtly hand her over to him, but she wasn't having it, and he picked up on her indicators of disinterest and let it drop. She stayed overnight but had work early in the morning and left before breakfast.

I was still caught in limbo for what I wanted from women. My overriding objectives were to flesh out my Game skills and to clack new girls. I was process-driven, treating the girls as foils for my own advance through the daygame and dating skill tree. While I'd enjoy the dates and very much enjoy fucking the girls, I would always prioritise The Game. I'd lie in bed after sex, re-running the set over and over in my mind trying to glean whatever lessons I could. It wouldn't really matter that the girl was still lying next to me.

This ambivalence and instrumentalism towards the girls meant I wasn't keeping them around. Except for Dovile and Zaria, it was one-and-done.

I met Flavia again a month later, taking her to a South American bar in Leicester Square. I wanted her on my rotation, but I'd been too cold over the preceding weeks and she wasn't interested. She refused to come home with me and soon dropped off my radar.

Almost two years later, in June 2013, I booked a flight to Bucharest to spend a week with Gabriella, a new Romanian girl I'd started dating. Gabriella had been dating a billionaire when I met her in London, and we'd had sex in Barcelona soon afterwards. She was hung up on me and promised to drive me around Transylvania. So once she assured me we could visit Castle Bran (otherwise known as Castle Dracula), I was sold.

I was queuing to get through security at Luton Airport, and it was rammed. Passengers snaked in a long line all the way back to immigration control. As I moved forwards at one of the turns, I looked around and saw Flavia standing literally two feet away from me on the other side of the fabric rail.

She looked hot. *Really* hot. Her shoulder-length hair had now grown out to almost reach her arse, and it was thick and glossy. She also had nice make-up and clearer skin. A solid eight now.

"Bloody hell, Flavia! Fancy meeting you here," I said.

We exchanged small talk before the queue's progress pulled us apart. She was distant and seemed uncomfortable.

"Anyway, you have my number. Call me if you fancy a coffee sometime," I threw out speculatively.

She didn't call.

This is how I wrote it up for the blog

I BANG MY THIRD 20-SOMETHING ROMANIAN STUDENT

📅 September 25, 2011
👤 krauserpua

Aside from vampires and gypsies, Romania's biggest export is girls up for fucking British guys. My first post-game girlfriend was from there, as was my first free blowjob from a whore, and my first foursome. Now this young lady.

It began as a quickie ten-minute street number close as a demo set for students while I was doing one of Andy's bootcamps. She hooked hard but you just never know so I was pleased when the text game struck home and she was obviously keen to meet. That was a Sunday and the following Friday afternoon we meet for an English tea. The closing bait I'm using these days with foreigners is to ask if they could be an English lady and drink proper tea from proper china cups because I know a great tea shop. She buys into th...

Still dating lots

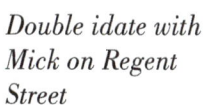

Double idate with Mick on Regent Street

CHAPTER

FOURTEEN

The Fake Valhalla

FOURTEEN

THE FAKE VALHALLA

he RSG experience taught me the value of a "rat pack." Humans are social animals and throughout history we've formed groups and managed delicate internal hierarchies. Back in the caveman era that moulded our present-day psychology, women became hard-wired to sit around the camp fire squabbling over trivialities, forming and breaking alliances as each tries to either become Queen Bee or to at least be her friend. Men went out into the world on hunting trips. That's a completely different dynamic because there is real danger out there and a real job to be done to sustain the tribe and repel invaders.

The hunting band values competence, loyalty, and a willingness to be a team player. Whether it's primal savages hunting mammoth with sharpened sticks or modern soldiers repelling primal savages from their foxholes and machine-gun nests, the code of conduct is the same: you work together for the group objective, and you watch each other's backs.

The need to interface with reality is the single biggest difference between men and women. Men act directly onto the world (hunting, warring, exploring) whereas women act onto the world *through men* (bitching, moaning, manipulating). These two different realities create sharply different value systems and psychological profiles.

The way for a man to improve his rank among other men is to become more competent or to work harder in ways that advance the group goal. Women advance by creating alliances. It's why men are fundamentally honest and women fundamentally duplicitous.

This gets messy when you add in the cognitive flaw of projection.

A useful heuristic in tribal life is to assume everyone sees the world as you do. Why wouldn't they? You shared almost identical formative experiences and continue to share both the same environment and same tribal goals. This means men naturally project onto women their own honesty, loyalty, and commitment to team-play while women project onto men their own dishonesty, selfishness, and commitment to their own ends. I should probably add here that it's absolutely crucial to the future of the human race that women are so extremely self-centred – without that, we'd have ended on the evolutionary scrap heap aeons ago.

Projection underlies every naïve man's trust in his woman's fidelity and every woman's never-ending suspicion that her man doesn't care about her. Every time you read a feminist magazine article accusing men of dishonesty, superficiality, and insecurity, keep this in mind: Criticism often tells you more about the critic than the subject under critique.

The natural next step after projection is to create moral systems around your own self-serving biases. Male morality will lionise competence, loyalty, and team play. We see this enforced constantly, such as sporting rivals shaking hands before and after competition, and common phrases such as "taking one for the team." Women struggle to appreciate this and will tend to see such morally upstanding men as easy marks, someone who has bound his own hands with a naïve moralistic code that she can use to bilk him of attention and resources. Thus women target the highest-tier men of strong moral character to attach to for marriage.

This is why the Secret Society is so interesting. Men who can avoid the responsibilities of team-play without being shunned by the group get the best of both worlds, and women recognise this. They understand and respect such Machiavellian psychology because it's what the women themselves have and the secret code they all live by. There will always be a small group of men who find a way to wriggle out of hunting / warring commitments and stay near that gaggle of women, banging them behind the backs of the warriors.

Bear in mind I'm just outlining evolved feral motivations buried deep within us. Whether they are actually acted upon depends a lot on culture, upbringing, opportunity, and a person's self-image.

2011 would be the year I had the best time with my own hunting band – RSG – and also my biggest trouble with the back-stabbers For now, I was thoroughly enjoying being in my own rat pack. We lived together, hung out together, chased women together, and now travelled together. Jimmy had drawn up an elaborate list of "wing rules" to ensure we were all pulling in the same direction to get each other laid.

Naturally, I projected this hunting band / rat pack ethos onto fellow players. Bad move.

Andy was looking for new territories to expand into and found Norway a likely candidate. The oil-rich country had high salaries, high cost of living, and was full of cerebral, pussified, metrosexual men who struggled with women. That meant his happy-clappy marketing would strike a chord, and the men would be thirsty enough and rich enough to pay top dollar for coaching. That summer he sent Tom and Jon Matrix over for three weekend boot camps and soon forged an alliance with a local "lifestyle guru" there.

As ever, Tom was wildly enthusiastic about a new city.

"Mate, Oslo is fucking awesome," he texted me the Monday after his first boot camp. "Shangri-la!"

He then regaled me with stories of good reactions, easy numbers, and both he and Jon getting laid. His enthusiasm grew over the summer, and before long, despite my indifference to blonde, chubby Norwegian girls, I was persuaded to give Olso a try. October was the first time our schedules were sufficiently clear to travel together in a big group so we booked in five days over a long weekend.

The plan was for Mick, Jimmy, and I to represent RSG, then Tom and Antony, too. I had visions of merging our two loosely-affiliated groups into one big rat pack of London's best daygamers. It was purely social, without any business angle. When Jimmy first met Tom, he was rather underwhelmed, taking an immediate dislike to him, but tagged along because it was the kind of fun adventure he craved.

Friday afternoon rolled around. Mick and I lounged on the big leather sofas in the Château common room, packed flight bags at our feet, waiting for Jimmy to get his act together upstairs. The flight was in a few hours. My phone buzzed.

"I can't come. I'm ill," messaged Tom.

A few minutes later, Antony confirmed he would come without Tom. I should've known better than to worry a German may cancel a plan at the last minute.

We arrived after dusk on Friday night and checked into our hotel, a mid-range business hotel a ten minute's walk from Oslo's main shopping street, the pedestrianised Karl Johanns Gate. Team RSG shared one room with three single beds while Antony's bigger budget paid for his own single room elsewhere in the building. Heading out into light rain, we had our first big shock: the prices. A slice of rotten pizza from a Turkish kebab shop cost £4, and the beer was £10 a pint in the nearest bar.

"I think we'll be eating Pot Noodles all week," moaned Mick.

I slept well and woke up to the patter of torrential rain against the floor-to-ceiling hotel room windows. Mick rolled out of bed, scratched his fat arse, and shuffled off to the en-suite toilet for an epic piss that made the downpour outside seem modest in comparison. Then he shuffled over to the window in his boxer shorts and commented, "It's not looking good for daygame, boys."

We dressed for wet weather then assembled in the hotel lobby where Antony was already waiting, tapping his watch. We ordered coffee and sat on lazy chairs by the window. There was a small glass table next to each, and we used complimentary copies of *The Economist* and *Investors Chronicle* as drinks coasters. It struck me as strangely fitting to how my life had changed since my career in finance.

"The rain has stopped," announced Antony. "We must hit the streets"

We'd barely stepped onto the daygame street at Karl Johanns Gate when I saw my first likely girl. I stood at the pedestrian crossing waiting for the lights to change, and just as I stepped out onto the road, I noticed a cute girl walking beside me, Heidi. Slim, blonde, and dressed like a rebel. I'd find out she was a dancer, which explained her lithe body.

"You look incongruous," I told her.

"Incon... what? What does that mean?" she asked, smiling.

I rambled on with some nonsense about her style being edgy, but her eyes were soft. It's an easy opener when you're out of ideas – just pick two seemingly incongruous parts to her style, and frame one as Good Girl and the other as Bad Girl. Express mock confusion that you're not sure what this means about her true personality and perhaps imply your mother warned you about such girls.

Heidi's nose piercing ticked the first box for an SDL.

We crossed the road together and sat on patio seats of a café a few metres away. It was obvious from her smiling and animated manner that she liked me.

"What did I interrupt by my talking to you?" I asked.

"Nothing much. I'm just wandering around, maybe a little shopping. I only came to Oslo a few weeks ago."

She had recently moved into a new flat share and didn't know many people there. The SDL boxes were getting ticked at an unbelievably fast rate: Rebel, new in town, no plans, compliant.

"I don't have a boyfriend," she added, unprompted. I was even newer in town.

"You know the city better than me" I said. "I just arrived last night. Do you know any good bars nearby?"

We finished the coffees, and she took me to a dark, metalhead place. It was about two in the afternoon with bright sunshine outside, but the moment we stepped into the bar, the vibe sexualised immeasurably. Metallica played over the speakers, and we talked about bands we both liked. Heidi sipped her beer, made relaxed conversation, and didn't once mention anything that could be construed as an obstacle to sex. She was making no effort to leave or even put a time limit on our i-date. We hadn't touched or kissed yet, but it was feeling good.

"Do you like gin & tonic?" I asked. I had a bottle of duty-free gin in my hotel room.

"It's nice," she said.

"Okay, let's drink some."

We stepped back into bright sunshine and light drizzle. I started walking her towards my hotel.

"There's a convenience store this way," I said. "We can buy some tonic water and lemons."

"Where are we drinking them?"

"My hotel."

She shrugged her shoulders in agreement and then followed me into the shop and minutes later into the hotel. Two contradictory emotions competed inside me, nervous anticipation that I might pull off another SDL, and zen-like calm borne of the confidence that she was totally up for it. At this point I'd only had two SDLs from daygame – rattling a teenage art student in the pub toilets in Krakow the previous autumn, and then Cherry in Tallinn. It still felt like I was winging it.

Once in my room I released the pressure, turning my back on her to mix the drinks and letting her check her mails. She pottered around without the slightest trace of anxiety, scrunching her forehead once or twice while replying to business emails. We were soon lying next to each other on Jimmy's bed so that any sex-related messiness wouldn't sully my own bedsheets. I was sure he'd be understanding.

I allowed the chat go for ten minutes before turning, pulling her in, and making my move for the kiss. She resisted the first couple of times without pulling away and then threw herself into it. Two minutes later she was naked.

Dare I say it, the sex was excellent. She moaned, gasped, and enthusiastically sucked me off. I interviewed her while she was face down on Jimmy's pillow.

"Do you like my dick in your ass?"

"Yes, it's great!"

"You knew I was going to fuck you, didn't you?"

"Yes!"

Two hours from street to bed. I was pleased with myself. I ordered her to her knees then came on her upturned face. She went to clean off while I sent a text to Mick that I was now F-Town.

Heidi was notable mainly for the speed with which I whizzed through my SDL model. It shouldn't matter whether you close a girl on the same day or a couple of weeks down the line, but there's no denying the reality-busting ego boost of rattling a girl the same day. It's the kind of "holy shit! This stuff is actually possible" moment that changes how you see the world. It's the kind of thing that should only happen in James Bond movies.

It's quite easy to pull a girl onto an instant date. She doesn't even need to fancy you or be single because many girls just enjoy the diversion of having an interesting man entertain them. Their lives are pretty boring, and all attention from decent-quality males is pleasing to them. However, progressing from the i-date to an SDL is a vastly more difficult leap. To an average man it might not seem like such a difference – surely she's only on the i-date because she fancies you, so keeping it going is little different to getting her on a Day 2, right?

Wrong.

The big difference between an i-date and a Day 2 is the bubble-bursting. A girl may easily agree to a quick coffee when she has an hour to kill. Agreeing to dress up for a date where the man will hit on her and try to fuck her is a different scenario entirely. It's like comparing a spud gun to an AK-47 in terms of a girl's assessment of the risk (of being fucked). Just because they both have grips, triggers, and barrels doesn't mean they are on the same planet in the important characteristics.

An i-date is little more than an enhanced telephone number. She gets a bit more time to become comfortable with you. Even then you're often better off just taking the number because then you retain your mystique and don't lose it until in a more favourable night-time scenario. The worst possible outcome is to have a benign mid-afternoon i-date where the girl walks home after an hour of polite chat having satisfied herself she has gotten to know you and thus has no curiosity to see you again. Should've just taken the number.

Given that SDLs are rare and i-dates can backfire, we figured out a checklist to guide the aspiring player. Try to tick off as many of these as possible on the street before deciding to i-date, and then tick the rest off inside thirty minutes of that coffee. If you *can't* tick them off, take the number and bail with your mystique intact. You want the girl to be:

- Easy.
- Disoriented.
- Ovulating.
- Single.
- Unoccupied.
- Sexually interested in you.

If you can recognize these factors, like I did with Heidi, then you can start thinking there's an SDL in the offing. Heidi was clearly of a rebel mindset as shown by her fashion and vibe. Dancers are also rather physical girls and more likely to be promiscuous for reasons I have never understood. That ticks the "easy" box. She was disoriented on a macro level by having recently moved to a new town without having yet built up the network of friends and daily routines that create stability. Her immediate sparkling reaction to me suggested she was horny and at least a little interested in me sexually. Then she soon overtly stated she was single and had nothing better to do that afternoon.

There's no mystery to an SDL. You probe for the factors and assign a weighted probability based on the answers. Salesmen would call it "qualifying a lead".

Don't go looking for Same Day Lays during sun-up, or you'll burn too many promising sets. Most girls are simply not up for it and pulling hard will put too much tension on the line, snapping it. Rather, just run your usual street game, and be alive to the opportunity whenever it presents itself. Such girls will often make up their mind to fuck you very early on. After that, it's about just taking off the handbrake and freewheeling downhill without crashing. That means you must lead with confidence and competence.

Heidi was lying naked in Jimmy's bed when both Mick and Antony texted to say the rain had washed all the girls off the street, and they wanted to come back to the hotel. Jimmy himself had wandered off somewhere.

"My friends are coming back," I told her.

"OK."

She showered and dressed, then hung around, curious to meet my friends. She struck me as socially confident and not at all phased by the situation. Perhaps I could pass her onto my friends for a threesome? A few minutes after I poured gin and tonics for the boys, Heidi went to the bathroom.

"I fucked her. I think she's dirty. Shall I try to pass her on?"

They eagerly agreed like horny schoolkids. We hatched a plan and then went suspiciously quiet when Heidi flushed the toilet and came back out.

"I have to get some milk from the store," I announced. "Am I okay leaving you three here?"

Ten minutes later I was killing time in the store while the rain thrashed down outside, large drops bouncing off the pavement several feet into the air it seemed. My phone buzzed. It was Mick:

"She's just punched Antony. I think it's safe to return."

I pulled my jacket over my head and rushed through the storm to find out what was going on back at the hotel. Apparently, they'd all been chatting and flirting comfortably, and Mick had started to think it might come off. However, Antony became impatient and had tried to escalate her too quickly, pulling her in suddenly and trying to kiss. She punched him and sat back on the bed.

Interestingly, she didn't lose her temper and didn't try to leave. She sat on a chair, legs crossed, utterly unperturbed.

So I came back in to find them all sitting spread out across the room making awkward polite conversation and sipping on duty-free alcohol. I'd expected fireworks – shouting and screaming – so it took me a few seconds to adjust. Mistakenly, I figured Heidi probably wanted to leave.

"Come on, I'll walk you out," I said.

As we stood in the elevator to the lobby, Heidi turned to me.

"I heard you talk about passing me on while I was in the bathroom," she said. "I don't mind. I don't even blame you, but I'm not interested."

Three days later she invited me around to her apartment and cooked pasta. We had a good deep chat across the small dining table, drinking red wine. Perhaps she was angling for something less transient than casual sex but I'd already decided I'd never return to Oslo. We went to her room, and I fucked her again.

"I love being mistreated," she said. "It's so exciting."

Heidi was the highlight of the trip, not surprisingly, but the rest of it was a washout literally and figuratively. It just wouldn't stop raining, and we were priced out of the city such that our vibes collapsed through accumulated calorie deficiencies. We were reduced to buying a bottle of mineral water from the convenience store then refilling it at McDonald's throughout the day.

I had two dates, both mid-afternoon coffee dates that went nowhere.

The first was promising, a pretty young brunette with great English and an easy-going vibe. We sat under a canopy outside a bar next to the train station entrance. A large metal statue of a bull was visible at the bottom of the steps to the street.

"Tell me a secret about you," I said.

"I used to be a heroin addict."

Yikes. A few minutes later, as I was asking for the check, a stringy, young skateboarder whizzed past. He had that meth-head look with bad skin, sunken cheeks, and shifty dishonest eyes.

"That's my ex-boyfriend," she said. I didn't order a second drink.

I can't even remember the other date. Uneventful dates have a way of blurring together.

Mick and Jimmy were more interested in horseplay than daygame. On the second day we were all walking from the hotel into the centre when Jimmy jumped onto Mick's back, slapped his arse, and shouted, "Run, horsey! Run!"

As Mick ran off down the street with Jimmy on his back, bumping him into branches to spill the accumulated rain water onto Jimmy's head, Antony looked at me perplexed.

"Why are they having fun? We are here to work!"

The girls of Oslo were a big disappointment. Time and again I'd spot a tall, well-dressed, curvy blond at a distance and think she was a stunner. As she ambled closer the hope would die in my heart as closer inspection revealed them all to be fat with poor skin. These were girls who were born lucky and threw it all away with fast food and late nights.

Mick and I gave it one last push on the last day, but we were rained off again. We got back to the hotel by early evening completely spent. I felt like a dog left out in the rain. Jimmy and Antony caught a second wind and decided to brave the beer prices and try some bar game.

Jimmy opened a tall brunette called Jenny while Antony occupied her short, fat, ugly friend. Jenny was twenty-five and had a catwalk model's figure, but her face was rather harsh and dragged her overall rating down to a mere seven. If you blurred her face out for an in-field video, everyone would think you're a superstar PUA. Jimmy does have bad eyesight and said he only opened her because Antony asked for a demonstration, so perhaps that explains it.

I'd seen Antony on dates in London with bona-fide eights, but I'd also seen him rattle some real stinkers. He's such a horndog it made him too indiscriminate for his own good, especially when drunk. That night he was *very* drunk.

Jimmy bounced the girls back to our hotel room, and this is the first we knew about it, as they crashed through the door and spilled into the room where Mick and I were fast asleep. Mick had set up a noise-activated iPhone app designed to record Jimmy's snoring, with a view to teasing him on the flight home. It turned itself on before we'd even woken up so what happened next is all on tape.

"Gentleman! Gentleman! I apologise for the lateness of this interruption," he shouted, his arm waving expansively towards the other three interlopers. Mick and I were still disoriented, sitting up in our respective beds and rubbing our eyes to the bright light.

"Ladies, the fat Aussie bastard sitting closest to you is my good friend Mick. Well, he's not a good friend. Not even a friend, really. He's a fat Aussie bastard. I don't know why I brought him along."

The girls tittered. Antony made his way to the remnants of the duty-free gin and poured himself a drink.

"That bald cunt by the window is Nick. He's a Geordie. Please safeguard your valuables in his presence."

We were wide awake now. Jimmy was in great form, his vibe pulling everyone along with him and taking the edge off our anger at being rudely woken up.

"And now, my esteemed friends. Let me introduce the ladies. This tall one is.... um..."

"You've forgotten our names, haven't you?" Jenny accused.

Jimmy thought a moment, rolled his eyes up, and tried to remember. "Yes. Yes I have," he replied then gestured to Jenny. "This is Girl A. And the shorter one is Girl B. Say hello, girls."

Everyone settled down onto the beds and chairs. I figured this might go on a long time, so I stacked my pillows and sat up, still under the covers. Jimmy was stretched out on his bed with Jenny next to him, then he pulled her tits out and started playing with them. We just carried on the conversation like nothing unusual was happening, and I'm pretty sure she'd have fucked there and then in front of us if Jimmy had tried it on.

The little troll was sitting cross-legged facing Antony trying to pull him into a deep conversation. Mick and I exchanged glances and decided it would be hilarious if Antony fucked her. He'd never live it down. So we encouraged her to escalate him.

"Do you like Germans?" we asked her. She said she did.

"He has big strong arms, doesn't he? Do you think they are sexy? Touch them, feel the strength."

Antony was barely lucid, he was so drunk. He kept chatting on with the little troll and didn't seem to object as she kept pawing at him. We could see the lust in her eyes – she was an unattractive mid-thirties single mother being handed a chance to fuck a cool, young, bad boy. She was clinging on to him by now. Antony seemed to like it and seemed up for it too.

"Here's your chance," we encouraged. "We'll hold him down for you."

Mick and I grabbed him by the shoulders and held him down while the troll straddled him and started unzipping his fly.

"Get off!" Antony cried. We thought he was joking. We certainly were, as we were ready to let him go the moment the troll started reaching into his boxer shorts.

Unfortunately, Antony had a shorter fuse than anticipated. His face mottled purple in rage, and we just let him go. He stood up in one fast aggressive movement, catapulting the troll off the bed. Then he started ranting at her.

"Fuck off, you ugly cunt! I don't want you touching me. You're ugly. Fuck off!"

Mick and I recovered from our initial shock that this horseplay had suddenly become serious. Then we both pressed "record" on our watch-cams and angled the lens to capture the scene. Antony was gesticulating aggressively now, his arm flying out and up as his genetic memories of Nazi rallies fired up. It was hilarious to see an angry German almost sieg-heiling in front of us, so we couldn't help sniggering.

"Get out!" he shouted at the shell-shocked girl. "Get out, or I'll punch you."

Jimmy and Jenny had sat up and the vibe was completely soured. Antony eventually shouted himself hoarse and ran out of steam, so he calmed down. He was still adamant that the little troll must leave. He looked over to Jimmy.

"Who are you backing, me or her?"

"You're my mate, so it has to be you," Jimmy said without enthusiasm. "Come on girls, let's get you a taxi."

The troll stormed off into the bathroom in floods of tears, quickly followed by Jenny, who went to comfort her. Antony stomped around in a foul mood but was calmed by the time the girls re-emerged. He started to apologise to them, but something set him off again on another rant, so Jimmy eased the girls outside and down to the lobby.

He waited with them for a taxi, smoothed them out a little, then came back up. Antony went off to his room. We spent a few minutes expressing our mutual shock at the German's outburst then went back to sleep. Our flight home was the next morning.

The Oslo trip was a key inflection point. Team RSG had remained solid throughout, having fun and supporting each other in every way. Tom had bailed with a weak excuse, while Antony had shown pick-up for him was a joyless obsession that deflected a barely-suppressed rage. I started to doubt the Daygame Rat Pack would ever come together. Just like the Angelina episode would set things in motion with Isabella that would surprise me later, the Oslo episode both created a rift and showed some cracks in a facade I'd never have guessed was fake to begin with.

I left Oslo behind, but Olso wasn't quite done with me, as I'd find out the following summer.

Karl Johanns Gate is a long pedestrian street with a refugee-infested train station at one end and a PUA-infested town house at the other. Antony was flirting with working for Andy so he'd been put in touch with Andy's new business partner who ran the house. Morton was a life coach in his early thirties who had set up his own equivalent Château RSG. Being rather more money-focused, he marketed an "immersion" program in lifestyle design. That meant ten keen, young men sublet rooms in the big house and spent a few months immersing themselves in self-development. They'd sit in the big common room listening to guest speakers lecture on confidence, social skills, fashion, and mindfulness.

On paper, it seemed like a good plan. In reality, it was ten frightened guys sitting in a house all day long, *reading* about taking action. Just a typical self-help commune.

Andy had arranged for Tom to upsell his Norwegian boot camps at a lecture there a month earlier. It went well, so now Antony was lined up to talk about his dating model. I tagged along and videoed it, which proved immensely helpful later when trying to integrate Antony's insights into my own model.

A few guys recognised me from my blog so they asked me to speak after Antony. I delivered an hour of mental masturbation about meta-game. I can't remember more than that as it was an impromptu lecture with little preparation. The weird little house dropped out of my awareness until we were rudely reintroduced while I was in Turkey the next summer, as we shall see.

My brothers dog

The chateaux was in its prime

With Daniella later

LONDON

Tomfoolery

FIFTEEN

TOMFOOLERY

I came back from Oslo feeling something was out of place, as if I'd woken up one morning to find all my furniture subtly re-arranged. I couldn't put my finger on it – there was just a general sense of unease in my gut. Perhaps it was Tom pulling out on the morning of the trip, it was sudden and he showed little interest in the trip. I imagine if I'd missed out on a holiday due to illness, I'd have been barraging my friends with questions about it; How's the weather? Are the streets good?

Tom seemed singularly uninterested in the trip, like he had something better to do. It was the second time in three months that a trip had fallen through with him. The first was a mooted boot camp we'd teach in Odessa, Ukraine.

Antony had been watching videos of the Ukrainian seaside resort and assured us it was the summer party capital of the Former Soviet Union – Ibiza with vodka and communists. Sure enough, YouTube is full of sensationalist documentaries showing wild parties there full of hot girls. The three of us decided to go and try and get a few students to pay for it.

I put up a blog post in late June to announce the trip for the following month, and a few students showed interest. We decided to book flights for August as that seemed peak season. Antony and Tom sat in his Earls Court apartment scouring price comparison sites for flights while Skyping me in Château RSG. We agreed times and dates and an hour later, they sent me their booking confirmation.

They'd booked September, not August. I told them the mistake.

"Oh shit! Sorry. Look, it's booked now. Can we just do September?"

I was excited about the trip so I reluctantly agreed to the later date, wondering if we'd miss the peak summer action. Something didn't sit right with me, but I dismissed it at the time: How did Oxford graduate Tom and PhD student Antony, men usually extremely detail-oriented, manage to make such a dumb error? They were sitting next to each other in the same room. How could they make such a mistake?

Of course it *wasn't* a mistake. They were playing me.

Three days before the flight, Antony messaged me with a long-winded, unconvincing excuse for why he couldn't go.

"My PhD funding is running out in a couple of months, and I'm still a long way from finished. I can't afford the expense of the trip, and I need all my time to get cracking in the library."

I shrugged my shoulders and accepted the inevitable. I didn't believe a word of it, but he'd made his decision.

"That's a shame," I replied. "Still, if Tom is still on I'll go."

"Um… well…. Tom isn't going now either."

Seeing as going by myself would be boring, I'd now missed out on a ten-day holiday I'd been looking forward to and was down £260 on flight costs that couldn't be recouped. I was furious with the pair.

Antony seemed to solve his money troubles in time for Oslo. Once back in London, I found Tom was rather evasive, but the cheerful German psychopath met me a few times for coffee. We were chatting about Tom.

"I must admit, I don't like it when he sends me his +1 texts," I confided. "Intellectually I'm happy for him but emotively, if I'm going through a slow patch his game success irritates me. I suppose I'm just too competitive."

Antony surprised me with his reply.

"Mate, if you think that's bad you should see how he is when you +1 text him. I've been with him a couple of times, and his face just drops. He hates it. I think we all have this problem. Me too."

I'd always been hard on myself for being overly competitive and touchy about my friends outperforming me. Evidently this weakness wasn't unique to myself. Then Antony surprised me again.

"You know, Tom wasn't ill for the Olso trip, right? He'd arranged to have a bird fly in from Switzerland for the weekend, and when she confirmed he ditched the trip."

There were numerous little red flags like this, plus Jimmy's immediate dislike of Tom and then our bizarre experience of Antony's freak-out in Oslo. Something didn't add up but I didn't want to think about it so I never tried to get to the bottom of it.

Zaria had spent all of 2011 trying to lock me into an exclusive relationship. She'd just turned thirty and decided I was the man she wanted to play home-maker to. I'd resisted the whole way and eventually put my foot down, telling her I'll continue my wandering ways indefinitely. She wasn't happy but for now she was tolerating it, seeing me every week or so for dates and sex. I preferred to kick the can down the road rather than formulate a solution.

During the summer Tom and I had a double date with Zaria and a pretty Slovak girl called Frantiska who was Tom's main squeeze. We were introduced to each other's girls for the first time in the *Sir John Snow* pub in Soho. It was a pleasant drink on a bright evening. There wasn't any attempt at another foursome, so don't get any pervy ideas.

I had mixed feelings about Zaria all summer. I didn't want to let her go completely because she was a six-foot-tall catwalk model, but on the other hand, I didn't fancy her as much as I thought I should, and my enthusiasm for fucking her had started to wane through repetition. Our weekly meetings became fortnightly, and we'd barely messaged while I was in Oslo.

Tom was still out daygaming every single evening after work, usually starting off at Leicester Square where his underground train came in at. Zaria lived just around the corner on Charing Cross Road so it's no surprise they bumped into each other one evening.

"Oh! Hi Zaria," said Tom. "Fancy meeting you here."

Or something. I wasn't there. This part of the story was all related to me by Zaria later. He saw her again a week later and this time he suggested a Facebook add.

"I'm around Leicester Square a lot," he said. "Perhaps we could have a cheeky coffee."

Again, I wouldn't take these as exact quotes but I recognised one of Tom's favourite terms for a date invite – cheeky coffee. The intention is rather obvious, he wanted to test the waters with Zaria, and then ramp it up if she showed any interest in him. Zaria took him at face value (so she said), replied to his Facebook chat, and agreed to a mid-afternoon coffee. I think she was curious if there was any way to pump Tom for information that would help forward her agenda of locking me down.

He didn't escalate her that first meeting.

"He was very friendly and chatty. It was not sexual at all," Zaria told me later. "And then he invited me for a ride to Greenwich on the Clipper boat. We walked around the park and chatted."

London daygamers know this is the standard adventure date Tom always used in 2011. He spent more time on the Clipper each week than the ticket inspector did. So, there's no question he was trying to fuck her, and Zaria was taking the hint. On the third "date" in late August, he took her out to a pub and ramped it up – physical and verbal escalation, trying to kiss her.

Maybe she made out with him, maybe not. This entire narrative was told to me by Zaria so I only heard what she wanted me to hear. It's the kind of thing a girl in her position would deny either way, and it's not like I could rely on Tom to tell the truth about it either. What this *did* do was make Zaria decide it was time to tell me about it all once I came back from Oslo.

This all began around the time he made a "mistake" on the Odessa booking and he was still at it while I was in Oslo with Antony.

We were all rather obsessive at chasing skirt but it appeared Tom and Antony were letting Game completely rule their lives. Together with Beckster, the three of them were often stealing each other's sets and backstabbing so much it was like an anti-RSG. Tom was constantly on the streets or in pubs on dates. His bedroom hadn't even looked lived-in the two times I visited him. It was a tough grind.

His one genuine hottie, a Turkish girl who dated a professional footballer, would constantly mess him around like she didn't respect him at all. He invited me out a couple of times to see her, as if to say, "Look! Look! I bang hotties."

At that point, he had never fucked a catwalk model. He'd get one the next year but in 2011 Zaria was his best shot at ticking that checkbox. On the one hand, Zaria was just another lead for him (one in a long line of girls) but on the other hand, she was a class above his usual fare. She was smart, poised, and an actual model. Not the hottest model (they rarely are up close) but she did get paid to strut the catwalk and frequently appeared on magazine covers.

More importantly, Zaria was *my* girl. Stealing her away would put one over on me, which was taking our intense daygame rivalry too far.

I was sitting in the garden reading adventure stories when my phone rang. It was Zaria. We hadn't spoken in nearly three weeks.

"Nick. I want to meet you. There is something you need to know."

"Tell me now. I'm listening."

"No, we should meet face-to-face."

Which of my guilty secrets had she stumbled upon, I wondered. Surely she couldn't know about the blog? I'd talked extensively about her on it and even briefly put up some of her pictures before thinking better of it and removing them. She is not the type of girl who would laugh that off, being a poised and stable girl without a trace of ratbag in her. Did she know I'd recorded our initial meeting in Piccadilly the previous autumn?

We met on a chilly night at Embankment, then crossed over the river bridge, and walked along the south side parallel to the water. Evening lights twinkled on the river and the air was damp. Zaria looked serious, and I was very concerned that I'd put my foot in it somewhere. I was probably more nervous than her.

"Tom isn't your friend, you know. He's going behind your back," she said.

She'd mentioned something similar two months earlier when I told her about our upcoming Odessa trip: "He's not really your friend – be careful." I'd ignored it then. She now spent ten minutes filling me in with a detailed version of his attempts to seduce her over the past two months.

It was surprising in the same way getting mugged is. You notice two suspicious louts checking you out, notice them cross the street towards you and follow at a distance, and yet when they actually run up and pull a knife, it's still a surprise because you suppressed your instinct's attempts to warn you. Most people like to give others the benefit of the doubt and I was no different.

I must've looked disbelieving because Zaria pulled her phone out. "Look, these are the text messages he has sent me."

His last few texts, from a day earlier, were particularly galling. She'd told him she wanted me, and Tom had replied that I'm a womanizer and had told him I didn't care for her at all. He said I'd brought a Lithuanian girl to stay with me and was dating her instead. It was all true, but hardly the point. It wasn't enough trying to steal my girl but he was also trying to bury me with her. The tone of messages was rather needy, which was the main reason I believed Zaria when she said she'd blocked his escalation. It didn't read like a man talking to a girl he's already fucked.

He'd messaged to say I only wanted booty calls (that bit is true) whereas *he* would take her out and date her properly (most definitely not true). Thanks for throwing me under the bus, Tom.

While I was stunned by his betrayal, it didn't shake my view of reality. What *did* rattle me was his scarcity mentality in going after my girl, and the middling quality of his attempts to do so. Would a successful seducer behave in this manner? Now I wondered if I'd misjudged not just his character but also his competence. Was he fucking any girls at all? Had he been lying about *everything*?

On the one hand, he'd trotted out a few non-compliant girls in front of me, such as the Aussie and the Turk, and then waited until they were out of earshot before claiming to have fucked them. It seemed odd how little control he had over these girls, certainly less than I did with girls I'd fucked. His lay count also varied widely each time I asked him about it to the point where I just assumed he was padding it with dozens of imaginary notches.

But then again there was also evidence that he was doing well with women. He'd invited me down to fuck Manuela, and that had been very real. He'd shown me a few hidden cam videos he'd shot in his bedroom with girls, back when we first met, and there was also a near-miss threesome attempt we tried with a Hungarian nanny he knew, where she definitely acted like he'd already banged her.

I just didn't know what to think. He could be telling the whole truth or none of it. That's the problem when you catch someone in a lie; it casts doubt upon everything they've ever claimed. At what point did the truth become embellishment? At what point did embellishment become outright fabrication? It was all very disconcerting, not least because if he and Antony *weren't* getting the success they claimed, then did our daygame really work? This was bigger than just falling out with Tom. I was questioning whether Game really held the tremendous upside I'd always assumed it did.

"What are you going to do?" I asked Zaria.

"I have no interest in Tom." she replied. "I thought he just wanted to be friends, and I want to be friends with your friends."

Zaria was trying to make me exclusive to her, so it was in her best interests to show herself as faithful and devoted. Perhaps she was also messing with my head to instil competition anxiety into me so I'd bend to her will. With the benefit of hindsight I know she's a straight-shooter, but at the time my mind was in a whirl, and I wondered if I could trust anyone at all.

We went back to her apartment on Charing Cross Road, and I fucked the life out of her. The swirl of strong emotions made it the best sex we'd had in months. Then I lay in her bed unable to sleep, thinking, *they never talked about this in the PUA marketing.*

We woke up late and had lunch in a patisserie then hung out in a cafe together reading. By about 5pm we fancied a walk so she dressed up nice and hung on my arm as we walked to Leicester Square. Tourists thronged the streets so we were jostled around in the crowd. Suddenly a space cleared right in front of us, and who should I notice walking a few paces ahead but Tom, out on his daygame!

He must've caught wind of us in his peripheral vision because I caught a look of recognition in his eye, then he tried to pretend he hadn't seen us. I decided to have fun with it and called his name, forcing him to turn around.

"Oh, hi Nick!" he gushed, then gave Zaria a curt nod before looking back at me for the rest of the conversation.

"I'm just having a walk with Zaria, how about you?"

"Oh, just shopping, you know," he muttered and shifted his feet uncomfortably.

I could sense his brain cogs whirring furiously behind the glib exterior: How much does he know? Have I been caught out? Is he going to knock me out? Can I spin it to my advantage? I'd had all night to think about it, and he was now dead to me. Just another daygame weirdo who can't be trusted.

After a minute or so of enjoying his discomfort, I said goodbye and walked off with Zaria. She chuckled.

Although I froze Tom out from that point onwards, I chose to keep the episode to myself and the rest of the RSG gang. The daygame community is small, and back then I actually gave a shit what it thought of me, so I didn't want to add to the already long list of coaches airing their dirty laundry in public. Antony went cold on me shortly afterwards, even Skyping me to give a long-winded explanation of why.

He'd been researching his PhD thesis at a hedge fund and they'd been sufficiently impressed to offer him an internship. It was a big career chance, and he seized it.

"Nick, I have to cut all links with the daygame community. Could you please remove the blog posts I wrote for you and delete my mentions?"

No problem. Good luck to him in his career, I thought, without bitterness.

"Also, I'm going to have to unfriend you on Facebook and Skype. I'm cutting all links."

That seemed to be something different entirely, especially as my own accounts are completely separate from my PUA accounts. Still, true to his word, Antony turned his back on the community and never publicly resurfaced. Last I heard he'd gotten fat, became an alcoholic, and was an avid dogger (a form of voyeurism) and swinger. It's a shame to see the demons take control of a man so genial and talented in Game.

That said, he was so tight with Tom he must've known about the plans to steal Zaria, so fuck him and the panzer he rode in on.

I thought I was done with Tom, but Tom wasn't done with me.

Dovile had finished her London internship with both a bang and a whimper (see *Balls Deep*). Now she was back in university in Lithuania, living with her parents, and wondering what the future held. We'd become very close and now enjoyed a Mr. & Mrs. easyJet arrangement. I flew out to see her once, and she came to London twice. After the Manuela episode I'd promised not to fuck any new girls while she was in London. We'd agreed formally to be exclusive until the end of her three-month London trip, then afterwards I could date other girls. At the time that felt like a massive imposition on my lifestyle freedoms but I very much liked Dovile and took great comfort from hanging out with her.

One evening in later October, a few weeks after the Zaria-Tom debacle and after Dovile had returned to Lithuania, Dovile hit me up on Facebook.

"Nick, what do you think of this?" she asked. "Tom sent me a Facebook invitation, and I accepted. He just started chatting to me ten minutes ago."

As they'd already seen each other naked, he'd fingered her and she'd given him a tit wank on the night of our foursome, it wasn't a big deal…except that the only way he'd have gotten her account details would be by clicking on her name as she liked or commented on one of my photos. My friends list was restricted.

So he'd gone on to my Facebook page, ripped her details, and not informed me. A suspicious start.

"What did he say?"

Dovile copy-pasted me the transcript. It was just a half dozen messages, each of the "hi-how-are-you" variety. Light and indirect.

Probing. The shark will always circle, then bump, and then bite. After laying the groundwork, he'd written this:

"I'm flying in to Vilnius this weekend to meet some friends. Maybe I'll have time for a cheeky coffee with you ;)"

"He's trying to fuck you," I concluded, not failing to notice he even used the same cheeky coffee terminology as with Zaria. "Let's draw him out."

Dovile agreed to continue chatting with him to see where he was going with this, copy-pasting me the chat in real time. Each time I instructed her on how to respond. She was loving the intrigue and thrilled at a chance to show her devotion to me.

"Play it straight and take all his statements at face value," I said. "Treat the whole thing as if he really is just wanting a friendly chat. I want to see just how underhand he is, so we can't try entrapping him. Any escalation and proactivity has to come from him alone. Don't flirt or lead him on because then he has a reasonable claim that you were mutually seducing him."

We gave him plenty of rope to see if he would hang himself. I absolutely trusted Dovile, whereas at this stage I was still a little wary of Zaria. My reasoning was that Dovile had exactly what she wanted from me and never complained, whereas Zaria clearly had an agenda to draw me closer because she wanted more from me. It was still possible that Zaria had fabricated the entire Tom story; highly unlikely but not impossible. Also, Dovile would always give me absolute full disclosure without trying to limit how much of her life I could see, which is a good indicator of honesty.

I found this type of intrigue both fascinating and completely alien. My brain felt dirty just contemplating such spook-like Spy-Vs-Spy behaviour. However, I was furious with Tom and very much on edge. I was stepping closer to the line beyond which lies open war. If the problem could be contained, I'd restrain myself. If he was actively attempting to subvert my entire sex life, I'd better collect evidence. My previous revenge attacks on people who'd crossed me at school and university had been so ruthless and destructive that I was loath to go off half-cocked.

It was a rather paranoid phase in my Game journey.

As luck would have it, I'd already booked tickets for Dovile to visit me that Friday, just a couple of days away.

"A coffee would be nice, but unfortunately I'm travelling to London on Friday to see Nick :(," I wrote for Dovile to send on to Tom.

"No worries," he replied. "If you're still in London on Monday we can meet then."

He hit her up on Sunday evening to confirm a Monday afternoon coffee in Covent Garden.

"Don't expect to meet in Covent Garden," I predicted to Dovile, who was now sitting in my bedroom, having come to London. I knew Tom's entire dating model even before he recorded it for *The Girlfriend Sequence* product with Andy. We'd spent the last six months discussing it in obsessive detail with Antony.

Predictably, he hit her up again on Monday, "Something has come up. Can we push the time back to 7pm?"

Dovile asked me what was going on. I explained he was angling for an evening date because then there'd be darkness and alcohol which both help the seductive vibe.

"Keep playing it straight," I advised, reading the messages over her shoulder.

"In fact, let's meet at Earls Court," Tom pressed. "I know some great English pubs there :)."

That was the clincher as far as unmasking his intentions, placing the noose around his neck. My earlier anger suddenly turned into cold resolve. I could feel the old demons waking up deep within me. Those demons scared me. I'd been a ruthless vindictive shit at school, getting a couple of kids expelled and one ostracised by his own father – all because they'd crossed me and I wouldn't let it lie.

It scared me that I enjoyed the destruction. It had felt so natural to scope out their vulnerabilities and then manipulate others into attacking them. I'd been sent to the school psychologist at age six because of my first such plot which almost got a boy expelled--all because he'd made my nose bleed in a fight.

Throughout my teenage years I'd been a normal, happy-go-lucky, friendly kid right up until the moment someone crossed me, and then I'd change in a heartbeat. It wasn't the person I wished to be. Half of my motivation to become a boxer was an attempt to externalise those demons and sublimate their power into open, formal, safe competition.

"What a dirty, underhand, cheating Welsh bastard," I muttered. "A million girls in London, and he goes after you. You told him you're visiting me in London?" I asked her.

"Yes, but not that I'm staying at your place."

"But he knows we are still in contact, sufficient that you'd come and visit me?"

"Yes."

"How on earth could he think I'd not find out about this?" I wondered. He'd already been caught out sneaking in on Zaria.

I can only assume he was completely under the thrall of his ego. Successful players all go through traumatic identity change during their journey and personality issues can pop up unexpectedly like a game of psychological whack-a-mole. That's why it's so important to pair the in-field practice talking to girls with lots of introspection when alone; in order to smoke out and kill the demons. This was a time in Tom's life when he was obsessed with daygame and had shaped his entire life to support his new obsession. He'd gotten it into his head that whatever girl I could get, he could get as well. It's no coincidence that the two girls he targeted were the two I'd deeply converted and so had the strongest emotional connection to me. They'd be quite a challenge for him but that would just make any possible victory sweeter.

I went next door to tell Jimmy the story. He rolled back onto his bed guffawing, holding his belly like it hurt from laughing.

"You are fucking kidding me? This is brilliant! Perfect! I love it."

Tears were streaming from his eyes. From Jimmy's perspective, there were no possible downsides – it was a fascinating and squalid story no matter how it shook out. I went back to my room and fucked Dovile in the ass. I'm not sure if that was to reward her for playing along or to impress my dominance onto her in the face of competition.

The next afternoon Dovile sat opposite me in the dining room with a pen and paper, upright and alert. I'd told her I was going to walk her through Tom's dating model so she'd know what to expect. She was rather keen to show me how good a student she could be.

It took an hour because she kept asking for clarification and coming up with *what-if?* scenarios. I also wired her up with a spy camera and audio recorder. Dovile assumed I wanted irrefutable evidence of Tom's perfidy, but the real reason was I wanted to check out his dating game and see if it was as good as he'd led me to believe it was. My sudden suspicions over his results meant I wanted to know if I could take his purported expertise seriously.

I briefly wondered whether Dovile would obey if I instructed her to let him fuck her. Then I'd get a solid report on his bedroom escalation routine as well.

"Remember, you must play this straight," I admonished her while doing a last check that the camera and microphone were well-hidden. "It invalidates the whole purpose if you start flirting with him. Let him lead, offer half-hearted resistance, and make him really work to move you along. He has to really try. Oh, and drop in my name a few times. Tell him we still meet and have sex."

It was important to me that he must know she's not single and that trying to fuck her is clearly underhanded.

We took the bus down to Earls Court together, and Jimmy and I spun off for a pint in the closest pub to the one in which Dovile was meeting Tom. I didn't observe any of the date in real time, so the following is a reconstruction based on the audio-video recording, Dovile's text messages to me in real time, and her reportage immediately after the fact.

"This pub is too busy. Let's just get some cans of beer from the off-license," he said before sitting down.

That's fast. I suppose having already seen her naked on my bed during the summer foursome meant he wasn't starting from zero in the escalation.

"No, thanks. I'd like to drink here," she replied.

Tom started his date model while Jimmy and I supped a beer next door, chortling to ourselves. Half an hour later, Dovile messaged me.

"We're in *The Blackbird* now."

Jimmy and I moved on to a bar next door to that and then again when they moved further down the road to O'Neils. They were having the third drink in the Irish bar just fifty metres from his flat. Dovile knew because I'd told her where he lived and that he would work his way closer to his place with each stop.

"He's trying to kiss me now," she messaged from the cover of a toilet break.

"How is his game?" I asked.

"So-so. Every time I throw up an obstacle, he seems to find a way to slip around it. I think he'll try to extract me soon. You should come now."

Jimmy and I still had half a pint each, sitting at the bar in an old English pub right next door.

"There's no rush," said Jimmy. "He's not going to walk out on her, and she knows how to keep him hanging on."

I agreed, so we decided to patiently finish our drinks. We didn't even have a plan for what to do when gatecrashing the date. I wasn't the slightest bit angry. If anything, I was underwhelmed and disappointed that things were proceeding so predictably. I'd hoped for something more dramatic or unexpected.

Suddenly the door to our pub opened, and Tom appeared. He stood there a few seconds to get his bearings, ignoring the bar. He was obviously not there for a drink, so I can only assume that when Dovile had taken her toilet break, he'd rushed next door to buy some condoms from the machine. That's the only reason that made sense, but I never got it confirmed one way or the other because it was at that moment he saw us.

Seeing him so unexpectedly was a surprise to us, but at least we were in on the whole caper. Imagine how surprised he was, especially given his guilty conscience.

He looked like he'd shat his pants.

He froze a few seconds, eyes popping out of his head, then turned tail and scurried next door. "Jimmy and Nick are next door," he told Dovile, breathlessly. Then he literally ran away towards Earls Court station.

The bar where Dovile was waiting for us after Tom's exit was a shitty wine bar restaurant. We bailed on it and went back to the pub next door. Dovile joined us at the bar, and we finished what was left of our drinks.

We were giddy with excitement.

"You did great," I told Dovile, kissing her. She beamed with pleasure.

She settled down to tell us all about her evening but was soon interrupted by a text from Tom.

"I'll be in the Earls Court Tavern in ten minutes. Can you get away?"

We couldn't believe it. Did he not realize what had just happened? Did he believe it was a wild coincidence that we'd just happened to be drinking in the next pub while he tried to steal my girlfriend? We'd just travelled all the way from Hampstead to Earls Court for a drink?

This is why I say he was blinded by his daygame obsession and cognitively captured by PUA values. Common sense had just upped and left. I told Dovile to agree, then we all went there and were sitting in position when he rolled in a few minutes later.

"Hey, Tom," we all greeted him. I raised my glass like in a toast.

He darted off to one side and rushed to the bar, where a group of six middle-aged American tourists were standing having a post-tour bus drink. He opened them indirectly, edging towards them for a chance to disappear into their huddle.

"This is too good!" beamed Jimmy then sidled over to give Tom the "I'm very disappointed in you, son" talk while he was waiting to be served. My anger had completely dissipated. Dovile and I shared a drink and chatted until Jimmy came back. The entire episode already felt like yesterday's news. We had another pint and then took a bus home.

Halfway home, Tom messaged Dovile again, this time an attempt at face-saving and recovering his frame. He wrote enthusiastically that he was in a plush hotel with the Americans having a grand old time.

"You should come join me ;)," he ended it.

Dovile grimaced, and we all just shook our heads.

Back at home I went through Tom's wall on Facebook and listed the names of every one of his FB friends that I could find, about seventy names, and saved it to a Word document, then unfriended him. I had no plans to contact them to expose his secret PUA identity, but it was one of the measures I took just in case he kept on messing with my girls. The date sting had just been harmless fun, sending a message of "I know what you're up to, back off." I'd never intended to beat him up that night. Still, I made several provisions in case things got more serious.

Living around PUAs can make you paranoid. They are rarely neurotypical.

Tom was seduced by the dark side of game, which can unbalance your moral compass. Game promises a world of sex with many pretty women and that's a strong lure. Once you get some success, it can crowd out every other part of your life. Beginners in particular will fall in with the various shifty people of questionable scruples who inhabit the PUA world. As you achieve greater success the pressures build because the lure becomes ever shinier, and your pre-Game social group thins out: old friends disappear and are replaced by mentally-damaged Game obsessives. It's a powerful echo-chamber.

It's easy to forget who you are and what you once valued. Both Tom and Antony tumbled into the abyss, aided and abetted by the likes of Beckster. I was lucky to have the RSG gang as my bulwark against it, and even with Jimmy's savvy mentoring setting the tone for us all, I still took many steps towards the dark side.

The whole affair triggered serious ethical self-reflection because I didn't want to become Tom. He was like the ghost of Christmas future. I was partly there already, having banged some ratbags, swapped them on, and of course the foursome. I never told lies or betrayed my friends, but I was hardly a paragon of virtue. I was still recording girls in the streets and on dates, then posting it on the internet to self-aggrandize. Now I'd become increasingly disturbed by my path. The lure of fast and furious grot-fucks with ratbags appealed to my adventurous side, and I wanted to collect the kind of stories that would make Charles Bukowski blush. However, after each episode I'd feel as guilty as a fatty sitting in front of an empty KFC bucket, wiping chicken juice off his face. And just like a KFC fatty, the guilt would subside I'd soon be back there ordering another bucket.

I didn't just want quality women. I wanted quality male friends too, and I wanted both sides of my life to be achieved on merit. Honestly and openly. I didn't want to lie to women and pass myself off as a potential boyfriend, and I didn't want to use my friends to feed a black hunger for sex. I'd be happy with less notches, higher quality, and equally as important, the clear conscience that comes from an honest, open process. My inner game was shifting, although it would be a few months before the big oil tanker changed course.

I was sufficiently troubled to seek out Colin again and do another session. He'd moved into a shared apartment in a grotty part of town with LSS big-shots, Dr. Yen and Sam Altitudes. I brought in a six-pack of good lager, and we sat on his dusty old sofa working our way through it all. It was great. Non-stop deep conversation for hours.

"You know what it is, right?" said an increasingly inebriated Colin in his Scottish accent. "It's the Dark Side."

"Very confusing you are," I replied.

"It's a common theme throughout fiction and mythology precisely because it's so fundamental to the human condition. The Dark Side is seductive because you get power quicker, by cheating. You sell out, you fuck people over, and you think you reach your goal faster. But it doesn't work. It's a pyrrhic victory. The challenge is to be patient, learn, and let the success happen the right way. It's only then that your power is real and you reach your goals."

"I don't like waiting," I said, crushing an empty beer can and tossing it across the room at the waste bin.

"Tom will apologise to you, mark my words," he said. "Right now he's in the dark place, but he'll pull out of it. He'll have his Road-To-Damascus moment and then go around apologising to all the people he fucked over. That too is an enduring theme in mythology. Nothing really changes in this world."

I didn't believe him, but Colin was right. A year later Tom would go through the wringer, unexpectedly falling in love with a French girl who he later found out had been sleeping around the whole time. That triggered introspection on his Game obsessiveness and he'd patch things up with friends and family, and also send me an email apologising for his behaviour with me.

I accepted the apology. I no longer held the Zaria and Dovile incidents against him because I was keenly aware that I had unpleasant sides to my own character too. Let he without sin cast the first stone. We met up for a beer and cleared the bad air. We'd both changed for the better over the course of 2012, and by early 2013, we'd strike up a friendship that would power us through a couple of years Euro Jaunting and helping each other's fledgling businesses. Time spent travelling and gaming together around Europe would also give me a better insight into the reality of his game. While I'd never reach a firm conclusion on the accuracy of his lay count, I did see ample direct evidence to convince myself he possessed high level daygame skills.

The Player's Journey is one of personal development and major psychological change. We are not the same men we were when starting on this path and falling out over girls seems to be a rite of passage for aspiring PUAs.

London

Norwegian Sandwich

CHAPTER
SIXTEEN

NORWEGIAN SANDWICH

As winter approached I'd run out of steam for game. London was boring me, and my mojo was depleted. I was also wondering if I really wanted to stay in the Game. The happiest times in the year had been hanging out with Dovile and then going on holiday to Barcelona with her and Gita. I'd also felt strangely at peace when sitting in cafes with Zaria just chatting and watching her reading. Add to that my deep introspection on where my life was headed, and I was suffering analysis-paralysis over and above the usual daygame revulsion.

I didn't want to give up on my path but my earlier burning desire had damped down into a weak sputter. On the one hand I hoped I'd rediscover the drive to keep chasing hot girls and to develop my skills, yet on the other hand I was calmed by the realisation that I enjoyed having a girlfriend.

I didn't do many sets and didn't pursue my leads very hard. I was happy to just blog and watch the sales of *Daygame Nitro*. It was hardly a best-seller, but by the end of the year it had made me about £7,000. Nice. I'd regularly get speculative emails from blog readers, often sending me a wall of text outlining their specific problem with a girl they obsessed over. One such email was from a Russian guy who got angry when I didn't reply to him how he wanted, so he went off and scanned a copy of the book and put it on all the pirate websites. Sales had already dried up, so it was nice to get the additional name recognition. Before long my book was everywhere in the daygame community.

At the time I was angry at the attack on my fledging business but now I realise I owe him a few drinks for his marketing nous.

I bought a stack of books from Amazon and a few games for the PlayStation 3. My free time was nicely scheduled until Christmas. Most of our days were spent sprawled on the sofas in the Château communal lounge throwing paper airplanes at each other or in Jimmy's bedroom taking turns progressing his Skyrim save game. Lee was studying for his accounting degree, so I gave him some coaching on that. He'd also set up a male escorting agency website called *Men For Hire* and created profiles for half of the RSG gang.

Jimmy took great pleasure from having the highest hourly rate. I declined Lee's invitation to be on the site as I couldn't imagine any pretty women paying for sex with a stranger booked on the internet. No one actually had any clients, except Lee using a more established existing agency. He banged a few old broads before finally tiring of it. The last straw was some cuckold guy hiring Lee to bang his wife while he hid in the wardrobe masturbating.

"That was a bit odd," said Lee, when he returned home afterwards.

The big team news for December was Fernando's imminent return to Brazil. He'd been the most-liked member of RSG since joining us in early 2010 and was my dependable daygame wing for two years. Almost ten years away from home had finally caught up with him, and he was homesick. He'd come to London as a chump of low ambition, working in a carpet-laying business but the relentless self-development of daygame had changed his outlook entirely. He was now a focused, driven man, and hanging out with him felt like you were in the cool gang. That's what I came to observe from Game – those who succeed develop extraordinary self-confidence on the way.

We wanted to throw him a farewell party. He found a Brazilian restaurant near Kensington and booked a table for fifteen. That evening we stuffed our faces, drank beer, and gave farewell speeches.

I can't remember the details of mine, but it was emotional at the time. I ended with this:

"...it's been a delight and a privilege to watch you become the cool, bad-ass player now sitting in front of us. I've learned a lot from you, and I'm very proud to call you my friend. I wish you the best of luck back in Brazil."

He stood up and gave me a big hug. We both teared up, so much so that if we weren't banging lots of hot girls you'd swear we were faggots. Jimmy and Tony also gave speeches. It felt special, like the end of an era.

Later that night we took taxis to Camden and got roaring drunk. Ten of us standing in a huddle near the bar of the Camden Head, we made a lot of noise. It was almost Christmas, so the bar was decorated in coloured lights and mistletoe, creating an almost magical atmosphere.

I noticed a couple on a date, sitting at a table by the door. It was a hipster white guy with a slim, pretty, black girl. She was a solid eight and thus by far the hottest girl in the bar, possibly in all of Camden. I couldn't help flicking my eyes to look at her, and over the next hour I became progressively more annoyed about the situation. It wasn't so much that she was hot and another guy was on a date with her, you can't get every hot girl. No, the problem was the dynamic between them. She was shamelessly tooling him. He reminded me of a dog trying to impress it's master by rolling over or fetching the stick.

Perhaps I was just externalising my own inner game conflicts, but it bothered me.

"This can't stand," I declared.

"What can't?" asked Fernando, handing me a whiskey from the round he'd bought.

"That little faggot sitting there. He's got no balls. It's painful to watch her tool him so badly."

Fernando observed for a minute or so, as the girl said something that put her date on the defensive, and he began frantically qualifying to her, waving his arms around.

"Yeah, he's weak."

"I'm going to intervene," I said and walked over to the pair.

It was a busy bar so people were jostling and walking past the whole time. The jukebox pumped out classic English Christmas tunes, such as Slade and Wizard. I was drunk. I sidled up to their table and leant over so I was facing the girl, but my back was blocking the man.

"Excuse me. Are you fucking this guy?" I asked, throwing a dismissive thumb in the hipster's direction.

Her eyes widened and sparkled.

"No."

"Great. Come here," I commanded, took both her hands, and stood her up to face me.

There was nothing the little hipster could do. Just think through how you'd handle it – you're on a date that isn't going well, with a girl you haven't kissed (it was obvious from body language that she'd not granted him any physical claim over her). She's hotter than your usual girls, and this has caused you to let her get unruly. Now a seemingly confident, cool guy walks over and says *that*. And she likes it!

What to do? He was boxed into a corner.

I chatted and eye-fucked the girl for five minutes or so then she glided away. She liked the experience but wasn't particularly interested in me. When I walked back to my gang, the little guy was still sitting speechless, fuming. Whether he was angry at me, her or himself seemed moot.

Ten minutes later the black girl ditched him and wandered over to our group. We were in a ragged circle so we could all partake in the same group conversation. Our energy was buzzing. She walked straight in like Moses parting the Red Sea and stood in the middle, revelling in her central position as Princess of the Camden Head. Evidently my earlier approach had emboldened her.

We all looked at each other. No words needed to be spoken, and I knew how this would go.

"It's Christmas," she declared, holding up a mistletoe leaf. "Who will kiss me?"

There was a hush as we all looked at each other then made an exaggerated show of looking away or at the ceiling, like Bernie Sanders had asked who could spare some change. Tony let out a low "cor-blimey, guvnor!" whistle.

"I don't want to," I said.

"Me neither," said Johnny.

"Count me out," said Jimmy.

She looked crestfallen, her eyes darting between each of us. I could read her mind: *who are these guys?*

"Lee, you should kiss her," said Tony.

Lee scrunched up his face and whined, "Do I have to?"

He beckoned her over, and they had a big make-out, then he sent her back to the hipster. We all cracked up laughing, raised a toast to Team RSG, and continued drinking. We hadn't even needed words to co-ordinate such a response. It felt like a perfect encapsulation of the trusting team dynamic that Jimmy had worked so hard to encourage in us all.

A few days after Christmas, Jimmy came into my room with an exaggerated show of diffidence. That meant he was eager to show off. I patiently let him unfurl his banner at his own pace.

"What are you doing on Friday?" he asked.

That would be the night before New Year's Eve. Lee and Hayley had been hard at work organising a party at Château Hampstead. For years I'd always stayed home on NYE to avoid the crushing crowds, so having a party in my home seemed just fine.

"No plans," I said. "Just gonna drink the day after."

"Do you remember the tall bint from Oslo, the one who's mate Antony wanted to punch?" he said, referring to Jenny. "I've been chatting to her on Facebook, and she's coming to London with her little friend for New Year's."

Not exactly scintillating news.

"Good luck," I said, unmoved.

"Well, the thing is," he said, slowing his words into the drawl he always used when announcing something big while pretending he was too cool to care. "She's meeting another friend who lives in London. So there's three of them going out. I need a wing."

"Yeah okay, I'll do it. Do you know anything about the other girl?"

"She's a Norwegian fashion model. Really hot, apparently. Just help me out with Jenny, and you can have a go at her."

The girls flew in late on Thursday, and we met them the following evening on Oxford Street. They were already tipsy and excitable, buzzing around. Camilla was hot. She was a fashion model, not catwalk, and thus was curvy and of average height. Her features were of the photogenic type – high cheekbones, big eyes, full lips. She was an eight but not a head-turner. I was interested.

As per the well-drilled RSG wing rules, I let Jimmy have the play. My role was primarily to get him laid, and it became immediately obvious from Jenny's reactions to him that it was a slam dunk. Okay, I felt free to run more attraction material. Jimmy had already monopolised Jenny's attention, so that left me free to run the other two girls without treading on his toes as overall gang leader.

This night would be the high water-mark for my ability to make a previously-uninterested girl attracted to me by running quality attraction material. It was as if I walked over a Quad Damage power-up coming out the Underground. Years later I still wouldn't recapture such perfection.

There was only one problem – the little, fat, single mother called Lisbeth was there, and she was tighter with Jenny than Camilla was. As we walked off towards Bradley's Spanish Bar, she looked at me and said to the other two girls – in Norwegian – "He's mine."

Yikes. I was already unknowingly facing an uphill battle.

On the plus side, it stoked the fires of rivalry between Camilla and Lisbeth. I needed to make a decision over how to handle the evening. Conditions were optimal for Mystery Method: Camilla was part of the group and committed to stick around for a few hours, thus I needn't worry about hook point – that was baked into the situation. There was no need to make a strong display of intent like I would in a daygame set. Rather, I could mostly ignore her, drop DHVs on a carefully-planned timetable, and repel her first few IOIs. At no point would I risk her dropping off and leaving the group. Jimmy would be tied up with Jenny, and thus Camilla could either talk to me or get bored.

Game is so easy in these situations. It's like dropping down from the Premiership to the Scottish League.

Camilla was a gregarious attractive girl who was used to men throwing themselves at her, so my initial disinterest marked me out as different. I played the cool, laconic guy who sits back chilling and choosing his conversational interventions and words very carefully, leaving the field clear for Jimmy to rule the roost while increasing my value in the eyes of Camilla.

We took our drinks to a corner sofa area in Bradley's, and Jimmy and I conspired to sit Camilla on a wonky stool at the very edge of the group, forcing her to lean in and work hard to remain in the conversation. We'd crack jokes and tell stories then break out laughing at our own awesomeness. Jenny and Lisbeth ate it up because they were so keen to get laid, and that forced Camilla to fall in line too, basking in the happy energy.

Any time a girl tried to grab the conversation, either Jimmy or I would interrupt them and grab it back. Bradley's Spanish Bar is very cramped. Not being used to being out on the fringes, Camilla tried to butt in on several occasions. Each time she did, I just shooed her away, saying something like, "Shush! Men talking." The group would guffaw, and Camilla was left with steam coming out of her ears. It was all just playful nonsense and teasing, and she took it in good humour, joining in even though she was the butt of our jokes.

I kept it up for an hour or so with Jimmy's help. A few times he'd have Jenny eating out of his hand then look over at me and exchange a knowing glance. He loved to see telepathic wing work. It was like a football team in such perfect harmony that the striker can make his runs in full confidence the winger's cross will land at his feet. By the time we left Bradley's, at about nine o'clock, I knew Camilla was into me. She took the banter, kept grabbing my shoulder when she wanted to push herself into the conversation, and slapped my thigh when she wanted to make a point. There was still a long way to go before I could get inside her pants, but it was a sound start.

We took the Underground to Camden Town, and I continued to smash Camilla to the amusement of the whole carriage. I'd crossed over from Game to performance art. Being Friday night the train was busy so we stood pushed up together in the vestibule. Camilla was right in front of me, deliberately. The train shuddered as it slowed for a red light, making Camilla lose balance and fall into me.

"Don't touch me, you pervert!" I admonished, which of course made her touch me.

"Help! Rape!" I called to the carriage.

"I want your phone number," she said. Win.

A couple of passengers alighted at Warren Street, and as we rushed for the empty seats, I held Camilla's shoulders and announced, "Wait young lady. That's the VIP seat. You have to stand," then stole the seat out from under her.

I sat down with a big shitlord grin on my face. Camilla was indignant.

"Sorry, young lady. There are no gentlemen in this gang. We are ignorant oafs," said Jimmy.

All eyes in the carriage turned to us.

"Okay, you can sit on my knee," I said and tapped my leg like I was calling a cat to jump up onto me. Camilla leapt on, squirming her arse all the way into my lap. She was qualifying hard.

"Ooooh, aaahhh!" I exclaimed in mock pain. "Fuckin hell, Jimmy. It's like a hippo just sat on me. I can't feel my legs!"

The whole carriage tittered. Camilla just loved it and played along well. Then I held her wrists and started moving her like a ventriloquist puppet, making conversation between Jimmy and her using funny voices.

"Hey Jimmy. Hey, cool, tall guy," I said in a squeaky, annoying voice, waving Camilla's hands to get his attention.

"What is it, dear?" he replied, addressing Camilla like she'd actually been speaking.

"Your friend Nick is so cool. He's like a super-hero. He is Ultra Charisma Man. I love him so, so much! I very much hope he likes me too, even though I have cheeks like a hamster."

By the time we reached Camden I had such a rapt audience in the train I was tempted to pass around my hat for tips. Camilla hung on to my arm as we walked up to Camden Blues Bar. I felt good.

We found a horseshoe corner booth with a low table in the middle. It was big, and a few couples were on the opposite side on dates. A live band played at the other end of the room. We squeezed in along one side. The average client in the bar was young, in their twenties, and sported a wide variety of alternative types such as hipsters and metallers. The vibe was good.

There comes a point in Mystery Method where you've built your value, received the IOIs, and now you must declare your interest. Mystery calls it A-3, the male-to-female interest stage. It means you've already opened to initiate a conversation (A-1) and spent time displaying attractive traits that will make her fancy you (A-2) . I'd done all that. That time was ripe for me to show interest in her, after having pushed her away for most of the past hour.

Camilla tried to impress me with her travel and modelling stories then she did a sexy dance for me squeezed in between my legs and the low table. The two men across the table were mesmerized, gawping at her and ignoring their dates.

"That's good," I encouraged her. "Now turn around."

Camilla smiled and pivoted away from me, gyrating her ass. I immediately picked up her pint and took a huge gulp then high-fived Jimmy. The entire table broke out in guffaws. Camilla was indignant again, realising I'd just suckered her into turning her back on her drink.

It was all very nudge-wink performance art.

So Camilla played along, putting her hands on her hips and growling at me in an exaggerated display of mock anger.

"Come here, woman," I said. "I'm going to kiss you."

I pulled her down on to my lap and kiss-closed her for about ten seconds then pushed her off and spoke to Jimmy. He had Jenny curled up against him, gagging for it. Meanwhile, Lisbeth was sitting in the corner with her arms folded, hating every minute of it.

Jimmy could see the window of opportunity was open for us both.

"Come on. It's time for Team Jimmy to move on," he announced.

We flagged down a taxi, headed home, and hustled the girls up to the Hemingway Suite. It was time to heat up Camilla with make-outs, but Lisbeth picked *that* moment to reassert her claim to me, coming and trying to sit on my lap. Camilla recognised her position at the bottom of the three-girl hierarchy and slid off, disappointed. Fuck.

Gloriously, Lee's mate Alex stuck his head through the door to ask where Lee was. It was house rules that only Jimmy, Mick, and

I were allowed in the Hemingway Suite without invitation because we'd spent all the time and money creating it.

"Alex, mate!" I rejoiced, spotting a window of opportunity to rescue my set. "Come in. Pour yourself a drink. There's vodka and rum in the cabinet."

Lisbeth realised she might get laid after all and switched her attention to Alex. He knew his role and did me the favour of occupying her long enough for Camilla and I to slip out. As the Norwegian fashion model skipped down the hall towards my room with me, I felt great.

I poured some drinks, put on some music, and lay on the bed. It was a done deal. Extraction successful.

Camilla started dancing again, bursting with pent-up sexual energy. She pulled off her shirt and bra, dancing topless in front of me. It was an awesome sight. I pulled her in towards me and started unbuttoning her jeans.

"No. I can't."

The happy party mood screeched to a jarring stop, like a Muslim had just walked into a gay club.

"I'm on my period."

I wasn't sure whether to believe her, but she held firm. Her jeans remained firmly zipped and clipped. She got into bed next to me and went to sleep. Next door I could hear Jimmy rattling Jenny.

Camilla left early, and I didn't try to stop her. The three girls went off to do some shopping, Lisbeth with a healthy glow to her smile.

"Alex, you didn't, did you?" I asked.

He hung his head and shuffled off to the kitchen next door where he lived. Jimmy agreed with me that Camilla's period excuse was false.

"No way she's acting that sexual while on her period. Something went wrong at the end," he concluded.

I couldn't figure it out. Maybe I'd put a foot wrong and betrayed I wasn't really the super-cool, charismatic man I'd appeared to be. Maybe she enjoyed flirting and necking-on but had a line in the sand about sex. Maybe she needed more comfort. Whatever the answer I felt like she'd taken the piss, and I wanted nothing more to do with her. Sure, I wanted to fuck her, but I didn't want to put forth such effort again just to get a similar result.

We killed time all afternoon then helped Hayley and Lee set up the party.

About fifty or sixty showed up, most of whom were Lee and Hayley's friends. I knew most of them by sight but tended to keep my distance from them. There were a few from the wider London PUA community who I thought, quite frankly, were clowns. I invited Steve Jabba as we'd just started hanging out with him a month earlier.

The three stooges in the Hemingway Suite

I spent most of the party talking to my usual friends and doing just the minimum circulation around guests. It was pretty good, and I enjoyed it immensely – a table of finger food, lots of beers, small groups milling around chatting excitedly. Mostly I was talking to Steve, trying to learn what I could about his mindset. It was the fourth time we'd met, and I was well aware of his reputation in the London community.

I almost completely ignored Camilla who sat on a sofa in her own little world, fending off the attempts of the PUA guests to fuck her. Quite accidentally I was giving her a gigantic push-away, neutralizing the weakness I'd shown the previous night when I'd started pulling too hard in the bedroom.

After the midnight countdown to the New Year, revellers began to drift off or fall asleep in the guest rooms. About ten people remained, so in a mood of temporary festive cheer, we invited them up to the Hemingway Suite. I had to throw out a couple of Lee's young friends because they were very drunk and started misbehaving in a manner that risked damaging the ornaments. They went without causing any trouble, and Camilla was watching intently as I took control and ushered them out. It was a display of dominance and she liked it.

Another hour passed where Jimmy mixed us his favourite cocktail, the Dark & Stormy, and soon we were down to six. The three girls, plus Jimmy, Alex, and I. Lisbeth dragged Alex outside, wanting a repeat of the previous night. Perfect.

I had still barely spoken to Camilla and when I had, it was without sexual intent. Jenny was sitting next to Jimmy on a double-seater Chesterfield, every now and then reaching in to kiss him. I was perched on the other sofa while Camilla sat cross-legged on the floor puzzling over an intricate ornament from our display case. She looked like a small child trying with a Rubik Cube. The mood was calm, pleasant, and still. Soft 1940s jazz played over the speakers.

My phone buzzed with a secret text from Jimmy.

"I think a foursome is on."

That had never crossed my mind, but I knew to trust Jimmy's legendary calibration. I put my phone aside and nodded acknowledgement. He nodded back. With the benefit of hindsight I can see the conditions were there. The girls had already shown interest in us, they'd stayed behind as the party ran down, and they had that soft, passive energy that often precedes sex. Jimmy told me later he'd tested out Jenny verbally the night before and concluded they were both dirty.

Jimmy stood up and walked over to my sofa, sitting next to me. It was a two-seater so we were right up against each other, almost touching. We chatted a few minutes about nothing then he called over Jenny to sit on his lap. She smiled and padded over. Camilla continued to investigate the room's collection of ornaments, her back to us.

"What do you think of Jenny's legs?" he asked me, lifting them and placing them across my lap while she sat in his.

"Very sexy," I said, giving her calf a squeeze.

The penny dropped, and she started giggling.

"How about her hair?" said Jimmy.

I brushed it over her shoulders, tucked some behind her ears, and commented that, yes, it's sexy hair. If this continued, I was going to work in Red Riding Hood jokes about her eyes being all the better to see me with.

"What do you think of Nick?" he asked her.

"He's cool and funny," she said.

All this time I was running my hands up and down her legs and the insides of her thighs, which she accepted without a murmur of protest. It was on. I moved my hand up to her pussy and started gently fingering her through her tights. She cooed and giggled some more.

I looked at Jimmy, and he at me. Jenny would be fucking me tonight. Now we just needed to see if Camilla was part of it too.

I was very gratified because at no time had I thought I'd fuck Jenny – she was Jimmy's set. Camilla looked over. She'd been so engrossed in her ornaments that she hadn't noticed what was going on, but Jenny's giggle had caught her attention. She looked intently at us for a few seconds and then her eyes lit up and sparkled.

"Wow," she said. "Are we going to have an orgy?"

Three voices replied, "Yes."

"Great!"

She jumped to her feet and bounded over like an excitable puppy, launching herself on to my lap, straddling my legs so her knees were either side of me and she was looking me in the eye. Then she planted her lips on me. After twenty seconds of that, Jimmy led us all down to his room.

"Kiss each other," he told the girls.

As they made out on the bed we took the opportunity to touch them up and pull their clothes off. Jimmy made out with Jenny, and I with Camilla. I could tell Camilla had a preference for fucking Jimmy that night despite all my solid work the previous evening, and Jenny a preference for me, but I had to wait for Jimmy's lead as he was the "player" in this set and I was the wingman. Camilla tried to give him a blow job, but he couldn't get it up because I was in the room. The same had happened with Tom a few months earlier.

Totally unfazed, he got up, put on his dressing gown and went downstairs to make a cup of tea. The girls transferred their full attention to me, and I fucked the pair of them.

Ten minutes later Jimmy came back in with his cup of tea and sat in his lounge chair to watch as I fucked both girls for about twenty minutes. It only struck me as *slightly* odd. Once I'd satisfied myself hammering at them both it dawned on me that I was doing Jimmy a disservice – my presence was stopping him from getting laid.

"If you don't mind, James," I said in a mock aristocratic accent. "I'd like to take this fine lady next door and bang her brains out forthwith." I gestured to Jenny, who was lying on her back while I fucked Camilla doggy style over the top of her. "I promise I'll return her to you in full working order."

He was happy with that, so I took Jenny off to my room. She had a fantastic body, was super horny, and totally wanton. We had a pretty wild time until I sent her back to Jimmy as promised.

I went to bed a happy man and rather grateful towards Jimmy. I hadn't seen it coming at all, racing from "no sex tonight" to "wild threesome" in about fifteen minutes because of him. All I'd needed to do was get Camilla to like me the night before.

The girls spent most of New Year's Day in Jimmy's room, making up for lost time the night before both in sleep and in fooling around with Jimmy. I fucked Jenny again in the afternoon but nothing further happened with Camilla. I came to the conclusion that she wasn't that much into me after all, and I'd only got to fuck her due to circumstances, whereas Jenny did actually like me.

Camilla went off to Brazil a month later for modelling work, and Jenny got married six months later and had a baby. Jenny was satisfied with her last great adventure while I suspect Camilla was just getting started with all of hers.

The Hemingway Suite

We were nothing if not grandiose. If Rock Solid Game had a larger budget we'd have carved our faces into Mount Rushmore or bought ourselves an island and declared independence. We'd then take great joy in attending United Nations assemblies and trolling the shit out of them.

"Could the ambassador for Trollistan please leave the chamber," would become a common refrain in such a future.

We were determined to build ourselves up both in reality and within our own imaginations. This was something Jimmy had become world-class at. When you met him he had a rock-star vibe and would regal you with some tales that seemed eminently plausible to hear but preposterous should you ever write a bullet-point list of the information they conveyed. He had some established favourites but was quite capable of spinning such yarns on the fly.

"I've only been to Malta once. It's the last of the Mediterranean islands I needed to tick off the list," Jimmy would drop in to a conversation with a girl. "I've heard it's great for scuba diving; crystal clear water and underwater wrecks from World War Two. But unfortunately I never really got a chance to try it. I'd taken my band there as a celebration for finishing our demo, so we could all hang out, try the local foods, and try scuba."

"You can scuba?" asks the girl.

"No, that's why I took us there. To learn. It must be fantastic to glide through the water, totally weightless, hearing shoals of colourful fish swim by while you're investigating sunken warships. I'm sure that's how freedom feels."

The girl grips her drink, and her eyes go wide at the imagery.

"But my nephew had a motorbike accident on his holiday in Cyprus the same evening I arrived in Malta. His friends had rung me up, frantic. Jimmy! Jimmy! Dave is in hospital with a broken leg, and the police are sniffing around because he had no motorbike insurance."

"Oh my god!" the girl gasps.

"I know. We were all sitting in a Maltese restaurant built into the fort walls of Valletta harbour, drinking wine and looking out over the water. A bunch of local girls we'd just met were going to take us nightclubbing, and then my phone is ringing."

"What did you do?" asks the girl, leaning forwards, hanging on his every word.

"I had no choice, he's my nephew. So I booked a flight that night and rushed over to Cyprus. Once the doctors assured me his cast was solid and he could be moved, I took him back to Manchester. I must admit, once we got back, he was safe, and his mum stopped crying, I lost my temper a bit and bawled him out for being so careless and putting us all through so much worry."

Just stop and think of the impression that kind of story makes on you. It's basically a story about a group of mates who went on a cheap holiday to Malta, got drunk, and had to abort on the first night. A cluster-fuck and yet somehow Jimmy emerges looking like an international traveller, rock star, and adventure sport enthusiast who is king of his gang yet loves and protects his family.

That's the power of DHVs, and I learned it from him. When we first met, he was a low-level project manager living in a squalid flat by Elephant & Castle. That's all. And yet sitting, listening to him in a bar you'd think George Clooney felt lucky at the chance to buy him a drink.

Château Hampstead was itself an exercise in grandiosity, taking a battered Jewish care home and rebranding it as a hotbed of rebellious adventure. No stone was left unturned, and when we finally got done redecorating the ground floor common rooms our attention turned to a small office room on the top floor.

"We could create our own member's lodge, like Milk & Honey," I suggested to Mick as we lay in hammocks in the garden on

a warm spring day earlier in the year. We convened a house meeting and made the proposal.

We asked the house to chip in money and labour towards the project, but they all declined. So Jimmy, Mick, and I pooled £500 and set to work. Or rather, Mick and I set to work. Jimmy bumbled around making a great show of interest but did almost nothing until we'd already finished repainting the entire room.

The walls were split horizontally at hip-height by a runner, so we painted the upper section and the ceiling dark brown and the lower walls dark green. Heavy velvet blackout curtains covered the windows and both inner door and fire exit to give a permanent late-evening mood. I found two deep green leather Chesterfield sofas on Gumtree and had them delivered. The room was finished off with 1940s style furniture – a low table with a world map underneath the glass surface, a chest of drawers with an art deco lamp perched on top, and then Jimmy finally made himself useful discovering a portable drinks cabinet disguised as a globe. We filled that with bottles of rum, vodka, and whiskey. Discreet lighting tucked behind the sofas completed the classy, speak-easy vibe.

The next day Mick came knocking on my bedroom door.

"Nick, put your shoes on! Someone has left a cabinet on the road outside. It's perfect for the suite."

So Mick and I ran across Finchley Road, each took one end of the abandoned cabinet, and hefted it two hundred metres and up the fire escape stairs into the room. We'd claimed it literally one minute before another pair of locals who'd also meant to nab the free furniture and instead stood on the pavement bemused, scratching their heads.

Despite us feeling like a pair of gypsies, Mick had found a gem. The hip-height thick oak cabinet was fronted by two glass doors and perfectly suited the room.

We'd created a time capsule of the 1940s, our very own Red Room from Milk & Honey.

"What are we going to call it?" we mused, the three of us standing in the middle of the room absolutely amazed at how much better than expected it had turned out to be. Various names were mooted, each trying to capture something of our philosophical or aesthetic spirit.

"The Roark Room," suggested Jimmy, who'd just finished reading The Fountainhead and was very much enamoured with Ayn Rand.

"The Atlas Library," I thought, blending the twin influences of Atlas Shrugged and the Bioshock video game we all played.

"But there's no books," said Mick. We fixed that by putting up a small bookshelf in the corner and filling it with the Penguin Classics series of Tolstoy, Dumas, and Dickens that none of us read.

Finally one of us, I forget which, uttered "The Hemingway Suite," and we immediately seized on it. It captured the time period, the manliness of Hemingway's writing, and the upgrading of our mere "room" to the grander "suite". I had a brass nameplate engraved and superglued to the outside of the door to the corridor.

"We'll need some rules. Member's Clubs always have rules."

We quickly settled on a list that made us laugh and also feel so very important and sophisticated.

- *Non members are only allowed in when invited by a member.*

- *No music recorded later than 1959.*

- *No television or YouTube.*

- *Women may be invited in, but they must never express an opinion on any topic whatsoever.*

- *No member may raise his voice or use profanities.*

The rule that created the most fun was this: All insults must be delivered from a seated position. It was intended to minimise the chance of fisticuffs and ensure gentlemanly discourse. What actually happened is we'd wait until someone stood up to mix some drinks at the bar, then we'd brutalise him with insults. To respond, they'd have to run back over to a seat, sit down, hit back, then return to the drinks.

We had a grand old time. We'd suit up and hang out there every evening for weeks on end, drinking whisky and smoking Cuban cigars while listening to jazz greats like Django Reinhardt in the dank atmospheric surroundings. We'd tell stories or debate issues, the end result of which always seemed to demonstrate that we were cooler than everyone else in the world. We each felt like the Most Interesting Man In The World from the Dos Equis beer commercials.

We also consumed great quantities of liquor.

It was during our Hemingway Suite reveries that we'd develop various theories about women, lifestyle, and how to achieve the financial and geographical freedom we aspired to. We felt completely unplugged. We weren't even in the same decade as all the traffic whizzing by outside on Finchley Road.

We were James Bond. All three of us.

Predictably, the Suite was a tremendous aid in seducing girls. We'd be sitting in the bright, airy, tumultuous environment of the common rooms downstairs and then whisper confidentially, "Let's go up to the Hemingway Suite."

"What's that?" the girl would ask.

"It's our own special members room. Like a whiskey and jazz room. Come on, let's walk up."

The girl would be led through the maze of corridors up to a thick wooden door with the brass nameplate on it. The door opens, and she's led into a time-warp. We'd already arranged a deal in advance where the player could text one of the other members to set the room up in advance once he was about to pull the trigger. More than once, Mick would have a girl in the lounge and message me so I'd run upstairs, turn on the lamps, set the music playing, then squeeze out the fire exit a moment before Mick rolled in with his girl.

Once inside, it was game over. They'd fall in with the rules, accept a drink, and ease into the languid atmosphere. It was the Lust Bubble expressed in architecture, an escape from reality for just two people.

It was also a thirty second's walk from our bedrooms.

Grandiose even in our garden

CHAPTER

SEVENTEEN

Apocalyptico

CHAPTER
SEVENTEEN

APOCALYPTICO

W e soon developed a Hemingway Suite Theory Of Everything.
It goes like this:

The vast majority of people spend their lives rooted to one place. For example, a recent statistic publicised in the UK is that sixty percent of Brits live within twenty miles of where they lived when they were fourteen years old. Presumably these numbers include immigrants who will hopefully be deported soon, and thus the percentage is likely even higher than sixty among actual real British people. Even the relatively mobile university graduates who move to London for work will normally adopt it as their new town and stay there.

By and large, people find a steady job, find a partner, take out a mortgage, and settle down to start a family. The prudent few strive to pay off the mortgage as quickly as possible, but most will throw any salary raises into bigger homes and flashier cars. Most people will enthusiastically chain themselves to one place throughout their lives, as naturally as the air that we breathe.

It's an old adage that taxes fall on those least able to avoid them. For me, buying a house and taking salaried employment is like painting a target on your back. The government will rape you good and hard. I once calculated that during my pre-Game life in London

I was paying an effective tax rate of 70%. Let's just do the math. Here is an actual calculation I did based upon my 2008 salary:

- Gross salary including bonus: £85,000
- Income Tax: £24,628
- National Insurance: £4,256
- Take home pay: £56,116

So that's an effective tax rate of 29%: not so bad you say? Well, let's consider all the other taxes: Council Tax for my rental apartment was £948 per year. Almost every other purchase with my remaining money was subject to 20% VAT sales tax. So suddenly the government is costing me £40,832 per year, a tax rate of 48%.

But it gets worse.

Inflation is a tax on everybody who uses money and is approximately 2% per year, so now I'm up to 50%. The government stole, under the implied threat of violence, literally half of the money I worked for. Just for comparison, consider the tax rates levied on medieval serfs in England under the supposedly unfair feudal system:

"The tax rates in medieval England varied, depending on the king and events at any given time. Still, taxes rarely rose above 15%. In fact, 10% was the norm. Taxes were generally paid on land ownership, so those taxed were barons and lords. Serfs were exempt. What the serfs did pay, however, were tithes. The Saladin Tithe was created in 1188 by Henry II, requiring farmers to pay 10% of their labour (usually paid in wheat) and requiring tradesmen to pay 10% in goods and services. The standard benchmark was described as 'One day's labour in ten.' Such payment might be made directly to the king, or it might be made to a liege lord, a trade guild, or even a town.

Of course, like today, the king might attempt a further tax. In 1377, a flat tax was attempted, which was replaced in 1379 with a graduated tax. The increasing taxes led to the Peasants' Revolt in 1381. Generally speaking, when the tax level began to approach 30%, it was treated as intolerable."

Jeff Thomas, *Paying Your Fair Share*, internationalman.com.

I was being robbed far more viciously than an actual serf. I tried to find how much of their labour a plantation slave was allowed to keep, but there were no readily available statistics on Google. I suspect the modern Englishman is taxed at near-slavery levels.

And yet it gets worse.

Western governments have baked a ton of special taxes into the price tag of the purchases we make. Alcohol, fuel, and airline flights are the most outrageous examples. If you doubt me, just look at the invoice for your next flight – often taxation is seventy percent of a ticket price, and this is what you pay with money that's already been taxed at fifty percent!

And yet it gets *worse*.

The view from my room in Winter

Consider all the stealth taxes arising from government interference with your life. The London average for housing benefit in private accommodation, that is, my money stolen and handed over to the welfare scroungers who compete against me in the rental market, was £135 per week. Government spending sets a price floor in every market it floods with subsidies, thus pushing up overall prices. It's quite likely that government action was adding an extra £3,000 to my annual rental bill.

Then consider the Diversity Tax. Most white Londoners pay a massive premium to live in accommodation tucked safely away from the criminality and squalor of 'vibrants'. This means prices can literally double and treble for identical accommodation in a majority white area. The same goes for bars, restaurants, and other entertainment.

Adding it all together, it's a fair bet the government was robbing me of literally seventy percent of my income and then handing that money to my enemies, even going so far as to import more of them to take over my country. To say I was non-plussed with this situation is an understatement.

I quickly found that pointing this out in polite company was "racist."

Team RSG had no desire for this trap. Once you're aware of the matrix, there's no excuse for remaining trapped inside it. Game had already freed us from most financial outlays. Once you stop trying to impress girls with your car, your watch, your bachelor pad, and your fancy-pants restaurants, you suddenly realise how little money you need. Daygame freed us from even needing to pay nightclub entry fees. Château RSG broke more financial chains because it cost each of us only £300 a month all-inclusive to live in a gigantic mansion. We'd re-purposed it to contain a cinema room, a boxing gym, plus all the common areas that meant we'd socialise together for free, at low cost.

Some may look at us and say, "You're unemployed wasters living in grotty little rooms in a dilapidated old people's home."

And they'd be right, but that's not the point.

I was still living on my savings accumulated in my banking job, supplemented with a small income from pick-up coaching. Jimmy, too. Towards the end of 2011 Mick returned to Australia to help out with his father's wheeler-dealer business. Complete financial freedom was still a pipe dream. We travelled abroad most months for a week or two at a time, enjoying some geographical freedom from our UK base.

We were Semi-international Men of Moderate Mystery.

While Mick was having his send-off drinks in the Hemingway Suite in late Autumn, we racked our minds for any way to increase our freedoms.

"I see no reason why I should spend winter in Europe. Snow, cold, and weak daylight should be part of my history," I declared.

"I'm going to save like a Jew for a few months in Oz and then trek through South America," replied Mick, once more returning to his great adventuring dream. He hadn't yet seen the *Uncharted* game franchise, but he'd fit right in as main character Nathan Drake.

"I'll start in San Diego then head south through Mexico and maybe even as far as Brazil."

I thought it sounded pretty good. I also liked that as Mick was an experienced and savvy traveller, I could piggyback all his research and decision-making.

"Let's do a boot camp in San Diego in December," I said. "Then I'll fly back out after Christmas and join you in Mexico for a month."

We both posted our plans on our blogs and soon found five students keen to take the weekend boot camp. Unfortunately we knew nothing of West Coast culture and its seasonal variations, so we scheduled it for the week after the university had split for its seasonal vacation. Mick arrived two weeks before me and enthused over Facebook how much excitement was to be had, but by the time I flew in it was a ghost town.

I usually like American people, but I dislike America. The West Coast in particular is full of weirdos with all their dope-smoking, hippy mysticism, and latte-sipping vacuous superficiality. The a-historical towns feel like they've been hurriedly built up from zero the day before I arrived.

We made the best of it, and the students seemed happy. There wasn't any action on the seaside boardwalk so we took taxis to the open-air mall and found a few girls to open. I did two demo sets that became i-dates. In between them I was chatting to a husky, big white guy, the kind you'd see at a Trump rally in 2016 trolling Hillary voters.

"What's your job?" I asked.

"I work in law enforcement. My unit specialises in apprehending criminals who exploit minors, such as child porn, statutory rape, and so on."

Ten minutes later, while bouncing a Mexican girl to the ice cream stand, she told me: "I'm fourteen."

Oops.

Mick and I stayed in a hostel on the seafront and enjoyed ourselves in the bars and eateries, walking along the beach at dusk. As a holiday it was pleasant, but there were no hot girls. The closest we got to sex was when Mick was climbing the sea wall and singing one evening. A pair of twenty-ish black girls walked by, the only people within eyesight, and laughed at him.

"Look at his singing," they teased.

"Look at your face," he replied.

They laughed, and Mick leapt on the IOI. We took them to a nearby bar, and it seemed promising until they disappeared on the dance floor. We just left them to it and ate late-night street tacos.

San Diego beach and a happy dog

On the last day we went to a big box store, and I bought the then-new Kindle Touch on Mick's recommendation, and we also each bought a Nintendo 3DS. They cost about 2/3 the price as in England, thanks to our EU membership and outrageous tax system. Mick was leaving early the next morning so while I was sleeping he "accidentally" took my brand new Kindle and left his behind, which had a defective battery that could only hold a charge for two days.

I flew back to London after five days in San Diego, enjoying Christmas and of course the Norwegian threesome from the previous chapter, while Mick headed off for Mexico.

Team RSG connects

The second week of January 2012 saw me on a transatlantic flight bound for Cancun, the Las Vegas of Mexico. I didn't want to endure the huge Ibiza-style foam parties and braying American students there, and doubted I'd get much action anyway given my particular strengths and weaknesses. Instead, I took a shuttle bus further south to Playa del Carmen where Mick had set himself up in a hostel.

At this early stage I was utterly unprepared for the state of Mexico's infrastructure, and Cancun was an idyllic Elysium bubble of prosperity compared to what was to come. The first thing I noticed when stepping off the bus in Playa was the lack of pavements. Or roads.

Except for the main boulevard, a pristine pedestrianised street equivalent to any in a Greek island resort, it was a shit hole. Mick's hostel was only three streets off the centre, but two of those were uneven, pot-holed dirt tracks. Little kids sat on broken kerbs playing with sticks. I wouldn't have been surprised to see someone defecate in the street.

Speaking of which, of all my friends the one most likely to have already defecated in a public place was waiting for me outside the hostel.

"Hello, Mick," I called, and we shook hands. Team RSG – Mexico Branch, had made a connection.

Being an outgoing, chatty man, he'd already befriended the two middle-aged Mayan men who owned the hostel. He'd spent most of his time sitting in their courtyard area passing the time of day with them while drinking tequila and fine-tuning the music playlist. Every couple of hours he'd swim in the sea and eat street tacos. It was his lazy, London daily routine adapted for brighter sun and a swimmier sea.

I have a reclusive personality so I was grateful Mick introduced me to his new social circle; the two owners, a Greek called George, and a couple of *Eat, Pray, Love* post-wall backpacker women. They were all friendly and fun in a non-game context. It took me a while to adjust to having conversations that weren't focused on Hemingway Suite topics.

George made a particularly strong impression on me. He was a bulky forty-two-year-old from Mykonos, the popular Greek resort island. Imagine 1980s English ska singer Buster Bloodvessel on Valium. George was cool, relaxed, and very masculine. He'd spent his adult life working as a tour guide on the islands steadily racking up a 250+ notch count from the tourists. He knew little of technical game, and nothing at all of proactively picking up, but what he did have was an exceptional vibe. He managed to combine an almost non-existent ego with a solid happy-go-lucky vibe. From the very first moment we met I knew he was a likeable, trustworthy man.

It also turned out he was far more than just a big, hairy, Greek guy. He would travel Europe in chess tournaments, once beating the national champion of Moldova (or Macedonia, or Albania, or some other shit-box country). He also read widely and was carrying a big hefty tome of Osho's *Book of Secrets*. If he'd been Japanese and carried a sword, he'd have been Musashi Miyamoto.

Any time I saw a guy claim success with women I'd immediately think two things: is it true, and if so, how is he doing it? I wanted to judge my own results against external benchmarks and learn what I could where I could. Hanging out for a week with George made me appreciate his stories were eminently believable and as I asked him, he analysed his own game.

"There were a small number of hotels where my company would provide the welcome tours. Every week a new crop of tourists check in so I'd pick them up at the airport, wrangle them into the hotel, and then give them a resort welcome by the hotel pool on the first morning."

Scuba in Mexico

He sipped Ouzo, his favourite, and continued the self-analysis.

"I never hit on the girls. I'd chat with everyone and get to know them. We'd spend lots of time together in groups, taking them places, sitting in the same restaurants, and so on. Then it was just a waiting game. At some point during the week, if one of the girls fancied me she'd get drunk and crack onto me. Sometimes they'd fuck, sometimes they wouldn't. Then on check-out they'd all write nice things about me in the hotel scrapbook."

This system got him laid about once a month for ten years. I couldn't help but admire how well he'd integrated it into his work and social life.

He started reading my blog and was fascinated by the idea that this was a controllable pro-active process. For my part, I wanted to figure out his vibe. He was so easy-going and pleasant to talk to, yet never appeared weak or en-faggoted. The closest famous comparison I can give is Vincent Chase, the main character from the *Entourage* TV show. George projected an attitude that he was happy to go with the flow because it would always turn out well for him.

Mexico was all blue skies and blue sea. Mick wanted a relaxing holiday and not a daygame jaunt, which suited me fine. There's no game to be had on the east coast of Mexico anyway unless you're a hyperactive young nightclub player. The east is Mayan, and Mayans all look like semi-shaven hobbits. They waddle along with stunted height, ugly faces, little T. Rex arms, no neck, and many, many layers of fat. The ones we chatted to were naively pleasant but not a single female was fuckable. Literally not one.

We didn't even try daygame on the tourists. Our normal walkabouts between the hostel and beach confirmed the complete absence of sets. I saw three attractive girls in all the time I was there. I opened all three, two of which led to i-dates. I happily fell in with what Mick had been doing before I arrived – dicking around on the beach, swimming in the sea, ambling about and stuffing ourselves with burritos, tacos and any other little "delights" available from the street stall vendors.

That was the whole point of it – a relaxing trip that avoided both the European winter and the constant Game pressure to be out procuring new women.

After a week in Playa del Carmen, we moved on to Tulum. Mexico being a third-world shit hole, there was no public bus service and no trains. Except for the main highway south from the airport, every side road was little more than a mud track. Occasionally there'd be a real tarmac road if it led to a cluster of higher-end beach hotels. We took a private minibus with "Tulum" scrawled on a piece of cardboard propped up against the windscreen. At first it was exciting, travelling with the locals, but after a few stops at shit-box towns, the bus filled up, and I was squeezed in between a fat peasant lady and a man carrying chickens in a portable cage. There was no air-conditioning.

Once in Tulum, our mood improved. The main drag was a newly touristed shopping street, with a handful of restaurants, bars, and souvenir shops having clearly sprung up only very recently. It had a far newer feel to Playa: Tulum was far less-developed and far less-commercialized. The main part of the town is slightly inland, so we found a cycle hire shop and rented three bikes to get down to the beach, passing through the middle-class hotel/timeshare/luxury apartment area with its nice, neat gardens and golf course before reaching the beach road that wound its way through palm trees, forest, and a mini-jungle.

Tulum

It felt very much off-the-beaten-track. The last mile of our ride was along a road that threaded between thick over-hanging palm trees with the ocean barely visible through the gaps in fauna. It was beautiful.

Mick led us to our hotel complex. In keeping with the Mayan style, the building housing the reception area and communal room was as small and squat as the workers who'd built it. We'd booked one of the dozen wooden beach huts ("cabana") dotted under the palm trees on the very edges of the sand. Each had a hammock outside and several inside, hanging over sandy concrete floors. It was spartan. They could only be reached on foot, walking across the beach – which caused me no end of bellyache as I tried dragging my 20kg suitcase along the soft sand. I resolved to travel lighter next time.

It was idyllic, like the backdrop for a tequila or pineapple juice commercial. For the first hour we just lay in our hammocks listening to the waves breaking on the shore. Later we took a day trip to dive into a local cenote, snorkelling around the rocks underground. It's the closest I've ever come to understanding why people like Bob Marley.

Nothing happened for the three days we stayed. We lay around on the beach or in hammocks, swam in the sea without any other people in sight, and rode our bicycles into "town" to eat. George got me interested in reading Osho, and I got through the first hundred densely-packed pages of his *Book Of Secrets*.

A rare sniff of pussy in Playa

It was just what I needed at that point in my development. I'd become increasingly restless and dissatisfied with chasing grotty birds and the pomposity of our recent Hemingway Suite theatrics had somewhat unmoored us from reality. While my technical abilities, lifestyle, and self-image were all improving, I was in some way losing my soul. It was nice to turn down the volume of life and focus on simple things such as sand, sea and friends.

Perhaps not quite as dramatic as that, but I was still chastened by the episode with Tom, and I was also reading Roosh's blog – then the centre of the Manosphere – which was at that time a pit of negativity. I felt like my vibe was what needed the most work.

George was really into Osho, living it every day with his cool, unruffled calm. Tulum is an historic centre for Mayan ruins so we took the time to poke our noses around those as well. Adding these to the laconic beach lifestyle really encouraged me to slow my mind and focus on the lessons from the book. Osho was great for focusing my mind on life advice outside the PUA paradigm, so I felt like I was escaping the PUA cognitive capture and learning from a different world-view. Here is a sample of some quotations I'd ruminate over:

> *"Experience life in all possible ways – good-bad, bitter-sweet, dark-light, summer-winter. Experience all the dualities. Don't be afraid of experience, because the more experience you have, the more mature you become."*

> *"Listen to your being. It is continuously giving you hints; it is a still, small voice. It does not shout at you, that is true. And if you are a little silent you will start feeling your way. Be the person you are. Never try to be another, and you will become mature. Maturity is accepting the responsibility of being oneself, whatsoever the cost. Risking all to be oneself, that's what maturity is all about."*

On the last night we went to a seafood restaurant that was always full of locals – the best heuristic for finding good food in a new town. I was unlucky: Within ten minutes of the fish hitting my stomach, I ran outside to vomit. It was a virulent food poisoning, so bad that George and Mick had to help me into the taxi like I was Hillary Clinton climbing stairs. I spent the next twelve hours shivering and sweating in my hammock, crawling out on my hands and knees to vomit because I was too weak to walk. I finally passed out.

The next morning I woke up completely healthy. It was as if the previous night's attack had never even happened.

Mick had talked us into trying Cuba next. That entailed another nightmare minibus journey back up to the Cancun airport, stopping off in Playa briefly to collect some luggage from the previous hostel. While I waited for Mick, I talked to the owner.

"Cuba, eh?" he mused, chewing on tobacco. "You should buy some, how do you say, accessories, for the girls."

This was interesting.

"Every time I visit Cuba, I take a bag of accessories. Hair clips, colourful bracelets, broaches. The girls in Cuba have nothing. They go crazy if you give them a ballpoint pen."

It seemed ridiculous, but nonetheless we each bought $10 worth of cheap plastic necklaces, pens, and other worthless trinkets.

"Surely they can't want this tat," groaned Mick.

Two hours later we were buying a visa from the Cuban "embassy," a little kiosk in the airport arrivals hall immediately next door to the Cuban Air kiosk where we bought tickets. It was all done with pen, paper, and cash. The Cubans don't stamp your passport because then the Americans who make up over half the flights would get into trouble upon returning to the USA. Instead a printed cardboard voucher is slipped into your passport which you can throw away upon leaving the Worker's Paradise.

We sat in the departure lounge for an hour and were then called for boarding onto the small Cuban Air jet. Mick, George and myself sat in a row together, seatbelts buckled while the hostess demonstrated safety procedures to the passengers. We wondered excitedly what Havana had to offer.

HAVANA

Tropico

EIGHTEEN

TROPICO

We might hit Cuba while we're there," I'd told Jimmy back in London a week before flying out to Mexico.

"Nice place. Went five years ago. I liked it. Fucked eight girls in two weeks. You can't *not* get laid in Cuba."

When pressed, he went on to explain thus:

"Girls will approach you all the time. If there's a particular girl you like, all you need to do is to say 'hello' and start a trivial conversation. Be nice, and they'll come on to you. Take them around for a couple of hours, have a slap-up meal and a few beers in a nice bar, then go back to your private apartment to fuck them."

"Is cash changing hands?" I asked. In my world, paying for sex renders the whole act meaningless.

Jimmy took a long drag on his cigar – Cuban – and a sip of rum – also Cuban. We were in the Hemingway Suite trying to get into the mood.

"It's soft prostitution, mate. You don't need Game, just convertible currency and a foreign passport. Girls will flock to you for the novelty and the chance to get into the tourist-only venues they are normally excluded from."

There is a shady world of international sex tourists called "mongers," and they also maintain a network of blogs and forums detailing their exploits. It's like a parallel world to PUA, several rungs further down the SMV ladder. Whereas we share tips on how to pick up local girls for free, the mongers do likewise, but where to find the best value whores and semi-pros (part-time and amateur prostitutes)? It's not my world but I can understand their drive. It's like what I do without any of the difficulty. If you've given up on getting women to freely give their love, it's the next best thing.

I read through their Cuba sub-forums, and it bore out what Jimmy said. He was playing a grey area of part-Game / part-monging. The full-monger route worked thus in Havana: Your taxi driver ropes you in asking if you're looking for girls then drives you off to a brothel. You pay his commission then give the girl $30, and she fucks you. That's it.

Now I was sitting on the Cuban Air flight making its descent into Havana. I turned to Mick on my left and George on my right.

"Paying for it doesn't count, either hard or soft transfers."

They agreed and we drafted our rules of engagement:

- No lays were to go on the official notch count/flag count/lay reports. They didn't count as Game
- F-Town would be suspended until we touched down back in Mexico
- To the extent we could call a lay an achievement, the girl had to be hot, a non-pro, selected by us in a normal cold approach encounter (i.e. not pimped and not selecting us), stay around until we dismissed her, and not get uppity if we didn't pay her.

These rules were equivalent to saying we weren't gaming Cuba. It was just a holiday where sex would probably happen but couldn't be counted like picking up a lost tourist from the streets of London could be counted.

Havana is one of the few truly unique places in the world. Almost all cities follow a seen-one-seen-them-all pattern, whether it's every Japanese city having the same "eki-mae" square outside its train stations housing franchises for Doutor Cafe, Shane English, Lawson and FamilyMart, or the repetitive Old Town streets of Central and

Eastern Europe. My world travel through business and then Game had begun to strip each city of its individuality in my mind.

Havana, like Barcelona or Minsk, is truly unique. Nowhere else throws together black Africans, Caribbean weather, and Soviet communism into one big messy shit hole. The remnants of communism that I'd see in in suburban Vilnius or central Newcastle were the same: bleak, grey modernist buildings fouling the skyline, their weathered facades in tatters. But at least those countries were white. Cuba had all that but was filled with the same people who turned Rhodesia into modern-day Zimbabwe.

The ruins of Communism

It was like Detroit. Smashed windows everywhere, collapsed staircases leading to vacant upper floors, and rootless, aimless locals sitting on steps doing nothing all day. What Cuba did have going for it was natural beauty. Any patch of land spared development was still beautiful sand, grass, palm trees, and azure water.

After checking into our apartment, we took a walk around downtown Havana.

"This looks pretty dangerous," I said, noting gangs of black youths hanging out, talking animatedly over their loud music, and drinking cans of beer. In an English city that's a signal of impending crime so naturally we applied the same rationale to Havana. We were wrong. There's virtually no street violence in the city. The whole economy is reliant upon the money tourists bring in, so anyone who predates on them is in big trouble with the Law.

Mick and I shared an apartment with its owner, and George took a place a few hundred metres further away.

Being a police state, the Cuban rental system is tightly regulated and licensed. Everyone entering an apartment must show their ID and have the resident apartment owner sign them into a log book. Our apartment owner, who was very much in the closet because we didn't twig he was gay until we noticed a couple of gay-looking guys hanging around the kitchen chatting to him every afternoon, looked like Penfold from Dangermouse cartoons. He was friendly towards us.

Before Castro, Cuba was an off-shore rich man's paradise, and that history is still reflected in Havana's architecture. The city is dotted with many colonial style houses in Spanish and old American style as the former governors were displaced by the latter immediately after the war for Independence. Just as palaeontologists can date dinosaur bones from the layer of rock they are found in, an enquiring mind could infer that date of Castro's takeover of Havana by the layers of grime on every window. It looks like nobody has cleaned a window since 1959. Even the main parliament building has many unrepaired smashed windows.

I imagine the Soviet aid and US embargo cancelled each other out economically, but is that really an excuse for allowing the place to fall apart? It isn't like there's a shortage of labour as there are always people hanging about on street corners. Socialism plus Africans plus hot weather is a recipe for poverty.

Compare this to Vienna. Any such buildings would be art galleries or theatres, in pristine condition, lines of well-dressed socialites sipping wine as the tinkling of pretty women's laughter fills the air. In Cuba, you often can't go upstairs because either the staircase or ceiling has collapsed. I lost count of the number of front doors which had gone missing and the number of windows that had been smashed. The desolation reminded me of the post-pandemic movie *Twelve Monkeys*.

"It's sad and quite freaky to see," I told Mick as we sat on plastic chairs outside a street vendor selling cheese sandwiches.

"Mmmmmph, mmmph" he replied.

Four days into the trip I woke up to a text message from Jimmy.

"Someone has hacked your Facebooks. PUAhate, I think. Get onto the internet."

One does not simply *get onto the internet* in Cuba. There was literally one place online, the Imperial Hotel. They had a tiny internet café/room with a 56kb dial-up modem and computers that looked donated from my old comprehensive school. We handed the receptionist an extortionate sum of money, tapped our feet impatiently for Windows 95 to boot up, then waited for the browser to load.

It was indeed a PUAhate thing. "PUAhate" is the name of an old public internet forum of freaks and involuntary celibates who spend their days hating on the men who *do* fuck women. The forum was shut down two years later when one of its members, Elliot Rodger, went on a rampage in California and killed six people.

Being a PUAhate clown, his massacre was incompetent and unfocused. Although claiming to hate women, his first three victims were his male Asian flatmates and after shooting and missing many people, he finally killed another man and two women. Then he crashed his car and shot himself.

So, the self-claimed "misogynist" killer actually killed more men than women. That's the kind of incompetence you'd get on PUAhate.

One of the shooter's online associates had somehow managed to get the names of seven girls from each of Mick's and my Facebook along with pictures of us. He messaged Mick's girls claiming Mick was a travelling rapist with STDs and he was trying to spread AIDS. A couple of the girls blocked Mick while the rest messaged to ask what was going on. A couple got angry with him because the hater had also sent them a link to Mick's blog. We didn't mind that girls knew we slept around – we were brazen about that – but girls like to think players are free-wheeling naturals rather than determined strategists following a theory.

Strangely, the guy never messaged my girls. I checked with a few girls who would've been easily identified by him if he'd access to the comments they left on my Facebook wall. Nothing.

He also started a thread on the PUAhate forum "exposing" our real identities and photos, but it was laughably mistake-ridden. For example, he put up photos of Tony and called him Jimmy (they look nothing alike) and then went on a rant that I was carrying a gun in my profile picture because I wanted to look tough, and that those handguns are illegal in the UK, so I could be reported to the police. It escaped his notice that the photo was actually a publicity still of Jason Statham from the movie *Crank 2*.

The end result was that nothing really happened. The other PUAhaters called him a faggot and went back to their real hobby – bitching about Real Social Dynamics, the largest PUA company in the world.

It took us a couple of hours to sort it out on the slow dial-up connection, but we concluded that our Facebook accounts hadn't been hacked at all. The hater must have picked up information as a friend or associate of someone on the fringes of our social group. We logged off and tried some daygame downtown.

While Mick and I walked the streets, George sat in the central park playing chess with the local old men who set up on tables there. He'd spend four or five hours with them every day, chatting and playing, having a great time.

Our style of daygame is best suited to a particular narrow band of countries – Europe and North America. Certain conditions need to be in place: pedestrian traffic, hot girls, English language, safe streets, amenability to chatting, and girls with enough money to get by without a permanent boyfriend but not so much they become fat feminists.

Some countries are so poor you just can't do it. For example, in Africa the girls all suffer some combination of malnourishment, poor health care, a complete lack of fashion, and oppressive social pressure. Many have STDs or HIV. They have to whore themselves out to feed and clothe themselves and their families. It just wouldn't occur to them to have sex for free unless you caught them at a moment of extreme opportunity. The Dominican Republic is like that, and so is Cuba.

In contrast, in highly-developed countries such as America and Norway, girls have been liberated from concerns over diet, fashion, and manners. A large proportion of them become fat, insufferable cunts so we wouldn't even bother with them.

We saw two pretty girls walking down the main street to the park so Mick sidled up and tried his Spanish. One girl slowed down to chat while her friend quickly picked up her pace and kept distance with us twenty metres ahead.

"What's up with your friend?" he asked.

"She's on her way to the police station. She was reported for talking to a foreigner in a bar, so she has to give a statement. She can't be seen talking to you, too."

This was rather unexpected. The girl explained that prostitution is illegal in Cuba, and the police actively try to stop it. Most whoring is with semi-pros who meet men on streets and in bars, so the policing strategy is to harass all girls seen talking to foreigners. There are a small number of tolerated official brothel bars – we actually walked past one of them during this chat – and an equally tolerated small subculture within certain nightclubs.

Mick on the lookout

Normal girls who just want to meet foreign guys are out of luck, even though there is no money involved. As a result, there's no daygame to be had. The only way would be the slow 'social circle game' of befriending groups and meeting them regularly under normal social conditions – something we had no time for. Cold approach was literally forbidden.

We'd find out later that rule was also for our protection.

Humans adapt, and the curvy fertile girls who want to sell themselves for sex have adapted a way to skirt the law. We noticed that wherever we walked, girls would glide past and give us the eye. It wasn't subtle, either. They'd literally turn their heads as they strolled past in order to maintain a "come hither" gaze.

"Finally, I know how Steve Jabba feels," I said.

We quickly figured out the system based on watching the girls and following their lead a few times. An interested man would give the girl an acknowledging nod or some other signal then walk towards his apartment. The girls would follow at a distance of at least twenty metres, a few more looks exchanged to confirm both sides were on the same page. Once inside the girl would sign the apartment register, be paid twenty or thirty dollars in the convertible currency (exchanged at a rate of one-for-one with the US dollar). Then she'd fuck.

The most notable pattern in this ad-hoc prostitution was that *all* the girls were black despite Cuba's population being only 63% black. Hilariously, in a 2002 census only 11% of Cubans described themselves as black. Walking around Havana that is truly laughable. Many of these semi-pros were actually quite fuckable in a curvy, fertile kind of way, but all were clustered around the 6 range.

It wasn't just the black girls who were after our money, and at least they were delivering what they promised. Just about everyone in Havana seemed to be on the take or working a scam. Intellectually, I'm aware that 'adverse selection' was in effect: the scammers would pick us out and target us, whereas the honest folk wouldn't. This means we'd encounter an out-sized proportion of scammers relative to honest folk than that which occurred in the general population. Nonetheless it *felt* like Havana was wall-to-wall scammers.

I opened a couple of late-teenage girls in the park who were sitting on a bench chatting and who hadn't noticed us coming. We took them for a juice nearby, but just when everything seemed to be going well, they tried to bounce us to another bar. Adventurous men the world over have all learned that two girls telling you "there's a great bar I know" is a big red flag and you're being led into a clip joint – a bar that uses pretty girls to ensnare men and then massively overcharges them for drinks. We demurred.

"There's a cigar sale today," they said.

Again, this was a red flag because a common tourist scam worldwide is to claim special one-day-only access to a local market of grey-area jewels or local products. However, we actually wanted some cigars so we tagged along to investigate the deal. The "set" was dead; this was now business. The girls took us through a couple of back streets to a tiny ground floor apartment where a man sat behind a counter like a trader in a Zelda role-playing video game. There was a barred security gate in the hallway they wanted us to step through.

"I'm not going through that," I said. "If it shuts we are literally trapped."

Mick walked through while I stayed street-side of the gate.

"It's $100 for twenty Cohiba robustos," called Mick. "He claims they've been stolen from the factory."

"That's a tall story. Five dollars per knock-off is too expensive. I'm not paying more than a dollar."

We walked away from the deal and from the girls. We weren't at all unhappy because they'd given us a little black market experience in a Cuban back alley. Osho had advised me to live life in all its different ways and this was a story I could file away with pleasure.

One thing Cuba does brilliantly is live entertainment. It's a cash-poor, time-rich country so if there's any skill that requires only the latter (and doesn't need high-IQ), Cuba will have lots of it. Nearly every bar in Havana has good quality live music, often with accompanying dancers. There is fantastic music to be had, and it goes a long way in compensating for the general crappiness of the country. It's probably the only thing that keeps the average Cuban sane.

George was playing chess with locals again while Mick and I kicked back in an open-air bar in the tourist area. A small group played mambo on the low stage in front of a water fountain. The afternoon sun was blocked by palm trees overhead, keeping us in the shade. Two tables away we noticed a cool Negro chatting to staff.

His size, flamboyant fashion, and expansive gestures reminded me of Baron Samedi from *Live and Let Die*. He was legitimately cool.

He saw us and sauntered over.

"Hey guys," he said and gave a wide toothy grin. "Do you mind if I join you?"

Mick indicated to an empty seat with his beer bottle, and we shook hands with our new guest. He told us he worked security in the bar but often came just to hang out. I recognise and value charisma so I let him draw me out of my shell whereas typically I'll just shut down such uninvited guests. After an hour chatting to Baron Samedi, we became hungry.

"Ah, right, but be careful of the restaurants 'round here. Some are not very good. But if you like, I know someone who owns a good one, and I can take you there."

That's the oldest game in town, but in our defence we were a little drunk and having spent an hour or so chatting to us, the guy didn't fit the usual profile of a restaurant tout. He walked us across the road and to a side entrance in a back alley. We went on up the stairs to a nicely furnished but completely empty restaurant.

Such an inaccessible restaurant relies upon on word-of-mouth amongst locals or touts roping in tourists for commission. We took a look at the menu, which was reasonably priced. Nonetheless I could feel a rising anger at being played. I can forgive hustlers who take advantage of his mark's greed or stupidity, that's just evolution asserting itself. I don't forgive hustlers preying upon a mark's virtues because that is punishing good behaviour. I'd like to see more good behaviour in this world. We hustlers have a code!

That's why I'd support the summary execution of any robbers who lure a victim by having their confederate lie by the roadside faking injury. Put them against the wall, and I'll pull the trigger myself. If there are no bullets, I'll gleefully beat their skulls in with the butt of the rifle. Or a nearby rock.

"I don't know, Mick. I'm losing my appetite."

As we prevaricated, Baron Samedi's mask began to slip. He glanced nervously at the waiters, his commission in jeopardy. That was the clincher for me.

"Nope. I'm not eating here," I announced, and stood up.

He followed us down the stairs, spinning a story about how his baby needed formula milk. His kid's milk could curdle for all we cared; it was our mood that was soured. We thought we'd made a friend when all the time he was working a sales angle. We gave up on trying to make any more friends in Havana. Cubans are like taxi drivers – there are so many who try to scam that you can't take a chance with the honest ones either. Biologists have found that when the population of cheats rises sufficiently to outnumber the suckers they take advantage of, the whole ecosystem collapses. It would appear Havana long passed that point.

I'd now been in two Central American countries as a low budget adventurer and during my earlier finance career I'd had long business trips to Brazil and Chile where I stayed in five-star hotels and ate out with affluent professionals. Having seen Latin America from two sides, my major learning point was, "Europe is better."

En route to the beach with George

It wasn't our responsibility to alleviate the poverty brought about by low-IQs and a corrupt political system, even though we did feel for people whose average monthly salary was $30. Poverty is everywhere, and all the food is shit. Locals queue up at street stands for cheap pizza or cheese sandwiches washed down with a local brand Cola that tastes like oil. If I wanted that kind of squalor, I'd go back to Newcastle and ask my mother to cook.

Shops, as we know them in the decadent capitalist West, only exist in the tourist zone. Goods are bought with Convertibles rather than the worthless local currency, and the only decent food is in tourist-only restaurants. It epitomizes the dual nature of the country's economy. Tourists and those lucky Cubans who work with them have access to an almost European quality of life. Everyone else has to go fuck themselves. That's socialism.

Given these opportunities you can hardly blame local girls for whoring. An hour on her back being rutted by a gringo is worth a month of actual work shuffling papers in a government office or slamming a pick-axe into tarmac for a construction crew.

On our second night in Havana I decided to do the decent thing and give a lucky girl just this opportunity. Mexico had been fruitless, and I hadn't been laid since New Year's Eve, some three weeks earlier.

"I'm going out to fuck a whore," I told Mick and George, leaving them in a salsa bar.

I flagged down a Cuban equivalent of a tuk-tuk, this one pedal-powered. The twenty-something guy running it spoke English so when I told him I wanted a whore, he pulled out his phone and called up his female friends.

I mean that literally, by the way. He didn't call a brothel. He called his actual female friends from his own neighbourhood.

"They'll be very happy with me," he grinned, like the Milky Bar kid handing out chocolate bars. I guess it was foreign direct investment.

He stopped in a wide back street outside a small restaurant for locals, and I sat in the back of the taxi while he set off on foot to fetch the girls from their homes.

"Just wait five minutes. The girls must get dressed."

They'd been at home, watching TV with their family no doubt, when they got the call.

"Benita, it's Fernan. I've got a gringo wants to fuck. Put your shoes on and bring your sister, too."

Soon five girls stood in a line in front of me, all about eighteen and obviously friends with each other. They dressed in the kind of clothes that any girl would wear on a hot day in Cuba, sneakers, shorts, and t-shirt. They were clean-skinned and smiled pleasantly. Definitely not professional sex workers. They just stood there expectantly, letting me look them over.

I didn't fancy any of them, not for a price. If I'd been drunk and pulling them for free, a couple might've been worth a try. This being only my second day in town I still assumed Cuba had many hot women and that this quintet just wasn't up to local standards. I'd find out soon enough Cuban girls simply aren't very hot.

"You don't like?" the taxi driver pimp asked. "I can get more girls."

They wandered off back to their respective homes and he rang up another bunch of girls. Five more came out. One was really hot and stood out from a distance as she walked up a gentle incline towards me. Tall, slim, big eyes, and long black hair – like Laura Gemser from the old Emmanuelle mucky movies. I didn't want to window shop all night so I told the driver she was nice and she'd do.

"Okay, I arrange it. Wait here," he said.

Some jibber-jabber ensued, and the girl looked at me and nodded her head. Then he disappeared into a nearby doorway and emerged a couple of minutes later with an old crone still in her kitchen apron. The whole time the cute girl just stood with her feet together and head down, smiling shyly. She didn't speak a word of English.

"You pay me $50. I'll pay the girl and the room."

I handed over the cash and he handed me over to the crone. She called the girl over and walked us up a flight of stairs and into a bedroom clearly designed for exactly this type of activity.

"I wait here," called the taxi driver and lit up a cigarette.

It was all a little surreal walking into a room that looked like the interior of a Himalayan shack from *Far Cry 4*. Reds, yellows, and browns made the place feel warm and some soft lighting helped too. The girl seemed to be at a total loss as to what to do next, standing there dumbly in the middle of the room. So I treated her as if I'd just pulled her out of a nightclub. I escalated her normally, but much faster, seeing as LMR wasn't a factor.

Sex was pretty good. Being a normal girl she hadn't separated sex from desire like real whores do, so she let herself enjoy it which was fine by me.

Afterwards, she still seemed unsure how to proceed, so I motioned to her to put her clothes back on. Communication was all gestures and noises as we couldn't verbally communicate at all. We went back outside. The driver was waiting and took me back to my apartment.

"How was it, you dirty scoundrel?" asked Mick, stretched out on his bed flicking his eyes up at me over the top of his Jack Kerouac paperback.

"I don't know. I really don't know what to think about it."

That was the truth. It had been yet another weird episode, each of them contributing to the gradual upending of my mind as the holiday progressed. I felt like Game had ruined whoring for me.

Everything breaks down in Cuba

HAVANA

Bing
A Ling
A Ming
Ming

CHAPTER
NINTEEN

BING A LING
A MING MING

Since committing ourselves to the Hemingway Suite, it seemed only natural that we'd seek out Ernest Hemingway's favourite watering hole in Havana, a bar called Floridita. The great writer had emigrated to Cuba and cosied up to Fidel Castro as he spent the rest of his life fishing, smoking, and writing.

"Let's go to Floridita and have daiquiris, then rock back puffing on big fat cigars," enthused Mick.

We walked in just as a live band was starting up on a space cleared on the floor by the entrance. The female singer looked like a heavily-tanned Jessica Rabbit. Her body was sensational, and the red figure-hugging cocktail dress clung to her like a wet t-shirt. We sat ourselves down at a rickety table and perused the cigar menu. A bow-tied waiter took our order, Mick and George asking for Cohiba while I felt slightly Edmund Dante-like for ordering a Monte Cristo cigar.

As soon as the cigars came I dragged Mick over to a life-sized bust of Hemingway at the bar and took some photos puffing on mine. Then I leant on the bar and ordered a daiquiri.

This was it. We were now International Men of Mystery. I felt five IQ points smarter and ever so dashing.

I noticed a little Chinese girl sitting all by herself at the bar, so I said hello and took her back to our table. Her English was good and she told us she lived in Beijing but had taken a few months off work to *Eat-Pray-Love* herself around the world.

When the last ember of our cigars had burned out, the four of us set off down the street to another salsa bar. Again a live band was playing and the dance floor was thronged with keen salsa dancers spinning and jiving in that awkward robotic manner they all have. Vivid colours were everywhere, like a Babylonian garden. Green vines snaked up mesh wooden screens placed artfully around the room and hanging flower baskets rounded off the kaleidoscope.

A meeting of legends in Floridita bar

I sat at the bar knocking back sweet mojitos with the Chinese girl. We couldn't pronounce her name as it sounded like a snippet of a summer sing-song. So I called her Ming Ming. She found it cute.

She was obviously really into me, smiling, gazing and touching the whole time.

An hour in, Mick was keen to try another bar.

"It's raining outside," I complained. A sudden tropical storm had broken up the hot summer evening. Torrents lashed at the road forming small streams by every kerb. Nonetheless we agreed to rush through it to a smart looking place fifty metres up the street.

I stood up and the world spun around. I put my hand out to steady myself against the bar and missed, stumbling sideways into it.

"Fucking hell," I said.

"How many mojitos did you drink?" asked George.

"I don't know. They just kept bringing them. It tastes like fruit juice."

Evidently Cubans are as free with their rum rations as was Kitchener's Army the first morning of the Somme battle. It was shocking, and I stumbled out like Hillary Clinton walking to a podium. The sky was dark, and rain continued to pour down. I guessed it was around midnight. Ming Ming was clinging onto my arm as we tarried twenty metres behind Mick and George.

I looked at her slanty eyes and bobbed haircut. She wore a white dress. I fancied fucking her.

"Come here," I said and walked her over to a nearby doorway. Then I pushed her up against the wall and kissed her.

"Get off me!" she screeched and started batting her fists against my shoulders, then she squirmed out and ran into the middle of the road. Fortunately, Cubans can't afford petrol so there's very little traffic. She stood there fuming, her shoulders heaving up and down with her deep breaths.

"Don't be a silly cunt," I said and started walking towards her. It took a while because I fell over twice.

The second time I fell face-first and just lay in the road at her feet, laughing. Rivers of rainwater washed by me, and it was delightfully cool. I could feel rivulets run down the back of my neck and others down to the tip of my nose. It was like a cold shower on a burning hot day. A couple of cars drove past, catching me with a spray of water from the tires.

I felt great. Semi-conscious, inebriated, and now finally at rest on a bed of cool, fresh water.

Ming Ming hit me with her umbrella.

"You pervert! You beast!" she screeched, attracting the attention of my friends further up the street. She was still hitting me as George dragged her off, and Mick helped me to my feet.

I don't remember anything else from that evening. I think Mick put me in a taxi home. I don't know where Ming Ming went.

A couple of days later Mick announced that he wanted to go clubbing. It was Friday.

"There's a club called Casa de la Musica just down the road. Apparently it's the top club in town. All the hottest whores go there. I think that's my best chance of shoring one of the tarts."

Mick had only two goals in Game: Firstly, to fuck girls from fifty different countries, and thus collect fifty flags. Secondly, to fuck a whore for free. He already had over thirty flags but hadn't yet come close to 'shoring' a whore.

We arranged to meet George outside the club but had a few hours to kill so we walked down to the nearest Convertibles store and bought the most expensive rum in the shop – it cost maybe £20 for a litre of Bacardi's top-level brand. It was damn good, too.

By 8pm we'd had a couple of cuba libres and grown tired of sitting on our beds indoors. Mick had a small bedroom further down the corridor but we hung out in my much bigger twin room. He put some Ray Charles on his Spotify player.

"Jimmy was wrong about game here," he said. "There's no way into these girls for free."

"You know what his stories are like," I said. While sure, Jimmy had given us a factually accurate version of his Cuba adventure, I had come to appreciate just how favourably he reframes every story to present himself well.

"I'll keep trying, though."

I nodded my head in agreement. The rum had put a nice buzz on.

"Let's go outside and see how quickly we can drag girls home. We won't offer them money, but maybe they'll come just for the rum and our shininess," I said. We use the term 'shiny' to describe a child's tendency to be distracted easily when a flashy object is waved in front of him and it thus seemed appropriate to describe women's love of men who stand out from their usual company. Foreign men have an in-built advantage in shininess over the locals.

Our apartment was midway up a small hill, at the bottom of which our road connected to a main thoroughfare that bisected downtown, the central park, and ended up at the harbour. The hill was clustered with concrete three-story houses and tenements, one of which was ours. It took a minute's relaxed stroll to reach the end of our little street, and as we approached the corner, we saw a girl standing there alone. She couldn't have been more than eighteen, she wasn't very hot, and her chubby belly was hanging out a bit.

"I think she likes those kiosk pizza slices," I commented.

"She looks like a whore. Brilliant!" said Mick and made a beeline towards her. She smiled as he tried to say hello in his rapidly improving Spanish.

"Mi a no-have dinero," he said. "But mi habla Barcardi in mi casa."

Whatever her options were at that moment, Mick was evidently the best of them, poor girl. She beamed at us to display her crooked teeth and followed along. Two minutes after leaving our apartment we were back in my room.

She signed in with the gay owner while Mick mixed another round of drinks. After that it became awkward. She sipped her drink like it was nectar of the gods while she flipped through the books we'd left lying around, trying to take it all in. I lay back on the spare bed and let Mick take the lead. After ten minutes of fumbling Spanish conversation had stalled him out, he made a desperation move and dragged her out of the room to his own bedroom.

Ten minutes later they came back and she sat on the other bed playing with the Nintendo 3DS I'd handed her. She sat entranced by Zelda, the headphones shutting her out of the world. It was like watching a toddler see a horse for the first time.

"She took all her clothes off and wanked me off, but when I wanted to stick it in her she demanded money," he said. "No way. It has to be free."

She had no idea how video games worked, but once I demonstrated how the d-pad made Link walk around, she just cooed and gasped as she made him walk around Hyrule taking in the sites. So we left her to it and kept drinking.

An hour later we shook her out of her Nintendo trance and showed her the door. She smiled and kissed Mick on the cheek. We'd see her hanging out in the neighbourhood a few more times that week, and she'd always smile and wave at us. Perhaps she too shared Osho's wish to experience life in all it's different forms and chalked up her time with us as an interesting story rather than as a failure to earn money.

"Let's try it again. Why don't we go out and see if we can get a really fast bounce-back?" I said.

We went back out and passed the same Zelda girl who was sitting on a door step smoking a cigarette. We joined up to the main road another fifty metres down the bank where it opened out by a park. Almost immediately I saw two slim, black girls walking past a cheap local bar on the other side of the street. They were teenagers dressed up for a night out and obviously best friends.

I crossed the road, hollered to ask if they spoke English (which they did, a little) and quickly introduced myself as Mick caught up.

"We have rum and music in our apartment. It is there," I said, pointing up the hill. "Would you like to join us?"

The girls looked at each other and nodded expectantly. We walked right back up the hill. We'd spent a total of five minutes on the street, and it was our second bounce-back. Poverty is a wonderful thing, I thought, despite it rendering Game superfluous on our trip.

Again we poured drinks and listened to music. We soon paired off and Mick grabbed his girl and pulled her up to her feet to dance. That seemed a good plan so I did the same. We gyrated a little, fooling around and flirting.

"Let's go to my room," Mick told his girl, topped up their glasses, then led her out by the hand.

I was left with mine. She had tight vibrant skin, a flat stomach, and good-sized ass and tits. For some reason I thought she belonged in a historical adventure story where a scoundrel sneaks into a Cuban sugar plantation and fucks the most fertile slave girl. I kissed her. She pushed back into me for a minute and then suddenly started laughing coyly.

"I must ask twenty dollars," she said then did a slow spin to show herself off.

She was a solid seven, late-teenage, and ready to go. We'd only met twenty minutes ago. It was a simple choice to try for a legit notch by holding my frame and gaming her, or just hand over the equivalent cash as the profit of one copy of this memoir then fuck her right now. Easy choice. I took out my wallet.

If a Russian or Croatian girl asked for money I'd probably throw her out (and indeed I'd do that twice in 2015 to a Polish and a Ukrainian girl) because those girls have easily enough to get by. However, Cuba is especially poor. To deny her a month's average salary on a point of player's principle just struck me as cheap. I liked the girl and had no appetite for trying to diddle her out of what was pocket change to me.

Exploring Havana with my Greek
friend

She trousered the money into the back pocket of her short yellow denim skirt and then the vibe was back to normal again. We danced a bit more, kissed, and I started grabbing her firm ass. Just as I tried to pull off her panties, she conveyed in a series of elaborate gestures at her body and the calendar on my nightstand that she was on her period.

"Okay, I'll do you in the arse instead."

She blinked several times in incomprehension so I put her hand on my dick and then softly prodded her arse with my finger. She blinked again, this time in surprise.

"I never do," she said, meaning she hadn't done it. There wasn't any real resistance in her manner.

"There is always a first time. This is yours" I replied. I think she understood the meaning from my body language rather than the words.

She laughed nervously and let me take control. I pushed her head down and got an enthusiastic blow job then I rolled her onto her stomach on the bed, in front of the long horizontal mirror on the wall. Her face was just inches away, looking at her own reflection and no doubt ruminating on life as I slowly squeezed my dick into her arse.

There was a half-minute of tense resistance, and then she suddenly relaxed. I slid all the way in and her eyes opened wide, staring at herself as if to ask, "What are you doing here?" Then she looked back over her shoulder and gave me a tremendous smile.

The whole time I was railing her, she'd gasp, pout, wince, and smile at herself in the mirror, clearly enjoying the escapade. It was a new experience for her, and she was both fascinated and excited. At one point, I put her in a jujitsu rear choke. It's a controlling and dominant move that almost all girls like, especially when you're smashing them in the ass. As I squeezed the hold a little her eyes popped out again and she made gestures as if waving a fan in her own face to cool down. The rougher I got the more she freaked out, always smiling in between episodes of eye-popping and hand-waving. It was adorable.

Then she sucked me off again and shuffled off to the bathroom to clean up wearing just a very short skirt, which she amusingly pulled down for the sake of her modesty. We chatted amiably for a few minutes, just killing time.

Hang on, surely I can push this harder, I thought.

"Let's see what your friend is doing."

She was in full adventure mode now and milking it for all she was worth. Still semi-naked, we sneaked around the corner of the little hallway that led to Mick's room and then quietly opened his door.

We peeked through the narrow gap with her head below mine just like a Scooby Doo cartoon. It was not a pretty sight in there.

Mick, who was well overweight at the time, sat naked in a chair, masturbating, while the other girl lap-danced around him, also naked. I threw up into my mouth and swallowed it down again. My girl looked at me for guidance, so I made a series of improvised hand gestures that I was handing her over, pointing at her, the room, then her friend, then me. She put her hand over her mouth to suppress her excited giggle. Then I suddenly pushed the door wide open, pushed my girl in, then dragged Mick's girl out by the wrist. It took about two seconds then I was high-tailing it back to my room with a different girl while Mick swore loudly at me.

These girls really were up for adventure. Mick's girl offered not a peep of protest, just completely falling in with the sudden switch in partners.

We made out, and she also asked for twenty dollars. This time I held my frame.

"I gave your friend twenty dollars already."

It wasn't logical, paying her friend but fucking her for free, but she seemed to accept it, suggesting she was just asking as a matter of form. Still, I felt like a cheapskate, so as soon as she started sucking me off I gave her ten dollars anyway, meeting her halfway.

"Call it a tip," I said as she trousered it in her shorts back pocket.

I was tired and sweaty by then, so I lay on my back and made her ride on top. A few minutes in, the bedroom door burst open, and Mick and my original girl both came in and sat on the other bed to watch. How many men were going to watch me have sex? This was the third time, including Tom and Jimmy. Not that I cared.

Before long the two spectators were chatting, giggling, and throwing in words of encouragement. Mick started taking photos. The girl on top of me started playing to her new audience, waving her arms in the air and whooping while her friend cheered her on. A few more minutes and I was happy to just roll her off, pull on my boxer shorts, and take another drink. We all sat in a group drinking another quarter hour relying on mostly gestures to communicate, and then showed the girls out. I'm pretty sure we could've had them back for free any other day, but we just didn't care. Easy come, easy go. They tittered, smiled, and waved goodbye. A pleasant experience for us all.

As the door clicked shut Mick turned and said to me, "You know that girl who you were just kissing? My one."

"Yeah"

"Just before you dragged her out with you, she'd been licking my arsehole" he said with a triumphant smirk.

"What time is it now?" asked Mick, who rarely wore a watch.

"Nearly 11pm."

We both looked at each other. "Oh shit! George!"

Mick and George exploring

We rushed down to Casa de la Musica. Fortunately just a five-minute walk from our apartment, and George was waiting outside chatting to a taxi driver. It took a good fifteen minutes to get to the front of the queue, and we almost brawled with a couple of Germans trying to push in. It was lively, and the evening had taken on a warm, balmy feel.

What greeted us once we stepped inside was a surprise. This club was so fancy (and clean) that it didn't belong in Cuba. For a start, everything *worked* – the doors had handles, the toilets flushed, and the carpet covered the whole of the floor it was meant to cover. From the lobby, a low, carpeted walkway split the main hall into two raised areas on either side with bars, tables, and a throng of mingling revellers. A big stage for live performances stood at the far end. A live cabaret continued all night with dancers, singers, guitarists, magicians, and gymnasts. Every single one of them was excellent. This was high-quality entertainment. The ten dollar cover charge was a steal.

I got talking to some Irish guy who'd lived in Cuba for six years and ran a local business. "That guy singing now," he said, indicating a Julio Iglesias style crooner, "he's a star. He sells CDs throughout Latin America."

The bar areas were lively, and I felt like I'd stumbled into the "hot" club of the moment. The three of us elbowed our way between a few fat American tourists and ordered a round of Sol. We posted up a few metres away against a thick bronze railing that stopped people from falling off the raised platform into the walkway below. Surveying the clientele, I quickly noticed a pattern.

On the one side, across the walkway stood all middle-class Cubans who had access to convertible currency: tourist workers, government officials, import-exporters, plus ex-pats who lived in the country teaching at the university – affluent locals. They seemed to all know each other and mostly watched the cabaret. On the other side – our side – were the sex tourists. Fat, fifty-year-old Germans and Americans were in their own huddles looking at the whores.

And oh my, there were lots of pretty whores!

"I told you so," Mick crowed. "Word on the street is this is where the crème-de-la-creme of the whores ply their trade. No crusty street walkers here."

"I see this is where all the pretty women were hiding," I said, having barely seen an eight in the five days prior.

I later found out from chatting to a couple of them that they only do four or five clients a year, but at $100 a pop, that gives them the national average annual income of $500 for literally a few night's work. We were absolutely astonished by the quality of the women, although we *were* scanning the dark room with our night-vision beer goggles. We'd been starved of hot girls ever since arriving in South America so our standards were probably equal to a San Quentin prisoner on the day of his parole. Nonetheless, at that moment in time, beer and all, we were overwhelmed with the sheer beauty on show. It had an impact I wouldn't feel again inside a nightclub until Ibiza club in Odessa, Ukraine in 2016.

The Odessa girls were way hotter but also all whores.

The planets had aligned for us. Not only were we suddenly thrown into an abundance of beautiful women in a lively club, but our emotional state was just off the scale. Both Mick and I bubbled with energy, similar to the first night I'd been trolling Camilla in London. We'd had just a few sips of beer before the first few whores sidled up and started their pitch.

"Hi. My name is Rosy," said the first girl, fluttering her eyelashes. More girls flocked over, feeling our vibe, until six beautiful girls surrounded us.

We were quite aware what was going on, that these were whores, not normal girls taking an interest in us, but it was still a shock to the system on a primal level to have half a dozen truly beautiful girls competing for our attention at any one time. I said to Mick, "Hang on, we're in a great mood. Let's entertain ourselves. How many times in London are we going to get loads of eights and nines hitting on us, trying to get us into conversation and willing to put up with any bullshit we give them? Let's do it."

Compare this to sifting through the land-whales and broken minds on OkCupid in London, and *still* rarely getting a reply to your messages.

The first girl touched me softly on the shoulder, smiling. I immediately brushed her hand off and recoiled as if she'd told me she was a Syrian refugee.

"Whoa, don't touch me. That's five dollars."

She was startled, just freezing for several heartbeats. Clearly she hadn't read *The Mystery Method*.

"Wha.... wha.... what?"

I was smirking like a Jew writing a bad cheque. She touched me again.

"That's ten dollars now. Do you want to run a tab?"

We continued in that vein, recycling classic PUA lines that
Mystery and Style had pioneered in Los Angeles ten years earlier.
That just perked our spirits higher, Mick and I competing for who
could do the cheesiest lines, throwing in obscure references to see if
the other could identify which famous old PUA we were lampooning.
George stood and watched, mesmerized.

We were soon playing the girls off against each other, teasing them
and moving them around. They'd clearly never been douchebag-gamed
before and loved the novelty. For us it was like toying with a parade of
Miss Caribbean contestants. We each had three different eights eating
out of our hands, laughing at all our jokes, and trying to out-do each
other. You can imagine how that felt. Our vibe propelled ever higher.

At one point, I'd just finished teasing Rosy when another girl
walked over to try her pitch. I watched her approach, and before
she could say anything I pulled Rosy in, spun her around so she was
in front of me facing the new girl, then took her wrists and started
shadow-boxing the new-comer. Rosy giggled and cooed, playing
along so the new girl pretended to box, too.

Two eights shadow-boxing in cocktail dresses and high-heels in
this posh club. We were nearly on the floor laughing. I pulled them
both in confidentially to either side of me and whispered in their ears.

"You are my bodyguards. Protect me from other girls."

Mick had his own horseshoe of girls in front of him while he posted
up against the railing trolling them. George just stood between us,
drinking his beer, chuckling. He said later he'd never seen anything
like it. I overheard Mick admonishing two girls, who both cocked
their heads and listened in rapt attention like NFL players listening
to a coach explain a play.

"You look like a bad girl, and you look like the good girl," he
said. "She has higher heels than you. You must be really clumsy
when you walk."

"No, no, I can walk really well," she protested, so Mick had her
walk up and down the walkway like it was a catwalk. She came back
and puffed herself up proudly. "See! I'm an elegant girl!"

By our second drink we'd sucked all the air out of the room.
Literally every single prostitute, about thirty of them, was either in
our group by the railings or lingering on the fringe, hoping to be invited

in. We drank our beers, leant back, and chatted. We'd reached the point of critical mass where the girls forgot they were whores and started getting off on the energy and the fun of it. They'd all given up their pitches and just wanted to chat. Even the other patrons began keeping an eye on us rather than the cabaret performers, whether from jealousy or suspicion I don't know. We'd made such a stir.

The whole time I'd had my eye on one particular girl, the most beautiful I'd seen all year. At the time I rated her a ten, though when I sobered up and saw a photo Mick had taken, I re-rated her down to an eight. Still, "Samantha" was a formidably pretty girl. She'd been hanging around me since early on, and I'd always thrown her a bone while focusing my attention on other girls. It was standard Mystery Method – don't directly hit on the target, but give her enough attention that she doesn't lose hope and wander off. It was now time to make a move and qualify her.

"There are many beautiful girls in this club," I said to Samantha. Mick overheard and rolled his eyes. He knew what was coming.

"Do you think Cuban girls are beautiful?" she said. "Do you think I'm beautiful?"

I shrugged. "You're a pretty girl, but beauty is common, as you can see," and I waved expansively at the other girls around us. "What's so special about you?"

"What do you mean?" she asked. I think she'd never been asked this question before.

"Well, what are you good at? Can you play piano? Are you good at cooking?"

She paused to think, putting her finger to her lips and looking at the ceiling. It took a little while, but then she hit on an answer and looked back at me with satisfaction.

"I play volleyball. I was on my high school team."

I then asked her if she still played, to which she replied sometimes, so I asked her, "What's your balance and coordination like?"

"Very good," she replied.

"So can you pat your head and rub your stomach at the same time?" I challenged, showing with my own hands what I meant.

"Of course."

"Show me."

It took a few attempts to co-ordinate herself and then she got the hang of it. "Look, look, I can do it!" she shrieked with pride. I think that's the moment George spat out his beer.

I nodded and turned to my two bodyguards who'd been smiling silently the whole time, just thrilled to be there.

"That's very impressive isn't it," I said. "I don't think you can do it."

Mick got his girls to rise to the challenge, so we soon had a clutch of whores demonstrating the pat-head-rub-stomach trick. Over at the bar, the fat sex tourists looked forlorn. One even took out his bulging wallet and placed it ostentatiously on the bar, but only I seemed to notice.

"That's impressive, Samantha, but as you can see everyone can do it. Can you do it standing on one leg?"

"Oh, I don't know," she pondered, but the other girls cheered her on.

Thirty seconds later we had seven beautiful prostitutes in a line, standing on one leg, patting their heads, and rubbing their stomachs. Everyone was looking. The girls even got a small round of applause when they finished. I was almost crying laughing.

"It's never going to get better than this," Mick whispered in my ear. "I've got to choose one horse to back and go for it."

He was right. Our value was at its maximum possible level, and it was time to pull the trigger. I pulled in Samantha and started running rapport. She opened up nicely. I figured fifteen minutes of this, and I could give her the "I don't pay for sex" talk and go for the extraction.

Suddenly, an unexpected outside variable intruded.

"Nick! Nick! Nick!" I heard a girl yell behind me from down on the walkway.

How does any girl in here know my name? I turned around to be greeted by the moon-faced smile of Ming Ming, who I'd last seen standing over me wielding an umbrella. Evidently her attitude had softened towards me.

There wasn't anything I could do to stop her from joining us as she rather unceremoniously elbowed her way through the ho-train then literally threw herself at me, kissing me like I was a long, lost love.

"Oh, how lucky it is I met you again," she gushed. "It's my last night in Cuba. I want to have a special night!"

She was as horny as hell. "Any one of us could have fucked her," Mick said the next day. "I even think we could have spit-roasted her." I don't doubt it.

I now had a dilemma. I could...

- Take home the mediocre Chinese girl for free for a dead-cert notch and new flag, or
- Game the far hotter Cuban whore and hope she'd agree to let me do her for free

In my Gaming world paying for sex is utterly pointless, so it never crossed my mind to include a third option of "haggle a price and fuck the whore." I asked Mick for advice.

"Why don't you fuck both of them? Take Ming Ming home now, nail her, then come back and get the other one."

It was midnight, so I could probably just about manage it. Ming Ming was nuzzling my neck and pawing at my chest, repeatedly telling me she wanted "something exciting" to happen to her.

"Right then. You, you're coming with me," I said to Ming Ming. "And you, wait here. I'll be back soon."

Samantha nodded. "I'll wait."

Ming Ming came straight up to my bedroom. There was still some high-end Bacardi left in the bottle so I poured us drinks, put on some music, and started escalating. She gave me fearsome LMR. I've since learnt that that is very common for Chinese girls the first time. No matter how much they want to fuck, something in their brain tells them that they're not allowed to consent to sex the first time. Ming Ming was moaning and groaning to my touch, writhing about on the bed, thrusting her tits in my mouth, but she just wouldn't let me fuck her. Finally I got her undressed. Even then, she kept disengaging and telling me she wasn't "that type of girl."

Fuck it. I pinned her down and pushed my dick into her. She resisted, grabbing my dick and moaning, "No, don't!"

"Get your hand off my dick, you stupid chinky whore," I said, exasperated. "I'm going to fuck you now."

Either she'd go limp or my dick would. She looked searchingly into my eyes for brief seconds, then just flopped backwards in surrender. I slammed my dick in, and she responded with the sexual fury of the goddess Aphrodite riding a hurricane of lust. It got wild.

We got dressed and went out to a street stall for a slice of pizza and a Cuban coke. Then I took her back to the apartment and fucked her again. This time she was all over me and couldn't get enough. She agreed to let me do her in the arse but she was too tight, and I couldn't get it in. Then I came in her mouth. She told me that she was twenty-eight and that I was the fifth guy to fuck her.

I'm sure Ming Ming would've gone all night, but I had pressing business back at the club. I peeled her off me and pushed her into a taxi. Then I strolled back to the club. It was getting on to 3am, but I figured that's peak time for such a club. Ominously, I saw plenty of people walking away from the club and none towards. It looked like chucking out time. I walked in, and it was practically empty. All the whores had paired up or gone home. Evidently Samantha had either cooled off or received a paid offer because she was gone.

I must've just missed Mick on the street because by the time I came home again, there was an unmistakable rhythmic thudding emanating from his room. I wondered whether he'd held firm, or capitulated and paid for it.

Waiting to get scammed

George was playing chess

Back to Floridita

HAVANA

Whores and Semi-Pros

TWENTY

WHORES AND SEMI-PROS

ick was jittery with anticipation all through Saturday. The sound of the front door opening and closing registered somewhere as I dozed, sleeping off the hangover. I think it was the whore leaving. I also heard Mick's thunderous T-Rex steps up and down the hallway as he went to the toilet for several pisses which, added end-to-end, probably lasted longer than the *Lord of the Rings* trilogy.

Finally around 2pm he sat in my room to run down the previous evening's events. He'd taken a pretty whore home and finally given in to her insistence he pay $50.

"A knock-down price, mate. $100 is the going rate. It's like a semi-shore," he boasted, puffed up by his non-achievement.

"Doesn't count," I said, pulling the blanket back over my face to blank out both the bright sunlight and also the sight of Mick's testicles that threatened to escape from his baggy boxer shorts each time he leaned forwards to scratch his arse.

"Whatever. She's coming around this evening for a proper date. We'll watch a movie and have dinner. I think this is the night."

We spent the afternoon exploring Havana by the harbour and the usual mid-day drinking, this time under a red and white awning of a patio cafe that overlooked a small town square by the old fort. It dawned on me that Ernest Hemingway and Hunter S. Thompson probably weren't alcoholics by personal disposition, pasty white expats in the Caribbean can't help but down cold drinks as a coping strategy for the baking sun. Our trip was increasingly resembling a real-life version of *The Rum Diaries.*

Downtown Havana

Around 7pm Mick took his leave saying, "Time to meet the whore."

George and I raised our eyebrows then raised our drinks.

"Good luck, give her one from me!"

We tried a few more local bars including a bohemian back alley dive bar that was so stereotypically Cuban that it'll probably feature as a set location in the next Bond movie filmed there. Tattered old mambo and salsa gig posters were pasted over each other on chipped plaster walls while old men in panama hats played chess on battered wooden tables. It reminded me of the Mexican bar Antonio Banderas shot up in the iconic opening firefight from *Desperado*.

George patiently explained to me the key stylistic differences between Karpov and Kasparov, then delivered a polemic on why Capablanca – Cuba's greatest chess player – was a natural talent who cared little for orthodoxy. I think I understood it all at the time, but the tequila we'd started drinking interfered with my retention. He taught me his pet theories on Osho and also the Greek tourist industry. Those lessons are also lost to the alcohol-addled mists of time.

I do remember a story about his best mate banging a Bulgarian tennis star.

"A real natural, he is," said George in reverential tones. "He's about my age and fiercely ugly, but he's so bad-ass. This girl was in her early twenties."

Sounds like a man I'd get on with.

"I wonder how Mick is doing," I mused aloud.

A few streets away, Mick was standing in a line at a cheap pizza kiosk to buy his date dinner, then they washed the dismal slices down with the local cola and returned to our apartment to watch *Kung Fu Panda 2* on his MacBook. He was determined to show he wasn't a wallet for his date to tap. We'd agreed to stay well away until Mick gave the all clear. By 11pm George and I were drunk and restless.

"Let's try Casa de la Musica again," I said.

On the way there we walked past our own street. Three girls dolled up for a night out walked past us, and I very much liked the look of the tallest. We said hello and pulled them into a bright cafeteria-style bar immediately next to where we stopped them. I bought them a beer each then George and I invited them to my apartment for rum. We'd forgotten about the promise we'd given Mick three hours earlier. The girls agreed and tottered behind us on high heels, giggling.

Our apartment homo – the owner, not Mick – raised a fuss.

"No, no, no! The rules only allow two girls. Two tenants, two guests. That's the rules. Your friend already has one girl here. So, one more only."

There was no convincing him, so our party came to a screeching halt at his officious little wooden desk at the top of the staircase.

The girls' vibe popped like a PUA's reputation and they had a quick huddled conversation. The girl I liked turned back to me.

"I can stay fifteen minutes, but my friends are leaving."

Again the mask had fallen and the peculiarly business-like manner of opportunistic Cuban girls came to the fore. George went out to sit on the door step while I paid the girl $30, bent her over my chest of drawers, and fucked her from behind. She pulled up her knickers, waved goodbye, and rushed out the door.

"That was quick," moaned George, standing up and dusting off the seat of his pants. "I was just getting settled."

Unsurprisingly, we couldn't recapture the *Casa de la Musica* magic of the previous evening. Our moods were flat, and the club itself seemed to have undergone dialysis to remove all the fun. We sat at a table for a tête-à-tête, knocking back all manner of drinks while we entwined ourselves in a deep manly conversation about manly topics. Again, I can't remember a word of it. Maybe four hours passed and the nightclub was chucking out again. We hid our half-drunk beer bottles inside our shirts and stumbled out into the balmy air. We had no intention of calling it a night – we were fourteen hours into a bender and wanted to go full-Hunter S. Thompson.

There was a small park at the bottom of our street, not much bigger than a tennis court, with benches and a couple of swings. As we lumbered forwards on unsteady feet, we noticed a group of Uni-aged locals sitting around a park bench, drinking from a cheap-looking bottle of rum. *Teenagers the world over are the same*, I thought.

We started chatting, and their English was passable. George went off and fetched our reserve bottle of high-end rum from his room, then we shared it with the kids. Finally we'd met some Cubans who weren't trying to get money out of us. One of the girls looked very nice indeed, a white nineteen-year-old with thick, brown hair. She was responding well to me. Gradually we found ourselves edging away from the group, in deep rapport. Or at least that's how it felt to me, I was smashed out of my mind.

After about an hour I started escalating by touching her a bit, squeezing her thigh and shoulders, flicking her hair, just testing the waters. She smiled and took it. Behind her, George had the rest of the group enraptured with tales of Greece and Mexico.

"My apartment is up that street; let's go have a drink and listen to music together."

"Okay."

And that's how I started walking hand-in-hand with a hot young Cuban after picking her up from a park bench. It felt like a scene from a movie, where the bad guy stands on his castle ramparts with a crossbow then tells his prisoner below, "If you make it to the tree line, you are a free man." The whole time I felt like there was a target on my back.

I tried to project psychic interference to her friends, "Please don't look our way. Just keep talking to George. We are not the droids you're looking for."

About ten yards from the street corner, beyond which we'd disappear out of sight and mind, I heard footsteps running up behind me. Then her best friend leapt in front of us, a little out of breath from sprinting.

"No, no!" she said. "You can't go with her."

We stopped, and I turned and said, "What?"

"A hundred dollars," she replied, literally with her palm out.

I tried to laugh it off, just in case her conviction was weak. "No, I'm free. Don't worry about it. It's a special discount" I said.

She wasn't to be discouraged and insisted I pay her friend for sex. The girl herself stood meekly next to me, still holding my hand. She'd surrendered the play to her friend. I was starting to get angry now. The accumulated disgust I'd felt against money-grubbing Cubans mixed with my horniness, disappointment, and utterly inebriated state.

"Fuck that," I said. "I'm not paying a hundred dollars for her. Goodbye."

Then I turned and walked off home, cursing Cuba and its people. I hadn't actually verbalised my anger or vented at them, so it didn't create any hard feelings for George, who stayed chatting until sun-up.

"Friendly kids," he said the next day.

I was that close to banging a solid local girl for free and calling it a notch. Even now, I'm convinced she was well up for it and only cultural pressure stopped her. It was 6am now, and I collapsed onto my bed exhausted and dissatisfied.

What felt like the very next second, Mick was shaking me awake with a look of wild anxiety in his eyes. "Up! Up! We have to leave. We have to leave Havana right now!"

"Fuck off... Fuck off..." I muttered, flailing my arms like I was dispersing a crowd of enraged hornets. I'd been blacked out for an hour and wanted to remain that way. It was 7am.

He shook me again a minute later, but now my suitcase was open on the floor, and he was throwing all my gear into it. My eyes were only half-open. That was the limit of my energy. I was still blind drunk.

"Really. Get up you fat, Geordie cunt. There's a taxi coming in five minutes."

Even in my drunken haze I could sense Mick's mood was bordering on panic, and my danger sensors started to jar me awake. I pushed my feet out onto the floor and hoisted myself to a sitting position. It took a minute to collect myself, my head thick and vision still blurry. Mick was now on his knees peering under the beds to see if he'd missed any of my stuff. He swept a hand underneath to bring out my boots.

There was a heavy knock on the door. Mick's eyes widened, and he put his finger to his lips. We remained motionless, Mick on his knees in his boxer shorts and string vest, me swaying slightly perched on the edge of the bed.

The gay owner walked down the corridor and opened the door while we sat straining our ears to hear the drama through the thin bedroom walls. Fortunately, our curtains were closed so nobody could look inside. There was a short back-and-forth in Spanish as what sounded like three men pressed the owner for information. Then the door closed, and the owner came into our room.

"There are three big gentlemen looking for you," he said, looking at Mick. "Where's the Australian, they say, he owe us money."

I was half-dressed by now, pulling on my jeans and fumbling into my boots.

"I told them you ran away without paying my rent. I asked them to look for you."

Mick let out a long whistle, then thanked the owner for covering for him. Evidently the time Mick had spent chatting with the owner on his smoking balcony was time well spent.

"Hurry up. The taxi is coming" said the owner. "You can climb out the kitchen window on the other side." He then stole a look through the curtains. "Yes, I thought so. There are people watching the door."

Mick went through the window arse first and knocked a plant pot off the small balcony, wincing at the clatter it made on the cobbles below. Then he slid down the fire escape ladder and helped me hand the suitcases down to street-level. We both stood looking up at the owner who waved us off, closed the window, then went to the other side of the house to answer the door again.

Escape

A red fifties Chevrolet "yankee taxi" was waiting for us with the motor running. Mick gave the driver instructions in garbled Spanish to drive two kilometres towards the harbour. Then we paid him off, flagged down another taxi, and he took us to George's front door.

"You know, I want to feel like James Bond, but I meant the martinis and women, not the getting-chased-by-murderous-communists," I complained. Eventually, I'd live the James Bond dream as I'd always imagined it, I told myself.

I waited in the taxi, my head lolling against the hot leather back seat, while Mick woke up George and half his neighbours by banging on his front door and shouting up at the window. After a few minutes, George appeared at the first-floor window as drunk and confused as I'd been ten minutes earlier. He hadn't even been to bed yet. I was getting tired of seeing my fat friends in boxer shorts.

"We have to leave, *now!*" Mick called. George soon emerged, slid into the back seat next to me, then Mick sat in the front passenger seat haggling with the driver for a fare to the village of Vinales, a couple hour's drive away into the interior. An agreement was reached, and we screeched off.

We trundled along the coast road towards the city limits, azure sea on my left and low foothills and palm trees on the right, behind which the Havana cityscape peeped through. The sun was well up by that hour, baking the metal and vinyl car like a tin can left in the desert. I was already dehydrated and could feel what little moisture remained in my body evaporating into the air. A smell of gasoline and hot leather filled the car. When Mick wound down his window, we'd just get more of the former to offset the decrease in the latter. I imagined this is how necklacing smells to the citizens of Johannesburg townships.

"You owe us an explanation," I said.

Mick turned around in his seat just as the Chevy went over a pothole, and its shitty suspension threw us about. He banged his head on the roof then was sat down heavily on his rump. Any other day this might've been a delightfully scenic trip through a tropical paradise. On this day I was hungover, dehydrated, exhausted, and irritable.

"The whore came around. After watching the movie we started fucking. It was all great. She never asked for money. I fucked the hell out of her."

Great. Please continue.

"But this morning at 6am, I woke up to find her fully dressed. She starts demanding a hundred dollars. I kept saying 'no dinero, no dinero' and that just got her angry."

There's a joke about that – how you make a hormone.

"Then she just went mental. She picked up my laptop and waved it above her head, threatening to smash it. I took that off her, so she starts lunging for my wallet. I pinned her arms back and she starts yelling and screaming. That woke up the apartment owner."

Clearly I'd been in a deeper sleep than him.

"Anyway, it ended with us grabbing an arm and leg each then carrying her outside and dumping her on the pavement. She screamed some curses, and the owner said she was coming back with local muscle. He said it's a bad neighbourhood and could get violent. That's when I thought I should wake you," he added.

So we'd been run out of town by local thugs because Mick had ripped off a whore. Thanks, buddy.

"I still didn't pay her," he said, leaning back with a smug grin of self-satisfaction, gazing out of the window at some cows in a passing field. He sipped from a bottle of water, and I felt a deep ache inside watching the cold liquid slosh around.

"You paid her the night before. Doesn't count," I said.

"Fuck off," he replied. "I'm Ernest fucking Hemingway now. Jack fucking Kerouac. My stories are much better than your squalid little adventures."

Two hours in the heat was even less bearable than when we'd started the journey, and we desperately needed a pit stop. Mountains surrounded us now, and as the road snaked up the incline we passed a tourist attraction, a viewing point over a huge lake. A few tour buses were parked up, and I spotted a cafe bar.

"Stop here!" I frantically indicated to the driver, and he'd barely come to a rest before I was out the door and ordering the largest orange juice they could pour.

"This is a famous landmark," Mick said, checking his battered Lonely Planet guide.

"Don't care," I muttered and ordered more juice. It was blissful to rest in the shade. My whole body ached from lack of sleep and the bumpy ride. I was also coming down off the adrenal high that comes from narrowly escaping a beating. *Experience life in all its different forms*, Osho seemed to whisper to me. I didn't feel at all angry at Mick's shenanigans.

The juice, shade, and fixed seating soon improved my mood. I joined Mick and George at a viewing platform of chopped logs, and we looked over the lake. It was beautiful.

"Take a look at this," said Mick, and whipped out his phone to show me the photos he'd taken of me banging one of those Cuban ratbags earlier – taken without my permission, I should add. It was gross. I looked like an obese rhino squashing a gazelle. Was I really so fat?

"And you say I'm the fat cunt," he laughed. George had a quick peek and shook his head disapprovingly.

I'd been a vegetarian for twenty-three years and only started eating meat again six months earlier. My vegetarianism had been for bullshit "ethical" reasons when I was too young and stupid to know better, and by the time I hit my teenage years, it was an ingrained habit enmeshed in a web of self-supporting beliefs. It had kept me slim but at the cost of forgoing the muscle mass my martial arts training should've piled on in my twenties. I'd also denied myself all manner of delicious food.

Vegetarianism was the single biggest mistake of my life. It cratered my mood, my physique, and my hormones. If you're a vegetarian I implore you to close this book now, go to your nearest steak house, and order yourself the juiciest meat on the menu. Let the fatty juice dribble down your chin and hands. Enjoy the savagery of being at the top of the food chain. That'll help your game more than any textbook can. Chase it down with a double whiskey, fuck a whore, then punch a policeman.

While daygaming with Mick throughout the summer of 2011 he'd kept dragging me into his favourite Italian deli behind Top Shop on Oxford Street. I'd nibble away on a flavourless egg mayonnaise sandwich from Greggs while he feasted on chicken escalope and beef pastramis. Back at Château Hampstead he'd conjure up the most amazing-smelling dishes that left me salivating.

It was all too much.

"I want to eat meat. Now show me the best stuff," I asked him.

For the next week Mick took me around his favourite deli stores, butchers, and supermarkets. I ate farm-fresh sausage rolls, tapas, and learned to cook steak. I couldn't get enough. I started eating meat every single meal.

I'd developed a childhood emotional attachment to McDonald's cheeseburgers and sausage rolls from Greggs, my all-time favourite foods. I'd denied myself for twenty-three years but now I was off the leash it became a problem. I went crazy. I couldn't get enough meat so the flab piled on.

By the time Mick took those photos in Havana, I was coming off several months of cheeseburgers, two weeks of Mexican street food, and all-day drinking. This was in addition to a lack of sleep and exercise. I looked disgusting. I remembered something Camilla had told me while I was fucking her in early January.

"Nick, you sweat a lot."

I'd break out in hot flashes, get pinkish-red skin from over-exertion, and then huff and puff like a steam train. My fitness was still great; I was sparring, hitting the heavy bag, and doing my push-ups the same as ever. But I did sweat an awful lot nowadays. Not only was my moral compass broken, but if I stepped onto a pair of bathroom scales, I suspect I'd break them too.

We rolled up at the paradise village of Vinales early afternoon, and what a contrast to Havana. Tucked between forested mountains it felt like a level from *Far Cry*. A dozen stalls formed a market on the main square selling local arts and crafts, like wooden artefacts and trinkets. There was a salsa bar next door to the church, and that was it for public buildings. A few hundred houses were clustered around small roads leading out from the main square like spokes on a wheel. Then it was pure farmland.

The oddest thing about Vinales was the tourist population. Of the twenty-five or so tourists in the village's sole bar that evening, every single one of them was a white Western woman at or around thirty years of age. We were witnessing *Eat Pray Love: the Holiday Resort*.

Each woman was paired off with a Cuban man, every one of whom was good-looking and ten years younger than the women. The penny dropped. The Cubans were gigolos, actual real-life gigolos. I'd always thought such men were a contrivance for the lovers in romance fiction and suspects in Miss Marple stories. Each was ripped like an amateur boxer and dressed like a restrained version of Russell Brand. It was like the tourist resorts of Thailand with the script flipped.

I have no problem with sex tourism. The free market remains the single most effective method of balancing individual human freedom with aggregate societal good. It's not perfect, but every other method is worse. So long as the participants are entering into a free exchange, then it's their business not mine nor the government's. Problems only arise when outside parties apply force, such as Arab sex traffickers or the government externalising the attendant costs (e.g. healthcare for STD treatment) onto the non-participant population.

The view from our porch

My attitude is the same towards sex tourists as it is towards homosexuals and Africans: leave them to it – discreetly, away from public spaces – then let them deal with the costs and benefits themselves as it shakes out. Just leave me out of it, and don't try and steal any of my shit to relieve them of the consequences of their behaviour.

I believe in the "night watchman state" of classic English liberalism. The government has three jobs: defend the borders, keep the peace, and provide a means of settling contracts through the courts. Nothing else is the government's business. There should be no ministries of education, health, energy, or social justice. Protect us from foreign invasions, criminals, and fraudsters. That's it.

Put this way, the only three things Western governments *should* do are exactly the three things they have *failed* to do. They've put their thieving claws into everything but those. Our borders are dismantled, and foreign savages are actively imported to attack the citizens. The criminal justice system is subverted to protect criminals and harass the law-abiding. And contract law only functions if you can afford the legal fees.

A change of pace

That's the essence of Cultural Marxism; to subvert the core functions of government until chaos reigns and civilisation collapses.

In a functioning nation-state, interpersonal behaviour should be mostly free association. If some girl wants to sell herself to some guy, that's fine because that's her business, and vice versa. If they structure the interaction to humour and indulge the buyer's ego by hiding the fact that it's a paid transaction, good luck to them both. Not my business.

While sitting at a table watching the dance floor, we ended up in conversation with a gigolo at the next table. He'd be the only Cuban I'd meet the whole holiday who befriended me without asking me to buy him something; he even bought *us* a couple of rounds and refused to let us buy him drinks in return.

"I'm from Trinidad, a city further to the east. I meet tourist girls there. I charm them, dance with them, then they pay me to be their boyfriend for the week."

He was a charming guy with a roughish glint in his eye. I'd have put him at twenty-two years old, and he was clearly loving his life. His client today was a late-twenties German girl of frumpy appearance, but she was slim and well-mannered. She got a little annoyed that he talked to us so long, but he had a strong hand over her. It was a seller's market.

We met him for coffee the next day, and he told us a little about Vinales and the surrounding area then put me in contact with a local knock-off cigar dealer who sold me a hundred at a dollar each. They looked the part, too; a box each of fake Cohiba esplendidos and robustos, Monte Cristo number fours, and a box of Romeo Y Juliet.

That evening I sat with Mick and George in the back garden of our small, single-story house. We were on the edge of the village so pigs and cows wandered around the dirt tracks, drinking from a stream that ran alongside the house. We puffed on a new cigar each, sipping yet more rum. We were all non-smokers so it felt cool to hold the fat tobacco rolls in our hands. An hour passed, gazing at the darkening sky and talking nonsense.

"I can't feel my face," said George, patting and prodding his forehead and nose with a finger. "It's all numb."

I did the same. "Fucking hell, me neither!"

I felt like I'd come from the dentist after he'd mistakenly injected anaesthetic into my forehead. We both looked at the cigars.

"I think we'd best take it easy with these," I said. George agreed.

Belize
Please

TWENTY ONE

BELIZE PLEASE

We stayed in Vinales a couple more nights before making our way back to Havana for just one night, cooped up in our rooms lest we were still wanted men. I popped out to Casa de la Musica and brought back a pretty whore while Mick kept well-clear in case anyone recognised him there. And then we were on a flight to Mexico and in Playa del Carmen the next afternoon.

Stepping off the bus and over potholes, we made our way to the same hostel as before to find the owners sitting at a long table stacked with beer and snacks.

"Welcome home, men!" they greeted us, already pouring our drinks.

We kicked back, put up our feet, and relaxed in the relative familiarity of Mexico's east coast. Cuba had rattled us due to the constant duplicity of its hustlers. By comparison, Mexico was keeping it real, and I'd started to think kindly of the squat little Mayans who made up most of the local population.

"Let's have a look at these," said the shorter fatter of the two owners as I pulled four cigar boxes out of my suitcase. He was called Pepe and looked like a mini-me of the fat stoner from *Lost*.

"Nice smell," he said, holding a long Cohiba esplendido to his nose. Both men were cigar aficionados. A thick cloud of smoke soon enveloped the room as we all sat puffing away, sharing Cuba stories.

"You need to store these in a humidor," stated Pepe, a little bleary-eyed now from booze and nicotine. "The heat will dry them out. My friend has a cigar shop on the boardwalk. He'll store them for you."

That relieved me of the cigars for the next week and was yet another good turn the Mayans did me.

Our Playa return was just a stop-over on our way south to Belize. I spent the last evening there in George's monthly-rental apartment lying in the hammock he'd strewn across his lounge. I was back into reading his Osho hardback, trying to re-base my mind after the swirling vortex of Cuba. As the sun set, George grew excitable.

"Let's go clubbing," he said. "It's the last night."

We called in on Mick at the hostel and warmed up with cans of beer in the front yard then walked the few streets to the lively tourist boardwalk. I felt like I was in a British resort on the Greek islands, the type where tour groups of young men and women drink themselves into a coma or get fucked off their nuts on party drugs for the reality TV cameras. It was already dark and the thumping music of competing nightclubs blurred together to sound like an artillery barrage. Throngs of party-goers milled around us, all of them younger and more excited than myself.

We turned into the main bar street, and it was rammed. *I'll need to get seriously drunk*, I thought. Psychologically, I could feel my wheels spinning fast and about to fly off the axle. For months on end I'd been tumbling down the rabbit hole, further and further away from my core pre-Game personality. I was aboard the good ship of Hedonism as it was buffeted around wild seas, its captain below deck sleeping off a bottle of rum.

I sensed things were coming to a climax, like I was about to hit bottom.

The nightclub area may have a reputation for the hottest girls in Playa del Carmen, but I never saw anything above a seven and precious few of those. The bars were maybe half tourists, who were American or North European, and half locals, who were Mayans. We pushed our way into a crowded bar and bought bottles of Dos Equis, the beer advertised by *The Most Interesting Man In The World* commercials. That felt very "Hemingway."

There was no hope of getting a table so we posted up against the wall by the small dance-floor and watched all the inebriated floozies gyrating and waving their arms around. After two more drinks my libido stirred. It was dark, the music thumped in my ears, and we were hemmed in by a crowd of sweaty revellers. People were having fun. Animal spirits awoke.

"I still don't have my Mexican flag," I declared, to myself.

I looked around and judged the standard of girls to be very poor. There was nothing to shoot at. There were plenty of girls, but they were just ugly, fat, or both. I opened a Mexican girl next to me who was hopping up and down on the spot in time to the music. She wasn't very hot, maybe a high six, but she was the best I could see in the bar and after twenty minutes of teasing and chatting, I felt warmed up. In my peripheral vision, I saw a genuinely pretty girl come out of the bathrooms and walk past me. I made eye contact with her and she gave me a come-on look, so without a word I pulled her into me and started making out. She was drunk and really up for it, pushing into me like she was auditioning for a steamy love scene. The other girl was still standing next to me, surprised, and let herself be swept away in the throng on the dance floor.

My tongue down her throat, I flicked my eyes over to where Mick and George stood drinking. They raised their bottles to me. Looking good. A minute later I felt a hand on my shoulder and another pushed between us, peeling the girl off me. It was her boyfriend. He didn't even address me, just rattled off something in a language I couldn't recognise then dragged her off to the bar. I saw them arguing for the next ten minutes.

Our makeout had been hot and heavy. Now I had a boner. My skin felt hot, and my mind whirled.

I immediately grabbed a fat Mayan girl who may have been a five, possibly not even that. Her pretty, young face was perched atop a blubbery body with T. Rex arms and waddling legs, like a Cabbage Patch Kids doll. I didn't care. I knew she was fat, but my inner voice was determined to help me find bottom. I was determined to disgrace myself.

We danced together, touching and groping under the flashing strobe lights. I leaned in to kiss her and then once more felt a hand on my shoulder, this time heavier like a bear's paw. It was George. He waved off the girl and shouted into my ear.

"Look mate, you're too drunk. You should go home. I know you better than this. You shouldn't be doing this."

I told him to fuck off. Fortunately he didn't take it personally and instead ushered me outside to sit on the kerb, confiscated my beer, and let me absorb the cool night air. Mick was caught between backing him up as my friend and encouraging me to do something embarrassing that he could use to rip on me for weeks.

The streets pulsated with party energy. Music pumped from every window, groups of revellers chatted animatedly, and many couples were making out on the street, on benches, and against the walls. George went to the toilet and Mick went to buy a round. I was sitting down staring vacantly into space when a Mexican girl walked over and started hitting on me. She was slim, dressed in a tight black dress and heels. Not bad.

She was pawing me immediately, giving me big eyes and prattling on in Mexican which I couldn't understand. It was clear she was absolutely gagging for it.

"No dinero," I said, a few times.

She smiled. "No dinero," she agreed, sitting down next to me and leaning in so I could smell her perfume.

Rapid escalation, I thought. It was the only thing on my mind. I stood up, took her hand, then led her across the road to a quieter bar. We walked past the dance floor and directly into the toilets. There were two tiny cubicles side-by-side painted black like the bar interior and with flimsy door bolts to close them. I pushed her inside and she giggled. We'd met less than five minutes ago and hadn't shared a single word in a common language except "no dinero."

This is how booze, horniness, and a stupid determination to tick a PUA Achievement checkbox can lead you into strange situations. She was horny and up for a fast toilet fuck. I pulled the door shut and she was all over me, clawing at my jeans to get my dick out. I grabbed her dress and started lifting it up.

"No, no, not like this," she bleated (that's my assumed Mexican translation) while trying to turn around at the same time to show me her ass. Doing her from behind was the natural position in such a cramped cubicle. Nonetheless I wanted to finger her pussy and get her to suck me off, so I spun her back around and tried again to lift her dress. Again, she resisted and offered her ass.

Something clicked in my brain. I couldn't put my finger on it any better than I could put my finger on her pussy, but I sensed something was off. She reached back round to undo my trousers, undoing my belt.

At the very moment my dick flopped out, two things happened. First, my mind finally pieced together all the red flags and I was hit by the sudden realisation – *she's a tranny!* Second, the toilet door was kicked open and George was there. He yanked me backwards and frogmarched me outside where Mick waited, sniggering.

"Plus one," he said. "Well done."

Then they escorted me to George's flat, put me to bed, and locked the door.

Looking back, I can't believe I'd let it get that far. I'd ignored so many red flags, the most obvious of which is that no hot girl just walks up to you, paws at you, then lets you drag her into the toilet for sex in five minutes. I'm aware fast toilet pulls do happen, but not *this* easily and especially not to me.

I'd almost fucked a Mexican transexual in a piss-sodden toilet cubicle. I think that's what alcoholics call "rock bottom." If any one pivotal incident led me to re-assess my game and turn my back on the Dark Side, it was this. Things had been building up: weight gain, alcoholism, rootlessness, shifty pseudo-friends, grot-notching. I'd already seen other PUAs stare into the abyss, and now it was happening to me.

This is not what I'd gotten into the Game for. I wanted satisfying sex and dating with young, pretty, chaste girls. I wanted the type of girls you see on lingerie posters or in James Bond movies. I'd rather have a handful of them than a bucketful of cheap trollops like Isabella or Chiara.

The next morning Mick and I waved goodbye to George and took a bus south towards Belize. I didn't even know it was a country, I'd always thought it's just an English school franchise. Mick is a born traveller, never happier than when getting off the beaten path and hanging out with new friends found in a dive bar or halfway up an Inca trial. Whereas I'm reclusive and unadventurous, Mick is gregarious and constantly looking for new places to see. Letting him take me off to a tiny fishing island for a week sounded perfect.

George had fallen into a mini-relationship with a European backpacker girl he'd met at the hostel before I first arrived in Mexico. She moved in with him for a few weeks so he stayed there and wished us well on our travels. I was so strangely sad to say goodbye to him that I almost wondered if the tranny experience wasn't such an outlier and I'd actually turned into a faggot.

Our bus took us through Tulum and right down to the border with Belize. We didn't hang around in town but took a taxi straight out to the jetty where we'd catch the ferry out to the islands. We sat for an hour clearing immigration then waited for the little boat to show. It was only slightly bigger than the craft from *Jaws*, and the twenty passengers were crowded together.

The sun roasted us, and it was hard to pick out the horizon because both sky and sea were the same azure blue. I felt like I was taking a boat directly into a Bounty bar "taste of paradise" TV commercial.

There were a couple of islands, but apparently ours was the designated tourist one. I forget its name now although I'm not even certain I knew what it was while we were there. I'd delegated every decision to Mick and just followed his lead like I was on the business end of a Same Day Lay. We pulled up to another *Dr. No*-esque jetty and paid off the customs officials with another cash "administration fee" that went directly into their trouser pockets. Then Mick walked off along the beach to find accommodation while I dragged my twenty kilo suitcase through the sand on its tiny wheels, bitterly cursing my decision to bring it from London.

The island was beautiful and as different from Havana as anywhere in the Caribbean can be, considering it's ultimately all just sand, surf, and black people. It was quaint and rustic, with wooden shanty town buildings leaning against each other for mutual support. Little dive bars opened out onto the beach and small two-man fishing boats dotted the horizon. I felt like Captain Jack Sparrow. I was overcome with how quiet the island was. There was only one road, and you could go an hour without a car driving past. In fact, I don't recall seeing one the whole time we were there.

Belize harbour

Mick found us lodgings in a ramshackle wooden hotel straight out of a *Deadwood* movie set. The wood had warped so badly that walls were not vertical nor the staircase horizontal. Clinging to the banister as the steps creaked under me, I felt like a kid walking in the Funhouse at a gypsy fair. The mirrors made me look fat, but I reminded myself that might actually be accurate rather than just a Hall Of Mirrors illusion. Our room was small, damp, and dingy, with a nearly-zero-watt light bulb hanging naked from the ceiling.

We were staying in a fire-trap. It amused us to no end.

A short distance from our hovel, at the tip of the small island, was a little beach with a large shack selling booze. This was the social focal point. Everybody on the island, locals and backpackers alike, seemed to spend all their time there, sunbathing, drinking, and swimming. The water was clean, and it was possible to swim out two hundred metres to another, untamed, island full of trees and high grass. No doubt the only remnants of human activity left there would be empty beer cans and discarded condoms.

A few upscale bars lined the beach near the main jetty, so Mick and I got our meals and evening drinks there. For the past month my mind had felt like a radio being dialled to an increasingly high frequency, the wavelength getting ever shorter until I was an attention-deficit thrill-seeking monkey. Kicking back on the island slowed me right down again, turning the dial to a lower frequency. I was now able to hold full conversations and even sit reading a book without getting antsy. Nonetheless there was nothing to do on the island but swim and drink, so after a few days we'd seen it all and gotten impatient from the slow pace of life there. There wasn't any game to be had, every girl was either travelling with her boyfriend or an under-age local.

Mick did try charming the cute, underage receptionist at our hotel, but it didn't go beyond a few snippets of Spanish and shy smiles. We explored the area where locals lived but couldn't find any whores.

Surprisingly, the island had internet. I logged on and found John Bodi was online. He'd been hanging around us a little in London for the past year, just dropping in and out for the occasional daygame or drinking session, and he'd tagged along to our Riga trip a year before. He was now in Singapore visiting a friend, experimenting with his own unplugging from the matrix.

"What's the plan?" I asked, idly wondering if his period of winter calm had been more fulfilling than mine.

"I've arranged to go to Thailand. I want to try Chiang Mai in the north, it's a bit of an arts and crafts town, not like the sex tourism of the south. I'm going to find a kick-boxing gym and do a weight-loss holiday."

I thought about this. He's not the only fat Geordie with an interest in Muay Thai. I'd done a few years training in Tokyo and even had some amateur kick-boxing fights there. I hadn't really done any martial arts since I was married. My Château RSG training used the fitness and drills from kick-boxing, but I never actually did sparring or pad-work anymore. I missed it. I missed being in the ring, working angles, and trying to confuse my opponent until I can land a solid shot.

"When are you going?"

"Next week," he replied. "For two months."

I made my mind up immediately. I knew what I was getting into, and it was exactly what I needed.

"If you're good with it, I'll join you. I've got a few days left in South America, and then I'll need a week or two in London."

We agreed. He'd done all the work to find a gym and monthly rental apartments. I'd just piggy back off that like I had Mick for the past month in Mexico and Cuba. I doubted there'd be any Game up in the north of Thailand, and that suited me fine. I just wanted to get in shape and reconnect to normality.

Mick and I returned to Playa where I picked up my cigars and we had a drink with George. Then I boarded a flight back to London.

A re-up for the Hemingway Suite

Drinking by the sea with Mick

Paradise

Hail To The King, Baby

TWENTY TWO

HAIL TO THE KING, BABY

There's a term popular among international travelling men called "pipe-lining." It means initiating contact with women online before you show up in town in an attempt to have dates lined up in advance. Naturally online dating sites and Tinder (with a spoofed GPS location) are the primary means.

Having never been to Thailand to game, I didn't know what to expect, so I decided to try pipe-lining. Tinder wasn't popular back in early 2012, so I used DateInAsia.com which was a standard online dating membership site. I plagiarized Mick's profile verbatim and copied Jimmy's message principle of "push-pull-push." It was like I'd put on my White Man God superhero costume and within hours I had a dozen girls messaging me. There were just three problems.

First, they were nearly all Filipinos not Thais. Only a few girls were from Chiang Mai. All the rest were in shit-box villages a thousand miles away in the Philippines and thus logistic dead-ends.

Second, they weren't hot. Their profile photos were what I'd term "gamma-hot," meaning that if you're a no-game loser frozen out of his own country's dating market (like I was in my late-twenties), then encountering a slim, young woman who wears make-up and a dress gives the illusion she's hot. Seeing a whole bunch of them in a line in your DateInAsia inbox gives the illusion they are *all* hot. Kind of like seeing a Spice Girls poster for the first time, the illusion dissolves upon closer inspection. Many Asian girls look like average pre-pubescent boys dolled up in careful make-up.

After a few days I'd whittled my leads down to half a dozen girls who could be anywhere between a 5 or 7 depending on how representative their photos were. I moved a few of them over to my Facebook and Skype. Having given up on the Filipinos, I just hassled those island-dwellers for naked photos. A few obliged.

The third problem came when I proposed dates to the keenest girls. Four times they said: "There's one thing I must tell you. I'm a ladyboy." My half-arsed pipe-lining experiment ultimately left me with three good leads from real women who lived in Chiang Mai: Peach, Zaza, and Angel.

I stepped out of the taxi at the apartment complex Bodi had lined up for us, a ten-story, white-washed square block that must've had several hundred units in it. He emerged from the small breakfast cafe on the ground floor and quickly took me through my induction. I completed papers in the reception, let them photocopy my passport, and then signed a one-month lease that worked out at three pounds per day.

Yes, three pounds. The coffee I'm drinking as I write these words in a Moscow cafe also cost three pounds. You buying this book just paid me half a week's rent in Chiang Mai.

"This way," said John, walking off to the elevator. I think he enjoyed playing the host and showing me what a cushy deal he'd lined up.

Our rooms were next door to each other on the fifth floor. I clicked open the lock and stepped into a sparsely furnished, small whitewashed room, like a hospital room in a third-world hospital. There was a separate walk-in shower bathroom and floor-to-ceiling sliding windows onto a balcony. I had a good view over the city and could just spot the old town away to my left. We walked into John's room, and he'd already set up a little Haribo Cave. He had an extra mattress and pillows, a few scenic pictures blue-tacked to the wall for atmosphere, and a line of male grooming products so long you'd think he'd ram-raided Superdrug for deodorant and shower gel. And several bags of candy. I was to learn much about John's idiosyncrasies through 2012.

He'd done a great job organising our digs. I wanted to pat him on the head and say, "good boy."

"Now let's get you a scooter," he said.

We trotted downstairs and along the apartment complex driveway. In the two minutes it took to reach the main road I was already sweating under the burning sun. Sometimes my high-status skin colour is a curse. Just around the corner was a small bike rental business that filled out two garages with a selection of motorbikes and scooters.

Perhaps this is a good time to tell you about my relationship to auto mobiles.

Way up in the mountains

I've never owned a car and don't even have a driver's license. It just never seemed worth the effort for someone living in a highly-centralised metropolis with excellent metro systems (Newcastle, London, Tokyo). I'd look at how much my friends invested into car ownership versus how often they drove and concluded it's better to just order taxis anytime walking or public transport can't meet my needs. Later in 2012 I'd rent a car in Croatia with Jimmy, and though it would be a great road trip, it was a ton of hassle and only worth it as an occasional jaunt.

While I think cars are a waste of time, I do love them. I have every kind of Bugatti, Ferrari, and Aston Martin in my garage in the *Need For Speed* video game. I grew up playing the wild driving game *Burnout* and thus cannot trust myself in a real car on a real road. I've been conditioned to thinking braking for corners is what faggots do, and if you want to overtake a car, it's best to ram it into the wall for a takedown. Now that I'm an International Man of Mystery with an independent income, driving your own car is just "something poor people do."

"This one looks good," I said, gawping at a Japanese superbike. It looked like you could do great wheelies on it up the motorway. John subtly eased me away from that deathtrap and stood me in front of a tiny, Italian-style scooter I'd expect my granny to ride.

"You need a scooter commensurate with your competence," he said.

"Does it have an engine?" I asked, peering at a square block the size of a Big Mac carton which had lots of tubes coming out of it.

I persuaded John to let me have a bigger scooter, with red and white stripes on it like a Hulk Hogan poster. I signed the contract, laid a damage deposit, and took a shiny potty-bowl helmet too. I was never asked to show a driving license. John already had a slightly bigger and better scooter.

"These are perfect for Chiang Mai roads, you'll see," he said. "Top speed is nothing here – you need something that can accelerate quickly and nip around with a short turning circle."

I nodded.

"Right, there's a back lane past the next lights. Let's go up there and get you used to the machine."

I sat on my scooter, kicked up the stand, turned on the engine, and immediately shot forward into the main road like a dwarf from a cannon. Fortunately, a red stop sign down the road had cleared a path, and I didn't hit anything. My player's journey had almost ended right there.

John stuck to me like a grammar school hall monitor, glancing over every two seconds as we putt-putted up the road to the next stop sign.

"This lane!" he called angrily and waved me over.

We made it to a curving back lane surrounded by houses and without traffic. For ten minutes he explained the gears, braking, turning circles, and so on. Twice my scooter tipped over on turns, but I soon got the hang of it.

"Are you ready for the road? We'll pick up our stuff, and I'll show you the gym."

"Yessir!"

"It's a fifteen-minute ride including a big roundabout and an actual motorway. Are you sure?"

"I've got it. Red light is go. Green light is stop. No problem!"

He didn't realise I was joking so I had to show him another few turns, signals, and braking exercises before he let us rejoin the real road.

This would be the first time we'd hung out together for an extended period, and you never really know how you'll get on with someone until you try. I'd seen him out on the streets of London daygaming, and he'd gradually ingratiated himself into the RSG circle. What I didn't fully appreciate was how much trouble he was having with Game and unplugging. He'd make the occasional allusion to locking himself in his room for three days to eat chocolate and weep uncontrollably, but I'd assumed it an exaggeration. I'd assumed he was opening sets while on the streets, rather than walking around locked in a death spiral as his subconscious tried to convince him to commit suicide. This is something into which his own memoir *Death By A Thousand Sluts* goes into excruciating detail. I arrived in Thailand just assuming he'd gotten his shit together and, quirks aside, was a stable normal man.

He'd quit his job a couple of months earlier to have a Game sabbatical, aiming to "live the dream." Thailand was the third country on his world tour having recently finished with Singapore and China. He'd arrived two weeks ahead of me and already started at the local KC Muay Thai gym. He'd pipelined a couple of local girls who were clearly up for it, but he was chronically incapable of escalating them.

Whizzing around the chaotic streets of Chiang Mai was great fun even though I frequently failed to notice traffic lights and shot through red lights at junctions at least five times each week. I came to appreciate why the scooter is ubiquitous. It's the only way to weave through all that traffic. The roads would be swarming with traffic like an ant colony, but the pavements would be empty. It's like nobody walked anywhere in this town. That didn't bode well for daygame.

We looped around a ring road that encircled Chiang Mai's little central park, a long strip of grass prettified by banks of coloured flowers and large portraits of the king. This was the tourist area judging by the shops, the rope-haired backpackers, and the various bar streets branching off from our road. I fell in behind John and mimicked all his signals and lane changes. It felt great to dodge traffic and whizz around, just yanking on the throttle any time I wanted a speed boost. John led us off the ring road and soon pulled onto the motorway. He cranked the gas, and I looked at my speedometer to find myself doing forty miles an hour.

"This is fast enough that if I fall off I could die," I thought, equal parts thrilled and terrified. It didn't feel like a video game anymore.

We were rapidly leaving the town behind, zipping past a few big box supermarkets and hardware stores until we saw only cheap, old, one-story houses with broken wooden fences and washing hanging from poles in the gardens. John flipped his indicator and turned left into a dusty back road and followed it around a gentle curve until we arrived at KC gym.

It was an open air gym, the roof held up by pillars so that the fresh air could sweep through the training area unimpeded by walls. We pulled up in a small parking spot and walked in. I let my eyes rove to get a feel for the place and how legit it was. There was a full-size ring in the middle, currently occupied by two local pros doing light sparring, and a couple of students in the corners being taken on the pads. A line of six heavy bags was on a matted area, and on the other side of the ring were some full-length mirrors, more bags, and another larger matted area that I guessed was for attribute training and stretching. It looked fine. All the students were white foreigners – mostly skinny-fat backpackers and a couple of hardcore Muay Thai enthusiasts with a visible "gamma pull" to their facial expressions. They were like looking into a mirror at 2003-era me in Japan.

A pint-sized local introduced himself in broken English.

First day of training

"I'm Chun," he said. "I'm manager of gym. Welcome."

He was smaller than most of the girls I fuck, but he looked absolutely legit. His body was of the limber, recently-retired pro look, like a resting jaguar. He was poised, confident, and it was no surprise to learn he was a former Lumpinee champion. A fact confirmed by the photos on the walls of him wearing a championship belt and being presented with large trophies in ring-centre.

I signed up, and we agreed to return the next day to begin training.

I'd first visited Thailand in early 1999 when I'd had two weeks off work but couldn't get any friends to come on holiday in that window. So I flew to Bangkok for a week, almost fucked an *Eat-Pray-Love* Japanese girl called Junko who I'd met in the airport bus queue, then went to Phuket. I was twenty-four years old, and it was only my second time outside Western Europe. I was amazed by the beaches and sea and couldn't believe how hot the women seemed compared to the sloggoths who lumbered around my office in London. So I fucked a couple of whores and also completely failed to close a dirty, Spanish girl who looked like a young Helena Christensen. She was subletting me a room and came onto me while sitting in the lounge. It's one of those head-scratching events where I cannot understand how I didn't fuck her.

So she gave up trying to fuck and instead told me she'd been raped the month before at a music festival. That evening she brought home a big young backpacker and fucked him. She was insane, quite likely a Borderline Personality Disorder sufferer, but definitely a solid eight. So I regretted being too inept to seduce her.

I'd enjoyed Thailand in 1999 and returned with my ex-wife in 2002, spending two weeks in Phi Phi before the tsunami hit. That was a fantastic holiday, living in a rustic beach hut and hanging out in bars and cafes all day. When John had suggested Chiang Mai I knew it only by reputation, as the artsy Northern town that the more mystically-inclined backpackers liked to visit.

Daily temperatures were well into the nineties and then dropped to a chill at night. There was plenty to see, such as large craft markets, temples, and a beautiful Buddhist shrine tucked high into the surrounding mountain side. On the downside, the air quality was awful, and the nightlife was worse.

One minor surprise was learning that there are no comfortable beds in the whole of Chiang Mai. The first night I lay down to sleep, I thought they'd forgotten to give me a mattress. The mattress they'd provided was so hard it was like sleeping on a kitchen table. I later spoke to a few locals, and they told me that's just the preference there.

John and I very quickly settled into a routine that would last the whole month: wake up, go down to the restaurant on the ground floor overlooking a nice little garden for breakfast, jump on our scooters, and look around town. Then we'd take the KC kick-boxing class from 2pm to 5pm, shower off there, then ride our scooters to the local shopping mall for a massage. Eat at a street cafe near the apartment, then scooter home, and read until lights out. Every few days we'd go to a bar to make at least a half-hearted attempt to scope out women. That was the month. It was a Spartan existence compared to the excesses I'd been indulging myself in just a few weeks previously in South America. I loved the asceticism of it.

The coaches at KC pushed us extremely hard. They'd begin by hustling us around the neighbourhood, jogging under the burning sun for half an hour, which nearly killed me the first few times. I felt like a WWI Armenian under Turkish occupation. Then we'd pour cold water over our heads, sit down a few minutes to recover, and begin a long stretching and calisthenics workout. The second hour would be light technique training, bag-work, and every fourth round I'd get called into the ring for pad-work with a junior coach. Maybe once every two sessions Chun himself would take the pads or spar me. While the fitness regime was punishingly fun, I was disappointed with the technique coaching.

The gym was set up for foreigners, or *farang* as they're called locally, who are hobbyists or don't really know the sport. Most gyms have pro fighters milling around and a connection to all the local fight promotions. KC had a few young Thai pros as coaches, using the income generated by the gym to fund their own training. They were real professionals and very good at a local level. What was missing was pro fighters who trained and fought without being on the coaching staff: that's a key indicator for a quality gym.

I'd taken five kick-boxing matches in Japan ten years earlier, so I knew a bit about fighting, though I was now very rusty. The pros were well above my level, but the farang were well below, standing awkwardly and extending their arms in a manner I'd hesitate to call a "punch." I was the only person in the whole gym who had the boxers' weave, bobbing my head from side to side and up and down while rolling my shoulders and working angles. It looks a little weird at first but it's an essential skill if you're not to get laid out within ten seconds of starting a bout.

Everybody else just stood like statues. When shadow boxing, they just moved their arms robotically, chins up and head stationary. They'd hit the heavy bag with a combination and stand there waiting for a receipt. Any time I watched them spar I had their measure within thirty seconds, already spotting every opening they left: dropping their right hand when jabbing with the left, raising their hands too high to block combination punching and so on.

I'm not trying to present myself as a bad-ass, I'm not, just to drive home the point this was a holiday fitness gym disguised as a fight gym. Once in a while a farang who fought competitively would come down and give me a run for my money. John and I could only handle four sessions a week before our middle-aged bodies broke down under the strain and sun. A month of gruelling training and a gruel-based diet toned me up nicely until I was in pretty good shape. I'd never get a six-pack, but I no longer looked like a Hungry Hippo.

I'd leave the gym each afternoon a broken, beaten-down man, and I absolutely loved it. My muscles would feel like stretched-and-released rubber, the satisfaction of exhaustion penetrating through to the bone. The showers were cold so two minutes under that brought my body temperature back to normality and allowed my brain to function again.

The post-workout massage was always very welcome. I'd sit on my scooter waiting for John to patiently repack his gym bag, put on my pudding bowl helmet, then we'd ride off together to the nearby supermarket. The ground floor had a square of micro-business kiosks, such as nail salons and mobile phone repair. The biggest was a Thai massage parlour that charged maybe two pounds for a half-hour rub down. We'd lie on adjacent hard beds with hand towels over our faces, letting the adolescent female staff prod, twist, and batter our muscles. It was completely non-sexual and felt great.

It was a slow month. Just a few days of this routine had calmed me right down. I'd sit in the apartment-block cafe sipping on a cappuccino, looking contentedly across the small garden at all the colourful flowers and the insects that buzzed around them. I was working my way through *The Count of Monte Cristo* and reconnecting to nature and to my intellectual passions. I'd been stumbling drunk around Mexican bars trying to fuck trannies a fortnight earlier but it seemed another world away.

Chiang Mai is not a party town, and we found it was almost ungameable. Local people descend on bars in mixed groups of half a dozen or more and just sit around the table eating. Each group has its own hermetically-sealed bubble which ignores everything around it. This is a logistical nightmare, as there is no smooth way to get at the girls. The nightclubs are colourful and busy, but the volume is cranked up precisely to prevent conversation, and the dance floors are so rammed that revellers can just hop up and down on the spot.

We did some sight seeing

Remember what it's like to go drinking on News Year's Eve in an Irish bar? It takes half an hour to get served, then the only place free to stand is on the route to the toilets, so every second you're bumped from behind as someone mutters "excuse me" and pushes past. That's a Chiang Mai nightclub.

Always alert for patterns and opportunities, we quickly noticed something among the university-aged girls we wanted. They'd always show up in a group of six girls and one boy. That boy was always – without exception – an Estrogen Slug. He'd shuffle in with his thigh-fat rubbing together, his eye's narrowed from cheek fat, and his skin smooth like a baby. He'd always – without exception – be ostentatiously dressed in a shiny blazer, gold stud earrings, and leather loafers like he'd been invited to a cocktail party on 1970s Fantasy Island and was just waiting for the Time Machine to take him there. His job was to buy the big bottle of whiskey on the table then stand there looking pleased with himself. The girls would giggle, check their phones, and drink his whiskey. They'd occasionally dance. Then they'd go home. That was it. I never saw anyone ever touch each other, much less kiss.

I was left thinking: "why do they even go out to the club?" They seemed like automatons living out a caricature of what the TV commercials told them was "having fun."

Thailand had noticeably crumbled in the ten years since my previous visit. There's no longer any testosterone outside of the Muay Thai gyms and the taxi drivers. The men look like fat women. They have the same smooth skin and silky hair as the girls. They have no facial hair and all displayed effeminate mannerisms and a Milo-level obsession with clean, neat fashion. Did they go to the hospital every week to have their testosterone removed by dialysis?

Korean boy bands were very popular. Every TV turned to a music channel had clip-after-clip of slanty-eyed rent boys dancing in formation until their fat producer was ready to sodomise them.

The upside of staying in a high-estrogen country littered with broken effeminate males is that the girls are not getting their "real man" needs satisfied. They throw themselves at white Western men, even the gamma and beta nerds who have no success with women back in their home country. It's a case of market arbitrage finding a win-win for both sides. We just needed to find some hot enough to open, and that wasn't easy. So many of the girls looked like little boys with painted faces and long-hair wigs. John owned the biggest breasts I saw all month.

"Asian girls are a phase that betas and gammas go through," said John, tipping his whiskey glass. "What all these inter-race couples have in common is the man is a dorky pencil-armed fag, and the girl is slim but fundamentally unsexy. Each side doesn't realise how weird and aspy his partner is because it's all they've ever known."

I thought back to my pre-game life in Japan, and the hat fit.

Southeast Asia is a transition stage for men who are shit with girls in their own country. They find their little "in" in Asia and activate White Man God mode to rattle girls whose petite frames and obsession with fashion makes them worth fucking despite their fundamentally average genetics. I know from experience that it feels great to be wanted, and I could quickly become blind to the top end of real beauty that I was frozen out of. As far as I was concerned back then, these nicely-dressed giggly sixes were really eights. I was blind to the real eights: those girls lived in that fantasy world of pop stars, cosmetic adverts, and yacht parties.

As of March 2012, sitting in a Chiang Mai noodle bar by a busy side-road, I hadn't yet transitioned over to regularly banging Slavic girls. I'd meet and date some eights but I'd only fucked a few. My rating scale was still skewed from an ego-investment in the girls who would let me fuck them.

"A bitch is just a woman who fucks other men instead of you" is a funny manosphere aphorism. I'd add that for a trainee player, "an eight is just a seven who let you be the one to fuck her."

I was unimpressed with Thai girls, which meant these last few years had really changed me. Thai girls had no personality, social skills, or social acuity. I find Asians as a whole rather difficult to relate to compared to Europeans. The North Asians, such as Koreans and Chinese, strike me as all lying on the autistic spectrum and rather materialistic. I'd already noticed that they frequently didn't understand you are teasing them in set, even the girls with excellent English. The Southeast Asians were empty-headed sex pots. However, just because such girls are very feminine and come across as submissive, don't run away with the idea that they're pushovers in a relationship. That's just a myth. Every girl has her body agenda and places herself at the centre of the universe. Spend time on the ex-pat forums, and you'll read some real horror stories of angels turning into devils.

I spent considerable time sitting in that apartment cafe, usually with a cheese toastie or buttered croissant, ruminating on how my mindset and preferences had changed in the three years since starting my player's journey. Only a week into the Thailand trip, I'd realised I just don't fancy Asian girls any more (except Japanese, who are the Brits of Asia). I'd dated Bangkok native Tasanee in London for nine months up to early 2011 and really enjoyed her company, but looking back at photos of her now she just didn't seem hot. She was a pretty girl, and at the time I'd considered her a low eight. But now, she just had a weird Thai look to her. It wasn't rational or objective. My tastes were shifting, and I didn't know why.

It wasn't as simple as having raised my standards. Of the other girls I'd dated that year, I hadn't re-assessed any of them more than one point downwards. With Tasanee I'd gone from "she's really cute, I very much want to fuck her" to "meh, not interested."

So there I was in 2012, walking around Chiang Mai streets, malls, and the university campus asking Bodi where all the hot girls were. As much as I enjoyed a month focusing on kick-boxing, scootering, and absorbing atmosphere, I was still faintly disappointed that there wasn't any local box worth plundering. My method and preferences had found their kryptonite in Northern Thailand. Chiang Mai was set up wrong for daygame, and I felt I ought to have it out with the urban planning department who'd fucked it up for me. What were they thinking in not building more pavements, or in putting shopping malls out of town, or in encouraging scooter ownership?

Frankly, it was irresponsible of them.

As if to emphasise the point, when John and I returned to pick up our scooters after a walk through the old town, a cop had chained them up and given us a ticket. We had to take a taxi to the police station, pay a fine, then wait hours for the wheel clamp guy to unlock the bikes.

I couldn't read the parking ticket, but my guess was it listed the transgression as "attempted daygame in daygame-free zone."

Getting laid is often a "horses for courses" scenario. I sucked in Chiang Mai. A networking social-circle guy on a six-month student visa would probably do great gradually insinuating his way into university circles and knocking over girls on the down-low. I'm told by internet forums that Bangkok and Pattaya are completely different – way better for daygame and nightclub cold approach. The irony is that guys who do well in countries like Thailand don't know where to begin in countries like Russia, Ukraine, and Belarus, whereas I now excel in those countries.

It's a conundrum, but there's no getting away from the fact that I just couldn't get started in Chiang Mai.

CHAPTER

TWENTY THREE

Shoot and Scoot

CHAPTER
TWENTY THREE

SHOOT AND SCOOT

I wasn't completely shit, mind.

I still had my three remaining pipelined leads. Peach was a 24-year-old local girl who worked in an international company. She spoke great English and seemed very keen to meet. I set up a date at the end of the first week at a small nearby nightclub that had a large open-air bar area outside.

"Fancy coming along to watch my date?" I said to John. I wasn't much fussed about Peach and knew John struggled with escalation. He'd related to me a farcical story of completely failing with a DTF girl in the two weeks before I arrived, so I wanted to knock it on the head and set him on the right track.

We walked along back lanes for the three hundred metres from my apartment to the club then sat outside wondering how Peach would match up against her online profile photos. I was pleasantly surprised. She had silky black hair right down to her arse, and that arse was for real, too: wide hips, round butt-cheeks. She looked like a real woman, not a little boy in make-up. A solid seven I wanted to fuck. I was happy with that.

She came in and sat down at our table, smiling but a little nervous. I'd already told her John might be there a little while at first. We ordered drinks, sipped them, and I eased her into rapport. The main thing I wanted to demonstrate to John was how to pull a girl into your frame and spike her.

"Do you like Thai girls?" she asked.

"Tigers? Yes, I love tigers. Roooooaaaarrr," I replied, making a clawing action on her thighs.

"No, no. Thai girls!" she protested, her accent dropping the final 'l' sound unintentionally.

"Yes. Tigers. Big scary cats! Are you a big scary cat? I don't think so. You look like a silly, little kitten."

This kind of playful bantering ensued for half an hour, exasperating her and finding endless opportunities to touch her and move her around. Before long she was sitting next to me on the small wicker sofa. John made his excuses and left. Now it was time to find where she was really at.

"There are two things that girls *always* overestimate their abilities at," I stated.

"What are they?" she asked, leaning in to me.

"Kissing and blow jobs. Every single girl thinks she's excellent at them."

She jolted upright, excited with a chance to impress me. Her eyes sparkled. "I really am excellent with blow jobs. A ladyboy gave me secret tips."

I looked suitably unimpressed. "I don't believe you," I said then changed the subject.

An hour later I pulled her out of the bar and walked down the back lane. She was giddy and playful so I threw her over my shoulder, slapped her ass, and carried her fifty metres down the street. When I set her back on her feet she'd completely lost her mind: cheeks flushed, eyes shining, and a huge smile. She followed me home no doubt feeling very lucky to be there.

Up in my room there wasn't the slightest hint of resistance.

"Right then, let's see these blow job skills of yours," I said and got my dick out.

She dropped to her knees and gave it her best effort. Yep, it was quite good. Then I stripped her off, and as she knelt on the bed I fingered her from behind as she collapsed her head into the pillow and gyrated her ass in front of my face. Then I stuck my dick in and smashed her. It was good sex.

Twenty minutes later she climbed onto the back of my scooter and sang delicate love songs in a happy lilt as I drove her back to the club to pick up her own scooter.

"+1. Day 2. I'm F-Town now," I texted Mick then went to sleep.

I woke up for breakfast to find a message from Mick.

"+1. SDL. I'm F-Town now."

He was in Mexico City and had found a solo rock-chick wandering aimlessly past the bar he was chilling in. Bastard. I sat reading *The Count of Monte Cristo* then John and I went to the late session at KC gym. I felt thoroughly refreshed after training, but the supermarket massage stall was closed for the evening.

We scootered home and parked up in the courtyard next to a line of small shops – a massage parlour, a launderette, and a restaurant.

"There's a nice bird works there," he said, pointing out a woman at the desk of the massage parlour. "I've had my eye on her awhile."

My body was stiffening up now that the adrenalin from training had worn off, and I was cooling down. There was only one woman in the shop, and she seemed to be closing up, turning off some lamps and turning the open sign on the door to "closed." I knocked, and she came over.

"Can you do one more massage?"

She was quite cute. She looked early-thirties but still in yoga-shape. Long hair, decent face. Not bad at all but not enough to get me interested. I was drained from training and just wanted the aches to get smoothed out.

"Okay. One more," she said and pulled the door open. John said goodnight and went off to his room.

She indicated a futon on a raised platform behind a folding Chinese screen wall then brought over a complimentary tea. I lay down, closed my eyes, and reviewed my thoughts on the book I'd been reading. She got to work and silently kneaded my muscles for half an hour. I could feel her digging her thumbs into pressure points and grinding her elbow against my muscles.

I began to slip out of my reverie. Something didn't seem quite right. Too much of her body came into contact with mine. It wasn't overtly sexual, but her thighs seemed to rest heavily against mine. She asked me to sit up so she could work my shoulders. Sitting behind me she pushed herself right up to me, her crotch against my back. She wasn't gyrating like one of those "happy finish" deals, this was a standard massage place for normal people. Nonetheless, all those other massage girls had kept far more distance and only ever really used hands and elbows on me. My spider sense was tingling.

"You have strong shoulders," she said, kneading them. "Your back, too. It's strong."

It was getting on to 10 pm. She looked as sleepy as I did. The massage finished, and I assumed she'd ask for the money then kick me out. Instead, she sat down next to me on the futon with a fresh cup of green tea and carried on making small talk.

I read her for indicators of disinterest. Is she giving me the hint to get up and leave? I watched to see if she'd eye the door, look out the window, put away the tea, or do anything else suggesting I should leave. I left long pauses after my sentences. Those IODs never came. She fancied me and wanted something. I switched on and gradually took control of the conversation. Before long she was showing me photos of her family.

"My house is forty kilometres from here. It's late, so tonight I sleep in the shop," she said.

This was entirely inappropriate for a customer-client frame. Time for a compliance test.

"That was a nice massage. You must also be tired. Turn around, I will give you a shoulder massage," I said.

That went well, and I began combing out her hair with my fingers. She closed her eyes and purred.

"Let me show you my photos," I said. "They are on my laptop upstairs."

She offered a little polite resistance then let me cajole her up to my room. She sat on the corner of the bed while I loaded Facebook and Spotify. I knew she was up for it and just needed to be pressed enough that it "just happened."

My first two kisses were rebuffed then she jumped into the third. I moved it along gently but firmly until she was rubbing my cock, and I knew it was a done deal.

"No, we shouldn't," she said as I pulled her skirt up and got between her legs. Then I slid my dick in, and she pulled me close. The sex was no big deal. It was hard to get excited about fucking a girl over thirty, even such a pleasant and well-toned one. I shot my bolt then she re-ordered her clothes and went back to the shop.

She never asked me to pay for the massage.

"+1. SDL. I'm F-town," I texted Mick. We'd swapped the title three times in under twenty-four hours. I also texted John, which probably wasn't a good idea because he'd fancied her for weeks then I'd just barged in on a whim and fucked her almost without effort.

For the next couple of weeks we'd catch eye contact through her shop window every day as I came to and from my parked scooter. We'd smile and nod, but I never went into the shop again. For some reason, that eye-code was more romantic than the escalation and sex. She'd told me that first evening that her younger brother had died in a motorbike accident late last year, and she had only recently gotten over the grieving.

I like to think I added a little happiness to her life, one thrust at a time.

Peach was evasive the couple of times I messaged her, but towards the end of the trip she agreed to meet again. I rode the scooter to her apartment building, a nicer version of mine and went straight to her room. She cooked pasta, and we chatted while drinking wine. I genuinely liked her – she was chatty and pleasant.

Then I stripped her naked and got a better blow job. I very much enjoyed doing her from behind, watching her bounce and moan, her thick long hair splayed out across her back and shoulders.

"I can't believe you came on my face again," she said, fifteen minutes later. "Nobody has done that. It's disrespectful."

"You liked it, though."

"That's not the point."

She was a foreigner groupie and had gone online specifically to meet another farang. "I only ever dated one Thai man," she said. "He was my first boyfriend, before university. Then I dated my English teacher when I was twenty. Since then, I only like foreigners."

"How many men did you sleep with?" I asked.

"Nine, including you. I slept with American, French, and Australian."

I doubt anyone in London would bat an eyelid at a girl averaging two men a year, but by Northern Thailand standards that was a scandalous total. I wasn't sure what I thought about it. A year later she relocated to New York, no doubt living her dream.

CHAPTER

TWENTY FOUR

Domestic
Violence

TWENTY FOUR

DOMESTIC VIOLENCE

There's something strangely satisfying about punching fat girls in the face. I got to do it for five minutes straight in KC Gym. Let's see if we can unpack my pathos and figure out if it was all fair and above board.

Ex-pats are a bizarre group, seemingly polarised between a small number of fully-actualised digital nomads pursuing their passions and the Good Life abroad, surrounded by a morass of creepy lost idiots who were pretty much chased out of their own country. I'd like to think I'm in the former group. This ecosystem was expressed in microcosm at KC Gym.

John had done a little boxing in the UK years ago but wasn't much better than an enthusiastic bag-puncher, so despite being a big strong man, he was near the bottom of the gym in ability. Unlike a normal boxing gym, this Thai ex-pat gym was a weird status-jockeying world so his lesser ability put him at the bottom in social status too. The fat girls there acted like it was the high school from Mean Girls. Nonetheless, he'd come to learn so he was watching fight videos on YouTube, reading technique books I'd recommended, and making a real effort to "learn the craft."

Good grief, those gym girls! Think of how awful the typical female UFC fighter is, and then imagine she was fatter and had even less talent.

Shok was a fat, American-born Singaporean with bad acne. She was in her early twenties but she had a tired battered look like she'd been frying omelettes in a Filipino island favela cafe for twenty years. The gym was part of her mating strategy. She sought personal lessons from Chun until she could bully him into sleeping with her. Melanie was a fresh graduate from a So-Cal university. Blonde, pretty-faced, and *very* chubby. I'd guess she was heavier than me.

Then there were two obsessive old maids, hardcore gym-junkies who used high intensity training to drown out the screaming of their empty wombs. Thirty-year-old Svetlana was beautiful once, but age and hard training had done for her. If the nightclub was dark enough and her make-up good enough you might try to take her home, only to be shocked in the morning. Amy was Asian-American. A big broad-shouldered girl who really did make a serious go of becoming a fighter. She trained hardest of anyone in the gym, was super-fit, and ready and willing to fight professionally in any show Chun could find for her.

Silly girl. She just didn't get it. Her prime fertile years pissed away because she'd rather become a cheap parody of a tough guy than raise a family. She also didn't *get* Thai boxing. Her shadow boxing and sparring was just aspy spamming of robotic combinations without any understanding of the interplay inherent to the sport. She took to the fitness regime because it was repetitive grind work that appealed to her Aspergers, but she couldn't grasp the art form. Two weeks after beating a fellow ex-pat they threw her into a fight with a "ringer" – a vastly experienced local pro who brutalised her for five minutes then knocked her out. I actually felt sorry for her.

All four girls would huddle around together during breaks. They formed a clique who looked down on every man bar the Thai professionals. There were a few white men who were okay company in a dorky backpacker kind of way. I got on best with an Aussie who fought competitively, was six inches taller than me, and used to absolutely punish me with long right kicks when I grew too tired to pop in and out of range. Unfortunately, he rarely trained the same sessions I did.

Well, fortunately, now that I come to think of it. Those kicks hurt.

When John showed up two weeks before me, the girls had status-scanned him and assessed him as "not worth being friendly to" and this was clearly evident when I watched their interactions during my first class. That all switched 180 degrees when I showed up, and suddenly John and I were playing off each other, having fun in the gym, working on technique together, and paying absolutely no attention to the girls. We had our own nexus, not subservient to theirs. Their ears pricked up and they were soon ingratiating themselves into our party, sliding up on the bench during post-workout food, or asking us to adjust their gloves.

That shit annoys me. It's so transparent – someone ignores you, sniffs out some value to glom onto, then suddenly takes a keen interest. Melanie annoyed me most because she was so deluded – she couldn't fight at all but was pestering Chun to get her a match. Finally, he relented.

Light sparring with Chun

"I'm buying tickets for this one," I said to John, eager to watch the carnage.

"Me too," he agreed. "Any time I spar with her, she cheats. Tries to cheap shot me, the bitch."

Let's take a moment to reflect on the bizarre world of ex-pat fight shows in Thailand. There are two completely different circuits. First is what you see on Thai TV and is discussed in fight forums on the internet – each Thai city has a big arena that holds weekly shows where real local pros eke out a career. Big cities will have numerous small hall shows for lower-level or rookie pros, not unlike boxing in England. This is real Muay Thai, and the quality is often very high. It's their national sport, after all.

It's boring as fuck though. The typical fight is five rounds and the first two are not scored – they are for fighters to move around a bit, letting the scrum of ringside gamblers form an opinion as to who will win. That's why there's a rush of betting mid-way through the match. Fat taxi drivers wave paper tickets in the air attempting to push to the front of the small betting kiosks set twenty metres from the ring. Then the last three rounds are mostly hugging and kneeing each other in the ribs (the fighters, not the gamblers) because this is what scores with judges. Getting kneed in the lower ribs for three rounds straight hurts like hell, but it is unlikely to knock out a seasoned pro. Thus real Muay Thai is soporific to the Western eye.

All of the crazy knock-outs and dramatic back-and-forth comes on an entirely different circuit targeted towards tourists. Whether it's Chiang Mai, Pattaya, or Phuket, it's the same deal. A large barn-like bar area popular with tourists (usually near the backpacker hostel region) will set up a ring once or twice a week, put in rows of folding plastic chairs, and double up the staff on the bars that ring the building. There'll be one or two farang-vs-Thai fights at the top of the card. These are real fights matching students from gyms such as KC, and the purpose is to access the "come see my fight" marketing of the white participants, bringing in some farang eager to drink beer. The undercard will be completely fake matches between local Thais who treat it the same as Tenerife actors dressing as cowboys and simulating Wild West bank robberies at the local Spaghetti Western entertainment park.

Every one of those fake fights, to the bleary-eyed uninitiated farang, is like the second coming of classic boxing battles such as Castillo-Corrales or Gatti-Ward. Clean shots, momentum shifts, and lots of knock-downs. It's really clear to anyone who knows kick-boxing that they are very careful not to actually hurt each other.

There's very little bone-on-bone contact, so kicks are always light, showy, and to the arms and gloves. Punches are wide and looping, without snap or follow-through. There's clear turn-taking rather than actual scrambles. The fighters are probably friends from the same gym.

But, it's fun to watch when you're beered up. Like pantomime.

At the first show I attended, they also had ten local teenagers blindfold themselves and step into a mass royal rumble. Just kids having fun cuffing each other softly before diving theatrically. All the drunk yahoos in the crowd ate it up, booing and hissing when appropriate.

One wag shouted, "he's behind you!" to a blindfolded boy.

"Oh no he's not!" shouted another. A team of drunken Brits took up the pantomime heckle.

Working on those love handles

The whole set-up is fixed. Any Westerner in a normal Chiang Mai gym can get a fight, and the opponents are usually chosen so that the Westerner wins. If necessary, the organizers will drag a taxi driver off the street to fight with him, although most of the time they'll be up against a guy from another of the local gyms who'll be told to fall over and feign a knockout just to keep the party rolling on another week. In Melanie and Amy's cases, they believed their own press clippings. Amy won two fights straight before they put her in against that girl trying to win who actually had a chance.

After a couple of weeks I wanted to fight but I just couldn't trust the match-making. It wasn't like Japan where I'd built up a year of regular training and the coaches had a personal bond of trust with me. I knew this was just a farang mill. I suspected the organizers may insert a ringer who is light years ahead of me, and I'd get absolutely crushed.

On the first weekend I arrived, John took me to such a show because his new mate – a middle-aged Italian ex-pat called Giorgio – was having his second fight. Giorgio talked a good game to John but as soon as we were introduced, I figured him as a fantasist. He wasn't in shape, moved oddly, talked in a glib manner, and sure enough in the ring he looked *kinda* like a kick-boxer but didn't really get it. His opponent was an equally past-it Tuk-Tuk driver who'd had a few fights a lifetime ago, to look at him move.

What followed was like watching two dairy cows fight underwater. Both guys showed grit, enthusiasm, and will-to-win, but it was just horrible – like watching fat people have sex. Giorgio broke his hand on the Thai guy's forehead then got dropped with a knee to the ribs. He lay grimacing as the referee counted him out and later went to the hospital to have his hand set and his two broken ribs strapped up.

This was a forty-five-year-old man. That stuff takes a long time to heal at his age. I admired him for trying, but I concluded he may as well be jumping in front of a bus. So I was rather wary about putting myself into that position, and then Amy getting crushed by a ringer took the last bit of wind out of my sails. I reminded myself just getting rid of my big, fat belly would make it a successful month for me.

Melanie's opponent for this, her second match, was a big, fat German girl making her debut. John and I hung around Melanie's corner pre-fight and helped encourage her. As much as we found her disagreeable, the fact was she was from *our* gym and had the courage to step into the ring – we actually wanted her to win.

The fight was awful. It was scheduled for five rounds, and a minute into the first, both girls had punched themselves out, unused to the speed with which unchecked adrenalin dumps drain your energy. Again I sympathised as I'd experienced precisely this in my first kick-boxing match, standing ring centre barely able to lift my arms, wondering where all my fitness had gone. They cuffed each other around in a sloppy manner for another nine minutes before the ref ruled it a technical draw. To keep myself entertained I'd given John a technical commentary, inadvertently picking up on all of Melanie's flaws.

"She turns away any time there's two punches together. If there's three she literally turns her back," I noted. "She never pulls her elbows down and in to protect her ribs. She literally never defends her body."

Two days later we were in KC, and Melanie was strutting around with the "I'm a fighter now, you're just a tourist" haughty vibe, as if we hadn't all seen her making a fool of herself against a lightly-talented opponent. She was leant up against the ring drinking water during a break. I was due to climb into the ring for pad-work, and she was in the way of getting to my gloves behind her. I asked her to let me at them, and she wouldn't move. It wasn't accidental – she was posturing, looking down at me.

As luck would have it, two rounds later Chun put us together. It was the first time I'd spar her. At this point I still intended to go easy on her. Just as the bell went, she tried to sneak in a hard right hand before I was ready. I put my gloves up and jabbed softly, sliding slowly back and to my right (I'm southpaw). I'm taller than her, already knew all her deficiencies, and my style is based on being crafty and using counter-punching to maximum effect.

Plus, she's a girl.

She became frustrated. I was only tippety-tapping her, but she'd swing, miss, and I'd lay a soft jab clean on her face. As beginners often do, she tried to assert herself by throwing progressively harder punches until before long she was swinging full-power. Anyone who spends time in boxing gyms sees this all the time and cuts the beginners some slack – just cover up, move, and wait for the coach's attention to be drawn by the loud thwacking noises. There's rarely a need to stiffen your training partner with a hard counter-shot.

But then she hit me behind the ear on a break. *Right, you silly, fat bitch. Enough is enough! Time to hit a woman.* I dare say if she'd been hotter, I might've gotten a boner.

The round ended, and I gave her one last chance to calm down. Instead she came out throwing for the next round. So I rolled back to let her right hand fall short then cracked her hard over the top with my southpaw left. Her eyes lit up with shock then anger. I threw a few half-arsed shots at her head to get her gloves up, and then just bulled forwards whacking left and right hooks to the body. I'd seen she couldn't throw proper uppercuts or hooks so she got flustered at close range, and I just bullied her around laying into her body. I wasn't hitting hard, just enough to be very uncomfortable, and must've gotten in about thirty-five clean shots. When it finally occurred to her to pull her elbows down and in, I cracked her with a right hook to the chin.

I saw Chun standing outside the ring looking up. We caught eye contact, and he was fine with it. He knew I was bringing her down a peg without actually hurting her. The bell went, and he pulled us both out.

About half an hour after we finished, she came over to me and said, "I lost my rag in there, didn't I?" I nodded in agreement, surprised by her uncharacteristic humility, and replied, "Yeah, but no worries."

I beat up a woman. That's how tough I am.

When John returned to Chiang Mai in late 2016 he would get quite a shock. KC Gym had closed down so that part of shared history had disappeared forever. More disturbingly, he discovered a newspaper article about a recent murder-suicide. A local woman had divorced her farang husband and taken both the child and the house. During a furious argument with him on the street, she'd pulled a gun from her purse and waved it at him. Distraught and overly-emotional, he took it from her, shot her twice in the head then shot himself.

It was a tragic story like I often used to read about on manosphere blogs. The man was Giorgio.

CHAPTER

TWENTY FIVE

Zaza
Da Whore

TWENTY FIVE

ZAZA DA WHORE

After three weeks or so, the spartan Thai lifestyle had worked its magic. My belly was back down to thirty-two inches, the same it had been throughout my twenties when I was training regularly. My fitness was way up – no more heat flashes walking up stairs, nor dripping sweat over the women I fucked. The downside was that my entire body ached right through to the bones. I had blisters, cracked skin, and nobblies all over my feet. My left shin was sensitive to the lightest of touches, and I sported two black eyes where John had caught me flush with a stiff jab in sparring. We'd started taking private classes with a seasoned pro in another gym to get the technical improvement that KC Gym didn't attempt to provide. Ten years after first kick-boxing in Japan, I'd finally learned how to *really* throw a mid-kick.

Despite all the training there was plenty of down time for us to zip around to explore the city on our scooters. Chiang Mai is famous for it's night market. A half dozen streets were swamped by street traders hawking t-shirts, souvenirs, knock-off handbags, and so on. Smoke and noodle odours from barbecues and fry-ups floated along the breeze. For the past few years I'd been steadily amassing a watch collection and already had twenty or so tucked into different drawers around my room in Hampstead. Naturally, I took great interest in the watch stalls here.

"This one is nice," I said, picking up a Panerai Luminor Marina with silver bezel, black face, and thick, black leather strap. It was a masterpiece of copyright infringement.

"Hurry up, you've been here five minutes," said John, looking impatiently left and right down the street, itching to move along to other stalls.

"Here, have a look at this one," I said, plucking out a Lange & Sohne concept watch that probably never previously existed outside the feverish imagination of the engineer at the Chinese knock-off factory where it was made. It was a lovely art deco piece and just what I was looking for.

"Watches are gay," John said, grudgingly handling the piece. "It's just a watch, all it does is tell the…oooooh, that *is* nice, isn't it!"

His eyes lit up, and at that very moment John developed a watch obsession that afflicts him to this day. "Let's have a look," he said, bending over to peruse the stall's hundred watches, mostly bad Rolex imitations. "Which ones are good?"

For the next week he'd knock on my bedroom door every evening at 11pm. "Let's go down to the night market and look at watches!" he'd plead.

We'd spend a couple of hours being led through the shuttered storerooms and shops where the street vendors kept the majority of stock. The little gook would stand patiently inside the door as John and I opened every last cabinet and scanned hundreds of watches at a time. By the end of the trip we had a half dozen each: Panerai, U-Boat, Breitling, Lange & Sohne. You name it; if it looked good and infringed a Swiss copyright, then we bought it. These were beautifully designed trinkets and in my world a heterosexual man is only allowed to build a collection two fashion items: watches and leather jackets.

We also explored a few riverside bars.

One night we scootered to a whorehouse and banged a ratbag each. We rode into a three-story hotel-casino complex forming a horseshoe around a parking lot, kicking our stands out and chaining the scooters to a concrete post. It was a tawdry watering hole, a light steady flow of local men parking up and walking in to the tables and slot machines, jingles and roars emanating from behind the front door for the few moments before it swung shut again. A few men stood outside in the balmy night air pulling on thin cigarettes, their tubby bellies poking out through button-down shirts, vacant eyes staring into the middle distance, no doubt wondering where their hopes and dreams had escaped to. We walked in a side entrance down a long, low corridor bathed in dreamy pink and blue lighting. It felt like an alternate-universe Travelodge. A few metres in the plain walls gave way to a long floor-to-ceiling internal window, like a theme-park aquarium, that continued on another twenty metres. Rather than fish, this aquarium had mermaids: slanty-eyed mermaids in bikinis who fucked for cash.

There were three long rows of concrete seating, like the first three steps of a staircase leading up to a giant's home. About twenty whores lounged about, dotted in little groups of three or four like high school girls waiting for the local football team to take to the pitch. Each had a circular plate pinned to her bikini bottoms showing a number.

John and I just stared at them. They were all sixes, maybe sevens if you like a bit of slant. I think he was drooling. The girls perked up a little, as monkeys in a zoo do when they hear your packet of crisps crackle. Number fourteen was the best of the bunch.

We continued down the corridor, paid about thirty pounds each to the old madam at reception, then waited a minute for each of our chosen girls to emerge. They led us away separately to private rooms bathed in that same odd blue and pink lighting. Then I fucked number fourteen in an utterly forgettable encounter. Had it not been for the oddness of scootering through Chiang Mai, then walking past the "aquarium," I'd be unable to remember the occasion at all. Banging a girl for money seemed utterly pointless. I don't even think I nutted. Riding back through the dark streets to our apartment complex I felt no more sexually satisfied than if I'd been to an actual zoo and masturbated in front of real monkeys. Yep, Game had ruined whoring for me.

I still had time for a few more bizarre Thai encounters.

Zaza was the third of my active leads from pipelining DateInAsia. I'd fucked Peach, and the second girl had been looking for English practice, so I'd ditched her as soon as it became apparent. Zaza was twenty-one and hailed from the type of mud-hut mountain village that Henry Kissinger wanted napalmed in Vietnam. She looked reasonably hot in her profile photos. Like Peach, she had extremely high oestrogen, giving her baby-like soft skin and long black shampoo-commercial hair. Unlike Peach, her English was terrible, and she was both flat-chested and narrow-hipped.

This made me rather suspicious.

Gook-fucking is a stage every intermediate player must pass through on his way to the hotter, tougher, white girls. I figured I'd try out a couple more, and then I'd be done with yellow fever.

When we finally met up on week three Zaza insisted on bringing along a friend, so I brought John. He'd found a bar called Riverside that commanded a tremendous view over the water. It was a lively place split evenly between young Thais and Western ex-pats. Local bands did passable covers of well-known rock and pop songs and the vibe was great, almost no sleazy vibe. The outside terrace went down to the riverbank. We saw little in the way of hook-ups between ex-pats and Thai girls. It seemed more like a friendly social-circle kind of bar.

I shot a few red lights, swerved around a speeding tuk-tuk, and entered the fray at Riverside. We bought a pint each and then found the girls sitting at a table overlooking the river.

"You like Pitbull," said Zaza, comparing me favourably to her bald-headed pop idol.

The date was mostly about typing into Google Translate then handing the phone back and forth. We'd dance a little and take the piss out of the creepy computer-nerd gamma Western guys who were scanning the room for drunk Thai girls with a white man fetish. *There but for the grace of God go I*, I thought in disgust, recognising among the creeps some elements of my younger pre-Game self in Japan (while conveniently ignoring having just exploited a similar dynamic to bang Peach). It's normal to externalise characteristics you dislike in yourself, project them onto others, and then hate on them. In early 2012 I was still attempting to transition away from my old chodey self but hadn't yet become comfortable with the new "player" identity. My ego was still up to its nefarious tricks.

I spent most of the date surreptitiously assessing Zaza's hands and neck for any tell-tale signs of a ladyboy. She seemed genuinely female, but I just couldn't be sure – the Mexico debacle was still only a month past, and I was excessively alert. After a couple of drinks, we took the girls for a ride home on our scooters but didn't try to kiss them nor bring them inside.

Two days later Zaza and I met in a club across the road from my apartment complex. Within half an hour she was sitting on the edge of my bed explaining via Google Translate that she would not have sex.

"I want to marry you," she said.

One of the problems with Thailand is you just can't trust any girl met on the internet or in a bar to be female. It really messed with my head. I've since had an American friend who lived in Thailand explain the tell-tale signs. He actually said the girls who look most curvy, dolled-up, and excessively sexy are *more* likely to be ladyboys because they are following a male conception of sexy rather than a female one.

I kept staring at Zaza for any signs but couldn't see anything obvious. No Adam's apple. No claw-like hands.

"I'm not marrying you," I said, pulling her in. She rested softly against me, female-sized hands in her lap. I felt she was ready to fuck, but I just couldn't pull the trigger. I was ninety percent sure she was legitimately female but...would you jump out of an air plane with a parachute that was only ninety percent sure to open? If I were to try confirming her gender by examination, there was the risk she turned out to be male after all. That would take me too close to staring into the abyss.

I passed up on the lay.

She wanted to meet again, but I declined, and for the next two months, when I was back in Europe, she kept sending me messages: "Hey, how are you my favourite boy?" and so on. She liked all my Facebook photos and eventually posted up some convincing bikini shots. I had no plans to return so I let her down gently and moved back to white girls.

Thai village girls are often on the make, seeing white men as piggy banks.

When a man is frozen out of his local dating market strange things happen to his mind. In Muslim countries they rape little boys, or parked cars (I wouldn't have believed it either if not for a video on LiveLeak), or join ISIS for the promise of sex slaves. In Europe they overdose on porn. An enterprising few look for a wife in dirt poor countries. Feminists have it ass-backwards (no surprise) because it's the *women* who are the predators, preying on sexless vulnerable men. The nerds loitering in Thai bars are usually lonely, broken, damaged individuals looking for affection and companionship as much as they are for sex. They probably realize deep down that the bar girl they marry doesn't love them, but it beats loneliness and celibacy. It's a pretty dark existence.

A lonely Western man goes online and is immediately flattered by younger, smooth-skinned, and very feminine girls contacting him. How different from his mundane life working all day in a cubicle in Milton Keynes and then reheating an M&S curry in his microwave while watching Netflix all evening, a life with no real contact with women except shop assistants and HR wildebeests. Having little experience with women, he is likely completely unaware that these cute "virginal" Thai brides-to-be are scheming bitches interested only in an exit from their shithole country. He doesn't realise girls in "acquisition" mode are very, *very* different from girls in "job done" mode.

Such girls will play several men simultaneously and pick the fattest cow for marriage. I remember in 1999 sitting on my bed with a pretty Thai whore next to me. My cum was still crusted across her face as she whipped out her purse and showed me a photo of her white Australian "boyfriend."

"He knows I do this work," she said. "He visits a few times and buys me nice things. Soon I will go to Australia with him."

Fucking hell. I'd paid twenty pounds to smash her into the mattress and cum on her face, and this dumb "boyfriend" sap was working hard in Melbourne saving money to bring her in to wife up.

The big problem is the Western legal system. The girls are not required to honour their side of the contract. Instead, if she waits five years for her Permanent Residence Visa, she can frivorce the man, take half his cash, and remain legally entitled to stay in the country. And yet the media tells us these women are the victims of "human trafficking." Thailand is full of desperate ex-pats who are wilfully blind to the sting. I'd see several of them at breakfast in my apartment block, talking about their latest love.

Ex-pats are a funny lot. My theory, based on my experience living in Japan, is they have all been chased out of their own country for one reason or another. They're always misfits, and the single guys are especially sleazy; rat-faced, unkempt, and broken down by life. They've cashed in their assets and relocated to places like Thailand to live like a king at third-world prices, run amok in the local sex industry, and then hook some bar girl at the tail end of her career who pretends to like them. There was a lot of that going on in Chiang Mai so I wouldn't have anything to do with the other ex-pats there.

Thailand is a corrupt country. Well, to say a country is corrupt is to say the people are corrupt. Genetics drives identity, identity drives culture, and culture drives politics. Thailand isn't just corrupt in a political sense – the whole sexual marketplace is extremely sleazy. Southeast Asia generally is simply abnormal. John would go to Jakarta two years later and try to game the nightclubs.

"Nick, all the girls in Jakarta clubs are whores," he messaged me.

"Come on, don't be so misogynistic. Up your game."

"No, really. I mean *literally* whores. Every single hot girl here is asking for money."

Prostitution is everywhere in Thailand, too, and if you're new to the country and haven't yet learned its local peculiarities you can never be sure if a girl is on the game or not. That's bad news for those girls who aren't because they get tarred with the same brush. I'd soon develop a radar for it and notice lots of shy, good girl university students in certain cafes, but that would present a different problem – zero English, uninterested in farang, and looking for a proper boyfriend rather than casual sex. I suspect it's a small population of adventurous girls like Peaches who service the entire Player population of Thailand.

I was already bored of Chiang Mai by the time it came to leave. My body was broken down from all the training, and I was exhausted to the point of feeling permanently ill. I was tired of being in the third world, tired of having a crappy old bed and crappy shower. Mosquitoes bit me every night. I didn't want to talk to any of the local men because they were all oestrogen faggots. I didn't want to talk to the creepy ex-pats. So it was just John and I keeping our heads down and grinding through the fitness regime.

"If I ever go back to Thailand, it's for the beaches," I told John as we stood outside the breakfast cafe waiting for my taxi to the airport. "I'll eat fruit on the beach, climb cliffs, scuba-dive, watch kick-boxing... I'll do all the lifestyle stuff, but I'm just not interested in gaming Thai girls."

I was done with the third world. I wanted tall, curvy, white girls with university degrees, low notch-counts, and good English.

Black eyes courtesy of John

Zadar For More

CHAPTER
TWENTY SIX

ZADAR FOR MORE

Croatia is full of tall, curvy, white girls with university degrees, low notch-counts, and good English. Having successfully avoided the chilly frosts and ravages of a British winter, I noticed the weather beginning to turn and my thoughts focused on the Continent.

Thank God I'm back in Europe, I thought, setting my suitcase down in my Hampstead room and turning on the Xbox. "No more third world, no more lady boys, no more fat Mayans, no more trannies, and no more whores."

I loaded up Call of Duty for the first time in over a month and let my mind wander into daydreams of what spring might bring: walking in medieval old towns past patios of sophisticated coffee drinkers, eating juicy steaks, and sipping cold beer under the hot sun. I knocked on Jimmy's door to find him still sitting in his underpants playing Skyrim. I'm not sure if he'd moved all month.

"I'm telling you mate, we need to give Yugoslavia another try," he said. I agreed. "You won't believe Dubrovnik. It's where all the rich Italians park their yachts for summer. The bars and restaurants are absolutely rammed with top-drawer tottie. Rammed, mate."

"Rammed," I echoed.

"And Sarajevo! Don't get me started on Sarajevo. The most beautiful girls I've seen in my life. I drove up there with my mate Richard from the band six years ago. I'm telling you, it's a lovely little city in the middle of all these big fuck-off mountains, and all the skirt is tall with long legs."

I looked over at the TV screen, where his Skyrim character was hacking his great-axe at some long-legged mountain bandits. I looked back at Jimmy, his eyes, misty with joy and nostalgia, turning a shimmering translucent grey. This was it – the Frame Control Singularity! – where fantasy and reality had merged and my northern house-mate slipped imperceptibly between them as expedient.

We agreed on a plan – Fly into the coastal town of Zadar for a week, then bus up to Zagreb for week two. We'd spend week three in Zadar again then back to Zagreb to hire a car to spend the final week driving through Dubrovnik, Sarajevo, and Belgrade before finishing up in Zagreb to return the car.

Jimmy in Zadar Old Town

That's what it's like making plans with Jimmy. There's no direct route from A to B. That's what they'd be *expecting* us to do!

Whereas I'd spent the winter travelling to warmer climes, Jimmy had found another way to amuse himself without leaving his Hampstead bedroom: PlentyOfFish online dating. He began by trolling girls, sending then a long rambling critique of their profile, and offering advice on how to look more attractive online. Some girls took the bait and sent angry responses, which was exactly what he planned for. As any player knows, emotional engagement is critical in capturing a girl's attention. You can work with any emotion except disgust or indifference.

So these girls would be triggered into an angry reply in order to re-establish their frame as "hot" and "desirable." Jimmy would reply in turn to continue the argument, but he'd soften his tone and stack his comments with DHVs. For example, he'd reply:

"Look, Angela. I'm sure you're really a much nicer girl than you appear online. You seem pretty so I can imagine some men would feel proud to walk into a nice restaurant with you on their arm. But the thing is – lots of girls are pretty. Men like me have a lot of options. I set up a small hotel business for my mother in the Lakes District so she can potter around cooking and dealing with guests (she loves fussing after people, so I figured a business dealing with sometimes irate customers would be great for her). Anyway, the thing is – I often have to go down there to help out or tweak the website and so on. After a few days of this, I want to just go to a nice restaurant or museum with a girl who is pleasant. I don't need hostility or challenge in my leisure time. So obviously we got off on the wrong foot, but when you do find that high-value guy you're looking for, you're up against girls just as pretty as you but who don't kick up such a fuss. That's why I said you need to bring out some of your warmer personality traits in your profile."

This back and forth would continue and the girl would visibly soften as she absorbed Jimmy's DHVs and his messages subtly increased comfort. Several girls asked him onto dates.

Like all things Jimmy, that soon ceased to amuse him and he looked for an even easier way to get girls out. He then settled on an original method (he even wrote a short book about it that he never published). It was really simple monkey-see-monkey-do stuff, but the genius was it incorporated everything you need. You'd start with a wildly illogical but colourful subject line and an initial three-line message with a push-pull-push structure. For example:

Title: I just fell off my pie
Message:

Your arms are stupidly long, like Mr Tickle. (Push)
You have really nice hair. Very sexy. (Pull)
You owe me £20. (Push)

The idea was to break through the clutter of a hot girl's inbox with irreverence and surrealism. She'd scan through fifty titles of "Hi" and "Hey baby" to see something like "My doctor's goldfish will eat you" and click it open. Jimmy's messages were often laugh-out-loud hilarious, and he'd spent winter banging a handful of these PlentyOfFish tarts on dates.

I was now entering my third straight year of plundering Jimmy's vault of game techniques, so why not copy his online game too? I fired off ten messages on OkCupid to girls in and around Zadar (PlentyOfFish didn't seem to have any girls using it there). Even in a quality country like Croatia, the online girls are pretty unappealing so I set myself a minimum threshold of "if I'd fuck her after three pints in a bar and didn't need to work hard for it."

Even then it was hard to find enough targets. I got very lucky in that by far the strongest response came from by far the hottest of the girls. My initial message to Zehra was this:

You sound crazy. Totally batshit crazy.
I like your hair. Cute, feminine, massive.
Weirdo.
Two hours later she sent me a thesis.

"Well, thank you for the compliments. Now prepare yourself for compliments for you :D hahahah Firstly – reading your profile, made me smile :) thats what I really like about it, :D secondly – you have there something untold which interests me very much ;) your birthdate :P and thirdly – that was the most interesting profile I read since I'm logged here – that contacted me :) Im very glad to have read that nice profile on this boooring evening :D hahaha guess that flu isn't that bad, when having someone interesting contact me :D Greetings from Croatia, btw ;)"

You can imagine how I perked up reading that. After two months of rattling gooks and whores, I'd gotten a strong hook from a proper, hot, white girl. I wrote a normal somewhat try-hard message telling her we'd arrive in Zadar in a few days and instructed her to sleep off the flu so she can show me around. She eagerly agreed but I hadn't yet hit on her so I wasn't sure where I stood. I'll include a few message snippets, lest you totally overrate the quality of my message game back then when not corralled by Jimmy's prescriptions.

> *"Hmmmmmmmmmm. We'll be going to Zagreb later but Zadar looks nice, if a bit boring. Nothing like London or Tokyo, that's for sure. I think I'll avoid the crowded places so I don't get other people's sweat all over my suit. So a quiet relaxed lounge bar sounds perfect. I'll light up a fat cigar and enjoy the sea view. So tell me something about yourself. If I take you out are you going to be fun, lively and not too much of a stalker?*
>
> *Your hair is proper crazy. I hope you still have it this style. You look like a squirrel."*

That's a show-piece of Clumsy PUA Tactics #101. Heavy-handed DHVs on my travel, awkwardly setting myself up as the prize, then ending with a flourish of heavy-handed qualification. Ugh. Fortunately, she liked me and put up with it, sending very long and excitable messages. I've saved you the bother of reading the next six messages each. I took my laptop next door to show Jimmy.

"This is emotional engagement, right?"

For the record, this is the profile she responded to, shamelessly copied from Mick's template:

> **My self-summary** – *I'm straight to the point. There's too many push-over men in this world who don't know what they want and are too pussy to go out and take it. I'll lead you like a man should – decisive and dominant.*

I'm not "a laid-back guy," I don't initiate a conversation with a girl saying, "hey, how was your weekend?" Boring. I'm my own boss. I wake up when I please, I do as I please. I spend most of my life travelling through Europe.

I don't mind if you give me a bit of shit. That's how it's supposed to be. Just please, none of that "hey" or "hi" stuff. That's boring.

What I'm doing in life – *Making dinero and eating tapas*

I'm really good at – *Winning. Nobody ever wins against me.*

You should message me if – *You've got better things to do than window-shop, and you have some spark about you.*

Jimmy and I arrived in Zadar and spent the first night in a newly-opened hostel tucked away five kilometres along a rocky beach, a long walk from the centre. Zadar is a small town on the Adriatic coast that spills out from the fortified Old Town. It's a classical medieval town with turrets, ramparts and drawbridges on two sides and then town squares and winding alleys inside. April is tourist off-season and deathly quiet. A few students roamed around between classes and an occasional holidaymaker stared at his map then wandered off bemused.

Jimmy and I sat in a pub fronting the town square. Once in a while, a girl walked past so we took turns opening. Oxford Street it wasn't. Then we found a better hostel inside the Old Town and moved our stuff in the next day. Later that evening we had a double date with Zehra and her best friend.

We'd both brought our leather dress shoes, blazers, and cloth caps. Since watching the Dos Equis commercials for the Most Interesting Man In The World, we'd become awfully pompous and loved every self-referential minute of it. We sat at a high table in a pleasant corner bar on a cobbled street sipping whiskey and waiting for the girls to show.

Zehra walked in, and I was very pleased. Buxom, big-haired, pretty-faced, and a shy awkward smile. I'd soon find out she was cerebral, introverted, and suffered some social anxiety. Jimmy wasn't so pleased with her friend Julia – it was the female version of the Arnold Schwarzenegger / Danny DeVito double act in *Twins* with Julia as the 'left-over' DNA.

"You are dressed nice," said Zehra as we waved them to sit down at our table.

"Sartorial elegance," I said. "Thanks."

We over-egged the English gentleman shtick all evening, talking like Raffles and Sherlock Holmes. The first hour was an absolute masterclass in PUA teamwork, our telepathic understanding like the Brazil 1970 soccer team. Every joke, every comment, every witticism was delivered with perfect timing, bang on the nail as if we were working from a script.

Tease. DHV. Stack. Roll-off. Repeat. The girls were destroyed, deer in headlights, and loving every minute. Zehra was hooked.

Jimmy and his favourite hobby. Zadar

The night cut in, yet the sea breeze was mild. After two whiskeys we let the girls walk us to the sea front and the famous Sea Organ on the southwest corner where the waves lap against a specially-constructed feature that makes musical notes. Having already winged me to perfection in the bar, Jimmy dropped his walking speed to a snail's pace and tied up Julia in conversation, allowing me to take Zehra on ahead and weave my magic.

I was walking along the sea front in an old medieval town with a beautiful twenty-year-old girl next to me and my best friend ten metres behind running interference. It was a lovely evening.

Having gotten Zehra into "isolation," I engaged her in deep rapport. I probed into her hopes and dreams, her personality, the thesis she was doing at university, her lifestyle, and more. It wasn't just idle chit-chat. I was sinking my hooks deep into her soul, and her personality made her very amenable to it. I very much liked her.

"Zehra, I think you're the sort of person who is often very disappointed in the people around you because you have very high standards of behaviour, and you're the only person who meets them."

Being mystically inclined, she started thinking that fate that had thrown us together, and I did nothing to disabuse her of the notion. After a thoroughly enjoyable two and half hours, we said goodbye at the main entrance of the marina. I didn't try to kiss her – it seemed premature.

We met one-on-one the following evening.

"I'd like you to have this," she said, taking a moonstone from her purse. "Carry it close to your heart. It absorbs bad energy and imparts good vibes."

She was serious, which made it all the sweeter. I recognised in myself that tumbling shaky feeling of becoming attached to someone in a short amount of time. Zehra was having quite an effect on me.

After a couple of drinks in a local bar she came back to my hostel room, sitting on the edge of the bed nearest the door. We chatted some more, but I didn't escalate lest she fly out in a hurry. An hour later I walked her halfway home and tried to kiss her, but it was odd: we were in a standing hug on a narrow bridge over a stream. She pressed her lips tight together to prevent a real kiss but didn't move her head or feet to disengage. It was like she wanted to kiss but was scared.

So I grabbed her tits and ass. They were sensational. She let it happen but still wouldn't kiss properly. When we finally parted outside her place she gave me a long tight goodnight hug and told me, "You can see me so well, I feel naked. What you said was like a bullet in my head."

Deep rapport indeed.

The following day, Jimmy and I took a bus to Zagreb, looking out the windows as it inched up the dry scrub land and along tunnels cut into the mountainside. A week later we returned to Zadar for the afternoon, passing through with a hire car. Zehra and I had time for a short date before Jimmy and I began our road trip in earnest. We met Zehra and Julia in a yacht-side cafe restaurant. It was a narrow time window so I knew I couldn't take her anywhere. We just ran our Most Interesting Man In The World spiel then headed off down the Croatian Riviera.

Jimmy had a hard-on for Dubrovnik, a beautiful medieval fort town where episodes of *Game of Thrones* had been filmed due to its high city walls and picturesque winding alleys. It was like Zadar on a higher budget. The whole time we drove along the coast, Queen's greatest hits thumping on the stereo, Jimmy kept up a monologue of how amazing the women were.

"Any bar, you'll see eights and nines," he enthused. "All dolled up like they are going to the theatre. Classy skirt."

We arrived late evening and found our apartment in the foothills overlooking the fortified Old Town.

"Come on, let's get at them," said Jimmy, clapping his hands together and rubbing them with glee.

The water shimmered and reflected moonlight. Inky shadows were cast under the city walls as we walked across a stone bridge and through a medieval gate. I expected to be challenged by a night-watchman with a pike and plume. We wandered down to the main square struck by two conclusions: It was achingly beautiful and... deserted. Just a handful of couples ambled past us down the main street. We heard the soft sounds of live music around a corner so we investigated, finding an open-air restaurant with a few dozen locals enjoying a get-together. Wine flowed freely. We sat down and ate dinner.

"There were more birds last time," Jimmy said.

The next afternoon we explored more of the city and concluded we'd hit off-season. Jimmy did get a stroke of good fortune though.

We continued our lazy exploration of every back alley, soon finding ourselves at the foot of the outer edge of the city walls overlooking a large marina. A patio cafe stretched along the bottom of the wall, and as we approached Jimmy noticed a hot brunette eating alone. She was just enjoying the atmosphere breathing in the sea air, no doubt on a mini-holiday break. Jimmy sidled up and said hello, propping himself up against the low cafe wall from the outside while she sat at her table on the other side.

Outside the fortified town of Dubrovnik

It went well. She was visiting from Vienna. He took her number and arranged to meet later that evening. For some reason Jimmy wanted me along, perhaps eyeing a threesome. We agreed I'd do some attraction with her and we'd team up to bamboozle her back to our apartment, much like we'd done with Camilla and Zehra. There was a snag, though By the time we met her in a cafe on the main square, I was in a *very* exuberant mood.

I just smashed it out of the park. Over the first half hour she found out I'd been the smartest kid in school, travelled the world, lived in Japan and spoke Japanese, was a leader of men, kick-boxed, and so on. I even managed to squeeze in that I'd been BMX champion of Britain for my age-group. She lapped it up, leaning over her wine glass with starry eyes while Jimmy slouched in his seat barely saying a word.

"Jimmy, you're awfully quiet. Are you feeling okay?" I said.

That was the final nail in the coffin. He looked like Bruce Willis in *The Sixth Sense* finding out he'd been dead the whole time.

"I'm alright," he mumbled quietly.

We moved on to an Irish bar, and Jimmy recovered his mojo and started sexualizing.

"My mate back home had a threesome one night," he began, rattling off a long story full of DHVs and spikes. The Austrian brunette – a mid-twenties eight – was completely taken in, nodding her head enthusiastically and agreeing that yes, sometimes it's best to ignore social rules and throw yourself into interesting experiences. She was there for the taking, yet Jimmy never pulled the trigger. It was his set so I just followed his lead until we watched her walk away into the night. He'd stay in touch with her on Facebook, and she invited him to Vienna for sex but it just petered out over the next two months.

There was no way around the fact that I'd hijacked his set in the early going. "Shouldn't have done that, mate," he said as we walked up the hillside back to our apartment.

"Why didn't you take her home?"

"Wasn't feeling it. You'd taken the play away from me so even later in the Irish bar things weren't right."

That was the first real splinter between Jimmy and I. He'd done a few similar things to me in 2010 and 2011 so I didn't feel at all guilty. Nonetheless I respect wing rules and knew I'd erred. He didn't make a big deal of it, but I could see he was holding some resentment. Since the very beginning of *Rock Solid Game* Jimmy had laboured to create a rat pack where everyone had each other's back. He wanted us to be a class above the every-man-for-himself attitude that plagued most men's dealings with women.

I kept in touch with Zehra via Facebook the whole time. When we finally came back to Zadar to wrap up the trip, Jimmy and I found a private shared room in a hostel. Two beds in one room up on the fourth floor of a crusty historic building right in the middle of the Old Town.

It was our last night in Zadar, crunch time after nearly a month on the road, and I hadn't even properly kissed Zehra. Something had always come up to stop me escalating. I knew she was sold on me emotionally, but she was artfully avoiding the physical route. We arranged to meet that evening while Jimmy wandered around town by himself. He was oddly out of sorts, not interested in finding girls. Mind you, there was nothing to find.

Passing through Mostar in Bosnia

Zehra showed up in a fancy cocktail dress, her hair clearly styled specially at a salon and long earrings. As I watched her stumble and totter around the cobbled street in her high heels, I could see she'd made a big effort to look classy. It was sweet because her tits and ass were so buxom that she still looked like a stripper. She'd even look dirty in a burkha.

"Some of my classmates told me you and Jimmy had spoken to them on the street this month," she said, amused. "It's a small town!"

We'd only done a half-dozen sets each. Small town indeed.

We had a walk to the sea then a quiet drink. Jimmy wandered past us a couple of times that hour, such was the small size of the town. Zehra told me she liked old horror movies, so I enthused about Mario Bava's 1963 gothic horror *Black Sabbath*.

"I have it on my laptop," I said, affecting a careless tone like it hadn't been the plan all along. "We could go back and watch it."

"Okay" she agreed, without any hesitation. We both knew this was the last chance saloon, and while I doubted I'd break her down, she knew that was the next stage of the courtship dance.

"Extracting. Give me an hour," I messaged Jimmy. *Black Sabbath* is an anthology of three horror stories. I figured I'd lightly escalate her during *The Telephone*, go for the lay during *The Wurdulak*, then kick her out at the end of *The Drop Of Water*.

She got nervous as soon as we turned on to my street. "Let's walk some more," she asked.

Jimmy had stayed out, and as we turned a corner by a tobacco kiosk we almost bumped into him. It was a bit awkward because the streets were otherwise deserted, the bars were closed or closing, and the place was dead, so Jimmy had no obvious reason for wandering around.

"Hey.... um.... fancy seeing you here, Nick. I've just popped out to find a bottle of water. It's so nice out I got a bit carried away. I might go sit by the sea organ, and let it inspire me to write some music."

"Great idea. Catch you a bit later."

Zehra fretted again as we got back to the hostel, requiring me to walk her around town another ten minutes. I saw Jimmy in the distance again, but he was alert and ducked into a doorway before Zehra noticed. She was nervous, and I wondered if her previous sexual experience was limited. She instinctively knew what we were building towards, wanted it, but it seemed like she couldn't allow herself to keep moving forwards.

We walked about forty minutes then bumped into Jimmy yet again, ambling along with his hands in his pockets.

"Did you find a bottle of water?" Zehra asked.

"Yeah, delicious. Really hit the spot."

"How was the sea organ?"

"The what?.... oh yeah. Fantastic. Bloody fantastic," he blurted out. "I want to have a walk up to the marina. My dad asked me to get the lie of the land. He's considering a trip to Croatia in the summer."

Zehra came inside at the third pass. With Jimmy wandering around alone outside, there was no time to waste, so I put *Black*

Sabbath on my laptop, and we started watching. We were kissing after a quarter hour, but then she put up obstacle after obstacle.

An hour passed with very little progress.

"Can you give me another half hour?" I messaged Jimmy.

The outside temperature had plummeted to near zero under a cloudless sky. Another hour passed, and I had Zehra down to her underwear. It was midnight.

"I'm in the bathroom next door," Jimmy texted me. "Listening to podcasts. The Wi-Fi is too slow for YouTube."

Finally, at 4am, Zehra relented and threw herself at me. She was obviously gagging for it, and as soon as her forebrain allowed her to have sex, all that pent-up sexual frustration burst out. She was so energetic and sexy that I had to pull my dick out of her at least five times in the first five minutes because she was making me too horny – I thought I was going to come too quickly.

It was very good sex. Some of the best I've ever had. Finally after an hour I felt a bit guilty for Jimmy still sitting on the toilet seat next door in an unheated bathroom, reading Burnley Football Club team news.

"You did it. You sank my ship!" she said, triumphantly. "I was fighting you but you broke down all my defences. Thank you!"

"Why did you fight so hard?"

"I was worried I won't see you again."

I walked her home soon after and came back to find Jimmy stretched out on his bed, wrapped in multiple blankets, snoring. I think he'd inconvenienced himself for about seven hours to help me close. While that was sterling wing-work, it did carry an unforeseen downside – he'd just demonstrated a stark contrast to my own error winging him a few days earlier in Dubrovnik.

Zehra came to see us off at the bus stop to the airport and then we flew back to London. The Croatia road tour had been great fun but very little in the way of action with girls. I'd also gotten a near miss with a ratbag from OkCupid in Zagreb and Jimmy had come close in Sarajevo. However for the most part we'd spent most days in cafes and restaurants with precious little opening.

I very much liked Zehra and wanted to keep her around. We'd spent hours talking, and her cerebral and somewhat vulnerable character made me warm and fuzzy. She also had exactly the look which I like – thick dark hair, buxom body without turning fat, and a uniquely Croatian look that I can't quite describe; it combines a strong angular brow with deep set dark eyes and thick eyelashes. Google search 90s porn star Draghixa, and you'll see what I mean. Dovile was slipping in and out of my life by now, so I marked Zehra as her replacement.

Bringing Zehra to London

We kept up steady Skype chats, and I soon invited her to London, buying her a budget flight out of Zadar and meeting her at Golders Green bus station one late evening in May. She stepped off the bus in a loose-fitting tracksuit and gave me a nervous hug. She'd never been outside her own country and was now in the middle of London. We walked up to Château Hampstead and settled into my room. She put up a half-arsed struggle over fucking but soon relented, and then we were rolling around the bed naked for most of the next week.

We were lucky enough to catch a heatwave, so Zehra would sun-bathe on a rug in the back garden each day then I'd show her around the familiar tourist sites. On Friday evening the whole RSG gang went out to Old Street. By now Zehra had gotten over her social anxiety with us and spent half the evening talking to John, who'd recently moved into the mansion. This would become a pattern over the next year or so – I'd pull a hot girl and then sit back and let John befriend her. I knew he wasn't trying to fuck them behind my back, but he'd admitted he was still struggling with deep misogyny. I figured helping him spend time with hot young girls in a social context would eventually make him realise they weren't witches trying to hex him.

Sex with Zehra was excellent, and I very much enjoyed being the recipient of her first ever blow job.

We were both sad on her way back to the airport. I found myself wishing she lived in London. She had a brittle bird-with-a-broken-wing vibe at times and had recently done herself a serious knee injury playing volleyball causing her knee to ache constantly. I had the game discipline not to try fixing her problems but it still tugged at me on a deeper emotional level than I was used to with girls.

We kept up regular Skype contact but logistics went against us as either my trips or her classes would stop us meeting. I remember one video chat in particular, laying on a sofa in the Château lounge mid-afternoon.

"I've been thinking a lot, Nick," she said. "That week in London was magical. I dream about it still. I was thinking that, well, it would be nice to always be like that. In London with you."

She looked shyly down, blushing. She was trying to tell me she loved me and was frightened by the intimacy. Now I was torn. I very much wanted to keep her as a regular, but I had absolutely no plans to give up chasing fresh skirt. Whether her vulnerability was real or affected, I didn't want to hurt the girl by keeping her hanging on. Whereas girls like Dovile could keep themselves open to the potential of new boyfriends, Zehra was too reclusive. It would be me and nothing else.

She wasn't even from Zadar but from a tiny party island further down the coast that was swarmed by the drunken English summer crowd. Her entire experience of Englishmen before me was working as a waitress in the bars where the Brits got fucked off their nuts on drugs. She'd spend long evenings lying in bed reading dark fiction on vampires and serial killers, getting off on the taboo. There wasn't a nasty bone in her body – all her weirdness was just a fun way for her to cope with her world. Her father had been killed in the Bosnian war when she was six years old, and her mother had struggled to raise her on the small island. So there were probably some daddy issues motivating her to latch onto me.

It was quite the dilemma. Most men would rate her an eight, but for me she was exactly what I wanted in every way; age, looks, vibe, and character. I simply couldn't conceive of anything I'd change about her. Well, maybe bigger tits. Ultimately I laid it all on the line, overtly. I explained that I was a travelling man and while I hoped to bring her to London and see her out in Croatia, she needed to concentrate on finishing her studies. We remained friends but time and logistical trouble meant that by the end of summer her intense infatuation had cooled off.

Zehra at the Chateau

She's an adorable girl, and I still genuinely like her, so when she told me that she was having a hard time in 2015, I was very concerned. She'd broken her foot at her sports club and the injury was misdiagnosed. The doctor kept her on painkillers for a long time, and the stress brought on by her university work left her vulnerable to a weird bug which kept her laid up for months. I suspect hypochondria played a part, but it certainly depressed her, and she'd seem melancholy when we would chat. In addition, her family was having the usual financial problems.

I'll just point out that she never once asked me for money, nor did I offer. The only significant thing I'd ever bought her was a £79 return flight to London. She was no gold-digger. I'd told her I'll always have time for her and I meant it, so we had some long Skype video chats again. I figured she needed to reach outside her tiny reclusive world of study and lying in bed. So it was quite a surprise to see the direction our chat turned.

"Nick, I want to ask you about something in London," she began. Even in 2015 I'd not lost my interest in rattling her a few more times but something in her tone told me this was completely unrelated.

"I'm completely broke. I can't even go to the cafe for a coffee. Every penny I have goes on food. The work here is seasonal so I can only earn in summer doing waitress work. So, I've been browsing the internet, and I had the idea of working in London. I have an EU passport."

I agreed in principle. I'd have no qualms about advising her on setting up in the Big Smoke. "There are lots of jobs here if you're okay waitressing or working behind a bar or coffee machine," I said.

"Well." She paused and looked down shyly. "I need much more money, and I want to help my mother. I heard that escorts get rich in London."

Exploring Mostar in Bosnia

That was a surprise.

Now, if there is one person who *shouldn't* escort, it's Zehra. Whores are always unhinged, but they at least share the one absolutely crucial prerequisite for whoring: the ability to separate sex from love. In contrast, Zehra took *everything* to heart.

"Zehra, you've got the body for it but not the mind."

I spent an hour explaining everything I knew about the sex industry, giving her all the reasons why she couldn't and shouldn't escort, emphasising the psychological damage it inflicts.

"If you must cash in on your body, get a job at a high-end strip club. You'll have to hustle hard, but you don't have to fuck, and with your shape you'll get lots of private dances. But even then, I really don't recommend it."

It seemed surreal to be telling a (now) twenty-three-year-old island girl with a notch count of three that fucking dozens of men per week for cash was a bad idea. I ended my lecture and waited for her reaction.

"That's what my brother said. He said I'm crazy and forbade me to do it."

Ultimately she fell for her sports coach in Zadar and moved in with him. I last spoke to her in early 2016, and she was pretty happy with how things were progressing. She showed me photos, and he looks a bit like me and the same age. I'd notice this a lot over the years – lots of the girls who took an immediate liking to me would date other middle-aged skinheads. I'd frequently transition into paternal relationships with my favourite girls once they'd drifted out of my sexual orbit. Dovile, Tasanee and now Zehra looked to me for advice and emotional support, which I'd happily provide. As the years wore on I'd value this type of friendship with several other girls I'd date too.

*Drinking at
Le Mans 24*

*We did see a bit
of the race*

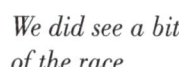

*Visiting French
villages on the
way home*

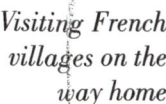

CHAPTER

TWENTY SEVEN

Language Exchange

TWENTY SEVEN

LANGUAGE EXCHANGE

Mick was in the kitchen rustling up another chicken escalope meal. The pan sizzled and various ingredients were laid carefully in the few spaces between all of Lee and Hayley's unwashed dishes.

"I've found a new in," he said, smugly.

"Do tell."

"Language exchange," he said, sprinkling salt and pepper over his chicken fillet before pressing it down hard into the pan until it smoked. "There's a Facebook group that meets in a bar by Tottenham Court Road station every three weeks. It'll be full of lonely fresh-off-the-boat Euro-tottie. They are meeting tomorrow."

We'd always studiously avoided using this type of weaselly 'in' to girls, where you pretend to meet for a shared activity but are really just on the pull. It felt dirty and bad for inner game in the long term. Nonetheless we fancied a change of pace so that Thursday I joined Mick, Johnny, and John in a large first floor bar that the language exchange organisers had hired for the event. It was rammed. Maybe two hundred people, split fifty-fifty between men and women. I might've been the oldest person in the room.

"What is your language?" asked the thin young dork registering entrants by the door. His Top Man suit fitted him like a Western condom on a Chinese man.

"English and Japanese," I muttered, scanning the sea of girls in the room behind him.

"We'll write English, then. Most of the people are here to practice that," he replied, then straightened out my five pound note and added it to the neat pile in his small strongbox on the table.

We stepped into the throng of Spanish, Brazilian, and Italian girls, all of whom had come in groups of two or three. There were plenty of foreign Euro-chumps buzzing around them but seeing as almost everyone was here to practice English with native speakers, we held home-court advantage.

"Fish in a barrel," Mick chortled and squeezed past me to a spot in the bar next to two pairs of girls.

"I'm not sure I approve of this," I said to Johnny. "Pretending we want to do language exchange while clearly trying to get laid. I don't like subterfuge."

"Do you think there's a single man in this bar who came for the language?" he countered.

"I give it two months tops before this place is invaded by the LSS," I said, thinking how quickly word would get around the London Seduction Society forum – the local internet group for Game enthusiasts. They were currently all swapping tips on which salsa class had more foreign women so the moment they got a sniff of the language exchange night they'd swarm in like badly-dressed semi-autistic locusts.

I looked around to find my first set. The girls weren't especially hot. If I squinted carefully then perhaps there were three or four eights. Most of the girls were little brown fives and sixes with chubby cheeks and thighs threatening to burst the stitching on their tight jeans. Still, the atmosphere was friendly and relaxed, and because everyone was on the lookout for new friends I soon took several numbers without effort.

"We need to build out vibe," I said to John. "Let's stand at the bar and talk loudly."

We ignored the room so as not to be caught value-scanning. Within a few minutes of animated gestures and forced laughs, we saw girls looking over at us. I got a round of drinks, and when I turned back around, there was a cute little Spanish brunette standing right in front of me. She was flanked by a Mexican guy and an Italian guy competing for her attention in good humour.

"Spanish, eh?" I opened, looking at her identifying badge. "You people are crazy."

She took an immediate liking to me, and I'd realise later she'd manoeuvred herself to precisely that spot as a proximity indicator of interest. She was nineteen years old and spoke appalling English.

"My name is Daniela," she said. "I from Madrid."

"Help me translate," I said to the Mexican guy, then tooled him as my conduit to picking her up. I don't think he was wise to my manipulating him. Perhaps he was too enthusiastic and happy to realize he was being "AMOGed." This is an old PUA term meaning "Alpha Male Of Group," wherein a man will try to establish himself above other men so that the girls see him as the leader and are thus more attracted to him. There's a whole library of techniques for how to AMOG, and I was using one now by setting him up as my translator – i.e. my underling.

"Tell her I think she looks like a hamster."

He translated while I arrogantly leaned back against the bar like Marlon Brando waiting for James Dean to introduce Carey Grant. Daniela looked at me and giggled, so I tweaked her cheeks and continued talking. Every now and then I threw the Italian guy a bone so that I could keep the Jimmy Horseshoe in front of me. I caught Daniela eyeing our set-up with a curious eye, and she seemed to quickly notice that I'd pushed both men into a subordinate position. I saw her brain process this and then her eyes immediately light up in response. After ten minutes I excused myself to find Mick elsewhere in the bar. It was game over – all I needed was to leave her hanging then collect her number before closing time.

She couldn't wait, and half an hour later she'd tracked me down for more awkward conversation, this time without the Mexican translator. I soon rolled off again but kept my eye on her, as she was my strongest lead, and I didn't want her to slip out before exchanging numbers. An hour later we'd all worked every set of interest, and Mick was keen to get home to eat. I wandered over to Daniela who was once more flanked by Mario and Luigi.

"Hey," I leaned over to the Mexican. "Tell her it was nice to meet her, and I'm going home now."

He conveyed my message then I slowly turned to leave. Daniela frantically tapped my shoulder, waving her smart phone in my face. "Do you have Facebook? I have Skype too! Here's my phone number. And can we take a photo?"

Daniela was on a tight time-frame. She'd been in London just a few days and was due back in Madrid within the week. "I think to move to London some time," she'd said in the bar. "This a looking trip."

Later that same night, she opened me with a Skype video chat, which I let run for an hour, consulting Google Translate, letting the comfort build, seeing how hard she was investing. That was followed up by a morning-after chat and agreement to meet for a drink later that evening.

Her English was so poor and London so new to her that I thought it safer and easier to meet near her hostel rather than risk a logistical fuck-up. Consequently, I embarked on a thirty-minute bus ride across the north London suburbs and met her in a bar. We had a couple of beers and the whole time her demeanour was signalling "on", it was just a question of when. She was a horny young minx who had fuck energy bubbling underneath everything she did. We made out in the last bar, and she climbed all over me, literally.

I like it when girls chase. It feels powerful. I leant back and acted like a dickhead, pushing her away with a cad's smirk on my face. Nineteen years old and as randy as they come – *this will be easy*, I thought. We walked through the quiet tree-lined streets to her hostel, then she unexpectedly fobbed me off at the door.

"No, you not come in," she said. "I not sure. Meet tomorrow, OK?"

The next evening we met outside West Hampstead tube and walked up to the Black Lion bar where we sat across a high table and knocked back bottles of Corona. A tipsy Brazilian girl intruded for a while, but she was good-natured and took some of the conversational weight off my shoulders. There was no question of Daniela losing interest in me, she'd been sold from the first moment she'd noticed me in the Language Exchange bar. The problem was her inexperience with men.

I walked her up the bank to my front door but she froze at the doorstep. She just wouldn't take that final step. "I only sex one man," she said, shivering despite the warm night air. "We date two years before."

She'd tell me later she'd had sex literally one time her whole life, six months earlier, and made this poor guy wait almost two years for it. Then she'd turned down his marriage proposal. What was it about me that attracted the inexperienced good girls? She also showed me a photo of him, and he looked eerily similar to me.

On this second date I walked her back down the road to a pub full of Poles where she jumped me again. The next night I met her once more in a pub and got her back to Château RSG. It was tortuous stuff getting her semi-naked on my bed, and she locked up tight when I tried to pull her jeans down.

The fourth night was her last in London and she wanted to come around to my house. "If we see each other again, we will have sex," I wrote, exasperated.

"I understand," she responded.

After an hour of canoodling and several half-hearted "we aren't having sex" protests, I squeezed my cock into her. It took about ten minutes to get it all in because she was so tight and tense. The sex was bad because of her worry and discomfort, and it became a chore just to get through it. An hour or so later, I bundled her into a taxi and went to sleep.

We kept in touch while she was in Madrid. The sex was so bad that I wasn't much enthused when she wanted to come visit me a fortnight later but I liked the idea of having another pretty teenage girl on my rotation, and besides, sex might improve as she became increasingly comfortable with me. She had visions of standing alone at Gatwick airport while I was out drinking, having forgotten all about her.

"You definitely come?" she asked.

I agreed to pay half of her fare, about thirty pounds, as a surety, to help relieve her paranoia of being left alone at the terminal. Two weeks later, she was visibly relieved to see me approach her at the Arrivals terminal. She'd still expected me to flake on her. I took her out for a few drinks then fucked her. She stayed at the Château a couple of days, and I fucked her a couple more times, but the sex didn't improve. She was too inexperienced, tight, and nervous.

In stark contrast to her sexual technique, Daniela was very confident in her sexuality. She'd come up close to the other guys in the house, touching their arms softly as she spoke and holding steady eye contact. One time when John was cooking she came up right behind him to talk – with me standing there filling the coffee machine two feet away – and his hands were shaking because of the sexual energy she projected. Elena had a similar vibe, a girl who also projected sexual confidence despite having had sex one time less than Daniela before she met me.

Ultimately the poor sex and weak communication sapped my will to date the little Spanish minx. On the last night, we lay in bed together with our smart phones to have The Talk.

"Do you want to date me?" she asked.

"I like you, and I want to see you again, but I don't want to be your boyfriend," I replied.

She thought a while then smiled, tapping into her Google Translate. "I'm glad I met you and had sex, but it's better we don't pretend. Let's just be friends."

It seemed rather easy. I'd expected her to be clingy. So I agreed and after seeing her onto the Gatwick Express train we waved goodbye for the final time. I did wonder if she really was going to go quietly, but as the months passed she made no effort to stick around and that suited me.

Return to Zagreb

TWENTY EIGHT

RETURN TO ZAGREB

ummer had arrived, and you couldn't keep us cooped up in London for love nor money. The Rock Solid Game business was ticking along nicely, and we'd had no trouble filling up boot camps every month or so.

"Let's spend a month in Yugoslavia and have students pay for it," I suggested. Mick and Jimmy had been throwing similar ideas around for months, and as John had sufficiently ingratiated his way into the Château it felt odd to charge him for tagging along. We posted on our blogs that we were offering one-week residentials on the road. Mick had two students sign up, and I had two. For the first week my student was a recently de-mobbed US army man, and then for the second week I had Ash, a British-Indian former boot camp student who would go on to become very successful with girls.

We arrived in Zagreb full of high spirits. The sun blazed in a bright blue sky, and the streets buzzed with tall, leggy, hot girls. We lazed in outdoor cafes until early afternoon then walked around daygaming. Unfortunately, the streets were misleading, and our prospects soon took a dive.

"Anyway, I think you're cute. Let's get a coffee later this week," we'd say towards the end of a street approach of a smiling enthusiastic girl.

"Oh!" she'd gasp. "I'd love to, but I'm going to Dubrovnik tomorrow morning. I'll be there all summer."

Zadar, Split, Dubrovnik, Montenegro... it was the same story with just the holiday destination interchangeable. At least half the girls we number-closed were packing suitcases for a summer on the Adriatic coast. Fuck. Before long we were getting frustrated at seeing so many promising leads deflate into nothing. Travelling together is high pressure at the best of times because every day brings the possibility that a wing will get laid while you don't, potentially side-swiping your ego enough to knock your own vibe and thus lead to poor street responses. Having all our leads collapse heaped on the pressure.

The Hemingway Suite Coat of Arms

Mick in particular was getting on my nerves. His usual playful banter had taken on a mean edge, and one lunchtime as we sat eating pasta in Nocturno café, a fairly innocuous jab struck me as one too many. "Hurry up eating, you bald Geordie bastard," he said and flicked a small sachet of sugar at me. "I've got two dates this afternoon. Can't have you holding me back."

We argued for real, and the mood on the street was icy as we walked around silently in a group of three. John stayed home. An hour earlier Jimmy and Mick had just walked out of the apartment to lunch while I was still in the shower, not having the decency to wait ten minutes until I was dressed. We remained on edge all week.

In an effort to counteract the petty vibe-crushing bullshit, we had a sit-down meeting on how to cut the negativity and boost our state. There wasn't much to discuss because we knew the problem and were all on board with Jimmy's wing rules. We agreed to tone down the banter and I walked out of the meeting buzzing with energy. And I mean *buzzing*. I felt indestructible. My vibe was so high, I walked down the street shooting six-guns from my fingers, hopping up and down and singing quietly to myself. My first few sets went great but didn't really stick. I knew I was doing high-quality work and just needed to bump into a girl who was available and into me. She was out there somewhere. Every fibre of my body pulsated with certainty I'd find her.

We turned off the main city square at Jelacic and walked through the park towards the train station. Trams clattered past, and I gazed down the long, straight road with its great lines of sight. From over fifty metres away, I spotted a likely girl walking towards me. Young, slim, punky-looking with a nose piercing, slightly dyed hair and rock-chick fashion. Her tight vest suggested a cracking pair of tits underneath. A dirty birdy if ever I saw one. My vibe was up, and my opportunity had come.

"Hey. Stop! I want to say hello. You look very punk rock."

Eighteen-year-old Dorota hooked immediately. We spoke for a full ten minutes, and both her replies and her body language made it clear she fancied me. As the conversation progressed everything slotted into place.

"I just arrived by train. I'm from Czech Republic. I wanted to visit for a day or two. My mum doesn't know I'm here," she said.

She'd been feeling bored in her small town and fancied a day out in the big city to take a look around, as she had nothing else going on. She couldn't stop batting her eyelids at me and giggling at my jokes.

"Let's cross the road," I said, pointing to an archway leading into a courtyard cafe. "There's a nice place to get a drink over there."

My spider-sense was tingling. We sat outside under a parasol and sipped local beer getting to know each other. As she didn't put up any obstacles and was clearly enjoying herself, I moved fast.

"Sorry, I was just looking at your breasts," I said as she told me her favourite music. "Repeat the list, please."

"I want tequila," she said.

With an hour gone I felt like she was comfortable with me and talking freely. She'd taken my oblique sexualisation without trying to block it. Time to make things more overt. I stood up and pulled out my wallet. "I'm going inside to pay the bill. This is your chance to escape. If you are still here when I come back, I shall assume you like me."

She was still sitting with a big smile on her face as I came back. I walked her to the second venue, a tiny rock bar called Alcatraz. Midway there I ramped it up again. "You are in danger of being kissed very soon. You may become a victim."

"What type of victim?" she asked.

"Sexual."

I could do no wrong. We kissed in a booth in Alcatraz bar, and she was massively into it, pushing into me with her big breasts. This was it, the window of opportunity had swung open.

"It's too dark. Let's get out of here," I said and hailed a cab. She followed, and I kept her talking about music for the short ride back to my apartment. We sat on the sofa watching YouTube for a few minutes, then I pulled her in to kiss. Her skin was hot to the touch and her cheeks flushed, but she broke away and retreated into the adjoining kitchen.

"I can't," she muttered, looking at the floor. "I like you, but I can't. Not today. It's the time of the month."

Damn! It's always gutting to ride the Same Day Lay roller-coaster right up to the end and then crash on the final bend. *Think fast, Nick!*

"I'll do you in the ass"

She freaked. "No! I've never done that!"

I sat her down in front of YouTube for another ten minutes and lightly groped her. Soon she started to squirm and push into me.

I pushed her onto her back and took my dick out, sticking it in her mouth. Her horniness overcame the final hurdle. A minute later she took my cock out of her mouth and looked me in the eyes while wanking me off.

"OK," she said.

These days I have developed a system to lead a girl to anal sex in the most exciting and least frightening manner I could conceive. Back in 2012 it was all new to me and rather crude. I flipped her around on the sofa, pulled her jeans down to mid-thigh and then put my dick in her ass. Surprisingly she didn't squeal much. I must've fucked her about ten minutes there, pushing her face into the cushions, before pulling her to her knees. I'd stripped off her vest and bra so she just knelt in front of me with those big teenage knockers forming a deep cleavage. Brilliant. I came all over them and then she scuttled back a few feet against the wall.

"That was a bit much," she said, sitting with her back to the wall looking down at herself. I don't know if she was expressing pleasure or disgust. Then she showered off and went out to find a hostel for the night.

Later that evening we all met up outside Alcatraz, and Dorota came out to join me. Jimmy had a cute new girl out who he'd met while she waited for a tram in the main Old Town square. She had big dimpled cheeks and thick brown hair so he called her Mouse. Mostly we posted up outside by a high table and let the girls press into us while we persuaded ourselves we were rock stars. I got Dorota to put her hands down my jeans then took her home again. This time she sucked me off on the bed but got cold feet at the thought of more anal sex. She freaked out for a few minutes at my clumsy manhandling of her then lay next to me dozing for an hour before going back to her hostel. I never did fuck her a second time.

Considering that she'd let herself be picked up outside a train station ten minutes after arriving in a foreign country, then lost her anal virginity two hours later to a stranger twice her age, you'd be forgiven for thinking Dorota was a dirty girl. You'd be wrong.

She'd had a moderately religious upbringing in a small town, and a day trip to Zagreb was her idea of a big adventure. She got rather more than she bargained for, caught up in the momentum of the occasion and overwhelmed by it all. She let herself go and enjoyed every minute, and my being in the right place at the right time worked for both of us. I got my lay, and she got an excuse to do something wild. Thinking through the psychology of the situation I began to formulate ideas about how Game could sweep a girl off her feet in what we'd soon term the Lust Bubble.

We kept in touch through Facebook and had a few abortive meet-up attempts when I was in Prague over the next two years. It never quite happened and eventually petered out. In March 2015, we'd get into an unexpected Facebook chat and discuss that first day for the first time.

"I look back on that day like it's a dream, like it happened many years ago," she wrote. "I enjoyed it and have absolutely no regrets, but it seems like another person. Getting fucked in the ass two hours after meeting a man just isn't me."

You don't say.

"It was essential to discovering myself," she continued. "I'm a good girl, and I never had sex quickly again. That was just a very strange day."

I cajoled her into sending me some topless photos and she briefly slipped back into the same Dorota I'd first met. "I don't understand how you make me do this. I haven't seen you in three years. We are chatting, and now I'm taking off my shirt and photographing my tits. I don't know. You compel me to do things I don't do."

When I'd first laid eyes on her, I was convinced that she was a dirty slut because she had that punky 'outsider' look and vibe. Although I'd been right that she was an SDL candidate, I'd been wrong about the reason — it was nothing about her look and everything about catching her at the best possible moment in her life for it. As I compiled more of these experiences over the next two years I'd come to develop of concept of 'Adventure Sex' to describe the service men like us provide to girls. While I've found punky-looking girls are indeed more likely to lack impulse control and more likely to jump into bed quickly, these are just surface-level markers and very unreliable. Her personality disposition, logistical timing, physical attraction for you, and current horniness are all far more important and these show themselves more in sub-communication than in fashion sense.

"It's as if all the hottest girls hang out in cafes," I moaned to Jimmy. "They must teleport in because we never see them on the street. Just groups of turbo-hotties sitting around a table gabbing on in their stupid language."

Jimmy clapped his hands together and rubbed them with enthusiasm. "We'd best figure out how to work the cafes, then!"

We soon hit upon a method. While walking past cafes we'd eyeball them for available sets. Ideally there'd be at least two different groups of girls and an empty table between them. If so we'd sit down, order coffee, and then build up our presence. Mostly that involved leaning back in our chairs and talking loudly about how awesome we were. Our peripheral vision would be alert to any glances in our direction that might wishfully be considered in IOI. After that, it was simple Mystery Method – open indirectly, stack a little bit with some kind of tease or playful push to gauge how receptive the girls seemed. If they responded well, we'd chat for a minute before rolling off. If they were too cool for school, we'd roll off immediately. We'd build more value, fish for more IOIs, and look for an opportune time to make a longer go of the conversation. After five or ten minutes, we would make an indirect statement of interest and take a phone number.

For a street gamer, that's an awful amount of fannying around to get a single number, but Jimmy loved the convoluted route, and Zagreb was the kind of place where cafes were stuffed full of hot girls like a boat out of Libya is with terrorists. Just half an hour in a Zagreb cafe gives you a shot at half a dozen hot girls. The fourth time we tried it, we were having difficulty pulling in IOIs from a table of three hot girls we liked. Furrowing our eyebrows, we considered strategy.

"We could pawn off that group of lads," suggested Jimmy. At the next table sat four high-school boys in baseball caps and t-shirts puffing on e-cigarettes. They were full of happy boisterous energy, eyeing every girl who walked past but never thinking of saying a word.

Jimmy and I on our first road trip

"Excuse me, lads," he opened, leaning over a little to the next table. "We were just talking about football and wondered who is the big team in this town. We mean with the locals, the Manchester City of this town, not the United."

Talking to teenage boys about football as an interested outsider wondering who he should support? Why, you couldn't ask for a better opener. The boys immediately sat up and enthusiastically outlined why Dynamo were the team to watch. We let them talk for five minutes, prodding them with follow-up questions while gradually leaning back and lowering our own voices. The girls we wanted had noticed the commotion, seeing two cool foreigners leaning back while a group of local boys seemed to be trying to impress them. We got our IOIs and opened the girls.

As it turned out the girls were, unsurprisingly, headed to the islands the next day so the set was dead. Acknowledging this, Jimmy segued off into doing the lads a good turn. "Girls, there are some cool young men I want you to meet," he said, waving his arm expansively to cover the teenage kids. "They've been helping us out with local knowledge."

He then introduced the two groups and left them to it, the boys eagerly changing seats to the table next to the hotties. Jimmy left a grandiose tip, pulled on his flat cap, and walked out.

"My work here is done."

This was the beginning of what we'd call the Value Tap. Jimmy had already tapped me for two years, but this was the first time we'd tried theorising it as an offensive manoeuvre on third parties. It was not simple AMOGing, a term to describe positioning yourself above a man who enters your set with the intent of stealing it (or conversely, invading his set). This was about using a neutral bystander to build your own value and work you into a set they have no connection to.

Consider a keg of beer on a rack behind a bar. Imagine you insert a small tap at the bottom out of view from everyone else. This allows you to siphon off a steady trickle of beer until eventually it's all been transferred from the keg to your stomach. When the keg owner finally goes for a drink, he's left with an empty barrel but can't understand why. That's how Jimmy worked his friends in social situations. He'd developed an arsenal of subtle tricks to leech value that were imperceptible to all except an expert in social dynamics who was looking precisely for them. His plan allowed him to drain his friends until he was subconsciously identified by nearby girls as "the cool one of the gang." He'd be the one leaning with his back against the bar, looking out at the dance floor, while all his friends crowded round, leaning in to hear whatever he might be saying. He was so known for it that we called that technique the Jimmy Horseshoe, and I'd used it effectively on Daniela a month earlier.

We'd been in an arms race since 2011, when I'd first figured him out and begun to develop defensive countermeasures to his value tap. For example, when he locked himself in at the bar to build a horseshoe, I'd lock myself in right next to him and then start to talk louder. That meant he had to talk even louder than me so I'd drop my voice *really* low. He'd damaged his hearing in his twenties playing in bands so he'd have to lean into me to hear what I was saying. If I kept the conversation interesting enough he wouldn't realise I was counter-tapping him, and now onlooking girls would identify *me* as the cool guy. It was the same in street game; I noticed that no matter how fast we walked, he was always half a step ahead of me in order to present himself as the leader to oncoming girls. At first my reaction was to take a few steps to the side so we were no longer a pair, but that wasn't ideal. So I had fun with it. I'd keep changing my walking pace, and he'd be forced to adapt his to maintain his coveted half-step advantage. Any time we walked uphill I'd pick up speed and he'd be out of breath by the summit. Him bending over gasping for air, red-cheeked, would negate any half-step advantage for ten minutes or more.

Now that we were co-operating on cafe sets, we developed a range of value taps for other customers and for staff. It became quite easy to draw IOIs. I'd always prioritise the efficiency of street game, but value-tapping is a useful strategy to chisel out a warm open in a closed environment. It may take fifteen minutes and a cup of coffee to establish your value and only thirty seconds to find the girl doesn't fancy you, so for me, the figures don't add up relative to street game. But it's another tool.

It was while searching for a value-tap that we met a Croatian waiter called Tom. He was a cool, young man with excellent English who we befriended while trying to draw the attention of a nearby two-set.

"Come out for a drink with me," he said. "I'll show you my favourite bar." Zagreb is a whole world away from Havana, both geographically and culturally, so we knew this wasn't a sting.

That's how we ended up in a small student bar tucked into a courtyard that was fashioned after a submarine from Jules Verne's *10,000 Leagues Below the Sea*. Tom introduced us to his social circle, one of whom was an Audrey Hepburn look-a-like called Sofija. That's no exaggeration, mind. She was just as hot as peak-Audrey and looked just like her. I didn't find out until later that she and Tom were friends-with-benefits.

Jimmy and I ran our usual Most Interesting Man In The World game on the group of half a dozen and had a blast. Sofija showed some interest in me, but I put away too many whiskeys, and I must have come across as a bit of a dick. She gave me her number nonetheless and came out for a coffee two weeks later when we revisited Zagreb. We met up at Jelacic Square, and she showed me her favourite beatnik cafe.

While the twenty-year-old Sofija looked like Audrey, she had a personality more befitting Brigitte Bardot – depraved. She told me that she'd been a wild child and her dad was in prison. Although she looked like an angel, she was definitely a dirty birdy and frequently hinted that she was a bad girl. Whereas nowadays I'd steam right in and fuck her, back in 2012 I wasn't so well-calibrated. I was into multiple dates and value-based Hemingway game, whereas when I moved over to a stronger "bad boy" game in 2014, I'd try to get laid within hours. With Sofija, I should've done the latter. As a result, her initial interest cooled and she friend-zoned me.

Men usually assume that if a girl is beautiful, then she's also psychologically balanced. Psychologists call it the halo effect: if someone has one noticeable positive trait you figure they have lots of others, too. Sofija's angelic looks tapped into my purity fantasy so I couldn't find it within me to get sleazy with her, and she lost interest in me. Live and learn.

I'd make the same mistake in the opposite direction that same week with a vampish girl called Gordana; long straight black hair, strong dark features and white twenty-two-year-old skin. Gordana trained hard in the gym and worked as a make-up artist. Although she looked like a very hot and very dirty slut, she was actually chaste and calm. Had I worked patience, comfort, and value-based Game, I'd have likely gotten her because she had a fierce sexual attraction to me from the beginning. Instead I leapt on the first show of attraction and over-cooked her.

I'd picked her up as she was waiting for a tram in Jelacic Square, and at the time I couldn't believe a girl so hot fancied me. We had some good text chats, and I took her on a date during the return leg to Zagreb in August. We went to Alcatraz Bar, and at the first hint of attraction I pulled hard. After about an hour we started making out, and I tried to pull her home. Nothing else came of it until later in the year when I was on my way to Belgrade via Zagreb. That time, I got her topless on my bed with my hand down her pants.

"No, no," she moaned. "I promised myself I wouldn't have sex tonight."

Unfortunately, there wasn't a third night, and one of the hottest girls to ever have my dick pushed against her clamped-shut mouth disappeared out of my life forever.

I failed with a different hot nineteen-year-old good girl the same week, putting my hands up her shirt in an upstairs ice cream bar but failing to get her home. Still, it was experiences like this that formed a strong positive impression of Zagreb, and it would take a couple of fruitless trips there in 2015 and 2016 to finally turn me off the city.

Drunk with Daniella

Neo Masculinity

TWENTY NINE

NEO MASCULINITY

ack in late 2009 I'd become acquainted with the burgeoning "manosphere." It was then nothing like the orderly little-boys club that it has since become. Readers coming to this book in 2017 will be entirely familiar with the main-streaming of "shitlord" culture that went as far as the US presidency with the God-Emperor Trump himself. We now know all about Pepe, meme magic, neo-masculinity, Gorilla Mindsets, the Alt-Right, "going Galt," and the rest of it. It wasn't always like that.

For those not familiar allow me to explain. There are two kinds of men in the West – Shitlords and Shitlibs. The former is a high-testosterone man who is combative, confident and mocks his enemies with a 'zero fucks given' nonchalance. Think of the kind of brawny white men who showed up alone at Hillary Clinton rallies wearing red Trump hats, heckling. He is an extreme embodiment of the K-selection mating strategy. The Shitlib is his opposite number: low-testosterone, snarky, and obsessed with signalling his moral virtue or political correctness in order to earn approval from his group. Think of an effeminate Silicon Valley tech employee with hunched shoulders and a Refugees Welcome t-shirt sipping a Starbucks latte while working on his Macbook. He represents an extreme of the r-selection mating strategy.

I hope it's clear by now that I'm a shitlord. If it's not, I've gone terribly wrong somewhere in my life.

The cultural explosion of 2016 had to start from somewhere, and in late 2009 the impending shitlord "red pill" tsunami began as a few ripples in a small pond. Back then blogs came and went; some classics like *Seasons of Tumult and Discord* or *The Better Beta* disappeared without trace while others such as *In Mala Fide* were springboards to surprisingly successful social media careers for their authors. The biggest were – excuse the extreme gayness of the name – "The Three Ro's": Roissy, Rollo, and Roosh.

While not as funny as the Three Stooges, they had just as large an impact on my intellectual development.

Together they accounted for probably 50% of all manosphere traffic and frequently blended PUA and manosphere themes. When Roosh set up his RooshV Forum and his Jezebel-for-men *Return Of Kings* online magazine, they were roaring successes, quickly catapulting him into position as the key community organiser.

Roosh is an American man of Middle Eastern lineage and a few years younger than me. He was the first manosphere/pick-up blogger, beginning his *DC Bachelor* blog (which soon became *Rooshv.com*) five years before I entered the fray as a wide-eyed novice. He blogged pseudonymously about his efforts to get laid in Washington DC, and in 2009, he released a simple pick-up guide called *Bang*. Available in e-book for $10, it substantially undercut the premium-priced pick-up books of the time and quickly became a standard text. Roissy (the all-time greatest manosphere blogger) was originally a commenter on his blog, and it was Roosh who encouraged him to blog under his own handle as *Roissy in DC*.

By 2012 I'd accrued a certain amount of notoriety after four years of blogging, and the release of my instructional manual *Daygame Nitro*. I was the first blogger to consistently post actual hidden-cam videos of my street pick-ups, dates, and even lays. This hyper-documentation of my daygame journey had netted me approximately two thousand daily readers, and I'd written the first competent daygame book. Roosh was aware of me, but we'd never met.

We swapped a few emails and realised we'd both be in Zagreb at the same time. He was living in Poland and Ukraine but had decided on some summer travel to check out alternative sites. He'd pioneered a modern iteration of the nomadic Euro-lifestyle, something that had been common as far back as the 1920s amongst Americans and upper-class British with money to burn – yet another indication that every generation has its adventurous men who will rediscover the same wheezes as those decades before them, and PUA was simply my generation's iteration. Roosh had recently released his own daygame book called *Day Bang*. Our styles were diametric opposites so I was very curious to meet him: Was he any good? Was he getting laid? If so, what was his quality like?

So at 8pm on a Wednesday night, Mick and I stood under the big horse statue in Jelacic Square waiting for Roosh to show. He finally came wandering over wearing blue jeans, trainers, and a zipped-up dark jacket. Just a regular guy. In fact, if there was any one phrase I'd use to describe Roosh and his instructional material it would be that: just a regular guy. He was calm, humble, and engaging. Although clearly confident and socially competent, he lacked the playful grandiosity that Jimmy, Mick, and I worked so hard to achieve. This was reflected in our daygame method: we'd accuse girls of being drug dealers or hamsters, pulling them off-balance, and weaving a web of nonsense around them. In contrast, Roosh recommended making inoffensive small talk and quietly filtering for the Yes Girls through a pick-up equivalent of the sales funnel. A salesman would say RSG carefully nurtured our leads whereas Roosh quickly filtered his, the different ethos in sales being mirrored in pick-up.

We had a couple of drinks sitting at a high table in the beer garden of a pub facing onto a heavily-wooded park. The streets were empty, and only a couple of mediocre girls flitted past us in the bar. Roosh made a half-arsed attempt pinging a set, but mostly we were talking about travel, game, and writing.

After saying goodbye a few hours later, Mick and I walked back to our apartment. "I liked him," I said. "He's not weird at all."

Roosh and I had drinks again a couple of days later. I'd been reading his blog for a couple of years now, so I had a pretty good handle on his ideas and values. I felt like he was missing a trick. Once we were sufficiently inebriated to dispense with social subtleties, I spoke my mind.

"Mate, whether you like it or not, you're in a unique position," I started up, gulping down some cold Croatian beer. "I can see you're pretty reclusive and unassuming, just pottering around in cafes on your laptop and looking to pick off a local Euro girl here and there."

"I like the life," he agreed.

"Sure, me too. But the thing is, you are now the de-facto leader of the manosphere. You have the traffic and the forum. It's all well and good writing *Bang Ukraine* or *Bang Iceland,* but that's not what you're built for."

I had to call him Bert because he'd decided to use fake names while travelling after an unpleasant episode in Estonia when locals had read his blog, realised he was in town, then organised a witch-hunt to run him out. It felt so weird sitting across from him and saying, "Bert."

"At the moment, you're using your notoriety to troll haters and sell books. I'm not saying you should stop, but you're in a position of leadership. Use it!"

"What do you mean?" he asked.

"You have an organisation. There are thousands of lost little boys on the internet looking to you for advice on how to live their lives. For years, you've mostly told them how to talk to girls or suggested some interesting books to read. You can leverage that audience and start to have a real impact on culture."

Bert/Roosh nodded. He'd been thinking along similar lines himself but hadn't yet actioned his plans. Although Roosh came across as chilled and calm, he didn't seem to be very happy. Travelling solo and living alone for months on end starves a man of male friendship, especially men who have the Game and red pill knowledge required to have serious conversations without biting your tongue or blowing up in exasperation. His player career was burning out, and he was at a loss as to the next big project to motivate him. I'd get a similar burn out in 2015.

We drank until closing time then stumbled through Jelacic Square. Before shaking hands and waving goodbye, Roosh said, "It was nice meeting you. I'll send you an email because I'd like you to do a guest post on my blog."

The next day he started a "Meeting Krauser" post on his forum and said very nice things about me. I replied on the forum there to return the favour. We had mutual respect. The more I thought about it, the more surreal it seemed. When I'd dipped my toes into the manosphere waters in 2009, Roosh was a big deal. I knew him as the creator of a small media empire, whereas I was just some pathetic chump living in a grotty apartment in South London, still waiting for my first kiss from the Game. Three years later we were meeting as equals in the middle of Zagreb and shooting the shit about girls, travel, and life.

It represented progress for me. I was smoothly transitioning from a wannabe to a somebody. The current version of me doesn't give a rat's ass for social hierarchies, climbing, or reputation. I've embraced my solo wanderer identity that is the natural me. But in 2012, I still felt like there was something above and beyond my current station in life. I imagined there was a "top table" to which I didn't yet belong, be that in business, society, girls, or anonymous internet writers who live in tiny apartments in the quiet suburbs of Warsaw Pact countries.

Roosh was head of the top table for the latter and my overriding impression of him was that he was of similar interests to myself and doing similar things with similar success. It was both satisfying and underwhelming.

Not long later he started *Return Of Kings*, initially with a mission to create an easy-to-read online magazine for male interests. Leveraging his high profile and online savvy, it became a rapid success. Together with his forum moderator "Tuthmosis" and former *In Male Fide* proprietor Matt Forney, he hit upon a formula to take his website viral: trolling mentally unstable degenerates for hate-clicks. They pumped out a series of Top Five list articles of reasons not to date fat girls and feminists, or troll-jobs about how rape should be legalised on private property. It was a roaring success. Delicate snowflake millennials were triggered the whole world over and hate-shared the articles on Facebook and Tumblr. Before long *Return of Kings* hit two million page views per month, and Roosh was laughing all the way to his Clickbank.

Return of Kings quickly raced to the bottom and became impossible to read due to increasing juvenile lowest-common-denominator writing, but I could see the social dynamics at work and couldn't help admire their ability to drive traffic. It was a pioneer of many current Alt-Right trolling tactics. For example, Roosh had been harassed by Social Justice Warriors for several years, accusing him of the most outlandish things. They'd really made his life in Europe uncomfortable, yet he'd been unable to hit back against the smears, death threats, and so on. BUT. He was now sitting on a two-million-views-a-month website that ranked high in Google searches. So what came next was the elusive obvious: He wrote hit pieces on his harassers.

Both mainstream and social media were infested with lying Marxists seeking to attack critics of the Leftist narrative. They had it in for Roosh because he advised men how to get laid and to stand up for themselves, something feminists cannot possibly allow. Roosh realised these SJWs were extremely vulnerable, they were usually fat, ugly, frequently on psychiatric medication, and possessed no employable skills. So whenever one attacked him, he'd dig up a little dirt on them (there was *always* dirt on this kind of person) and write an article displaying their real name and employer's company prominently. Bingo! Any Google search by prospective employers or romantic partners would find Roosh's article as the top search result, and the SJW would find people quietly disappearing from their lives.

As I write these words, Roosh has almost broken into the mainstream, reinventing himself as a public intellectual. His 2015 speaking tour took him to New York, Toronto, and London, where he lectured packed rooms about his conception of neo-masculinity. John went to the London talk and was unimpressed.

"Absolute shit. He just rambled on and loads of weird worshippers tried mobbing him," said John.

I think he was probably over-stating for dramatic effect, a habit of John's. *Return of Kings* also shifted direction around this time and became a much better and more high-brow publication. The manosphere had grown and now had many educated and eloquent writers, some of whom wrote for RoK.

Ever the savvy self-publicist, Roosh deliberately leaked the speaking tour meeting venues to the media in advance while actively baiting them online. Predictably, SJWs picketed the shows and called in bomb threats, creating dramatic stories for local television news to gossip about and raise his profile further. Roosh captured video footage of himself, the intellectual, having his free speech suppressed in Toronto. There was even a big campaign to deny him an entry visa to Canada, and the mayor of Toronto spoke out against him.

This played very well to his audience on the Roosh V Forum but rather less with his fellow "Three Ro" Rollo Tomassi, who accused him of bringing down hate, anger, and derision onto the manosphere for his own personal gain while risking the anonymity of his audience with such grandstanding. My own opinion is somewhere in the middle – he's a shameless and reckless self-promoter, but his message of renewing Western Civilisation and combating misandry is one I enthusiastically support, and thus I'm all in favour of his grandstanding to get that message into the mainstream.

I felt like I occupied a strange limbo, neither an anonymous chump nor an all-conquering superstar. I'd started my game journey as "outside the circle," as one of thousands who read books and blogs written by the well-known guys. Now I was inside the circle. I was friends with those of the big names in London who I wanted to know. My "arrival" on the international scene came when waking up on the morning of August 31st to find the "Three Ro's" all had their top blog-post about me on the same day.

Roosh had published my guest post "Direct Daygame For Beginners." Roissy had written about me and Steve Jabba in "Street Kiss Close Analysis." Rollo still had as his most recent post something he'd written about me in passing the day before. It was all a bit odd, especially as the three men didn't ever seem to collude with each other in planning content.

It never crossed my mind that I could be like the celebrity PUAs Mystery or Tyler or Neil Strauss. That would be like a kid picking up a guitar and thinking he was going to be Keith Richards. It never occurred to me back at the start of my daygame journey that I'd be a thought leader on my own little patch of the Game-Manosphere world. The upper echelons are reserved for superstars cut from a different cloth. Nonetheless as I progressed I began to catch up and then surpass people I'd looked up to. First I was outgrowing the noobs on the forums who'd been my first wings in 2009. Then RSG began to split between the active guys getting laid (Jimmy, Mick, Fernando, Lee, and myself) and the others who had girlfriends and were just enjoying the social scene. I'd also started outperforming Jimmy, the leader of the gang. I'd gotten laid on trips where he hadn't, and I'd completely shut him down that night in Dubrovnik.

Admittedly, when my hubris abated I'd realise the main reason Jimmy didn't get laid much was he just didn't try as hard as I did. It wasn't until 2014, when I finally surpassed one hundred notches, that I'd relate to Jimmy's ambivalence with cranking the handle on the notch conveyor belt. He'd banged over a hundred girls before we'd even met, so racking up notches for the sake of it was old news to him. Nonetheless, his losing that incremental edge in status he'd always enjoyed over us would change the group dynamic in ways I wasn't ready for.

This pattern appeared to me first behind a fog that gradually cleared until I could relate it to other areas of my life. My professional finance career had been the same way. I'd start at the bottom without ego, very conscientiously learning and improving. My ability would increase faster than my self-conception and then there'd be that moment when I'd look around and realise I'd surpassed everybody. I got lucky in the genetic jackpot that my brain finds it relatively easy to figure out patterns and how to do things. Then I do the work, and the results come.

In these moments, however, I'm at my least humble.

I still had to work hard. I lost more than I won, and there was an upper level of girls I hadn't yet cracked. Already people were recognizing me on the street, "Hey Nick, I read your blog and you said blah blah blah," and then they'd ask me technical questions. Men were willing to pay me £1,000 to hang out on holiday and learn Game. Life was changing.

I'm naturally reclusive, so it was often uncomfortable. People argued about me on the internet: "I think Krauser would say this," and someone replied, "No, no, I think he would say that." *Just ask me, lads!* I imagine Roosh had similar experiences on an exponentially grander scale.

Though I liked Roosh on a personal level and greatly admired his political activism, I just didn't rate his Game. I found his *Day Bang* book disappointing – it seemed like a manual for low-value men to have crushingly boring chats with disinterested girls. I kept my opinions to myself at first, but a schism soon opened up between the direct London style and the indirect Roosh style. Not long after Roosh visited London so I invited him for a drink with Steve Jabba and I. Steve is rarely able to hold his tongue, so he was soon berating Roosh over some trivial Game theory disagreement, and I didn't enjoy being in the middle of it. Steve thinks everyone should agree with him, and he was needled by Roosh's vastly superior public profile despite having (what Steve thought of as) vastly inferior game. The drinks didn't go well.

An uneasy peace held throughout 2013, but by the time my *Daygame Mastery* book came out in early 2014, things were strained. Any time Roosh posted on his blog about daygame, fans of my London style would descend on the comments to tell him he was wrong. I stayed completely out of it, but I was tarred with the same brush nonetheless, and Roosh ran out of patience. As far as he was concerned, he'd been polite and friendly, and the London guys were attacking him. Then the London daygamers started reviewing my products on his forum; competing products to his own. I didn't ask anyone to post reviews, but I didn't discourage it either. I think the guys just enjoyed winding him up.

His tolerance expired, and he began looking for a pretext to ban me from his websites. That pretext came when I posted in a "Post Your Controversial Opinions" thread in his off-topic forum. My post listed opinions more-or-less what Roosh himself now states publicly, but this was early 2015 and Donald Trump hadn't yet shifted the Overton Window of what opinions can be permissibly expressed in public. The moderator suspended me for seven days, and then shortly after Roosh made the ban permanent without letting me respond.

I had no problem with him banning me, but then he went on a dissembling dishonest tirade against me, accusing me of all kinds of things and changing his rationale several times over a few days. It was all very gay. That was the beginning of him disappearing up his own arse, banning me for blatantly obvious business and personal reasons (which were entirely understandable), but posturing like he was taking a moral position to protect his audience.

The Alt-Right forum MPC.dot got involved and trolled Roosh's platforms mercilessly, and it became another flash-in-the-pan manosphere controversy. One wag summed it up beautifully on Twitter:

"Banned for expressing controversial opinions in thread for controversial opinions on forum specialising in controversial opinions. Troll job: A+"

I was proud of that.

ISTANBUL

Shaken And Stirred

CHAPTER
THIRTY

SHAKEN AND STIRRED

ick and I sat at a table outside the Argyll Arms pub just around the corner from the Oxford Circus tube station. We were sipping ale and enjoying what remained of the September 2011 sunshine. He was explaining a hotel scam to me, and it hurt my brain. Mick *always* had a scam lined up. His dad was a used car salesman and very good at it. Putting one over on the punters was a proud family tradition.

"The thing with Latin America is they don't speak English well and don't use the same websites we do in the Anglosphere," he said. Well, he didn't actually use the word "Anglosphere" because it was much too high falutin' for him. He's from Tasmania.

"So my mate Justin has set up a hostel review site. He's padding it out with fake reviews of places he's stayed in. It's got graphics and comments and star reviews. Everything, mate. Looks totally legit."

"But it's not?" I queried.

"Pfffffff!" he responded, spraying spit into the pint of ale he now lifted to his lips to drink. "You think like a sap. Can't you see the angle?"

"No, frankly, I can't. I don't think like you do Mick. I go to work, I get paid. I don't have any schemes. My stuff is above-board."

Mick had landed a well-paid job as a credit controller in London despite possessing literally zero financial experience. He'd just invented fake jobs on his resume, lied convincingly at the interview, and arranged to have a genuine credit controller friend (who had coached him pre-interview) on speed dial for his first month at work to solve the problems that came up. That he was still working there a year later left me perturbed, being unable to figure who was to blame for the injustice; Mick the fraudster; the company for failing their due diligence; or the entire finance industry for requiring exam credentials for a job that literally any fat Aussie bullshitter could do with only minimal coaching.

Mick fumbled inside his blue leather racing jacket, custom made by an old lady in Clapham Junction, to pull out his phone. He tapped his fat fingers at the screen, and Justin's website loaded up. I'll admit, it looked legit.

"I've been helping him. When we tour Mexico we will send emails to every hostel owner promising to review their business if they give us free food and lodgings."

It actually worked. Long after I'd returned from Mexico, Mick would go back to Latin America for adventure and – ultimately – in order to find a wife. I think his website scam paid his accommodation costs for the first year.

As the months wore on, Mick would gradually talk me around into a more entrepreneurial view of the world. He could survey any environment like a con-man at an old folks home, identifying disparate items, alliances, and situations within any environment then piecing them together in novel ways to find an "angle" to make money. Game was just one of these scams, and it's why he took to it so naturally.

I was only half-listening. A tall, slim girl had just walked past, her thick, black hair flowing. She looked like a Bond Girl. Mick was rummaging around in his plastic carrier bag for half a sausage roll he'd bought at M&S earlier in the afternoon, so he didn't see her. I leapt from my chair – girls that hot were a rarity in London.

I pressed "Record" on the spy cam clipped into my jacket pocket then clip-clopped down the street to catch up with her just outside Bella Pasta on the corner.

"Excuse me!"

Sanaz was from Turkey and visiting London for a three-week crash course at a very expensive language school located inside Regent's Park. Her English was broken, but I managed to convey my interest and took a number. She didn't appear very animated so it felt flat, but she replied to my texts and agreed to a date the next evening.

We had tea in Camelia's Tea Shop and then went to the upstairs bar oft the John Snow on the other side of Carnaby Street. It was while we stood at the bar waiting to order pints that I noticed her two rings and decided it was a good way to test how she'd react to me touching her.

"Those two rings are nice," I said, scooping up her hand into mine. "Is there a story behind them?"

I absolutely didn't give a shit what the story may be, so when she gently withdrew her hand and said the smaller ring was a gift from her grandmother, I just nodded and pretended I was paying attention.

"This second ring is for good luck," she said, clutching it against her chest and looking skywards. "I'm auditioning for a new role."

"Oh, you're an actress?" I said. She'd told me the day before on the street, but I'd literally forgotten. Actress, waitress, toilet cleaner...it was all the same to me.

"Yes, this is a big role. I'm down to the shortlist of the last three candidates. The casting director told me privately that if I can improve my English, the job is mine. That's why I came to London, to study."

I paid the barman, gripped a packet of salted peanuts between my teeth, and picked up the two pints of Samuel Smiths Stout. We walked over to a corner booth and sat down.

"What's the role?" I asked, taking a sip of beer. I just assumed it was theatre or some other such cultural bullshit.

"Do you know James Bond? The next movie is shot in Istanbul, and they want a local actress to be the Bond Girl."

It's rare that I ever blow beer out of my nose, but this was one such occasion.

"Are you okay?" she gasped, fumbling in her bag for tissues. "Did something happen?"

"Fine, fine," I said, wiping snot off my nose with the back of my hand. "It just went down the wrong way. So, tell me about your grandmother."

That night I lay on my bed staring at the ceiling. The date had gone well. We hadn't kissed but she liked me and despite mediocre English, she'd been intelligent, thoughtful, and easy to talk to. Exactly my kind of girl. I let my mind wander into the realm of grandiosity, one of my favourite hobbies.

Every boy loves James Bond. Like the book jackets say, "Every man wants to be him. Every woman wants to be with him." He travels the world on Her Majesty's Secret Service, from Havana to Rio de Janeiro, from Moscow to Milan. He drinks vodka martinis shaken-not-stirred, plays baccarat, and has exquisite taste.

So do you, Nick, I thought. *So do you. Except for getting shot at, that's your life.*

Bond is cool because he fucks the hottest girls in the world. Bond Girls are the world's gold standard of "hot bird," and there's nothing so sultry as the girlfriend of the super-villain who Bond steals from under his nose. Sanaz had been offered the part to be that very girl in *Skyfall*.

> *Right, Nick, let's get this straight, I thought. James Bond gets into scrapes, gets shot, gets captured, and then, after saving the world from super villainy, right at the end he gets to fuck the hot girl. You, my cheeky, young Geordie lad, are going to fuck the same girl, but it's only going to cost you two pints and a cup of coffee. Maybe an M&S ready meal, too.*

The facts were clear. I was of higher value than James Bond. I slept well that night.

NICK KRAUSER

A few days later we had our second date, meeting at Camden Town to walk through the market eating street food and browsing boutiques. We followed the canal along to Primrose Hill and past the spot where I'd fucked Alla and come on Chiara's face. Then we sauntered through Regent's Park. It felt on. Sanaz was talking thoughtfully about her hopes and dreams and seemed to bump into me several times on uncrowded paths.

I took her to a wine bar midway between the park exit and the bus stop for the Number 13 up to Château Hampstead. I was in a daze. She was leaning into me, flipping through a slide-show on her phone of her with friends dolled-up for photo shoots. Then she'd sip her red wine and blush a little.

"Let's get a drink back at the Hemingway Suite," I suggested. She nodded in agreement, and I couldn't get us to the bus stop fast enough. As the Number 13 rattled through heavy traffic, I felt the Lust Bubble bursting but once we stepped into the hallowed halls of London's premier PUA nursing home, she was full of spark again. I gave her a quick tour then we settled into the comforting darkness of the Hemingway Suite, the bright afternoon sunshine completely blacked out by the heavy drapes.

I poured myself a whiskey and topped up her red wine. We sat together on a chesterfield sofa, thigh-to-thigh. She frequently turned into me and crossed her legs towards me. Time to make a move. I pulled her in.

She moaned softly and climbed across to straddle me, her breasts mere biting distance from my mouth and her crotch heavy on mine. I ran my hands up her outer leg and hips, up past her lower ribs. She moaned again and writhed a little. I couldn't wait to unwrap this Turkish delight. I pulled her closer and our lips met.

Suddenly she pulled away. "No! I can't do this. I want to, but I can't!"

She stood up and paced the room, then came back to stand right over me. Her face was a mask of tortured indecision. She looked at me, at the space on the sofa next to me, at the paintings on the walls. Twice she turned away and fussed with ornaments. I stayed on the sofa quietly watching, hoping she'd resolve her indecision in my favour.

"I like you Nick, really I do. I want this. But I just can't. This isn't me."

Fifteen minutes later she was getting into a cab home. Fuck.

That was it – my ego was fully invested. I literally could not imagine a better score than to be fucking a hot Bond Girl from a Bond movie that would be playing in the cinemas at that very moment. I had six months or so to make the fantasy real. Six months before I could walk into the HMV record store and watch other men pick up the Bond Girls 2012 calendar with her on the front.

If I could pull this off, it would be mission completed. There'd be nothing left to achieve in my life.

She left London two days later, but we stayed in touch with weekly video chats. I was surprised to find she was extremely down-to-earth, living with her brother and sister in a cosy apartment in the Bebek region of Istanbul. She had no time for the red-carpet lifestyle and never seemed to attend parties, galas, or ceremonies. Her life was little different from a girl who really was a waitress or student, she just happened to be very famous in the Middle East.

It seemed *on*. While I was in Mexico, our video chats were frequently an hour long, and she'd dress up nice for some of them. One time I told her to wear her favourite hat for me, and she did. Soon she was inviting me to Istanbul for a holiday.

"You can stay at my apartment," she said.

While Jimmy, Mick, and John travelled on from Zagreb to Sarajevo in July 2012, I took a flight to Istanbul with a plan to reconnect with them in the Bosnian capital a week later. I arrived at the shopping area Taksim full of hope, stepping down from the airport bus to see Sanaz through the throng waiting for me on a low wall. She lit up when she saw me and ran over to give me a hug.

"You came! You really came! It's so nice to see you!" she gushed then hustled me into a taxi to drop off my stuff at her apartment. Oh yes!

She buzzed around in the lobby and lounge them showed me through to the guest room. "You'll stay here," she said. "My brother is next door"

Oh.

We sat on the sofa eating pasta and watching Turkish television throughout the afternoon. It was simply too hot to go outside, and even with the blinds pulled down and the air-conditioner cranked up, we were still sweating. On the plus side, Sanaz was stripped down to shorts and a vest so I had a good ogle at her. Soon enough her brother came home, and we were introduced. He was a friendly, shy man who shared a similar interest in video games.

Walking around Bebek with Sanaz

"I want to show you my favourite restaurant," she said. "It's cool enough to go outside now."

We didn't have to wait for a taxi. Her house was midway down a steep bank, and the narrow street alongside was – no exaggeration – entirely composed of yellow taxis in gridlock honking their horns. I'd find out over the week this was a permanent state of affairs; taxis honking horns 24/7. Sanaz walked us to the bottom of the hill, and we jumped in the leading taxi. Istanbul felt like an ant mound. It was beautiful and awful in equal measure, with majestic monuments and beautiful bridges harking back to the days of Constantinople while head-scarved

Arab tourists scurried around in disorderly packs reminding me it had since been conquered by Islam and turned into Istanbul.

That first evening was the best of the trip, as I was full of energy. We sat around a table in a patio underneath whirring fans and ate traditional Turkish food. Four of her friends and her sister showed up, so we chatted and drank wine. Then at the end of the evening she gave me a hug, and I retired to my quarters. I lay in bed thinking, *how do I escalate her while her brother is here?*

Sanaz was very busy, deep in negotiations for a new role on a blockbuster TV show. Her phone never stopped ringing as her agents and lawyers discussed contract details. Nonetheless she was very kind to me and every morning we'd sit on her small balcony overlooking a courtyard and eat a breakfast of fresh fruits and pastries that she cooked.

The second day was eye-opening. We were winding through a back alley near Taksim, and I noticed a pair of shifty Iraqi men following us. They'd stare, confer in a huddle, then shadow us about twenty yards behind. Several times as we stopped for ice cream or coffee, they'd seem about to approach but then thought better of it.

I wonder if they recognise me, I thought. I'd heard Turkey had a daygame community.

I saw them snap off a few sly photos on their camera phones and then finally, as we were looking in a shop window, they had the courage to approach. The taller one opened in English.

"Hi! I hope it is okay to talk. Your television show is very popular in my country Iraq. Please make photo?"

Sanaz smiled and let them take a selfie with her while I stood off to one side holding the two ice creams, which by now were dripping onto my hands and down my wrists in the punishing Istanbul heat.

"This happens a lot," she said after the men had high-fived each other and walked off grinning. "My show is syndicated around the Middle East. One time a prince of Dubai was my fan and asked to marry me."

There was never any respite. Several times as we walked along the beautiful Bebek riverside at night, paparazzi would park up their scooters and ask to take photos.

"We have an agreement," she explained. "They don't take candid photos of me, and in return I pose naturally." She then walked twenty metres along the path pretending not to notice the paparazzi who scuttled along next to her like a crab snapping off photos. That weekend I saw the pictures on the cover of a glam rag.

She also requested that I stay a few yards away from her when paparazzi were around. "I don't want to explain in interviews who you are," she said. Given that I'd never told her about my secret daygame shenanigans, her circumspection over her reputation was even wiser than she knew.

Sanaz mixed with the elite of the Turkish glitterati, friends with billionaires, tycoons, actresses, and models, but only when it was professionally required. Most of the time she hung out with her brother, sister, and a few make-up artists she'd gotten close to on her way up. I'd expected her to be on yacht parties and walking the red carpet at film premieres. Her humble attitude was refreshing and made me like her more. I felt like I was an insider, seeing the real world behind the Great Gatsby.

Three days in, and I still hadn't managed to kiss her. There always seemed to be somebody else in the room. We were sitting on her balcony as I stuffed my face with some sandwiches she'd lovingly prepared.

"Are they good? Do you like them?" she asked hopefully.

"Mmmmnppph, mmmnp, gggmmmph," I replied and scooped a glob of hummus onto a cucumber stick and sent it down the hatch. Sanaz looked off into space, her eyes glazed and wistful. What she said next has stuck with me and represented a major inner-game breakthrough.

"Nick, you have the best life of anyone I know."

I put my sandwich down for a moment and thought about her lifestyle, her apartment, her friends, and her fame. "What do you mean?" She had Arab princes for suitors, and one of her best friends was married to a multi-billionaire shipping magnate.

She gave a wan smile, almost sad.

"Oh, you're so *free*. You can do whatever you want. Go anywhere you want. You have cool friends and complete control of your life. It's not like that for me. My friends and I get followed everywhere. We have all these parties where we must glad-hand everyone."

Now she was looking directly at me, inspecting my face. She looked like a child who'd fervently believed in Santa Claus and clung to that belief no matter how many adults tried to crush it, and was now sitting opposite the real live Santa Claus. Watching him stuff yet another cucumber and hummus stick into his gaping maw.

Breakfast overlooking the garden

"Money and fame are traps," she said. "The richest people I know are the least happy. The demons that drive them to get rich also tell them they are never rich enough. They have no freedom. No peace."

I was stunned. For a moment, I stopped eating.

I'd been very ego-based up until this moment. I had it in my head that there were ever higher layers of social life, with the rich and famous dining at the figurative top table. As a mere whipper-snapper from a council estate in Newcastle, I was like one of Fagin's street urchins who could only press his nose up against the restaurant window while the higher classes dined on delicacies inside. I'd never been one of the cool kids. I'd always suspected the whole concept of high society was a myth, that they were no better – nor any happier – than the common people, but being on the outside I wondered if it was merely sour grapes to think so. Now Sanaz was both showing and telling me my suspicion had been correct all along.

Think of *The Great Gatsby*. He throws ostentatious parties at his mansion with the social and political elite invited. It's all a massive front to persuade himself that he's "arrived" and worthy of his childhood sweetheart. Those parties are all sizzle and no steak. There *is* no cool gang. There *is* no higher level of socialising. It's still just four walls, bottles of alcohol, and lots of shaved chimps moving from room to room. It's just a student house party on a higher budget. While *Rock Solid Game* engaged in our own grandiosity, the elites engaged in theirs.

That's what Sanaz taught me. I was the guy on the outside looking in. I was the guy driving past the Great Gatsby's parties seeing the fireworks and hearing the raucous laughter thinking how amazing those parties must be and wondering what it must be like to be a part of it all, sitting at the top table. Sanaz had a place at that top table but rarely RSVP'd. She wanted to hang out with her sister, her brother, and make-up artist friends.

Thinking about this I realised her apartment only had one thing betraying her fame, an artistically shot portrait of herself that was framed and hung on the wall in the guest room. That aside, a Lloyd Grossman character shooting a *Through the Keyhole* show in her apartment would never guess her job. She was actually less grandiose than I was. I was living in a broken down Jewish care home with a motley crew of degenerate PUAs and bigging myself up like I'm better than James Bond. She was an actual Bond Girl who just sat on her sofa chatting to completely neurotypical friends like any other young lady. It was chastening. It was also *liberating*.

We went out a few more times that week, fishing from Galata Bridge and cooking our catch at a friend's house party that evening. We had coffee in a small hipster cafe tucked away in a Taksim back alley. She also drove us out to the city limits to a half-completed apartment complex where she had a modelling shoot, and then a dozen of us splashed around in the pool for an hour. By now I was really suffering from isolation as almost nobody spoke English. It was also dawning on me that five days in, and I was almost certainly in the friend-zone.

Fishing in Istanbul

I got Jimmy onto Facebook chat and brought him up to speed on the problem.

"I need help," I said. "I can't get her into a position to smoothly escalate. She's literally never alone. She's got exes hitting on her, the phone's always ringing. I don't know how to play it."

"You have to put your cards on the table. You have to say to her, look – I fancy you as a woman. That's how I see you."

"It's not that easy. I feel like I'm getting neutralised. Another two days of this and my balls will shrink and disappear."

"You have to bite the bullet," he advised. "There's no way you can fly into Sarajevo without having at least told her you want to fuck her. You'll regret that forever."

I lay in her guest room bed that evening knowing Jimmy was right. But why was it so difficult in this case whereas I'd fiercely escalated girls such as Dorota within an hour? Half of it was the situation, I was trapped in a foreign country, surrounded by people I didn't know and who couldn't speak my language, and Sanaz was outrageously busy closing a deal that was of critical importance to her career. The other half was my ego. I wasn't treating her as simply another hot girl. She was the *Bond Girl*. She was the trophy!

How gay. Only women care about their partner's social status.

Nick, I asked myself, *What would you prefer: A smoking hot girl with massive jugs and a tight ass who works the cash register in Argos, or a less hot girl with less massive jugs who is internationally famous for her talents?*

I had to admit, the massive jugs win out every time. I was reaching an important moment in my sexual preferences: It really doesn't matter what the rest of the world thinks of your girl. All that matters is: (I) do you fancy her? and (II) is your dick inside her?

Don't get me wrong; Sanaz was a beautiful woman and elegant in an Audrey Hepburn manner. But she was still an eight. The world is full of eights. She'd make a great wife, but I was interested in casual sex, so all that additional personality depth and accomplishment didn't really matter to me. At least not in that moment.

I kept thinking back to Sanaz sitting on her balcony watching me eat her food and finding out that she envied my freedom. It was a "light bulb" moment of clarity when I asked myself, why am I looking to magazines, TV, and other people to tell me what the high life is? Am I drawn to The Most Interesting Man In The World archetype for the superficial trappings of his success or for the substantive experiences of his life? What is it that's *actually* important to me? It didn't take long to settle on two things; my time and my freedom. Everything else was subservient to maximising those two core values.

It was great. Sanaz had helped me boil away the bullshit and get right down to the hard nucleus of what really mattered in my life. Time and freedom. That's it. Now that I knew my centre, I could build back up from it, certain that the foundation was solid.

This led to a new train of thought: What was the value I was offering girls? Why was someone with Sanaz's beauty and limitless options coming back to the Hemingway Suite with me, Skype chatting me every week, and inviting me to her home? What was I offering her that she wasn't getting better from a local Turkish guy? It was a genuine conundrum because I'd seen photos of her last boyfriend, he was a heartthrob television actor with sky-high SMV.

Taksim high street

Sanaz had led me to the answer; time and freedom. I personified a girl's release from the responsibilities and frustrations of regular life. A girl would be ambling down the street like any other day, and I'd suddenly smash into her world. My daygame patter would offer her a purity of emotional connection, an honesty and anonymity unavailable elsewhere – a means by which she can be her true self without pretence. I'd hear this many times from girls over the years, that they felt free and alive with me. I represented the spirit of adventure.

Girls love this emotional sensitivity. We can take them on a ride through all their emotional peaks and troughs, giving them excitement. The sex is almost incidental. I was edging closer to an understanding of the magic of daygame seduction and the adventure sex-frame. We offer them something billionaires cannot buy for them, and thus once in a while, we can steal a billionaire's girl like Bond steals the super villain's girl.

This was a massive step towards shedding a slavish external referencing and moving towards a more solid internal reference.

The next day Sanaz was clearing up the lunch plates, and her sister was in the bathroom. Finally, six days in, I had her alone. "Come here a minute," I said, walking into the guest room. "I want to tell you something private."

She followed me in, and I laid my cards on the table, telling her I fancied her, and I'd come on this trip because I wanted to move us forwards romantically. She knew it was coming and probably wondered why I'd taken so long. Her answer was clearly previously prepared.

"Nick. When we met I genuinely found you attractive, sexually. I still do. However, I've thought about it a lot. I'm twenty-nine years old, and I want a family. I'm looking for a husband. You're a casual sex guy so you can't give me what I need."

She had me there.

We got on fine after that. We knew where we stood and the elephant in the room was dismissed. Sanaz had a big contract signing on the penultimate day, so she recommended I take a ferry to the Prince's Islands in the river near Istanbul. They're beautiful old resorts, and I had a good day out like a normal tourist.

While kicking pebbles along a side street my phone rang again. It was the fourth time that day, always the same UK number. My Vodafone plan stiffed me for £2 every time I picked up overseas, and I'd already answered several times earlier that week to be greeted with automated marketing calls. I'd learned to reject the calls so I rejected this one for the fourth time that day.

A moment later I had a text message from the same number. "Mate, it's Tom. You need to take this call."

We hadn't spoken in nearly a year, and were most definitely not on speaking terms. This felt ominous. I replied okay, and he called.

"Mate, we're all in big trouble," he said, breathlessly. "Me and Jon Matrix are teaching in Oslo this week for Andy. Yesterday Jon was in a set and some local guy came up and started screaming at him. He whipped out his phone and started showing the girl YouTube videos of Jon doing daygame. He was proper white-knighting."

I could understand his consternation, but it was nothing to do with me. Oslo is a shithole with fat, ugly birds. I had no intention of ever returning.

"We went back to Morten's house," he continued. "It was just weird. Then a bit later we were sitting in that big lounge, and somehow the guys started talking about same day lays. Someone put your Oslo SDL up on the TV, the video of you fucking that dancer girl."

Uh-oh, *now* my spider-sense was tingling. I'd blurred her face, and there was nothing pornographic, but that video was skating close to the line.

"Well, there was this guy sitting at the back of the lounge. He recognised your girl. We just found out today that he told her and her boyfriend. They've freaked out and reported you to the police for rape."

"What?" I replied, totally confused. "How can I be reported for rape because of a video where a girl is literally saying 'I love your dick in my ass, fuck me harder.' I even fucked her again a few days later. It's ridiculous."

"I dunno, man. Maybe it was Antony groping her afterwards."

"What's that got to do with me? I wasn't even in the room. Anyway, like I said we met again a few days later, and she was happy. We chatted on Facebook a few times since."

"I'm just saying what happened," he said. He was rambling and in his panicky state not making much sense. "I'm flying back to Wales. I'm going to smash my hard drive and throw it into the sea."

I thanked him for the call and assured him it was all news to me. I'd been online earlier that day and not heard a whisper from

Heidi, the Oslo dancer, either on Facebook or my blog. I was now on a small Turkish island, without an internet connection, so I called my brother and gave him my login details so he could immediately remove the post, delete the YouTube video, and put Heidi on my restricted list on Facebook. Then I waited to see what would happen.

Nothing happened.

Heidi never contacted me, and she even liked some of my Facebook photos over the next few months. The only evidence that this entire drama even occurred was Tom telling me it had. There was no corroborating evidence. The whole thing was nonsensical. To this day I still don't know what, if anything, actually happened. Was Tom trying to do me a good turn to make up for his earlier bad behaviour, or was he covering his own arse after an unknown scheme of his went wrong?

I arrived in Sarajevo airport a defeated man, though serene and calm having learned about myself in Istanbul. The RSG boys were out drinking in a bar around the corner from where Franz Ferdinand was shot and World War One started. I joined them and brought a bottle of beer out to their table. Jimmy had already informed them of my failure with Sanaz.

"So let's get this straight," chuckled Mick, his manboobs wobbling under his t-shirt from the energy of his self-satisfied laughter. "She took the television series job and not the movie one?"

"Yes. Her agent said the TV role was much better for her career. There's the so-called curse of the Bond Girls. Their careers always tank afterwards."

He had to put down his plate of burek because his hands now had the gloat-tremors. Jimmy stayed quiet, probably feeling sorry for me.

"So, and I'm checking this just in the interests of science, you understand. You flew into Istanbul for a week and then *failed* to fuck a girl who *failed* to be the Bond Girl?"

There was heavy emphasis on the word "fail." I felt like he'd waited his whole life for a moment like this. He may never get such a gloating opportunity again.

"That's really not much of a story, now, is it?" he chortled.

Eating in Bebek

CHAPTER
THIRTY ONE

Siege of Sarajevo

CHAPTER
THIRTY ONE

SIEGE OF SARAJEVO

Most men consider themselves under-sexed. Those of us who hit upon a way to bang new girls regularly will go through a period of addiction, slaking our thirst for notches as if we'd just discovered an oasis in the desert. There eventually comes a point when you've banged enough women. I was a long way from that point but both Tony and Jimmy had reached it before I'd even met them. What does a man do next? Tony was at a loss so like a drug addict taking ever more frequent hits, he focused upon ever more notches and abandoned quality standards entirely. He stopped cold approaching and fell back on online dating to sneak a procession of fat ugly women into his room.

In contrast Jimmy stepped off the hamster wheel and became more choosy. He gave up on notch targets and instead raised the bar for what he'd chase. Mostly this was about quality – a pursuit of the Full Audreys – but he also sought more peculiar date set-ups or wilder sex. He took more satisfaction from the craftsmanship of the chase than the kill itself, as if it was all performance art. I'd recently benefited from his change in direction with the Norwegian threesome.

Yugoslavia would be Jimmy's big challenge. It had precisely the type of women he dreamt of but there were numerous obstacles towards getting them into bed. Their culture is more traditional than most of Central Europe and the population as a whole is more K-selected than ours; meaning girls value pair-bonding, family and monogamy. There will always be casual sex somewhere in a city, but in Yugoslavia the top tier girls were less likely to be the ones partaking in it. Jimmy faced what appeared to be an intractable problem; his quality standards led him to precisely the kind of chaste, K-selected girls who were least likely to have casual sex with a fly-by-night cad. Could he square the circle?

The Franz Ferdinand museum in Sarajevo

In contrast, I was still more than happy to rack up notches with any girl pretty enough to interest me.

In our quick visit to Sarajevo earlier that spring Jimmy and I had driven up via the historic old town of Mostar, wound our way through the mountains on what seemed to be the only tarmac road in the entire country and finally found ourselves in the capital. The whole time Queen and Steppenwolf blasted out of the car speakers, and we stopped off at tiny shacks to buy coffee and burek. I'd look out the car window at hamlets tucked into the valleys below and wonder two things: What must it be like to live in such isolation and, would one of those village girls run off with me for a dirty weekend in Sarajevo?

The answer to a third question (what would her recently-retired-after-Bosnian-war father do to me if he caught me deflowering his teenage daughter?) meant I chose not ask Jimmy to park up so we could try Bosnian hamlet daygame.

We'd spent three nights in the capital that April, and after his momentary disappointment that the authorities had repaired all the charming shell holes and bullet-scarred walls by now, Jimmy was in his element. We posted up in busy bars letting our vibe and outrageous "sartorial elegance" fashion draw IOIs. He left the city with Facebook adds from three very attractive local women. For the next two months he worked them until they were eating out of his hand.

"Look at this," he'd shout from his Château bedroom, expecting me to drop everything and run in. "I've got Emina taking pictures of hamsters at the pet shop. I told her if she finds one that looks just like her, I'll give her a prize."

Emina was twenty-two, a medical student with thick glossy wop-hair and long shapely legs--the kind of girl you could take into any venue in London and she'd be the hottest there. I watched impassively as Jimmy scrolled through the Facebook chat, and yes, I had to agree, she was eating out the palm of his hand. It was masterful long-game.

"I'm calling it," he said, meaning he was staking his reputation that he'd *definitely* fuck her.

He was also chatting to Angela, an equally hot and equally classy late-twenties girl from Zagreb. They'd met on the same April road trip, and she too was enmeshed in Jimmy's masterfully-spun spider's web.

"I'm calling it," he declared about Angela, too.

Jimmy tooling multiple classy hot girls on Facebook was nothing unusual. He'd call them all "Audrey" after the *Breakfast at Tiffany's* star he idolised. Deep in his fantasy world, Jimmy was Cary Grant, an international man of mystery both respected by the community and also desired by all the classiest skirt.

"I'm in it for the tens, mate," he'd say. "I've clacked enough sevens for five lifetimes. I'd rather have two coffees with an eight than sex five times with a seven."

The math confused me, but I nodded and walked back to my bedroom to continue with Call of Duty.

"Door!" Jimmy bellowed behind me. I knew if I didn't get back up and close his bedroom door he'd just keep shouting "Door" until the early hours.

We all had peculiarities to our strong frames and Jimmy was no different. His frame reminded me of a certain breed of goat. Apparently these goats cannot be domesticated nor held in captivity. If you enclose them in a pen they will just run full-speed at the gate and ram it with their head. If the gate doesn't smash open, they'll just repeat the run-and-ram routine until they literally headbutt themselves to death. That's Jimmy's frame right there. His bar game was based on pawning, value-tapping, and reframing everyone around him to ensure he had a slight status edge over them as group leader. He didn't always switch it off in Château Hampstead and would instead dig his heels in rather than give a little and lose the frame. We all knew this by now so to preserve group harmony we tended to accommodate him, such as hanging out in his room rather than someone else's. We suspected Jimmy would never, *ever* concede enough frame to sit on someone else's bed while *they* were centre of attention.

Jimmy's frame control dynamics were masterfully hidden and it fascinated me to deconstruct them so I'd turned it into a game. In addition to the usual friendship level of interactions there was this rich vein of social dynamics to explore. I developed a whole range of defensive frame control gambits that could be running in the background. It was rather odd to be relating to my friends on two different levels but I noticed Mick and John did it too. I think it's endemic in the PUA community because we are all hyper-aware of our social value in a given situation.

Naturally the group dynamic started to shift. By becoming increasingly aware of frame control we became increasingly irked by it and sought to impose our own more often. Mick and I became less accommodating of both Jimmy's and each other's peculiarities. This came to a head in Zagreb in July with our frame control battles, vibe-tapping, and shifting alliances. It was yet another ingredient into the toxic brew that was poisoning Rock Solid Game's previously iron-clad camaraderie.

The final straw for me came the first week in Zagreb when I was having a morning shower. Rather than wait for me as agreed, Jimmy and Mick snuck out to Nocturno for breakfast, and I just heard the door slamming. I turned off the shower and stood in the lounge with my towel around my waist, fuming. "Right, you bastards. I'm having you for that," I declared to an empty room (John was exploring a park five miles away from the nearest daygame spot).

Except for one really fun night in Alcatraz bar when I was with Dorota and Jimmy was with his new girl "Mouse," that week was strained. I had a few kiss-close dates that went nowhere. Jimmy met up with Angela, but the date was a disaster. She took him to a quiet bar owned by a "friend" who was really her desperate orbiter. The landlord was sniping at Jimmy so badly that my Burnley chum texted me to come down and help fight his corner. Within five minutes the landlord had pulled a huge ceremonial knife – like from a Conan comic book – from under the bar and held it to my neck. He'd talked jovially in full-Gamma fashion like it was all a big joke, but nobody believed him. He'd simply wanted to hold a knife to my neck because he was burning with jealously against Jimmy and trying desperately to look strong and powerful in front of Angela, since now he saw her showing attraction to Jimmy.

What a strange, squalid evening. Eventually Jimmy kiss-closed Angela but she explained to him that she was looking for a serious relationship. She walked off never to be seen again. Given the tenor of the trip we all leapt on that.

"You called it!" laughed Mick. "I was in your room, and I heard those very words – 'I'm. Calling. It.'"

"That's your problem, Jimmy," I added. "It's all well and good rattling a hundred grotty sevens, but the true class, the Audreys of this world, go for genuine high-value men like myself, not semi-literate Burnley criminals."

That's Mick with the bowler hat

We were as subtle as the knife-wielding landlord. Jimmy seethed more than I realised, taking a deep breath then walking slowly to his bedroom. Angela was one of his three high-value carefully-nurtured leads and he'd been unable to square that circle. John was hiding in the kitchen, swotting up on his Java programming. John couldn't handle the pressure at all and was trying hard to convince himself what he really wanted was to ignore girls and take in the cultural splendour of the former-Yugoslavia.

Jimmy filled me in on events in Sarajevo the week I'd been away in Turkey. He'd had been flaked on by one of his Sarajevo Audreys, and the other – Emina – had friend-zoned him on the date because she wanted a boyfriend and he wasn't sticking around. Once we teased him on it, he reframed the entire incident, spinning that they hadn't really clicked, and she was too classy a girl for him to "asset strip" by luring into casual sex.

"Humphrey Bogart wouldn't just pump and dump a girl of that class," he said, hiding his disappointment at being unable to reel these girls in.

We were sitting in a Turkish-style coffee shop in the Muslim quarter, and Jimmy reclined back, folding his arms behind his head, legs stretched out crossed at the ankles. He now looked like he hadn't a care in the world. His eyes glazed over in a tell-tale retreat into fantasy, probably visualising some kind of Skyrim-Casablanca hybrid where his armour-clad adventurer swigged an enchanted +4 French 75 cocktail of glory flanked by a posse of Nords.

"Of all the gin-joints, in all the towns, in all the world, she walked into mine," he mumbled to himself, eyes now closed.

While thinking about his failure with Emina and Angela, a thought suddenly jarred me. It was like first seeing that famous optical illusion isn't just a beautiful woman but is also a wizened old hag: *I've never known Jimmy to actually bang an eight.*

Shit! Hold the phones. Let's think about this:

- Approach 8s and 9s in the street, getting them laughing and flirting: **Yes.**
- Pull 8s and 9s into long message exchanges where they seem absolutely under his spell: **Yes.**
- Meet 8s and 9s on dates, the girls dolled up beautifully like they are DTF: **Yes.**

But actually bringing these girls home and fucking them? **Not so often.** Although he was trying hard to crack the top tier, it was mostly the sevens who came back to his room. In the three years I'd known him I'd only been genuinely impressed by three of the girls he banged; a classy Polish girl he girlfriended for a while in London, a motorbike racer chick in Vilnius, and a mouthy black trashbag from Manchester who was pretty hot. The other girls were all young and pretty but not the head turners we aspired to. He was caught in that awkward limbo where the girls he got didn't interest him anymore but he wasn't quite sealing the deal on the ones that did.

I was obsessed with the intra-RSG competition, and my own need to cut the apron strings with my former-mentor, so I was inclined to take the glass-half-empty conclusion. Looking back, I can see the clear pattern of the life-cycle of a narcissistic relationship. Allow me to explain.

Narcissists progress their relationships (sexual and platonic) through three phases: Idealisation, Devaluation, Discarding. In the beginning the narcissist will lavish attention upon his partner, creating an obsessive Idealisation. He treats the partner like a shiny new toy. The obsession is all about the narcissist's self-medication to avoid his ever-gnawing inner feelings of emptiness, aloneness, and being "defective" or "deficient." Readers of *Balls Deep* will be aware I began my player's journey as a man broken by divorce and facing the terrifying realisation that I wasn't as cool, stable, or even as likeable as I'd always assumed. I soon stumbled into an RSG boot camp and was taken into the inner circle of the coolest guys I'd ever met. I idealised them, and Jimmy was the leader. For at least two years I'd love the life, would work hard to change my identity and improve my game, and constantly defer to Jimmy's greater pick-up knowledge.

The professional wrestling industry has known for decades that the way to build up your hero (the "babyface") is to make his enemy (the "heel") terrifying so that his glory in victory is all the greater. For a narcissist, the glory is his narcissistic supply. The greater the narcissist believes the source of that supply, meaning the more impressive the subject of his idealisation, the better the narcissist feels. And naturally because the concept of the new partner is so magnified, it is not sustainable over time. It is a teetering pedestal which will inevitably topple when the wind starts to blow. I'd built up Game, RSG, and Jimmy into grandiose semi-mythical figures.

Admittedly, he'd encouraged me to do precisely that. We were all bigging ourselves up, constantly.

Next comes Devaluation. In the psychology literature, I've only ever seen the Devaluation phase written from the perspective of the victim rather than the narcissist, so I'm not entirely clear what motivates this phase. My guess is the narcissist develops a growing tolerance to the emotional spikes of receiving supply from his partner, and it no longer feeds his idealised false self. In my case the rose-tinted glasses had worn off regarding Jimmy. I was now seeing him as a talented but otherwise regular guy, rather than as a semi-mythical master PUA. At the same time I'd reached a level of success in game where simply being in RSG and hanging out with cool guys was no longer feeding my own idealised false self. I was plateauing. Mick too was up to his own version of this elaborate game with both of us, like a perverted love triangle. It was a heady cocktail.

Sitting in that Turkish coffee shop in Sarajevo, Jimmy and I were each coming to terms with our disappointment. From different directions we'd arrived at the same concern: would we ever crack the quality ceiling? Would the Game still move us forwards or had we reached a fixed limit?

This seed of doubt over our prospects led to further doubts over whether travelling around Europe as International Men Of Mystery was really the answer. From that it was only a small step to wonder if the RSG project was running out of steam and to move into the final stage of a narcissistic relationship: Discarding. We were already engaging in all the classic red flags of the devaluation phase: insults, gaslighting, threatening abandonment (verbally or physically), withholding information, demanding entitlement to information, projecting blame, accusations.

Narcissists need approval and lots of it. They need attention and lots of it. There are two different reasons (in the psychological literature) why a narcissist will discard you and seek another source of supply. First, because your usefulness as a source of narcissistic supply has run out. Second, because you threaten his idealised false self. My realisation that I was outperforming Jimmy (by my own metrics, mind, rather than by his own) and that his higher-end game didn't materialise into actual lays with an abundance of eights meant I felt like I'd outpaced him and had nothing to learn. The narcissistic supply I drew from him felt diluted and unsatisfying. My ambition to emulate him and his skills had waned.

The Devaluation phase is often accompanied by hubris and self-importance. And, yes, I'm fully aware how this sounds to the reader.

Jimmy could sense RSG was unravelling. He'd had a run of bad luck with his best leads and now his gang were mutinous. Additionally, he was dealing with some non-game-related family and business problems that were vastly more serious than I realised at the time (had I known, I'd have been considerably kinder to him). There was an imminent and grave danger that his bubble would pop and he'd fall back to earth as just a normal bloke after all. We'd flown into Yugoslavia as International Men Of Mystery but risked leaving it as just another trio of bullshitters.

Rock Solid Game had reached breaking point.

I'd arrived in Sarajevo as Ramadan began; more bad timing. It's a tough place at the best of times due to its cramped insular vibe and the constant social pressure from thirsty Muslim men just one Tweet away from joining global jihad. My friends had been there a week and barely had a sniff.

"I vow that I will drink a glass of my own cum if anyone gets laid in this town," said John, so sure of our failure was he.

Sarajevo is as unique a city as Havana or London. It's located on the only piece of flat land in an otherwise mountainous country, boxed in on all sides by towering peaks. Tiny, dirt-poor, vampire-like villages dot the countrywide in direct contrast to Sarajevo, a beautiful old Austro-Hungarian city. There's really nothing like it, and the girls are stunning.

We went to a nightclub on my second day. Being the first day of Ramadan, it was practically empty. There was one viable set, a table of four girls, of whom only one was hot. Mick beat me to the opener so I was now hamstrung by RSG wing-rules: whoever opens the set, runs the set. We all fell into our roles to support Mick by tying up the obstacles and laughing at all his jokes. He did well, but I noticed the hot girl stealing glances in my direction. Mick had us roll off for a while, but the girls suddenly stood up, grabbed their bags, and left.

Mick ran after them, chased them up the stairs, and held them in conversation on the street as they waited for a taxi. It just felt like another set to be thrown into the pick-up grinder. We joined him outside. A little gypsy kid wandered into our midst and started begging for money. He sensed Mick was trying to pull, so he latched onto him, tugging at Mick's jeans and aggressively thrusting his open palm at his face.

While Mick was distracted I briefly caught eye contact with the hot girl, Neira. She was staring at me hard, giving me the eye. So I eye-fucked her for almost a minute.

"Goblin," I heard from over my shoulder. It was RSG-code to complain a wing was usurping the player in a set. I didn't care. One week of blue balls, several hours of cocktails, and a general fuck-the-world attitude did it for me. Neira fancied me, not Mick. It seemed wrong to let her go to waste. I steamrollered the set and shut him out. She gave me her number and disappeared into a taxi.

Mick was furious. I think steam came out of his ears. He berated me all the way back to our apartment, quite rightly. His anger was fuelled by the thin week we'd all had. Non-stop rain had emptied the streets, and the much-anticipated weekend nightlife had been crushed by Ramadan. I'd taken the one good set by breaking the rules. Jimmy quietly fumed but said little.

I met Neira the next afternoon at five, sitting across from her in a delightful tiny Austro-Hungarian coffee shop recommended in all the guide books. I'd rediscovered my mojo and was full of stories. Neira beamed and cooed, "You're so self-confident."

That is the next best thing you can hear from a girl, and a precursor to, "do you have a condom?" It was on. I went through the motions of verbally spiking her. As she told me about her recent work trip to Belgrade, I let my eyes glaze over then seemed to come back to earth. "Sorry, I just looked at your breasts. I'll keep my eyes up."

She excused herself to the bathroom, so I said, "when you walk away, I'm gonna check you out." I then stared at her legs upon her return and gave an approving nod. These were all little gambits I'd been working on to get my message across and heat a girl up while sitting in a bright afternoon cafe separated by a table. It worked. She blushed.

"I'm going to kiss you in the next bar," I said, then patiently sipped my tea.

Those phrases perform a dual function: both escalation and compliance tests. If the girl doesn't want to fuck, she'll block or evade in an attempt to forestall your momentum and put you back into the friend-zone. With Neira, I got smiles, thanks, reciprocal compliments, and thus sexual tension. We kissed on the street outside, and her response was so enthusiastic that I switched plans.

Aptly named Balkan beer

"Let's not bother with another bar. We can go back to my place." I lived five minutes away, just up from the Muslim district. She agreed.

Back in 2012, I was usually slow in pulling the trigger, so to do that after just one café venue and no alcohol was highly unusual. I was outside my comfort zone but training myself to change plans on the fly as a girl's reactions determined the speed with which I could move.

We stood in line in a convenience store to buy wine, and I quickly texted John to ask if the coast was clear.

"No" John replied. "Everyone is here. They said they aren't moving for you."

I guess they felt justified cock-blocking me. Fair enough.

"I live alone," Neira offered. "We can take a taxi there."

The taxi took us five miles into the suburbs, a grotty, rundown, Tito-era neighbourhood and dropped us in a car park behind a tall grey concrete apartment block. It felt like the last level in *Stalker: Shadow of Chernobyl*. Whatever else would happen in Sarajevo, I was certainly getting local colour.

Her apartment was spacious and nice. She put a music channel on TV, and we sat on the sofa drinking wine. We made out and gradually escalated until her bra came off and she got antsy. I rolled off, we drank more, then twenty minutes later I sat behind her now-naked body and finger-fucked her to orgasm. Then she hurriedly put some clothes on.

"My friend Esma is coming here any minute! We go out tonight."

We adjourned to the kitchen, and after she brewed some tea I sat her on my lap, stripped her half-naked again, and chatted. I could feel from her squirming that she was getting very horny, and it was time for another try. I led her back to the lounge, undressed her fully, then laid her on the sofa. I slid my dick in, and after literally five strokes, the doorbell sounded.

Neira scurried away, threw some clothes on, then waited until I'd re-fastened my belt before opening the door. Her pretty blonde friend Esma came waltzing in with a smile, saw me, and then literally stopped and sniffed the air as if to say, "I smell pussy juice." We introduced ourselves and chatted over a glass of wine. Technically, I had my notch but was suffering blue balls. I kept looking at Neira's long brown hair and tanned skin, just aching to hammer her into the mattress.

"We go out now," she said. "Maybe we meet later tonight?"

Clearly she was suffering the same unfulfilled horniness as myself. Esma went off to the bathroom, and Neira whispered in my ear: "My friend is a slut. She loves sex."

"Remember my Australian friend Mick from last night?"

"Oh yes, funny guy!" she agreed.

"He's really cool when you get to know him. Let's try to set him up with Esma."

"Yes! She'll like that," chirped Neira.

I called Mick, and he was considerably mollified upon learning that a pretty young slut had agreed to a double date. From that moment on, all of his previous resentment dissipated. I thought the little crisis was over, and Jimmy and I went for a drink at Bar Havana for a couple of hours before the double date. He, too, seemed mollified, and our conversation turned to strategies for pawning off the staff at the bar.

"We are shiny here. If we act cool, make friendly conversation with the staff, and leave generous tips then I'm telling you – we can have this bar on lock down!" he enthused. He'd realised that our London salaries went a long way in the Balkans, and while he'd never pay a woman for sex, he was quite happy to spread cash around to feel like a big shot. It's what Humphrey Bogart would've done.

He gave a short lecture on the importance of wing rules but then seemed to let it drop. Mentally, I drew a line under the whole episode. I'd stolen Mick's set, and now I'd replaced it with an even hotter lead. Karma balanced.

Jimmy went home, and then Mick joined me in Bar Havana, and the girls joined soon after. The date was absolute child's play. Neira was giving me puppy dog eyes the whole time, just counting down the time till I'd take her home to fuck. That freed me of any need to game; I could just lean back, be cool, and give Mick the floor. He took full opportunity and performed a one-hour masterclass in playful attraction that had the admittedly easy target of Esma almost drooling. He kissed her early on and we just had fun and moved on to another bar. After three drinks, we were just two hundred metres from our apartment and ready to extract.

"Coming back now," I texted Jimmy. "Stay scarce!"

A minute later he pinged back. "No. Fuck off you cunt. Find somewhere else. You're not banging two rotten slags back at this place."

That surprised me, as I thought we were now square. I called John to check if he was joking. John answered in hushed tones. I think he was hiding under his duvet so Jimmy couldn't hear. "Jimmy has gone mental," he trembled, "He's pacing around the lounge right now, cursing to himself. He's slammed doors and punched the walls."

Yikes, I'd only ever seen Jimmy lose his temper once, and that was while blind drunk and throwing a few of Lee's shitbag work colleagues out of a house party. Even then he'd been fairly restrained. I'm not one to avoid confrontation, so I texted Jimmy. "I'm coming up now, alone. Let's talk about this," then I left Mick and the girls in the bar.

I was furious as I walked up the gentle incline to our first-floor apartment that overlooked a picturesque roundabout. Nonetheless, I controlled my state and was calm upon reaching the door. I couldn't get my key in. Unbelievably, Jimmy had locked me out and left his key in the lock. I banged on the door to no avail, and Jimmy didn't reply to my text to let me in. I called John.

"I can't let you in," he said. "I'm not getting involved."

"You can't not be involved," I said. "I'm locked out of the house, and Jimmy is cock-blocking Mick because he's angry at me. Either you side with him and let me stay locked out, or you unlock the door."

John snuck past Jimmy's bedroom door like he was playing *Splinter Cell* then quietly unlocked the door and slipped away into the shadows.

Jimmy came out of his room, raging. It was a cold, barely-suppressed rage that turned his eyes into pin holes and his lower lip trembled. I'd literally never seen him lose his rag; his diffident, zero-fucks-given calm was legendary. I was confident there wouldn't be a fight because we'd already sparred a few rounds in the Château Hampstead boxing gym and taken each other's measure. In the unlikely event he launched himself at me, I decided I'd smother him with a bear hug and wait for John to pull us apart.

It had become another perverse frame control battle. We were each determined not to give the other the "win" of losing our temper. Jimmy was using all of his willpower to prevent exploding completely, and it meant he had no ability to form coherent sentences.

"Just fuck off. How could you do this?" he said.

Keeping it logical, I said, "Look, I broke the wing rules. I apologised to Mick, and I found him another set. He's sitting in a bar two hundred metres away with a girl ready to fuck. It's done. We're square. He's happy about it all."

"No, fuck off. I'm not letting you bring those skanks in here."

He was sitting on the sofa now, glaring at me, arms crossed. His rage had subsided, but he was still very, *very* angry. I realised this wasn't an argument about wing rules at all. This was the culmination of our growing tensions over months that had just been exacerbated this trip. It was what I'd later realise was the Devaluation-to-Discard phase. John was probably hiding under his bed.

"You steal sets, you wanker," yelled Jimmy.

"This isn't about stealing sets, is it? Mick and I are square on that. This is about something else. What is it?"

"You aren't bringing those slags here. Find somewhere else."

We went round and round. He was gratuitously insulting me while simultaneously stonewalling rational discussion, and I realised this was a ploy to frustrate me into losing my temper. He wanted me to escalate it into an all-out slanging match so he could either vent his frustration or else take on serene calm and accuse me of being unstable. I had my own ploy, which was to box him in logically about how he was breaking wing-rules with Mick in a hypocritical attempt to get revenge on me, while simultaneously reframing him as being passive-aggressive about the deeper issues.

Even in the midst of temper tantrums, we played our insidious frame control games. I stayed polite and calm, without swearing or raising my voice, and remained on topic.

"Fuck this, I'm going for a walk. Do what you want!" he declared, got up, and strode out the door.

"Thank you. I appreciate it," I called after his receding figure, then went back to Mick and the girls. We took a taxi to Neira's apartment. I messaged Jimmy that we wouldn't need the apartment clear after all, but John told me later he'd tramped the streets for several hours all the same.

We stayed overnight at Neira's apartment. Mick banged Esma in the lounge, and I knocked the hell out of Neira in her bedroom. We broke her bed at one point, and it was fantastic sex. We swapped Facebooks the next morning and said goodbye to the girls when our taxi arrived.

Mick clapped a friendly hand on my shoulders, "Thanks mate, all is forgiven!"

Ethnic Cleansing

THIRTY TWO

ETHNIC CLEANSING

J ohn never did drink his own cum. Or at least not because of that incident.

Mick and I stayed at Neira's overnight and returned in the morning of what was to be our last full day in Sarajevo before taking a train to Belgrade. Jimmy was already up and out all day. When he finally rolled in that night he muttered a gruff "hello" then went to bed. I was sharing a bedroom with him, so he stretched out and was silent all night, bad vibes emanating off him like radiation. I heard him packing his suitcase early morning, and he disappeared again before breakfast.

Both Mick and I were in the doghouse, and even John got only a few brief grunts. The three of us dragged our suitcases down to the taxi rank nearest our apartment to find Jimmy already there. He nodded an acknowledgement then jumped into a taxi by himself. We saw him again waiting on the train platform because we'd all booked seats on the same train when buying tickets three days earlier. He sat in another carriage while the three of us shared a compartment the next carriage down. Nine hours later, rattling through the flat Serbian countryside, our train pulled into Belgrade Central Station.

"He'll get over it," mused Mick. "He's just chucked his toys out the pram, but it won't last long."

We agreed, assuming he'd pout another day or so then find a way to reframe it all so we could hang out again like nothing had happened. However, we only saw him a couple of times that week in Belgrade, walking up Knez Mihailova and pretending we didn't exist. He had his own apartment elsewhere. It dawned on us that this was a real disagreement and Jimmy evidently thought it was us who'd been in the wrong and owed him an apology. We'd notice a sudden uptick in posting activity on his blog, as every couple of days he'd post about what an awesome time he was having making new friends in a salsa bar or having coffee with a Serb girl who, by wild coincidence, was *just like* Audrey Hepburn. A few times he referred obliquely to a trio of "donuts" he'd ditched like unneeded baggage.

"I don't think he's coming back," said John. "This is a full-on reality weave. He's convincing himself he's better off alone."

We were concerned. One of our best friends was alone in a strange town, appeared to be having a mental breakdown, and had far too much pride to admit the falling out was his own fault. What could we do?

"Let's troll him," I suggested.

So Mick and I counter-posted on our blogs what an amazing time *we* were having, how vital camaraderie and friendship is while on the road, and how many delicious donut shops we'd found.

Belgrade is the old capital of the Former Yugoslavia, and it retains a majestic air. It's now considerably run-down from NATO blockades and from when the Clintons sent the US Air Force in 1999 to bomb it during the Kosovo War. Despite having a median per-capita income of just $400 a month, Serbs live quite well. They lack iPhones and high-end gaming PCs, but they are a fit, healthy country doing well to fight off the constant predations of globalists and the European Union.

As Jimmy and I had seen in our one evening there a couple of months earlier, the girls were stunning. Possibly the hottest in the world. We were aching for a crack at them.

While checking in at a fourth-floor apartment, a minute's walk down the hill from the central Republic Square, Mick kept hitting on our landlady until she made a pointed reference to her 'girlfriend'. Finally we dragged him off and walked up to the main street – Knez Mihailova. It's a long pedestrianised walk that ends in a park called Kalemegdan, the ruins of an old fortress at the point where the Danube river meets the Sava. It's Serbia's biggest tourist attraction, so every day there's a trickle of locals and tourists wandering around. The park is also popular with teenage couples who burrow into every secluded spot. You could call it the focal point of the Old Town.

The first impression on our Western eyes was of civilisation. Cafés and restaurants dotted the streets, and in the hot summer weather, their outdoor seating was thronged with locals sipping coffee and jabbering on. We couldn't understand a word of it so I invited myself to think they were discussing higher points of arts and philosophy, as opposed to whether so-and-so is really a slut or such-and-such is going fishing next weekend.

Serbs are dominated by the weather. Sunny skies bring packed streets and the slightest dribble of rain clears them out again faster than a NATO air raid siren. The atmosphere was wonderful: families, singles, and couples ambling around the park or sitting down to eat. Everyone was white, slim, and dressed in a careful, orderly fashion. It was the opposite of the classless, multicultural shithole of London, which was already beginning to feel like it was occupied by low-IQ foreign invaders. Simply sitting there drinking a milkshake was so pleasant. I thought wistfully, This is how England should be; this is what the globalists stole from us.

One of the local universities had all of its faculty buildings in the centre, mostly around a small grass park called Studentski Square. On sunny days, small groups of students sit on the grass sunbathing, and by evening they sit in circles around cans of beer and an acoustic guitar.

"This has everything," I cooed to Mick, walking in circles, my head spinning to take it all in. "Grand architecture, civil cafe culture, monoculturism, and shed loads of hot girls. I've found my home."

We rattled off a few sets that afternoon, unsure what to expect. It turned out to be rather similar to Zagreb. The younger girls were all students, and they shared the same Converse boots and denim jeans summer fashion. We were tired and frustrated following the late night in Sarajevo and the long uncomfortable train ride. Nonetheless the three of us had drinks in a salsa bar and took a few flaky numbers. It was fun.

By the third day, I was full of energy again. Most of the girls I spoke to claimed serious boyfriends, and I was getting more sudden blowouts than I was used to. I quickly realised that Serb girls have little patience with weak, timid men. If even the slightest faggotry enters your demeanour, that girl won't stop for you in Belgrade. I'd built up a little momentum when my eye caught a brunette wandering down Knez Mihailova just in front of Zara. I was feeling incredibly horny, and my eyes were popping out of my head every time I saw wide hips or tanned legs.

Anka looked great clad in tight denim shorts with shapely bare legs and big tits fighting to escape from her tight t-shirt. Up close she wasn't especially hot, a six, but she just oozed sex and oestrogen.

"You have the sexiest walk I've seen all day," I said. She giggled, batted her eyes, and we went for a coffee under a parasol near Republic Square. Her phone blew up with messages from some friends.

"My friends want to meet soon," she said.

"Will you go?"

"No, they can wait," she replied.

It took an hour to finish our coffees then I walked her to a bar opposite our apartment. She threw back a few vodkas, touched my forearm, and smiled constantly. I faced a technical dilemma regarding how fast to extract her. Ideally, I'd build more comfort over an hour then pull the trigger. However, her friends had taken to calling her, so clearly the bubble could burst at any moment. Fortune favours the brave. Ninety minutes in, I went for it.

"Let's watch some YouTube. I live there," I said, pointing across the road.

We settled the bill, walked across the road and she entered the lobby. We stood patiently for the lift to open, and it was then she got cold feet.

"No, I can't," she whimpered and stepped back.

I grabbed her, pushed her against the wall, and made out with her for the first time. "I want to take you upstairs, rip your clothes off, and fuck you hard," I growled, gambling that my boldness was what she liked most about me.

Her knees buckled and she moaned. Then she slid out from my grasp towards the door. "Here, take my number. I must meet my friends."

I took the number and she rushed off, turning back to wave and smile.

We met again the following day, and it was clear she'd come for sex. It was a balmy evening, and she'd dressed to show the maximum skin. I sat her down in the same whiskey bar on the corner of my street and then gazed at her deep cleavage and made a pretence of listening to her conversation. An hour in, I couldn't fake my patience any more.

"Let's go inside," I said.

"No. You said you share your apartment with three men," she bleated. For a moment I thought she was turning down the sex. Then she continued, "Let's get a taxi to my place."

It turns out her place was so far from the centre that we were winding through hills and tree-lined country roads, but in about twenty minutes we pulled into an apartment complex, and she took me up two floors to her nice, private apartment. She was a school teacher and clearly earning more than the median $400 per month despite being only twenty-six.

There wasn't any LMR. Her body was a little disappointing once she got naked because her huge hooters flopped around when freed. I much preferred them bound up into buoyant globes in her bra but didn't have the heart to ask her to put it back on. She had just finished her period and had that unpleasant musky smell that sometimes lingers a day or two later. That grossed me out a little so once I'd got my notch, I really just wanted to leave. She had it in mind to go for seconds and was a bit miffed when I told her to call me a cab home. I spent the next twenty minutes looking out of the window while she sat awkwardly, and neither of us knew what to say. My mood lifted when I got back to the apartment and made Mick hand over the F-town ring.

That same afternoon Mick and I had been trawling Knez Mihailova doing ten or so sets each. I'd become adept at spotting "hidden hotties," meaning girls of beauty who aren't dolled up to show it. I put it down to my hawk-like eyesight and very clear idea of what I wanted in a girl. One such girl rushed past in a fast walk, about thirty metres away. No make-up, her hair pulled back into a harsh bun and a loose-fitting tracksuit. She was hurrying by the same spot that I'd picked up Anka, outside Zara.

"That one," I said and ran off.

"She's gross," Mick called after me, lacking my discerning eye.

I just knew from her walk, figure, and facial structure that she was my kind of girl. It was a genuine DNA-tug: a girl whose perfectly complimentary genetic fit seems to make your blood bubble with excitement.

Branka stopped easily and seemed surprised a man would show interest. She was twenty-one, tall, and on her way home from belly dancing class. Everything clicked into place: introverted, intelligent, bookish, long-legged, exotic look, especially high cheekbones, and cat-like eyes, sexually inexperienced. I took her to Coffee Dream for a milkshake.

Whereas my natural inclination with Anka had been to push fast and sexual, what I'd later term "r-selection daygame", that same gut instinct told me Branka was a slow burn who would need time but would eventually fall hard. I made no attempt to touch or kiss her, but I liked her a lot, and we arranged to meet the next afternoon for a late coffee.

This time she'd prettied herself up nicely and just looking at her cat-like eyes and high cheekbones made me ache with a nostalgia for past summers, like staring at 1930s movie starlets or hearing a song from your childhood. She suggested Zmaj Bar, also known as the Philosopher's Café, her favourite hangout. The basement was wood-panelled and stacked with comfortable Chesterfield sofas; very much like a jazz bar, but without the band.

"I study philosophy," she told me, then discussed her thoughts on Aristotle and Plato. Her English was good, so we had a deep discussion and within an hour I felt we'd connected strongly. Branka was the most impressive girl I'd dated up to that point in my life, a combination of beauty, elegance, and cultural depth. She reminded me of Zaria the Russian catwalk model but was still just twenty-one years old.

Take your time. Don't rush this. She's a good girl, I thought to myself.

"I want to show you my university," she said, as we were paying off the coffees. "My faculty building is around the corner."

She walked me through Studentski Square, and I took a chance and kissed her. She responded passionately. It was on. Suddenly all my carefully-laid plans to slowly seduce her evaporated, and I lost patience. I walked her to the same whiskey bar by my house as I'd been with Anka. I was giddy at the thought of slotting such a top-quality girl.

We both ordered beer.

"Tell me about the book you're reading," I inquired.

"*Fifty Shades of Grey*. It's very interesting," she replied.

I couldn't believe my luck. She'd just handed me the opportunity to sexualise that I was looking for. It had only recently been published, so it was still the toast of the chattering classes, a rare chance to talk about dominance and sexual depravity in polite company, and I realized at once that it could be useful in my approach to girls. Since then it's been a go-to gambit for amping up sexual tension.

We talked about BDSM and other sexual preferences, allowing me to find out an awful lot about her sexual outlook and predilections. She'd had literally one boyfriend and only fucked him once, she said. We kissed a few times, and I saw the tell-tale widening of her eyes like the light of a boiler furnace had just ignited. Whether that was excitement, arousal or both didn't matter. I tried to pull her home.

Five minutes later she was topless in my bedroom while Mick and John sat in the lounge watching tennis on Serbian TV. Branka was in that familiar female battleground where she wanted to fuck but thought it a bad strategic move. So I just sucked her tits a bit and didn't fight too hard when she wouldn't let me unbutton her jeans. Half an hour later she wanted to go home.

I walked her to the bus stop on Knez Mihailova, and as we approached she turned her head up to look lovingly into my eyes and said, "Thanks for not raping me." I didn't know what to say to that so I just shrugged my shoulders.

We wouldn't meet again that trip, but we exchanged Skype details and video-chatted regularly. She was the kind of girl I'd always wanted from Game, and I was absolutely willing to return to Belgrade just for her.

Friday night rolled around, and we'd heard the nightclub boats on the Sava River were great fun. It was a twenty minute's walk from our apartment, and as we headed down, the signs were good – loads of dolly birds tottering up and down in their heels along the grass strip that runs along besides the boats.

Mick had arranged to meet a Russian tourist there he'd number-closed earlier that afternoon so he was in full Game Mode. John and I just wanted to get drunk. I'd gotten my lay and had a few decent dates so the pressure was off. When Mick's blonde turned up he took her straight into isolation so John and I went to the bar and ordered double vodkas.

John's state was improving after a couple of weeks wigging out so we knocked back drink after drink, watched all the hot girls, and talked about life, the universe, and everything. Unfortunately, despite all the hot girls they were still outnumbered four-to-one by good-looking local men entertaining them and locking us out.

Without warning my vibe exploded. Perhaps it was vodka, perhaps something else, but I was overtaken by a bulletproof confidence and the urge to rapidly escalate every girl I saw. John and I opened a few sets, groped them a little, and took their polite excuses in our stride. At my absolute peak state, I saw a girl out the corner of my eye who I really liked. Tall, leggy, high cheekbones, elegant fashion, and flowing brown hair. She and her six friends formed a small circle where they could all face each other while chatting and dancing. *How could I get into this set*, I wondered.

Mystery Method would have me open a set within her line of sight, build value and pre-selection, then perhaps open indirectly with an apparently off-the-cuff comment to one of her friends. Alternatively, I could wait until she went off to the bar or toilet and try to catch her alone or with just one female friend. Or perhaps I could go chump style and dance next to her flamboyantly and wait for a chance to turn to her and try to salsa spin her.

So many options for a seasoned player.

I took a more direct line. I crashed into her circle like a truck driver in Nice and walked right up into her face.

"Hi. I'm Nick," I said and put out my hand. I ignored everyone else, like we were the only two people on the boat.

"I'm Marijana."

She shook my hand and stared at me like a deer in headlights. I immediately caressed her hand, maintained laser eye contact, and babbled nonsensical bullshit that she probably couldn't hear. Her friends seemed to melt away and never interrupted. At the time I was too drunk to process it, but with hindsight I'm sure she eye-coded them that it was okay. After a minute I walked her backwards out of the circle to a nearby wall and locked in. She stayed with me for twenty minutes and much of that was kissing.

Even now, writing these words four years later, I shake my head and wonder how I pulled it off. She was one of the hottest girls on the boat, a twenty-three-year-old folk singer, and I'm not very good at night-club game.

John left me to it and knocked back more vodka. Later he lay under a tree on the grass verge and drifted in and out of consciousness. I stepped over him when I took Marijana down to the grass, and I lay there kissing this lovely Serbian girl. Ten minutes later, or what seemed like ten minutes but could have been half an hour or more, I became aware of a couple walking past.

"Ugh, that's disgusting, those two kissing in the dirt like that," I heard a girl say.

"Yes, disgusting," the man agreed. Then, "Hang on, that's my friend, Nick!"

Mick was taking the Russian for a walk but wouldn't quite manage to get her home. I tried to extract Marijana, but her friends found her and carried us both off to a house party deep in the Titoist projects of Novi Beograd.

It felt like all I did was eat

More Zagreb

THIRTY THREE

MORE ZAGREB

Our Belgrade adventure lasted a week, and then we took the motorway bus west to Zagreb. We were tired from three weeks on the road. Falling out with Jimmy had let all the steam out of our petty in-fighting, drawing away negative energy like lancing a boil. The three remaining musketeers were in good spirits now that Dogtanian had left.

John had completely binned daygame, his periodic "I'm just going to live in Thailand and bang whores" tantrums had grown so tiresome that even he gave up on them. He was now scouring a Lonely Planet guide for museum and theatre recommendations. Mick was starry-eyed over a twenty-one-year-old Croatian virgin called Bojana who he'd kiss-closed just before leaving Zagreb for Sarajevo. They'd stayed in touch, and he was pedestalising hard in anticipation of seeing her again.

He rested his hand on my shoulder, squeezing it like a father giving encouragement to his child before he steps up to the batter's plate in a Little League game. "Mate, this girl is special," he said.

I wasn't used to such intensity from him. He was almost maniacal. I think that's what happens when you acclimatise yourself to ratbags from bars and PlentyOfFish and then suddenly tumble into set with a genuine eight. His last lay before leaving London was a short, chubby Jew he picked up in a Camden Town blues bar. Bojana was a class above.

I was exuberant from having poked a bird in each of the three countries we'd visited. The F-town ring felt reassuringly heavy on my finger, a weight I could carry with confidence. We took a swish modern apartment overlooking a park a few minute's walk from the Old Town. Mick spent an hour or so drooling over the Apple TV systems before I dragged him out for more daygame.

My intent had dropped to zero because I'd had two new notches in seven days, a bunch of make-outs, and a couple of promising leads left over in Belgrade. I was content to game vicariously through Mick, picking out sets for him with my superior eyesight. He had a good day and found a girl he'd fuck later that week. We'd been walking around the Jelacic area for an hour, and Mick was in set while I stood at a discreet distance, waiting for him to finish when a hot girl walked past, and I felt the familiar blood-bubble. She seemed to glide past with her feet barely visible under her long colourful skirt wrapped tight like a sarong. Long black hair cascaded down her back, and she wore a form-fitting black vest.

I wavered. I was embodying what Buddhists would call "freedom from desire" and not happy about it. My feet wouldn't move. Alarm bells were ringing; *you cannot let this one go, she's literally the perfect set you always dream about.* Really she was: five-nine, long-legged, firm, round tits, long hair, big dreamy eyes, and a lazy cat-like walk. A solid eight.

Sometimes life is just nice to you. I said hello to Jelka, and within two minutes I knew she was my Set of Glory. She responded well to everything I said – each little tease, push, and pull – loving the moment. Out of the corner of my eye I could see Mick, finished with his squirrel, hanging about and waiting patiently for me to finish up. Instead I sat her down at an outdoor cafe right behind us, flashing Mick a satisfied grin. He wandered off and would soon find a blonde student who we'd see again the next evening.

It was maybe three in the afternoon. The sun burned into the pavement creating a shimmering effect as heat bounced back into the air. Locals darted from shop interiors to shaded sidewalks. I leant back, sipped coffee and ran my usual patter. Jelka leant into me halfway across the table, filled my inscrutable silences and told me all about herself. She was a Dalmatian, from Split on the south coast, and had moved to Zagreb for university and now worked at a cocktail bar. I took her to Alcatraz, where I was quickly developing a reputation with the staff.

I was freewheeling downhill to glory. We made out under a flashing neon sign with an embossed Marilyn Monroe on it. It felt so *on*.

"I have a meeting, I must go," she said, pulling herself upright and straightening her sarong. "We can meet later."

Ten minutes after she walked out, I ordered another whiskey and revelled in the rock 'n' roll atmosphere. The bar was dark and streaked with colour, while the door to the street was hazy with sun-bloom, like the lens-flare from a sniper scope. I was so satisfied. My phone buzzed with a message from Jelka. "It was pleasure to meet you, Nick. Thanks for kisses, very, very nice... ummm."

I joined up with Mick to shadow him around town, watching him work sets and keeping on top of the burgeoning text banter with Jelka. She'd already arranged to attend a house party that evening but was willing to ditch her friends at 11pm to see me.

"I'm catching an early train tomorrow," she wrote. "I'm returning to Split."

That told me she was up for it, and I hadn't any time to waste. This was a one-shot chance, zero or hero. With the benefit of hindsight, knowing what I do now, she'd ticked most of the same-day-lay checkboxes: walking around aimlessly with a horny, sexual vibe to put herself on display, intense eye sparkle, swaying upon my open, full compliance on the date. Things also flowed astonishingly well logistically. Just consider this:

- Living with a boyfriend for a couple of years but he was out of town today.
- She pinged me first after leaving the i-date
- Enthusiastic tone of her messages.
- Agreed to the date first time I asked.
- Agreed to a late-night date.
- Willing to ditch her friends to meet me.
- Explicitly outlined her time-frame.

Reading between the lines she was telling me, "I have a short time window later this evening for you to seduce me, and after that I'm gone." In an earlier life I'd have second-guessed myself thinking *this can't go anywhere, she's got a boyfriend and leaves town tomorrow*.

We met by the central train station, and I took her to the same bar I'd taken Dorota a couple of weeks earlier. It was dark now, so we sat inside and made inroads into shots of rum. We both knew what was going on, slipping into that strange vibe where our brains shut down, and she just leant in on me quietly while I scratched her head and let her absorb my presence. We barely spoke. My main enemy was her forebrain, perhaps feeling guilt over the boyfriend or the lightning speed of the seduction. The bar soon called last orders, and now it was make or break.

"Let's sit in the park," I suggested and walked her towards my apartment. It was a clear night, the sky a deep, dark blue. We lay on the grass under a tree and canoodled. My plan was simple: let her absorb my masculine energy until her hindbrain overpowered any remaining forebrain resistance. If I craned my head left, I could see our lounge window, the lights inside winking teasingly just a hundred metres away.

It was deathly quiet. Once or twice a dog-walker or couple walked past on their way home. We made out, and I sucked on her tits. The forebrain-hindbrain conflict was clearly visible on her face and in her body language, she was horny as a Turkish immigrant but fighting valiantly to control herself.

And then it happened. It was like a fog lifting, and now she was looking directly at me with clear, hungry eyes. It was unmistakable. Her final resistance had crumbled and she'd resolved whatever conflict that was holding her back.

"Let's get a cup of tea," I said, stood up, helped her up with my hand, and led her to my front door.

"Extraction. Be scarce," I texted Mick and John. A minute later I was walking her through the kitchen of a silent, deserted house. Jelka sat on my bed and looked around while I put on Fleetwood Mac. There was no preamble. She'd made her decision, and I wanted to act before she unmade it. I quickly undressed her and my eyes almost popped out of my head at her figure, she could've been a swimsuit model. Her body was the perfect combination of lithe slim lines and voluptuous curves. We got straight down to fucking.

She was lying underneath me, naked, while I smashed her.

"You fucking love this, don't you," I said, yanking on her hair. "You love that I just picked you up."

"Yes!" she gasped.

"You fucking love that I looked at you, thought *I'm fucking that*, and now here we are. Me fucking you."

"Yes!"

Afterwards, she knelt wide-eyed next to me on the bed, muttering. "I can't believe I just did that. I've never done such a thing before."

That is a very common reaction to Same Day Lays, a tell-tale sign of the cognitive dissonance that arises when a girl's hindbrain propels her into sex that her forebrain believes is in conflict with her self-image. So I ladled on the comfort. We lay together showing each other photos, music, and YouTube videos. An hour later she was ready to call a taxi home. I wanted to keep her on as a regular, but it was clear this was her one-time wild adventure while her boyfriend was away.

I made sure to parade her past Mick and John on her way out. As I strolled back from the taxi rank, I felt invincible. What a month I'd had! It was my best-ever run in Game, and if I was to wind the clock back to Zehra in April, I'd had a great run of younger-hotter-tighter for four months. Only Anka let the side down, but she was hardly a rotter. Was I finally cracking the quality ceiling? Had I reached a level where early-twenties eights were now the norm rather than the exception?

Mick brought that pretty blonde around the next night – not Bojana – and knobbed her. Jimmy was still ignoring us, but we saw him walking around Zagreb a couple of times. He was blogging about having met another stunner there, this time a red-headed Audrey. He walked past us one afternoon with her in tow.

"She looks a little…grotty," I said. She was tall, slim, and pretty, but rather more like Vivien Leigh in *Waterloo Bridge* than in *Gone with the Wind*.

"She looks like a sex worker," said John. He'd know. In fact, Jimmy actually told John she worked night shifts in a massage parlour giving hand jobs for money. Oh, how we laughed! Still, she *was* pretty.

A couple of days later we were back in England, riding the National Express bus home from Stansted Airport with a sickening feeling like we were riding to our own executions. We'd come to hate London now that we'd seen how much more civilised Central Europe was. London seemed to embody all the worst filth of socialism, immigration, crime, and the beta-chump rat race. The sheer joy of partying with friends in Yugoslavia, with its stable white culture and endless sea of beautiful women, had rendered us strangers in our own land.

This didn't hit Mick so hard, as he was from Australia and thus descended from the criminal classes.

Summer would end soon, and when I opened my pile of accumulated mail back at the Château, I checked my bank statements. Since quitting my job in mid-2010, the two years of unpaid woppery had made quite a dent in my savings. Back then I hadn't cared because I'd recklessly (and correctly) assumed that my life needed to change, and if that meant spending all my money on the transition, then so be it.

However, it couldn't last forever, and now there was a decision looming: do I keep living this way and run my savings down to zero, or do I figure out a way to restock my pile of "fuck you" money? I was also having increasing difficulty reconciling my Hemingway Suite self-image of the "fully-actualised renaissance man" with the reality that I was unemployed, lived in a dilapidated care home with assorted and equally unemployed riff-raff, and had fallen out with my best friend over a trifle.

Perhaps I should look for a job, I thought.

Russian Gambit

THIRTY FOUR

RUSSIAN GAMBIT

L et's cast our minds back to July 2010 and the very first Rock Solid Game euro-jaunt, the one that first opened our minds to the possibility of smash 'n' grab raids on other countries. We'd been in Vilnius a week, eight of us in adjacent rooms on the same corridor in a budget business hotel on a hill just outside the Old Town. I'd only been cold-approaching one year and only been laid five times from it so far. The Lithuania jaunt felt like one-part Game trip and one-part bachelor party, matching my own semi-chump state.

As opposed to the all-conquering dark triad shitlord that I am now. But I digress.

It was raining heavily outside.

"Let's go down to Maxima," said Mick. It was the largest supermarket chain in the country and just two hundred yards from our hotel. He'd finished picking at his toenails and his *Ren And Stimpy* TV series hadn't downloaded yet. "I want to stock up on cheese and chipotle dip."

I looked outside at the rain. The sky was a thick grey mist, torrents of rain pouring down to stab the pavement maniacally like shivs in the kidneys of a Mexican prisoner. Lightning flashed and thunder rolled in a few seconds behind. Yet it was strangely warm and pleasant.

"I've got nothing better to do, okay," I said, keen to avoid the rising cabin fever from being bottled up all afternoon. I felt like a travelling shoe salesman in that hotel.

On the way back from the supermarket half an hour later, two full carrier bags of white bread, hummus, and cheesy puff crisps in my hands, I spotted an extremely hot girl walking towards me. She held a large umbrella to protect her thick brown hair and long, black-tight-clad legs. Gorgeous. A solid eight. I said hello.

It was a Hollywood rom-com moment, chatting to her under the umbrella and creating a lust bubble while a biblical flood assailed the street around us and streams of fast-moving water snaked down the street into the drains. She was eighteen and studying fashion. I took her Facebook and never saw her again, but it lifted my mood.

I had several other Facebook messages waiting for me when I got home and logged onto the hotel Wi-Fi. Justina, a pretty brunette I'd number-closed the previous afternoon, had accepted my date request with one significant proviso, she wanted to bring her big, fat, gay best friend. Seeing as I had met her while with *my* big, fat, gay best friend Mick, it seemed like a sort of twisted revenge. We were all intending to try Bar 301 that evening anyway, a small two-level bar club that seemed to attract plenty of girls, so I invited her to join us. Fernando, Ace, and myself formed the advance party, getting to the club around ten o'clock. The rest of the gang rolled in an hour later.

It was midweek, so the night club wasn't very full. Justina was good fun but seemed like a typical time-waster, and her big, fat, gay friend clearly resented my presence. I've since come to believe that any young woman with a gay best friend is damaged goods and best avoided – there's something wrong with people who choose the mentally ill to be their lifestyle accessories. That said, she chatted excitedly to me and danced with me in front of the other punters, so it pre-selected me nicely.

I took a breather and sat with Fernando and Ace at the bar sipping the bottle of Corona they'd ordered me. I rarely had an opportunity to hang out with Ace, and I was trying to soak up as much as I could of his "douchebag" game. He was a Polish university student who'd modelled his look and accent on Hank Moody from *Californication*.

He was so convincing you'd easily believe he was an LA native. The three of us sprawled out on the bar stools like overflowing toilets, looking inscrutable and James Bond-like in our own imaginations.

"Look there," said Fernando, inclining his head and indicating with his chin. We were too cool to raise our hands and point at something. "Isn't that the girl you made out with last night?" he asked me.

Indeed it was. While drunk out of my mind in this same bar, I'd opened an nineteen year old former-gymnast, Kris, and rolled around with her on a sofa in the basement rooms. She was a tight seven and clearly insane:

"I was thrown off the Olympic team for alcoholism," she'd told me. "I was sixteen."

If I'd gotten to know her better, I'm sure she'd have some wild stories that would no doubt melt the mind of 2010-era me. She saw me and waltzed over, jabbering on in animated fashion. She wore a figure-hugging white dress and looked great.

"Crazy bitch," said Ace, intending her to hear. Her head snapped around, and she gave him a slow up-and-down appraisal with narrowed eyes and pursed lips. Ace held up to her gaze and threw back a jerk-boy sneer.

"Oh, you horrible man," she cooed, smiling, then turned back to me.

An hour later I was drunk, full of energy, and dancing with both Kris and Justina. They obviously hated each other even though neither seemed especially interested in sleeping with me. Their dance moves acted out the storyline of a symbolic battle as if choreographed by a contemporary dance artist. They'd stare, growl, and ignore each other in equal measure, the whole time orbiting me like rebel fighter pilots. I felt like a small child caught between divorcing parents. Looking up I noticed two tall hot girls, a blonde and a brunette, standing alone against the wall on the edge of the dance floor. They'd not moved since coming in half an hour earlier. Astonishingly, the dozen or so men at the bar had yet to try it on with either of them.

The brunette told me some considerable time later that they were living in Kaliningrad, a western outpost of Russia and a few hour's drive away by car. They'd driven into Lithuania to party and were on their last night, having run out of money and now drinking free tap water. They hadn't even eaten, but Julia – the brunette – would rather party than eat. I was the most interesting thing on the deserted dance floor, so they gawped at me. I looked up and caught Julia's eye so I went up in front of her and shot the Saturday Night Fever pose as my opener. They giggled and I went back to dance. Later I re-approached the two Russians and made small talk. They barely spoke a word of English.

Julia was one of the hottest girls I'd spoken to in my life so far. Remember I was just one year into cold approach and plying my trade in London which is thin on quality. I still lacked the confidence to properly hit on eights, and I remembered the previous summer where I couldn't even hold eye contact with such girls. I always went to pieces around hot girls, feeling a gnawing lack of entitlement. Additionally, Russian girls occupied a mythical status in our minds as if they are all savvy, street-wise adventuresses who twist men around their fingers while socially climbing their way to become oligarch mistresses.

Ironically, Julia wasn't far from that stereotype. She'd dated several millionaires and was kept in an apartment on a fat salary by a successful Moscow businessman. She looked exactly as the mental image you probably just conjured up; long legs, firm full tits and ass, long black hair, and smart, calculating eyes. Fortunately, I was too drunk to be intimidated, so I just messed around with her like she was an ankle-biting chihuahua.

A fight broke out behind us as some huge muscular guy came in and harassed a group of several men who'd look big and tough in comparison to anyone *but* this Goliath who towered over them jabbing his finger into their impassive Slavic faces. Ten minutes later the doormen hustled them all outside, and the group of five men mob-attacked the Goliath and kicked him all over the street. I never did learn what it was about, and instead I just chalked it up to the same Slavic thirst for brutal outbursts that had been extensively documented in *The Fall of Berlin* sixty-five years earlier.

The night club closed shortly after, and we were kicked out onto the street in rather less violent fashion. The two Russians were hanging around looking for trouble, so I re-approached them and they humoured Fernando and I until we swapped Facebooks. I tried a weak attempt to kiss-close Julia, but she easily deflected me, no doubt her teenage years spent in nightclubs had encouraged her to develop an entire toolkit for smoothly diverting unwanted male interest away from her. Fernando, Ace, and I walked off to a small whiskey bar, and I didn't think of Julia again. Too young, too hot, too savvy. I didn't have any hope chasing after hot twenty-year-old party girls.

A week later I was sitting in my lounge deep in the blackest shithole of South London, watching a movie with my Thai then-girlfriend Tasanee. My phone buzzed with a Facebook notification, and I was surprised to see Julia had accepted my request. Then I put my phone away and thought nothing of it. After Tasanee fell asleep I opened up Julia's profile and clicked through her photos. As expected there wasn't much on there, as Russians all use the Facebook clone "VK" as their primary social media site. Nonetheless she had a few dozen photos posing for nightclub photographers, amateur modelling in a park, and hanging with her gang of female friends. In these later photos, she always seemed to be sitting in a horizontal split. It was just too painful to see such beauty and flexibility that I'd never touch, so I closed the profile, stuck my dick in Tasanee's mouth to wake her up again, then once more forgot about the Russian.

Two months later, in September 2010, I'd moved into Château Hampstead. One evening Julia pinged me, and we started chatting for the first time. She still couldn't speak English so the conversation was mostly me accusing her of looking like small, furry animals and her replying with a stream of smileys. I'd write things like, "You're Russian. I bet you drink vodka every night," and so on. It was superficial nonsense, and it carried on once a week for about twenty minutes a time, for a year. She was learning English so the quality of her messages improved over time. I felt like it was a waste of time as I had no intention of ever visiting Kaliningrad and no reason to suppose she even fancied me. Nonetheless she continued to initiate chats, and I responded. I saw no harm in chatting to a hot young girl, even if she was just milking me for English practice.

By mid-2011 her English had noticeably stepped up, and I started to realise she was actually paying attention to my Facebook prattle.

She'd asked my favourite book, and when I waxed lyrically about Ayn Rand's *Atlas Shrugged* she'd gone off and read the Russian translation. The more we talked the more I realised she was not in fact a nightclub bimbo but actually much closer to the kind of intelligent and focused person that I can relate to. My preconceptions of hot young party girls were being shaken, Julia seemed to be both intelligent and somewhat attracted to me. How odd. I'd not expected either.

She'd grown up in an unremarkable working class family, and several years earlier her father had died in an accident, setting off a "wild child period" in her teens and creating the daddy issues that led her to desire older men. As a seventeen-year-old she'd suffered the same narrow horizons and lack of options as thousands of other girls in her city. Her life had turned upside down one night following a fateful encounter with a millionaire businessman who frequented the restaurant where she worked as a waitress. They'd dated, he'd installed her into a luxury apartment, and paid her a UK-level salary to be on call for him on the rare occasions he was back in her town for business.

"It was incredible," she'd say later. "I was a small-town girl at a dead-end, and this good-looking, charismatic millionaire wanted me as one of his mistresses. He was so cool I'd have fucked him for free, but he paid me a high salary anyway. My friends were so jealous."

Even as a seventeen-year-old waitress she'd had a hustler's mindset. "He dropped me off at my crappy apartment that I shared with three friends. He made a proposition, asking how much I wanted to become his mistress. I thought of a figure: how much money I needed to quit my job and live nicely. Then I trebled it. He said okay."

When we'd met in Vilnius she'd been dating him over two years and also acquired a boyfriend in Kaliningrad who didn't seem to protest the arrangement. Her intelligence and ambition surprised me. She always wanted more, and over the next few years she'd accumulate high-achieving men, be they businessmen, gangsters, athletes or fashion models. I sometimes wondered how I fit into all this. She also let slip her notch-count was slightly higher than mine.

Admittedly, I was only five lays into my pick-up career by then and not exactly a slayer in my pre-Game life. Her candid conversation would become a feature of our later friendship.

"I have visa for England!" she announced in late spring 2011. "I study English in London for two weeks."

I was the only person she knew in London and thus her only connection. Immediately the gamma section of my mind began to whir – *perhaps I can monopolise her attention and suck her in?* It's ludicrous for a man to think he'll get a savvy young girl just because she's slightly dependent upon him for local knowledge but – when boiled down to the core – isn't the whole essence of "gamma" about self-delusion?

She was staying in a hostel in a nice part of town slightly north of Old Street. We arranged to meet her very first night, and as soon as she arrived, she messaged me confirming to meet on a bridge over a canal in her area. I stood there waiting, feeling very odd indeed. Julia had been a phantasm for me, just a disembodied artificial intelligence at the other end of a Facebook chat. At no point had I ever expected to see her again, and even now I wouldn't be surprised if she no-showed. It was just too odd; a five-minute babble in a Lithuanian nightclub and a year of incidental short Facebook chat. That's not how men meet women, is it?

The dark streets were deserted, and I had a long unobstructed view of the cobbled roads and converted warehouse apartments. I saw her coming for two hundred yards away, and the closer she walked the longer her legs seemed to grow.

"Hello," she beamed and gave me a hug. I walked her to the closest pub, an old English affair with flowery-patterned seats and fox hunt paintings on the walls. We sat in a corner booth and proceeded to stumble through the language barrier.

Julia had a trophy girl vibe about her, a real head-turner who projected sexuality through nuance and body language intended to drive men crazy. She sat on the padded seat next to me, and I felt out of my depth, still lacking the ability to smoothly escalate. Fortunately, she liked me, loved England, and was in an adventurous new-town mood. We made out after an hour.

Julia visits London

We went around the corner to another pub and made out some more. Suddenly the alarm bells were ringing and my world-view was shaking. *Was it on? Could I fuck this girl?*

I felt like someone sitting in front of the TV watching his lottery numbers coming up one ball at a time, the numbers falling into place in rapid succession. There was a growing sense of unreality and excited anticipation. Surely this girl is too hot for me! Surely she had all kinds of options back home. And yet, here we were walking back to her hostel room two hours into the first date on her first night in town.

She tapped a code into the keypad at the entrance, and we walked upstairs and along a white-washed hallway. Her room reminded me of my halls of residence room in my first year at university – small, neat, new, and completely impersonal. Her unpacked suitcase sat in a corner underneath the window. We sat down on the bed to watch some YouTube videos. I tried to fuck her, and she said no.

We'd meet every couple of days over the next fortnight. By now I was increasingly comfortable spending time in the company of hot girls, having dated Soraya, Zaria, Dovile, and Angelina in the preceding months. I took her around the usual London tourist traps, parks, pubs, and cafes. She stayed over at my place three times, each time in progressively less clothes, and she got to meet the RSG gang. One evening she came over drunk with a Russian classmate who Mick cracked on with as we watched movies in the cinema room.

Fun though it was to fool around with a hot Russian girl, it was very frustrating. She clearly fancied me but was still dating her boyfriend of three years and the millionaire sugar-daddy. On her very last night in London she lay naked in my bed, drunk on red wine, and totally up for it. I knelt between her legs, got my dick out, and pushed it in.

This is it. I congratulated myself. *New notch. New flag!*

Before I got it all the way in she suddenly scurried backwards. "No! I don't want. Let's sleep!" Then she rolled over and started snoring theatrically. I was furious.

"That's enough! You play games!" I shouted, then picked up all her clothes and threw them at her. "Get out!"

She dressed in silence then I walked her down to the fire door by Tony's room. Her eyes blazed with a cocktail of emotion I didn't try to figure out. She turned to say goodbye, and I shut the door in her face. She returned to Russia the next afternoon.

I forgot all about her yet again, but a few months later she tentatively contacted me on Facebook, asking how I was and not referring to our earlier confrontation. I figured there was nothing to lose by replying, and by now her English had improved to the point where she could hold proper conversations. Another year of infrequent contact passed. In summer 2012 she made another announcement.

"I'm coming to London," she said. "I have a six-month student visa!"

Good lord, not again! I'd only just returned from banging Zehra in Zadar and was once more infused with my characteristically overly-optimistic assessment of my odds to get laid. Somehow I found myself waiting in the Arrivals lobby of Luton Airport for her to come through. We got a taxi to the train station then the train to West Hampstead. Her flat-share was a short bus ride away so I waved goodbye to her thinking, *why did I do that?*

Right from the beginning I felt an impending friend-zoning. Something wasn't quite right, as Julia threw off constantly mixed signals – she both liked and fancied me, yet wanted me kept at a distance. Usually that means there's another man in the picture. With her I knew of at least two such men in Russia, and she's the kind of girl who could fly solo to the moon and still come back with a gaggle of orbiting chumps filling her wine glass. She'd be all over me in public, hanging onto my arm and strutting down the streets in tight shorts and high heels, but then far more cautious indoors. I guessed she was tooling me but it still felt good to hang out with her. One time we bumped into my old friend Yasin in Soho and his jaw hit the ground at how sexually enticing she looked.

"Jesus Christ!" he typed into an SMS later that evening. "Is that the calibre of girl you're fucking nowadays?"

Well, no. I just couldn't make it happen.

Throughout that first month there was a simmering tension between Julia and I as we jostled over what, if anything, our relationship should be. Naturally I wanted to fuck her and hold her on a rotation. I don't know what she wanted from me. Just as I'd been building up to throwing her out of my room at midnight the year before, I could sense the powder kegs being stacked up underneath us this year too. It would take only a spark to explode the lot of them.

Jimmy and I were out drinking in Waxy O'Connors Irish bar with Steve Jabba in Piccadilly one summer evening, before the fateful trip to Yugoslavia. We'd been seeing Steve a few times a month since Christmas, but he hadn't yet moved into the Château.

"Fuck this shithole, let's go to a strip club," said Steve, necking his pint and putting on his leather biker jacket before waiting for an answer. "There's no tits in here. I want to see tits. Big, jiggling, sexy tits."

Jimmy and I looked at each other and slowly shook our heads. We lacked Steve's enthusiasm for the sex industry.

"Right then, I'm off to Spearmint Rhinos," Steve announced, his cheerful tone belying the intensity in his eyes. "Let's meet up again later this month," and off he went.

"I'm still well up for drinking," I said as the barmaid rang the bell for time. Jimmy agreed and we walked up Regent Street past Oxford Circus to a pub which I knew had a late-opening dance-floor area in the basement. Just as we reached the short queue outside I got a message from Julia.

"What are you doing?" she asked. I told her our location. "Okay, I come soon!"

She'd been hanging out with a pair of Aussie young professionals who'd rented a lavish Marble Arch apartment and would throw weekly parties full of booze and cocaine. I'd find out later they were PUAs in the London group although when Julia showed me photos I didn't recognise them. Half of the men in London dream of doing cocaine-party game; it's the capital's equivalent of the "pocket-square-faggot game," popular on America's west coast. Presumably this week's party was less than satisfying for her and she wanted adventure elsewhere.

Jimmy and I took up positions on bar stools in the basement and sipped at our beers, surveying the scene.

"It's pretty desperate here, all fat slags," he mused. "Nothing like Dubrovnik or Sarajevo. I'll tell you, the girls there...... you wouldn't believe how hot they are! Every cafe and restaurant is full of little Yugoslav Audrey Hepburns."

"Jimmy, we've been through this. It's a figment of your imagination. We just spent a month driving through those places."

He was not to be deterred, and he waxed lyrically for another ten minutes, staring dreamily at the ceiling so that the reality of awkwardly gyrating chubby office girls on the dance floor in front of him wouldn't disturb the fantasy. A shifty-looking rat-toothed guy of thirty sidled up next to me to order beer and threw a few curious glances our way. He was the distraction I needed before I was entirely co-opted into Jimmy's daydream.

I said hello. He immediately turned the conversation to girls.

"You two look like men of the world," he said, my mind immediately recalling Eric Idle's famous nudge-wink-say-no-more sketches in the *Monty Python* TV show. "This city is great for girls, isn't it? Ukrainians, Russians, they are all at it!"

Those words brought Jimmy out of his reverie. We looked at this cheerful degenerate and wanted to know more. He looked like a man with an angle, the type you'd never, *ever* buy electronics from in an open-air market.

"What do you mean, mate?" asked Jimmy, knowingly taking the bait. "Which girls do you like?"

Rat-man's eyes blazed with excitement, and he sat down and leaned in conspiratorially. "I'm fucking two Ukrainian blondes now. Proper hot girls. Look like models."

Let me take this moment to say my default attitude when men come up to me, seek conversation, and immediately start bragging about all the hot girls they fuck, is that he's either a liar or a PUA (but I repeat myself). They are always spinning a yarn, without exception. Nonetheless we were intrigued to find at just what moment this man's story would fall apart.

Green Park in London

"How do you meet them?" I probed.

Rat-man was sitting next to us now, gesturing arrogantly and clapping us on the shoulder like we were long lost friends. "Mate, it's really not hard. I'm a coke dealer. If they haven't got the money, I fuck them instead."

Around the time this bombshell dropped, a Russian girl I knew who liked cocaine messaged me to say she was at Oxford Circus in a taxi. The timing was almost Providential. I replied telling her to get out and I'd meet her there. I left our new drug dealer friend with Jimmy and nipped upstairs to fetch Julia. She seemed to be in an odd mood. No, not drunk nor on drugs – more like she was perplexed over a dilemma. I bought her a drink, we stood by the bar, and she started winding me up.

I don't know if it was deliberate, but she made a few tarty comments which pissed me off. She'd dance in a sexy sensual manner on the edge of the dance-floor next to us, then glide over to me and talk into my ear. Then she'd flit off again. Most of the room was checking us out because she was at least two points hotter than any other girl there. Rat-man's tongue was hanging out.

"Y-y-y-ou date girls like that?" he stammered, like I'd trumped him with Julia. When Ukraine sends its coke whores, they're not sending their best. Although some, I assume, are good people.

Julia continued her coquettish behaviour, gyrating like Salma Hayek in *From Dusk Till Dawn* then turning away and ignoring me for a minute. She'd come very close, gaze into my eyes, then wander off. I'll admit I enjoyed the show. I'd rather have this for free than join Steve in Spearmint Rhino to pay for it. She was a very sexy girl, and this was all directed at me.

The next time she turned her back on me, I did the most natural thing I could think of that would enforce my boundaries, in my inebriated and frustrated state. I gave Jimmy a look, put my foot on her arse, and sent her skidding across the dance floor into the speakers tower. Jimmy and I creased up laughing and rat-man sprayed beer through his nose. The whole room seemed to freeze.

Julia had skidded across half of the room but remained upright. She spun around with eyes blazing, grabbed her coat and stormed out. Jimmy and I still couldn't stop laughing.

"I think that's the last you'll see of her" he said. "Another bottle?"

A couple of months passed with radio silence. As far as I was concerned I'd given Julia all the time and all the information she needed to decide whether to fuck, and she'd decided no. So I was done pouring any more time into that bottomless pit. I went off to Yugoslavia with the gang and banged a few locals, as described earlier. Except for falling out with Jimmy, life was good.

We were all sprawled in hammocks in the Château garden, soaking up the sun. Lee was towelling himself off after Mick had thrown a pot of ice, cold water on him for a prank video. Jimmy still wasn't talking to us. He now haunted the hallways, an insouciant whistle announcing his presence, but he was never actually seen – kind of like a PUA poltergeist. Julia had started liking my photos again on Facebook.

"That's the first way to spot a girl's coming back on," advised Mick. "It's like when the shark nibbles at your toe before it comes back to bite your leg off."

Sure enough, a week later she began sending speculative messages. I replied in curt polite fashion, making no effort to joke around. I really couldn't care less about her, but if she wanted me, I was going to make sure she did all the chasing and work bloody hard for it. Eventually, she asked if we could meet for coffee. We agreed Caffe Nero at Fortune Green the following afternoon, a five minute walk down the bank from the Château.

I knew before she arrived that she'd made her mind up, finally, so watching her approach with her hip-swaying flair just confirmed the theory. She was dressed sexy, her eyes smouldered, and she immediately sat alongside me on the leather sofa. She stared, played with her hair, readjusted her skirt, and made a great display of conscious IOIs like a stripper trying to earn a lap dance fee. It was blindingly obvious and suddenly I took a liking to her again – now that I owned the frame. It seemed that the "pressure cooker" strategy would work best, giving her very little encouragement and refusing to act on her IOIs, in the hope she'd get increasingly frustrated and try ever harder. Then when the moment was ripe, on my bed, I'd finally pull her in and let her release the unbearable pent-up sexual energy.

So I continued to talk to her like we were comfortable in the friend-zone. I didn't gawk, touch, or kiss her. It was really satisfying watching her heat up and try new ploys to draw out my escalation. I knew it was in the bag. I was going to fuck this hot young player. We walked home and went up to my room. Steam seemed to hiss out of her ears. She was gagging for it, so I let her jump me. Clothes came flying off, she lay back with her legs open, and I pushed it in.

"No! I can't," she said again, this time I'd only made it a quarter of the way in before she scooted backwards. I fancy this is how Hitler felt getting turned back on the outskirts of Moscow knowing Napoleon had actually reached the Kremlin a hundred years earlier.

"No more, please!" This time I didn't have sufficient emotional investment to lose my rag and throw her out. I just switched off and went cold towards her. She'd been more up for it than at any previous moment. She'd quite obviously decided to fuck, pulled me in over Facebook, invited herself over, dressed to fuck, given me sex eyes in the cafe, and then undressed in my bed.

What madness was this? I suspect if I'd just held her down and forced my dick inside, no jury could call it rape.

"I'm sorry," she pleaded, pawing at my face. "I absolutely intended to have sex with you today. But something stopped me, I don't know. I don't understand it. Don't be angry!"

I stared deep into her eyes, trying to get a read on her. Was she just layering on yet more games playing? No, she seemed absolutely sincere. Blowing hot and cold wasn't a game, it was an expression of a genuine internal conflict.

"Okay, I understand, but we are finished," I said.

That seemed to be the crucial crack in the dam. Explanations tumbled from her in a torrent; she was still dating her boyfriend and didn't want to cheat on him, but it wasn't going well and she was thinking of dumping him. She really liked me but it's not in her character to cheat. Whatever. Not my problem. She dressed and left. There was no anger from me, just a resignation that I was to be forever cock-blocked by her messy private life. It would be smart to cut my losses.

The next morning she messaged me.

"I've broken up with my boyfriend. Can I come and see you? I promise it will be different this time."

She came over, and we fucked within five minutes of closing my bedroom door. It was weird in that she didn't just want sex but she also wanted to make restitution for her previous bad behaviour – it was like make-up sex without there having been a break-up first. It was also very *good* sex. High energy, dramatic, and wild. Perhaps it was even worth the wait.

We'd continue a sexual relationship for the two months she remained in London, her spending a lot of time around the Château and getting to know all my friends. Her English was excellent by now so there was little awkwardness plus the amount of time we'd spent messaging or hanging out before the sex had established a stronger than usual emotional connection. She went back to Russia, but we remained in close contact. We had a long weekend together in Barcelona the following January, and when I stopped over in Vilnius that April on my way to Belarus, both she and Dovile came around to fuck (unfortunately, not together).

It was always memorable. I remember doing her in the ass on a mattress in the loft of a warehouse conversion in a Vilnius industrial estate, watching her go absolutely insane with sexual abandon. She also fell into a drunken sleep on the sofa in Barcelona, so I woke her up by putting my dick into her ass then. too. Perhaps the most meta-level memory was in London in mid-2013. She'd gotten another short visa and came to visit me. We walked around central London so she could take in all the sights she loved. I spotted London daygamer Ed Lopez running around Trafalgar Square doing sets.

John and I used to call him "El Roido" because he's a short Peruvian who'd bulked up with steroids, making him look like Ray Mysterio Junior or perhaps the famous El Santos of 1960s Mexican exploitation movies. He was certainly a hard worker – in the ten minutes Julia and I were leaning over the high wall to watch him, he must've done five sets.

I noticed Julia was giving me "the look." Most girls get a recognisable "mong face" when desperately horny and anticipating sex. Their eyes go wide, deep, and seem to catch fire. Their mouths hang open dumbly while their head hangs down a little. Usually their conversation drops into mono-syllables and they move like a robot with its AI set to "follow." Once you recognise the look, you can spot it quickly. Julia had the least subtle version I'd ever seen. I turned around from watching Ed's set and saw her almost dripping with sexual energy.

Jesus, she wants to fuck right now, I thought.

She was only in town two days, and this was day two. We hadn't fucked yet. I walked her along The Strand and down Villiers Street towards Embankment. There's a Starbucks there with a disabled toilet I'd been meaning to check out. Naturally she didn't know about it, and I very deliberately turned my conversation to non-sexual topics for my own amusement in making the planned sex a bigger surprise. We stood in line for coffee and then sat at a table I chose which gave a view of who went in and out of the toilets.

She continued to give me that smouldering please-fuck-me look but never once verbalised it. I'm not even sure she knew she was throwing off the signals. No doubt her mind was just consumed by thoughts of hard dick and wet pussies.

"I need to use the toilet," I said and checked the disabled one. It was empty and clean, no queue. From the corner of my eye I could see the baristas fully engaged with customers. I stood outside the door and beckoned to Julia.

She looked confused for a moment, then the penny dropped. Her eyes opened in askance, and I nodded. She strode quickly across the floor and into the toilet. I locked her door, turned her against the raised baby-changing platform, and pulled her jeans down. Then I hammered her like I was drilling for oil. Five minutes later we exited the room past a middle-aged lady waiting in the queue.

I enjoyed the deeper emotional connection I had with Julia, as our familiarity and shared understanding made it very easy to get on with each other. I'd often consign (or be consigned by) girls to the one-and-done bucket but in Julia's case a number of factors stacked up well: she was hot enough that I felt not just pleased but *proud* in having banged her, she was smart enough and sufficiently self-aware to make good conversation, and her availability was the perfect balance of being around enough to keep a good connection but not so much that we slipped into the grinding mundane familiarity I'd experienced in the last year of my marriage.

Fucking Julia in a public toilet was the kind of adventure that reminded me I still had a zest for life. I never worried I was becoming a boring old man.

A holiday together to Barcelona

The Matrix

BELGRADE

CHAPTER
THIRTY FIVE

THE MATRIX

The Cold War continued in comical fashion. Jimmy and I were literally next-door neighbours but never spoke once in the following six months. I could hear him in his room, his door opening and closing, and his footsteps every time he walked into communal areas. That theatrically exaggerated whistling continued, and if it started up while I was asleep I'd invariably dream of PUA poltergeists haunting my mansion.

Obviously I wasn't going to crack first, maintaining frame was *far* more important than three years of solid friendship between liked-minded men who'd travelled the world together. *Far* more important. I once knocked on his door and returned a few of his Xbox games, but that was it. He'd still talk to Lee and Tony, but the rest of us were in the doghouse. He brought a few ugly whores around now and then to rut in his room. Well, I can't really say they were either ugly or whores – having barely caught a glimpse of them – but it felt better to just assume they were.

Mick, John, and I were ghoulishly fascinated, spending hours floating and dissecting complex theories on the psychology behind his blow-up. We were amateur psychologists diagnosing from afar.

"I think it's a reality implosion," said John. "He's spent years building up the mythology of Jimmy Jambone, the roguishly charming international cad, the Cary Grant for the new millennium, and now that reality has pricked the bubble, it's all crumbled."

"But isn't that the same thing *we* do?" asked Mick.

"It might be something more mundane," I said. "He'd pinned his dreams of financial and geographical independence on his new business back home, but it's hitting trouble. It can't be easy struggling to keep afloat, wondering if you're going to be stuck in an English office forever."

"And one of his close family members is seriously ill. That's hard on him," challenged Mick. "Losing friends, family, and business all at once can try a man's character."

"No no no," John interrupted, waving his finger like an impatient school teacher. "Let's stick to the psychology. That's far more interesting. Perhaps he's having an Adverse Bottom World Snapback Encounter."

"Have you just made up another bullshit word, John?" I asked. "Pray tell what fresh lunacy is this?"

John carefully placed his laptop to one side on the table by his sofa then leaned over, rubbing his hands in glee.

"It's like this. Jimmy is from a big family who all still live up North and are very tight. He's the lone offspring who went off to the big city to make something of himself. You know how us Northerners are about going down South where all the rich pufters live."

So far, so plausible.

"Well, haven't you noticed Jimmy only ever chases Trophy Girls? They all have to be tall, long-legged, and immaculately dressed. He's constantly dismissing the thought of getting little ratbags, or squirrels, or students. He wants to walk back to Manchester one day triumphantly showing off his girlfriend. He wants everyone in his town to say 'Hey, Jimmy is back after all these years, have you seen his bird? She's proper hot she is,' and he wants his dad to pat him on the back and say, 'Well done, son, she's a keeper.' That's it! That's always been his motivation in Game; the local boy done good."

"You can't claim that as your own," I said. "That entire Jimmy Girl-theory is something I concocted a month ago and told you. You're always nicking my ideas and putting your own names on them."

"Yes yes yes," John mumbled dismissively, waving his hand as if physically brushing uncomfortable facts aside. "Anyway, the point is this: It hasn't worked out. Instead of making it big in London, he's ended up in a dirty care home with a dozen unemployed pick-up artists. We get budget airline flights at 6am and stay in tiny box rooms in soviet apartment blocks. We spend most of the day in our underwear reading the internet."

"I do that in Tasmania, too," objected Mick, "and South America." He thought lying in a hammock doing absolutely nothing *was* living the dream.

"Jimmy dreams of greatness," John continued. "Travelling with us for a month has made him realise that he's failed. We live in Bottom World. What we are seeing is a bonfire raging out of control, and tied to the stake screaming in agony as the flames lick her feet is the Trophy Girl whom Jimmy fears he'll never get. Hopes and dreams, crushed by the squalor of PUA."

We didn't care that this was a spurious theory. Pathologising Jimmy's quest for top tier girls made us laugh, and we'd often spend entire weeks just stumbling from one lol to the next.

I'd had my own Adverse Bottom World Snapback Encounters over the past year, being my experiences with Tom, Antony, Cuba, and a pair of transexuals (if only they'd all occurred together in *the same story* imagine how cool it would be!). There wasn't any meltdown on my horizon, but I'd made a firm resolution to go after quality girls, the kind I could parade around Newcastle and people would say, "have you seen Nick's girl? She's classy and hot." It just so happened I had two of them in Belgrade talking to me on Skype and Facebook. Branka and Marijana had matured into Full Audrey leads.

I'd also decided to look for a real job. Two years of wopping around had gnawed away my sense of purpose. At first, resigning from my bank job had been liberating; I was escaping the matrix. Take *that*, Blue Pill World! I'm a Red-Piller now! I'd been free to hit on women, sleep in late, train hard, and travel the world. None of that would've been possible had I needed to wake up 7am every morning and commute into a stressful office job. The downside was that my sense of achievement was eroding. Without consistent challenge in all areas of my life I can become agitated, like I'm under-performing and losing my edge. I suspect that's my amygdala resisting early signs of atrophy, warning me that soft-living and dissipation make me less able to deal with the threats of this world, and thus it directs me to build it back up through struggle.

"I'll contract for three months over winter," I declared to Steve, as we lay on sofas in the lounge doing absolutely nothing. "That's the answer. Winter is shit for daygame anyway, and Europe will be properly snowed under. If I can stack some paper, it'll refill my war chest and bring my resume right up to date. It's the best of all worlds."

Steve agreed it was certainly, in theory, a wise move. "It's not as simple as just deciding to get a fat contract role and then making the money. It's a competitive market out there."

"Watch!" I said and picked up my phone. I'd already identified a few recruitment agents online earlier that morning and saved their phone numbers. I dialled the guy who'd least disgusted me in his web presence.

"Hi. My name is Nicholas, and I'd like to talk about a role you're handling."

I spent the next ten minutes summarising my resume to the agent and explaining my preferences. "I want a three-month role, and then I'm leaving," I said, steadfastly refusing to be considered for the more common six-month period. "I want to be free to travel by the end of February." I wrote down an email address he gave me and sent off my resume. One hour later the agent called me back.

"Your resume is great. I called my client, sent it on, and they want to interview you tomorrow. Now, could you tell us your salary expectations?"

The role was listed at £300 per day which seemed frankly absurdly high in the context of how much money I actually spent each week. I hadn't contracted before so I wasn't yet acclimatised to the nonsensical salaries they can pay. I still felt a little nervous because I'd been out of the industry for two years, and my requirements were very specific. I wanted a job right now, and it must end before the 2013 Euro Jaunt season began.

I put on my best suit and took a train into The City the next afternoon for a 2pm interview in a flashy office building fronted by a fully glass exterior. I walked through heavy revolving doors and across a wide lobby with marble floor and expensive black leather sofas around tables sporting the latest issues of *The Economist* and *Investors Chronicle*. Many eager and oh-so-professional workers buzzed around, and the secretary signed me in. I pressed my one-day plastic pass into the turnstile card reader and walked over to the elevator bank.

This was the centre of world finance, a high-level professional services firm, and I felt absolutely at home having worked many years in similar places. It was like slipping into a pair of long-lost favourite shoes. My body language immediately changed from the swaggering player's stroll to the upright efficient banker's walk. I could feel my brain click into another gear and even my grammar and vocabulary had shifted.

I was shown to a meeting room on the fourth floor and was supplied quality fresh coffee in a heavy white cup. Bottles of expensive spring water lined the low cupboard next to a stack of leather document wallets. It was all so familiar. Five minutes later a small man in his fifties came in carrying a thin file of papers. He shook my hand, introduced himself as Malcolm – the man running the team I was interviewing for – and began the interview.

I felt great, like I'd never lost a step. I self-consciously limited the more outrageously "alpha" body language and communication style I'd developed with girls, instead choosing to present myself as a calm and confident professional. The major Game learning point I followed was to avoid qualifying myself. My frame was that I had a ton of options, and I was investigating to see if this company was right for me.

We were done in twenty minutes. I'd passed the first test. My prospective manager Malcolm liked me. He'd satisfied himself that meat-space me was congruent with resume-me.

"Thank you very much for your time. I'd like you to talk to the office partner and the senior manager, but unfortunately they are busy today. Would you be willing to come back tomorrow?"

Indeed I would. I was impressed with the competence and professionalism of this outfit. Malcolm was the very picture of a seasoned, calm, oh-so-English finance professional. I liked him.

Twenty-four hours later, I was sitting in the same meeting room when the senior manager Toby strode in like he was between important presentations and really didn't have time for this shit. He introduced himself curtly, sat down, then ignored me for five minutes while reading my resume as if it were the first time he'd seen it. Then he looked up and held solid eye contact.

"This is a good resume, but I think you aren't as qualified for the role as we'd expect," he said. "Our office average is fifteen years post-qualification experience. You have five years."

I held eye contact, didn't fidget, and slowly nodded my head like he'd made a very good point. My calibration told me this was bluster – he was opening strong to steal the frame.

"I agree," I said and ever so slowly picked up my coffee and took a sip. "When interviewing me for my previous firm, my manager told me I had literally zero experience of that particular industry – which was true. He hired me because my academics and professional training were top-tier, and I showed the right amount of critical thinking, personality strength, and enthusiasm during the selection process."

Toby looked at me. He was a brawny masculine guy who I'd imagine voted UKIP, swore liberally in male company, and played rugby on Sunday afternoons. I was pleased to know the office senior manager was a man's man without a trace of faggotry in him. I knew what he'd respect.

"I applied for this particular role because it appears to be exactly in the middle of what my specific experience is. It is exactly the job I did, at the level I did, for the same niche of clients that I worked for with my previous employer."

This was all true. I knew this part of the finance industry inside and out. I spent the next ten minutes demonstrating it, giving him example after example and tying it all together with a coherent world view of global finance, many obscure technical anecdotes, and constantly displaying an old-timer's wisdom for how this industry really works. He was impressed, and it cost him immense energy to hide it and maintain his frame. I knew I had him convinced, so I went on the attack with a pre-prepared speech.

"The thing is, I don't need to work. I have enough money to live on a beach in Bali for the next ten years. However, after two years travelling the world with my friends I've come to miss the intellectual challenge of finance work. I love walking into a client's business, figuring out how it works, and then delivering on our promise. It keeps me sharp, and I'd very much like to stay sharp this winter. I already spoke to Malcolm, and he impressed me with his knowledge and attitude. I think this is a professional company."

I was pretty sure he'd lined up a tough question on why they shouldn't hire a man who'd been unemployed for two years as surely that represented a risk to the business. I'd pre-empted it and reframed the issue into me flying down from Mount Olympus to work with men who may, hopefully, be my equals.

Rob stepped out of the room and came back with the senior partner, a husky big Sikh man who embodied the larger-than-life persona of a high-level dealmaker. He shook my hand with a grip like a judo Olympian. This was not a man to be reframed easily, but I could also see he wasn't a "details" guy. I guessed Toby had recommended me, and he just wanted to perform a quick smell test and then close the deal. Five minutes of non-technical chat passed, and I knew they'd both agreed to hire me. "Okay, let's talk about salary expectations," he said.

"Roles like this usually pay around £450 per day," I said, gambling. It was almost true. "That seems about right."

The two men hastily conferred in low voices, hands over their mouths, then turned back to me.

"We feel that is too high. We were thinking of £400 per day."

My heart leapt like I'd just kiss-closed a catwalk model, but I kept my poker face. I nodded slowly, looked up and away as if I was making a decision, then looked back. "Okay. £400. I'm quite excited to work here."

We shook on it, and I walked out. I'd barely returned my security pass and reached the revolving doors when my agent called me up again. "Great interview! Well done!" he gushed, having earned the easiest commission of his career. "Let's just confirm the details."

Re entry to the Matrix

We confirmed. I was ecstatic. I'd worried that my two-year break had hurt my resume and if I'd lost the ability to function in the corporate world. Evidently not. I'd closed the deal at the first attempt. Forty-eight hours and one phone call after beginning my job search, I was slipping right back into my comfort zone on £75 per day more than I'd have been willing to take.

I walked on air all the way to Brick Lane market and bought a lightweight black biker jacket that cost exactly £75 because of the symbolism of the amount. That became my favourite daygame jacket, and it's the one I wear in *Daygame Overkill*.

I was chatting to Branka every few days. Her English was pretty good, and I enjoyed getting to know her well. Investing so much time in a girl online can be a time-sink, so I'd developed a structure to balance my investment with her willingness to be escalated. I'd already had girls like Martina in Lithuania milk me out of literally months of Facebook chat and then not spread their legs at the crucial moment. Now that I was signed up to work the next three months beginning in a week, I would have considerably less free time to waste and every solid lead was precious.

I resolved that Branka *must* talk about sex, her proclivities, and also send me racy photos. This was just the foundation of Long Game – a girl who won't do that is highly unlikely to have sex with you. If I can get her to reach the "let's have sex" decision from the comfort of Skype, then I'd feel much more secure booking a flight to Belgrade to close her. The last thing I wanted was to sit in a Belgrade apartment four days straight while it's too cold to daygame, and my leads won't come out.

"I've only had sex with one man" she told me, typing into Skype chat. "It was traumatic. He was a player, and he gave me an STD. It only cleared three months ago."

We shared a few sexual projection stories and dirty talk. I sent her a link to a pornographic blog run by a sex-positive feminist called *Sex Saves the Day*. The photos she collected from around the internet were all selected to appeal to women and ran the gamut from soft to very hard.

"Choose your favourite five images, and tell me what you like about them," I instructed her.

Whatever happened, it would get Branka thinking about sex and about me. I was pleased when she selected a few of the coy photos and two hardcore. My dick advanced one step closer to her vagina. I've found that girls who prefer to milk you of attention will rebuff attempts to engage them in these games. Even shy good girls will play along if they are sexually attracted to you – they'll just choose the least obscene pictures to prop up their good girl image.

One week she sent me photos of her wearing earrings of the letters N and K. She didn't know of my Krauser pick-up identity, just that Nick ends in that letter. In amongst the regular selfies I also had her perform a striptease on video chat then talked her into masturbating afterwards. It was all good fun and sucked her in. I found I was really taken by her, beginning to think she'd be a solid regular. She had everything I was looking for; young, smart, introverted, pretty, tall, sexually potent, chaste. I was chatting to Marijana, too, but she was considerably more reserved online so I focused those chats on rapport.

I remember my main feeling when seducing these girls online was one of power. It was a dirty, dark feeling of control. I needed to lie back and introspect on why that emotion bubbled up.

Thinking back to 2009 and my first foray into Game, my overwhelming feeling had been of powerlessness. I'd been thrust back onto the dating market without any skills to compete. If you were to describe my mindset that first year, you'd find a seething tangled mess of desperation, neediness, bitterness, and power lust. This all bubbled away and jostled for position with my more wholesome traits. By summer 2009 I'd experienced the eye-opening realisation that I could initiate conversations with precisely the pretty young girls that I fancied. As summer 2010 arrived, I found myself dating a sweet 22-year-old Thai girl and a concurrent relationship with an even sweeter 19-year-old French girl. Not only was I getting regular sex with girls who just one year previously would've seemed forever off-limits, but I had a second eye-opening realisation... those two girls were madly in love with me.

Holy shit! I felt like Smeagol wearing the One Ring.

The Men's Rights Activism websites I was still reading in 2010 reinforced the feelings of abandonment and injustice that I'd felt after my divorce. I'd become seriously mistrustful of women both in the abstract and in person and dealt with it by constructing a hard "alpha" shell around myself for protection. I deliberately screened for young, naive girls with limited sexual experience. Tasanee had only one previous sexual partner four years before meeting me, and the same with Adele.

I was probably the last person you'd ever want to learn the skill of "deep conversion," of making a girl fall for you hard. In early 2011, my game therapist Colin had been shocked at just how effectively I could rope in a girl, and he'd immediately dedicated himself to persuading me not to. When that failed, he switched tack and tried his best to pull me away from the Dark Side.

He was right, of course, but I wasn't giving up My Precious so easily. While I was scrupulously honest in my dealings with women (except for the one Big Lie of hiding my pick-up identity), I still felt compelled to suck girls in and make them fall for me. The hotter and more chaste the girl, the greater the achievement. I want a girl in Belgrade, I thought, so I'll damn well have one, and Branka very much fitted the bill as the new girlfriend.

"You know I'm staying in London, and I will date other girls," I told her.

"That's okay," she replied, giving me the moral fig leaf I needed to feel comfortable with my plan.

We agreed she'd come to London to visit me in November. Her parents agreed to pay for the flight, no doubt selling it to them as a sightseeing trip, and she'd stay at my place. She was ecstatic and so was I. Then towards the end of August I received my work schedule from Malcolm. My job involved specific self-contained projects that usually had three stages; planning, on-site work, and reporting. My contract paid me for billable days and nothing when I was idle. We'd agreed this suited us both fine because I was free to take short trips between stages and jobs. A five-day window had opened in late September.

"I'm coming to Serbia," I told Branka and she nearly wet herself in excitement.

I pre-framed myself that it wasn't to be a gaming holiday. It was a short trip, and I didn't want the pressure of relentlessly approaching. With that in mind, I set myself some easily attainable goals: close Branka and hang out with her like a girlfriend, try to persuade Marijana to take the five-hour bus from her hometown to Belgrade, travel back via Zagreb and try to close Gordana, the vampire make-up artist. I'd consider the trip successful if I knocked over any one of the girls and finished the Erle Stanley Gardner paperback I was reading.

Belgrade was cold. On my first night in town, I walked out of my little private apartment down by the park and onto the main promenade to meet Branka, enjoying the stroll through bustling streets and the early evening crowd. Within a minute my head was swivelling around like a bobble-head, girl after beautiful girl tottering past. In the short walk to Coffee Dream I saw at least twenty girls who excited me more than Branka. These were solid eights dolled up for Friday night. Heels, skirts, make-up...oh, it was unbearable.

It reminded me of July in Istanbul when I'd walk with Sanaz. While every male head was turning to gawp at her, my head was turning the other way to catch all the gorgeous tight-assed young Turkish girls who made my blood bubble far more than Sanaz did. It had happened with Zaria too, also in Istanbul, in early 2011. That had indicated some kind of inner-game issue, but the drama in Sarajevo and Zagreb had buried it. Now, feeling the same emotional reaction on my way to the date with Branka I realized I had a problem: even being on dates with the very high-quality girls I so pursued, I'd feel trapped and resentful that I can't chase after even more girls.

Closing time with Branka

What was wrong with me? Surely having one hot, young eight on your arm – a girl who adores you – is quite enough. Nope. No matter what I had now, I wanted more. No amount of women would ever be enough. I shelved these thoughts as I saw Branka approach.

"Be nice. Enjoy yourself," I told myself then stood up to greet her.

We walked to the traditional restaurant district, Skardarlja, and my sinking feeling continued. I couldn't stop various thoughts popping up: *she's dressed a bit dowdy, her hair seems dry, those tits are nothing special.* I realise now it was the narcissistic relationship phases playing out in rapid time – I'd Idealised her over the Skype chats and was now entering the Devaluation phase. How long until I tumbled into the Discard phase? I felt like I had no control over it – I very much wanted to stay attracted to her because I knew she was a great girl.

The restaurant was lovely, one of the best in the whole country. I was still into my International Man of Mystery vibe. After a few years living on savings, I felt so affluent on my new London salary that I didn't even need look at the restaurant prices.

This is it! This is what you've worked for all these years, Nick, I pleaded to myself, trying to reframe myself to ignore the sinking feelings. *You studied hard to be able to talk widely on these subjects. You worked hard to fund it all. You learned Game to get girls like this – girls exactly like Branka – to become attracted to you and go on dates with you.*

I ate a spicy meatball and commented that it was delicious. Branka enthusiastically agreed and stared at me with misty, lovestruck eyes.

This is exactly what you want Nick, I told myself. *Exactly. Close your eyes and dream. Imagine yourself in your city of choice, in your restaurant of choice. Now imagine your ideal woman. It's Belgrade, in Skadarlija, with Branka, isn't it?*

It wasn't working. Even during this weak attempt to reframe myself, the waitress had topped up my wine glass, and I wanted to fuck her more than Branka. Worse yet, I knew that if Branka and the waitress were to magically change roles, it would be Branka and not the waitress who I wanted.

I was trapped. I'd gotten exactly what I wanted but didn't want it any more. Was I condemned to be a perpetual malcontent?

Branka was blissfully unaware of my inner turmoil. We had a lovely meal and conversation, then I took her home and fucked her. I couldn't stop finding faults – her underwear is unattractive, her skin isn't sufficiently vibrant, her finger nails are painted the wrong colour. Then, ten minutes into the sex while Branka was on top and riding me, my brain dredged up the absolute perfect Devaluation pretext.

She'd admitted having an STD earlier in the year.

Perfect! This was reason to both Devalue *and* Discard her! I couldn't help it, I just started visualizing catching this no-longer-existent STD.

"Get off," I said, pushing her off me and standing up. "I just can't."

Then I went to shower, scrubbing myself to be sure. Never before or since have I been so obsessed with the thought of catching an STD – even as I was acting out, I knew it was a bullshit pretext because I always used condoms. I just couldn't help myself. I came back into the bedroom to find Branka's second big romantic moment in her life had been just as traumatic as her first. She was worried.

"What's the problem? Did I do something wrong?" she asked.

"I've had a big problem at work. It keeps pushing into my mind. I'm sorry," I said. I'd not lost my self-awareness, so I knew how deplorably I was behaving and was ashamed of it, so I tried to soften the blow for her.

We walked to her bus stop on a side-street and waited half an hour in the cold. I was impatient and wanted to go home and try to figure things out. We talked a little and finally she noticed a small printed notice explaining that her bus was temporarily withdrawn.

"Oh god, I'm so sorry!" she bleated, convinced this was some final straw that had broken our relationship. We went to Republic Square, and she caught a different bus. The whole time hot girls were swarming the square in their night-club clothes. It was horrible. I went to my apartment and lay on the sofa turning everything over in my mind.

Was this just another meltdown, or was it symptomatic of a larger problem?

I woke up to a text message from Marijana telling me she wanted to visit me in Belgrade, but her parents forbade it.

"You actually told them about me?" I replied, incredulous.

I pulled the curtains aside to see the sun was up. It was late Saturday morning, and I could no longer deny my natural instincts: I wanted to daygame. Solo daygame abroad is mentally taxing, and I hadn't been alone in a foreign country since visiting Adele in mid-2010. I knocked out a few sets (not literally, I wasn't *that* angry at the world) while wearing the work suit I'd worn when leaving the office the previous afternoon to go directly to the airport. It felt rather odd to daygame dressed as a banker. My smart leather shoes struggled to grip the slick pavement of Knez Mihailova.

I saw a very beautiful girl walk by, exactly the sort who'd turned my head the previous evening when I should've been paying attention to Branka. She was tall, dusky, and clearly too hot for me. Fuelled by the maniacal energy to open something-anything-everything, I ran up. I skidded on ahead but Milena stopped and smiled. She was a student from a small town in Bosnia, twenty years old, and the hottest girl I'd spoken to all year. She gave me what from her mannerisms appeared to be a flaky number so I was amazed when she replied to my ping. She'd later tell me the line which caught her interest was in reply to her telling me she was a student. I'd looked her up and down in her volleyball team tracksuit and said, "Well, not of fashion obviously."

Branka was texting to meet up that evening. I was mad at myself for treating her so badly and convinced this was just a minor wobble and everything would be fine if I'd just hold myself together and let the feeling pass. We watched the new *Total Recall* at the Tuckwood Cinema up by the parliament building. I didn't want to be in the cinema, I didn't want to be watching *Total Recall,* and I didn't want to be in Serbia. Branka knew something was badly wrong and became worried. I gave her a half-hearted kiss goodbye then on the way home I messaged her to say we weren't sexually compatible, and that I didn't want to see her again.

She was mortified and started blowing up my phone with messages. She suspected I'd planned to pump and dump her from the beginning, which was about as far from my original intentions as it could possibly have been.

Within a few weeks her hurt turned to anger. She said I was an arsehole and she hoped I got AIDS from all my philandering. There was some pretty nasty and vindictive stuff in those messages. I felt bad because her previous (and according to her, only) sexual partner had treated her like shit before dumping her hard, and she'd once told me that if I did the same to her, she'd break into little pieces. I wanted to let her down gently, but that would have been like kicking her to death while wearing slippers.

It's not easy to break up with a girl who has fallen for you, and I'd become quite smitten with Branka too. Timing is important. Sex triggers a cascade of hormonal and emotional responses within her that are not present prior to sex. Players are well-aware of the sudden dramatic shift in power in a relationship after the initial lay. The effect is pronounced once you've banged her three times, as the oxytocin addiction takes over and her final barriers crumble. An old pre-game maxim of mine is "bang a girl three times and you own her."

Girls have a purging mechanism. If you dump them hard – shutting off all hope of recovery – they'll cry their eyes out for three weeks, eat giant tubs of ice cream, and then one morning they'll wake up completely over you. Branka took a while longer.

Branka is one of my big regrets in Game. Through carelessness and a lack of emotional control, I managed to find exactly the wrong girl to mistreat. After six months of radio silence, she re-initiated Facebook contact. She'd blow hot and cold, sometimes sweet and nice, and other times sending angry messages. I took it all as part of my penance, letting her say whatever she needed to in order to get over me.

Finally, in September 2014, we met for coffee. I had a working theory that she wanted me to hit on her precisely so she could reject me and thus achieve closure. So I gave her precisely that. We had a nice drink, chatted, she nuzzled up against me, and we made out. She then refused to come back to my apartment, declaring she "didn't like me much anymore"

Great, my conscience was clear. I haven't seen or heard from her since.

While walking away from Branka outside the cinema, I'd pinged Milena. She'd finished studying at the library and was keen to meet. I could hardly believe it, doesn't she realise she's too hot for me?

I waited in Republic Square at 10pm and congratulated myself inwardly as I saw Milena arrive. We tried a couple of bars in the Strahinjica Bana region, ending up in the loft room of the "moustache bar" whose name I'll never remember but has dozens of moustaches painted on the walls. Milena kept herself on a tight rein and the deep rapport went beautifully. She warmed to the questions game, telling me she'd only ever kissed ten boys, her most embarrassing secret was she that she liked to lock herself in the bathroom and dance to her iPod, and that she'd broken up with her boyfriend one month earlier (and like Branka she claimed he was her only ever sexual partner). We parted with a non-committal peck on the lips, but I could tell she was somewhat into me.

The next morning, Sunday, I struggled out of bed at noon. I was to catch the bus to Zagreb the next day. I messaged Milena and she immediately struck up a text chat, so I invited her out.

"Let's walk to Zemun" she suggested. I had no idea what that was, but agreed.

That afternoon was the most enjoyable part of the trip, walking along the riverside and through quaint streets, sharing coffee, and sitting in the park. Five blissful hours with Milena on my arm. I teased her a little as onlookers gawped at us.

"You see that girl staring at us? I know what she's thinking"

"What?" she asked.

"She's looking at you then looking at me. She's thinking *how the hell did she find a guy like him? Where can I get one?*"

I tried to kiss-close, but she wasn't having it. I put it down to her K-selected village girl identity rather than any lack of attraction. We exchanged Skypes, and I left Belgrade the next morning. I felt strangely mercenary – I'd come to date one girl and ended up with another, an upgrade.

My first night in Zagreb was hit by a thunderstorm, so I headed out to my favourite restaurant for a steak then spent the rest of the evening in my apartment chatting on Facebook. Gordana confirmed our Tuesday evening tryst.

That next afternoon I had a weird date with Sofija, the girl who really did look like Audrey Hepburn. We drank coffee for a few hours, then whisky, and finally rum. There was no question she fancied me, but I could sense a barrier and knew it wasn't on. She stayed out of effective touching distance and didn't reciprocate my verbal escalation. It was a quandary. I couldn't allow a date with such an incredibly beautiful woman end without making an unambiguous statement of intent. Three hours in, I made my big move. I caught a 'hypnotic scanning' moment where we held deep eye contact and electricity seemed to spark between us. I went for it.

"I want to kiss you now," I said.

She held my eye contact, our faces quite close but not so close that I could just lean in to kiss. "You shouldn't try." I continued to gaze into her eyes, trying to turn her on. "I can tell you why, if you want," she said.

I asked her to do so and she launched into a long explanation about how, yes, she did find me attractive, and if we'd done this earlier in the year she'd indeed have had sex with me, but at that moment she was hung up on her ex-boyfriend and trying to get him back. Fuck. On the plus side, I had a solid nine admitting she would've had sex with me – that represented considerable progress from rattling the likes of Isabella and Chiara the previous summer.

Gordana met me that evening in Alcatraz. She was dolled up and immediately giving the eye. I settled into my drink and let things unfold as she knocked her own vodka back fast. I knew what *that* indicated. Within the hour, she was clambering all over me in the bar, so I started looking towards extracting her. She insisted on showing me a nearby bar which served a blueberry liquor (tasty, as it happened) which surprisingly was the very same bar where the landlord had held a knife to my throat. She agreed to the short, five-minute walk to my apartment, giving herself the pretext that she wanted to watch the rerun of the original *Mad Max* that started two hours later.

She was oh-so-hot but I couldn't get her tights off. We were writhing around on the bed topless and my dick tantalisingly close to her mouth but never quite inside. I rolled her over and bit her ass.

"Harder," she purred. "Leave marks."

In for a penny, in for a pound. I started yanking her tights down. "No!" she squeaked and fought me off, "I promised myself I wouldn't go that far tonight".

I couldn't surmount her LMR and never saw her again. I boarded my flight home to London with mixed feelings. I'd banged Branka but not enjoyed it, I'd met and dated Milena, then had both Sofija and Gordana admit they wanted sex with me but had decided it was a bad idea. They were all eights or better. At twenty-three years old, Gordana was the oldest.

What devilry was this? Was this success or failure?

I still feel bad about Branka

But at least the food was good

LONDON

Waltzing With Matilda

THIRTY SIX

WALTZING WITH MATILDA

My excitement at returning to work lasted about two weeks before it became a dull grind. I'd wake up in early-morning darkness and go through the laborious process of dressing up for work and shuffling down to West Hampstead underground station to join the other half-asleep zombies on the train. I took satisfaction in taking "right action" knowing that every week I endured as a corporate drone was banking money and polishing my resume, but I was amazed how boring it all was. For eight hours every day, I was forced to focus on what I *needed* to do rather than what I wanted to do. It felt like a contravention of my human rights.

"I've never been so bored," I'd tell John when we both came home from work. "It's made me realise that for the past two years I've never been genuinely bored. Any time one activity became tiresome I'd just switch to another one I was interested in – from daygame, to reading, to video games, to movies, to trolling Jimmy. Even the dullest parts of those days were better than now. Sometimes I just stare at my laptop screen and zone out – I can't do something else yet can't face doing what I'm supposed to."

"We are all broken men," Steve commented from the kitchen. It was his new go-to phrase.

All my London girls had dropped off, and I had no interest in daygaming locally. The moment I got home I just wanted to strip off my suit, put on my He-Man t-shirt, and hibernate. I kept up my Long Game with the Serbian girls but was otherwise an ex-player. A few weeks of that, and I was missing the sex. Even more, I was missing the thrill of chasing women.

"Just one more hit on the daygame crack pipe," I told John. "I need the thrill."

My second client had offices near Covent Garden, and I was on-site alone in a specially-prepared meeting room stacked with my papers and client files in piles around my desk. I'd spend all day there reading through reports, crunching data, and writing up workpapers. A few times each day I'd venture out to sit with a manager or trader and have them talk me through a system I was analysing, or fetch more data to crunch. I was so fully in my comfort zone that it bored me out of my mind. There was nothing unexpected, nothing I couldn't handle, and the lack of drama depressed me.

Mid-morning I was taking a break and chatting on Facebook to Neira from Sarajevo. She'd been close to visiting me in Belgrade but backed out when her work schedule changed. Now she was sending me naked selfies. I felt outrageously horny and couldn't stop thinking about girls for the rest of the day. That afternoon I was sitting at a currency trader's desk as he talked through his Forwards valuation model and gave sample transactions to lay off risk through OTC derivatives. I kept staring at my notepad, wondering if Neira would let me do her in the ass and if she'd have a threesome with Esma.

I had a late lunch from the nearby Pret-A-Manger and tried to focus on work. By half past three, I simply couldn't take it anymore. I packed up my briefcase and locked the meeting room door. On the way out I walked past the Head of Trading's office and popped my head in.

"I need to return to the office to write up my notes," I said, and he nodded.

"See you tomorrow," he chirped.

"I'm gonna fuck a whore," I texted John, then pressed the elevator call button and signed out at reception.

I stepped into the cool autumn air near Covent Garden station and felt great. I felt free. With a spring in my step I headed off to Soho. I wound up on Greek Street scanning the first-floor walk-ups between kebab shops and ethnic grocery stores.

"Busty Brazilian Model" declared a badly-written yellow card pinned on the wall inside one door. "Romanian Brunette Model" claimed another. I'd heard there wasn't much money to be made in the modelling industry, but it seemed these girls were really struggling between Chanel and Prada contracts. I walked up a couple of staircases and returned to street level quickly, unimpressed with the quality. "Even the whores are in decline," I grumbled. It seemed like nothing in London could interest me anymore.

A quarter hour later I was increasingly frustrated and ever more horny.

Finally I got lucky. On the second floor of my fourth walk-up, the grizzled old lady minding the reception lounge showed me upstairs and knocked on a tatty wooden door. The Spanish girl who opened it was legitimately pretty. She looked about twenty, a flat stomach, and a pretty face. She couldn't have been working long because she hadn't yet acquired the dull, burned-out eyes of a sex worker.

"Yes, I like her," I told the old maid.

"You can't take your sandwich inside," she admonished me then stood waiting as I wolfed down the rest of my brie, cranberry, and grape M&S sandwich. I handed her the empty cardboard carton and thirty pounds in crisp notes fresh from the ATM. She disappeared downstairs.

"Come in," cooed the Spaniard and walked me inside. She wore a dark grey basque, stockings up to mid-thigh, and a suspender belt. She was about as pretty as Daniela. Ironically, she gave off less of a slut vibe than her fellow Spaniard, Isabella.

"I'm in a rush, I'm not taking my suit off," I announced, then stood on the musty Turkish rug in room centre and got my dick out. She dropped to her knees and rolled a condom onto it using her mouth. After a short blow job, I told her to kneel on the bed then banged her doggy style. It took about ten minutes and somehow felt better than knobbing Branka. The sheer grottiness of the episode had a purging effect, as if an old Aztec demon had possessed me in Mexico and was finally exorcised. This Spaniard really did have a nice ass, and I had no trouble banging her until completion. It was nice to have sex without even a pretence of emotional connection.

"You cool man," she said afterwards. *Thanks hon, I loved you long time, too*, I thought. Thoroughly satisfied, I walked back to Charing Cross road, bought a collection of HP Lovecraft short stories and read it in a nearby Caffe Nero for a few hours.

My phone pinged with a message. "I'm getting a whore," said John. Clearly I'd set his mind moving in this direction, and he too couldn't focus on work. He left work at half past five and stopped off at a Chinese rub 'n' tug massage parlour on Finchley Road. A fat forty-year-old madam gave him a hand job, then he got the next Number 13 up the bank back to the mansion.

We arrived home within minutes of each other and were soon sitting in the lounge laughing about the sheer squalor of our lives. Steve wandered in with his laptop.

"It's good you're here," he started. "Let me show you the Google AdWords campaign I'm split-testing today."

"Don't care, mate," said John. "I just had a rub'n'tug."

Steve looked askance at me, sitting next to me on the sofa and manoeuvring his laptop into position so we could both see his Google Analytics. He patiently set up several tabs on his browser to aid explanation.

"I don't care either, mate. I just rattled a young Spanish whore."

He sat there, silently staring into space for a full minute. John chuckled in the pervert Eddie the Bastard laugh he reserved for his bottom-world escapades. It appeared we'd short-circuited Steve. He'd come barrelling in determined to boast of his marketing campaign, and now he just sat there, his eyes blank like Ted Bundy on the witness stand.

"I want one, too," he croaked. Another twenty seconds went by, and he recovered his customary gusto. His indecisive wobble passed, and he closed down his browser windows and opened a new one.

"How do I get a whore?" he asked. "Show me!"

We both chuckled and wandered out of the room. Let him figure it out for himself, we agreed.

Ten minutes later I came back downstairs to get some orange juice from my fridge. I could hear Steve on the phone in the lounge. "I want a whore. Can you send me a whore?" he said in his impatient demanding manner. There was a long silence and then, "Hello? Hello? Bitch, have you hung up on me?"

I was sitting with John in his room sharing my bottle of Johnnie Walker Double Black, ice rattling in our whiskey tumblers, when Steve rapped on the door. "Got one! You'll see!" he shouted through the door then stomped off in triumph. And hour later he messaged: "Fucked her. Big, fat, black mama!"

"We are all broken men," John said, raising his glass.

I'd have liked to say this was the end of my "squalid phase," but there was still a small amount of poison to be bled from the wound. A week later London was buffeted by wind, rain, and even hailstones. My

How this period of my life felt

mood turned greyer than the overcast skies, and I reached for OK Cupid. Online game has always been a waste of time for me, Zehra aside, I simply never get matches. I posted a new highly-belligerent profile and threw out thirty speculative messages. Six girls hooked and replied but things quickly whittled down to two: a black English girl and a Portuguese waitress. The black girl went bananas when I made some innocent joke about her climbing trees, and she started calling me racist, threatening to report me for calling her a monkey. It was an absolutely insane misinterpretation of an innocent joke, so I dared her: "Go on, report me. The admin will read the messages and conclude you are bat-shit insane and ban you."

Of course, OK Cupid was actually created by a creepy pedestalising gamma male and likely staffed by them too, so they were far more likely to simply play "side against the white man." I didn't care.

In contrast, Matilda from Portugal was delightfully sweet in her messages, responding with smilies, questions, and unsolicited information. She sent me a few pictures from which I deduced she was somewhere between a six and a seven. It's notoriously difficult to judge online. "She'll do," I thought, and we exchanged numbers. I was still wavering on whether to meet her, but a little text exchange convinced me I'd at least enjoy her company.

"I should warn you that although my grandmother says I'm a wonderful boy, I can also be a hungry wolf," I wrote.

"For our grandmothers and mothers, we are always a sweet angel lolololol but there comes a time when a hungry wolf comes and changes everything, but they don't need to know that :)" she replied and agreed to meet at West Hampstead tube station. Okay, she gets it. I'd pre-framed her for casual sex so I doubted she'd waste my time. Rather, I expected she'd give me the once over and decide within a few minutes if it was on.

"I'm going out to fuck a Portuguese slag," I called out to John as I put on my woolly hat and fur-lined flight jacket. Walking down to the station I was keenly aware of the big problem with internet dating: It's like filling out a ticket at Argos, the chances are that what you get is nothing like it looks in the catalogue. Fortunately, Matilda looked the same as her photos. She was twenty-nine and would have been very pretty in her early twenties. Cute face, thick luxuriant hair, and a sweet smile. A six with pleasant manner. Fine by me.

We kissed greetings on the cheek, and I walked her up the bank to a nearby bar. It was busy with the weekend after-work crowd so we settled in on stools by the bar, and I began my DHV stack. Right from the off, I knew I had her. She'd not had sex for a long time and was probably getting desperate from all the dross she must've already met through OK Cupid. Her facial expression had that wide-eyed look of happy disbelief, like I'd felt at the job interview when they offered 25% more cash than I'd expected.

I gave her the full date treatment, but on fast-forward. I DHV'd, ran rapport, and played with her hair. She was looking at me so imploringly it felt cruel to make her wait any longer, so after fifteen minutes I leant in and kissed her. The dam broke. She couldn't stop nuzzling me, running her hands over my face, scratching my beard and pawing me. I walked her further up the hill to another pub where we could sit together on a sofa at the back.

I dirty-talked her, accusing her of being a pervert trying to seduce me. Then I pulled her in and told her to grab my cock. She was tugging on it in the bar, her eyes unfocused and dreamy. "I can't have sex," she bleated. "I'm on my period." I backed off and ran comfort for the next drink, then sent her home.

The next day she flooded my phone with a stream of very uninhibited texts, and we arranged to meet for sex a few days later. That was a mistake; too explicit and too obvious. Doubts crept into her head. A couple of hours before the sex date she messaged me.

"Hey, I'm sorry I can't do this. You are amazing, and physical, you have everything I like in one man, but this is not what I'm looking for. I tried to tell to myself I could do it, go there, have some sex fun, whatever, and come back home like nothing happened but I can't."

That's the problem with creating an It's On moment and not sealing the deal. The window closes and may never reopen.

She was indicating that the problem was comfort – clearly there was no lack of attraction. I swiftly reframed the situation telling her we'd just go out for a drink and that nothing would happen. That was all the plausible deniability she needed. We did indeed have one drink, then I walked her home and fucked her.

"You know this is casual sex?" I checked, as she lay with her head on my chest.

"Yes, I know," she said. She seemed a little disappointed but shrugged and didn't make a fuss. We exchanged a couple of texts afterwards so I could give her a little more comfort, and then I let her go. I remembered that when I'd walked her into the house, John had been cooking and as her gaze lingered on him the look on her face made me pretty sure she fancied him. That gave me an idea. John had been striking out on dates because he was unable to escalate – it was like women had an aura he couldn't penetrate with touch. So a few days later as we sat in the lounge, I asked him about Matilda.

"Yeah, she's alright," he said.

"What do you think of my friend, John?" I asked Matilda over SMS. "He's the one you met in the kitchen."

"He is good looking and nice," she replied.

"He likes you, too. Shall I help you set up a date?" She agreed, so I facilitated it and passed on their numbers. He did pretty good on the date but fell at the last hurdle when she resisted being brought home to exactly the same house I'd fucked her in, to be fucked by a man who looked like me, was from the same hometown, and escalated her with exactly the same method. Perhaps it was a bit too weird for her.

Matilda was fun to be with, and I really enjoyed the dates, but she was the least attractive girl I'd fucked all year. My "normal" London life was not as appealing as my Balkans life. Collecting my Portuguese flag felt somehow grotty compared to posturing as the Most Interesting Man In The World.

I started planning a return to Belgrade.

Mount Awesome

CHAPTER
THIRTY SEVEN

MOUNT AWESOME

Milena had hooked strong. We'd chat late at night, and it fascinated me to burrow into her mind and discover how she thought. Every time we spoke, I'd learn more about her world view, and it constantly conflicted with my own limiting beliefs.

"I've never been to a nightclub," she told me over Skype. It seemed ridiculous to her that girls would dress up, go into a dark, sweaty room full of strangers, then wave their arms around on the dance floor until men groped them. This didn't compute. Surely it was PUA Fact that women loved attention and nightclubs were designed specifically to feed it to them?

"I don't want that kind of attention," she said. "I don't care what strangers think of me."

Milena was a village girl from the south of Bosnia, her dad a high-ranking policeman on the local force. She was the very definition of a greyhound: tall, curvy, intelligent, and with high self-esteem.

"Why do you like me?" I asked.

"I can't beat you. Every man collapses around me within five minutes. I can play with them, and they are weak. I know I can't do that to you. It makes you very interesting."

Interesting indeed.

"I want to hear you talk. Read me a story," she demanded.

"Wait," I said, going off to pour myself a whiskey. I sat down in front of my webcam, looking at her lying on her bed smiling.

"See! That's it! I can't control you," she gushed.

She told me my voice is hypnotically sexual, something many non-native speaker girls have mentioned. On dates I often pull out a paperback I'm carrying and read a few pages to them for precisely this reason. They'll often lose track of the words and just daydream, letting my voice wash over them. I did the same with Milena, reading from *The Count of Monte Cristo*. The more we chatted, the more I realised I'd sucked her in. These chats were becoming the highlight of my dreary workdays, and I suspected the feeling was mutual.

There remained a pressing issue – she'd rejected my kiss-close attempts back in September. To pursue Milena I'd need a few days off work, a flight to Serbia, and a centrally-located apartment. That's a big investment for a girl you've never kissed who has declared herself a chaste village girl. She was right up there among the prettiest girls I'd ever spoken to, so I was highly motivated. Was there any way to load the dice in my favour before rolling them?

I took a page out of Tony's book, creating an elaborate and romantic future projection where you both have sex, then walk her through it online. At the next video chat, I told her to lie comfortably, and I'd tell a story. I spun a yarn about us getting a ferry to a small Sicilian island then exploring the town and eating on the wharf. Somehow our fantasy selves ended up in bed fucking like animals.

I'd been trying these kinds of stories since seducing Zaria almost two years earlier so it had become a system. I'd start slow, set the scene with all its colours, sounds, and smells, then get the girl to buy in with small suggestions. The imaginary date would build emotional intensity and then ramp up smoothly until the sex happened. The whole time her reactions would let me know if I was moving too fast. For the first hour, I could see Milena sinking into the fantasy and her cheeks flushing red with excitement. Her eyes grew ever wider, and finally she became bashful and turned her camera off. I think it was pretty obvious what she was doing in her bedroom. She'd crossed the sexual Rubicon.

Girls have vivid imaginations so taking them all the way to the end of a sex chat is almost as effective as having actual sex. When you finally date them again, the first sex feels like the second sex to them. The enhanced comfort drastically reduces LMR. As the next week passed she sent me some pretty (and non-sexual) photos of her, and I inquired into her sexual preferences.

"I don't know. I haven't had a lot of sex. Normal things, I think."

I'd made my mind up. She was as close to fucking as I'd ever get her across the internet. I couldn't possibly let a girl of this quality drop off the hook so I made my move.

"I have a few days off from work soon. I think I'll visit Belgrade again."

"That's brilliant!" she said. "I can't wait!"

Forever the careful player, I also messaged Marijana to set her up as my back-up plan. We agreed to meet for coffee one afternoon on the same weekend I'd try to knock over Milena.

Finally living the dream

Flying out to Nikola Tesla Airport I was enthused, as excited as a small child riding in the driver's cabin on a steam train. After dropping off my bags I headed back out and met Milena in Snezana restaurant on the main Knez Mihailova boulevard. She walked in slowly, her hips swaying, like we were already lovers. Then she sat down at my table and just smiled dreamily, listening to my prattle.

I ate a bowl of spaghetti carbonara while she sipped coffee. The whole time she stared deep into my eyes, smiling to herself. Between mouthfuls, I touched her hands and hair, reassuring myself it was as on as it looked. I paid the bill and stood up.

"Let me show you where I'm staying," I suggested, expecting she'd wobble on the threshold and we'd need to walk around the park and drink a few beers. She agreed and fell in behind me during the short walk home. Despite her strong frame with others, she was now docile and easily led as if in a trance. Most girls enjoy following a leader, once they've ascertained you are worthy of leading.

She took off her shoes in the hallway, and my heart leapt. Hardly daring to hope, I nonchalantly put on some music and offered her a drink. Then we sat on the bed and kissed. Again, I kept expecting her to throw up barriers. Doesn't she know she's too hot for me? The barriers never appeared. Within five minutes, I was tugging at her jeans.

"Nick, this is really fast," she murmured.

"Yes it is, isn't it?" I agreed and ripped them off.

Ten minutes after entering the apartment, and half an hour after meeting in the cafe, I was fucking her. Even then it seemed unreal, so I fucked her again to be on the safe side, to reassure myself I wasn't dreaming. Then we lay together, and I just couldn't help thinking I'd won at life.

"I have to do some work soon," I eventually told her so she'd leave. Then I went off to meet Marijana for coffee.

Milena and I met again later that evening. This time she'd dolled up in a cocktail dress and high heels. It was both sweet that she'd tried so hard to look nice for me, and comical that she clearly didn't know how to walk in such heels. She towered above me, and I felt like Bernie Ecclestone taking his trophy wife down the red carpet at an F-1 opening event. Then I took her home and fucked her again.

The next day I took her to the Skadarlija restaurant district. We met at Republic Square, and as I stood at a pedestrian crossing with her on my arm, who would I bump into but Branka, who was getting off a bus. She looked at me in shocked disbelief. She obviously thought she'd never see me again and had sent mean messages just a week earlier. She can't have failed to notice Milena looked an awful lot like her too. Her face fell, and she stormed off.

"Who is that?" Milena asked.

"An ex-girlfriend," I said, stating the obvious. Over the coming years, I'd find out that Belgrade is an awfully small town and running into ex-girlfriends happens surprisingly often. I was shaken seeing Branka. Not so much because of the social awkwardness but because she looked so fucking hot. Damn! Did I really just discard that woman? Why hadn't I been able to tolerate a closer connection to a girl I still clearly very much liked?

Whatever bizarre wobbles I'd had with Branka were blissfully absent with Milena. I felt absolutely comfortable in every respect, whether we were chatting, fucking, or just sitting in silence on the wall of Kalemegdan fortress gazing across the Danube river. We'd meet for coffee in the lobby of Hotel Moskova or eat in traditional restaurants in Skardarlja. The first time we ate there Milena tapped my forearm and whispered conspiratorially.

"Can you see that couple there?" she said, meaning an athletic-looking man in his mid-twenties and his beautiful girlfriend eating a few tables behind me. "He's the star player of Partizan Belgrade. She's a famous television presenter."

And there they were on a Saturday night date in the same restaurant as me, a barely-employed layabout living in a dilapidated nursing home. If there was any one moment that made me feel like Ernest Hemingway, it was now.

Milena was my first legitimately top-tier beauty in her prime. I'd had the Russian catwalk model Zaria in early 2011 but she'd been a few years past her prime and didn't look as good in real life as her perfect-ten photos. Zaria also gave me shit because of my lack of commitment. In contrast, Milena was twenty and had all the time in the world. Like many young women, she simply didn't feel the need to lock me down.

This is it, I kept thinking. *You've won. This is the prize you'd had your eyes on since the very beginning.* I'd pulled, laid, and deeply converted a woman who was exactly what I wanted; physically, temperamentally, intellectually, in the absolute prime of her life. I couldn't think of anything I wanted more. I returned to London warm with the glow of satisfaction.

Astonishingly like Sophia Loren

International Man Of Mystery

THIRTY EIGHT

INTERNATIONAL MAN OF MYSTERY

I stayed on my Milena high for well over a week, reminding myself that notch fatigue is more a symptom of working too hard for mediocre quality than it is any general repetitiveness in clacking skirt. We stayed in touch and slipped into a stable communication pattern. My coffee date with Marijana that same weekend had gone well too, her having shown quite high investment by taking a four-hour bus ride just for that.

"I have to return today," she'd said, "My parents don't know I'm here."

Marijana was twenty-three years old. Her (self-reported) extreme chastity and somewhat diva-like personality intrigued me. I'd come to learn daygame granted me access to the type of girl you can rarely find on the bar scene, yet it was quite a surprise to get a rare nightgame hit, too. She lived in a second-tier town with her stable Serbian family headed by a strong father figure. Like many such girls, she kept them informed of her movements rather than sneaking off secretly.

Marijana was definitely not a party girl. We'd met in August when she was in Belgrade for a week-long rehearsal with her choir, and her best friend there wanted to celebrate her birthday on the nightclub boats. She'd tolerated me barging in so aggressively because she'd been in a great mood, liked the look of me, and loved the English accent. My boldness merely supercharged an already-existing instant attraction. She'd dated one previous boyfriend (a musician / struggling artist type) for two years before breaking it off twelve months earlier. She obviously liked bad boys but was not the type to go on a promiscuous tear with them. I was in the right place at the right time, a more important factor in getting laid than any system ever is.

I was developing a good sense for when I'd caught a chaste girl at the "right" time rather than simply catching a promiscuous girl at "any" time. If I sensed I was bringing out something deep within a girl, something that rarely surfaced, it gave me considerably more pleasure than rattling a promiscuous girl who just happened to be choosing me as the stunt cock for when she wanted to get her rocks off. My behaviour towards them must have been perceptibly different to the girls too because it was the chaste girls who hooked stronger, often for as long as several years.

Shortly after Mick had disturbed us rolling around on the grass outside the nightclub boat, her friends flooded out and took us with them. We walked down the riverside in the breeze and across a long bridge, finally stopping outside at a McDonald's to catch the bus. It felt like venturing into the heart of darkness.

There were four girls and three men. One of the men was a bald mid-twenties guy whose eyes burned with jealous rage. He kept badmouthing me in Serbo-Croat to the group and a few times said in English that I should "go home." The girls were instinctively repulsed by his jealousy and equally disapproving of his lack of hospitality to an invited guest.

"I don't want to spoil your party," I told Marijana as we stood up on the bus, holding on to one of the leather straps hanging from the ceiling. "We can meet another time if you prefer."

"Oh, ignore him. He's just angry because I'm the only single girl, and he thought I'd been picked for him. He's been after me all night."

Girls know what men are doing. One foolish assumption men make, and this is baked into indirect game techniques, too, is that girls can't see their seduction attempts. There is a world of difference between nudge-wink covert intent, and pretending you have no intent. Just own it, or girls will be disgusted by you.

The bus disgorged us outside a Tito-era housing project with a dozen high-rise apartment blocks. Our host, a genial young man, lived on the third floor. We sat in his lounge, Marijana resting on me like a girlfriend, as we drank more beer and partook of the inane chit-chat that dominates these parties. Twice I dragged her into a bedroom and tried to fuck her but couldn't get further than her tits in my mouth and my finger in her pussy. If the apartment had been empty, I'm sure she'd have fucked, this was a social pressure problem. Eventually dawn broke, and I took her number then got a bus back into the centre. She was returning to her hometown that afternoon so a date was impossible.

The coffee we had in October was pleasant. It was a cold day so I waited in a small cafe looking out over Republic Square. She'd made a big effort with fashion and make-up.

"My family really cares about looking your best," she explained. "One time I visited my grandmother without wearing any make-up and she scolded me. 'How can you walk around in public looking so plain?' she'd said."

Marijana was quite the talker. Mostly I listened and threw out bait to direct her. We made out a little and walked through the fortress grounds. I did try pulling her home but she wasn't having it. I took her back to the bus stop and said goodbye, promising to stay in touch. We continued our regular Facebook chats and occasional Skype video calls. I could see she was falling for me, becoming increasingly emotionally invested and reactive to me. I arranged to take a long weekend off from work in December and visit her hometown.

"Ho, ho, ho," said my manager Malcolm as we took an elevator after a business meeting. I'd told him I was returning to Serbia for the second time in as many months. "Got a secret girl in Serbia have you?"

"A gentleman never tells," I said, resisting the urge to disclose any aspect of my lifestyle to my co-workers.

That December, I spent Thursday night in Belgrade fucking Milena then took the painfully slow bus to Nis the next morning, arriving mid-afternoon. It was a noticeable step-down from Belgrade. Immediately upon getting off the bus I felt like I was in the middle of a Kosovan market – lots of dirty, rat-faced men ran tiny market stalls selling mobile phone cases, cheap socks, and other tat. It was a reminder that Central and Eastern Europe are considerably less attractive countries than their Old Town capitals would have you believe. It felt like Albania; ramshackle lean-tos and huts abounded, each with a selection of grotty-looking fruit or second-hand shoes or similar. The vendors wore threadbare tracksuits and dirty old shapeless Metallica t-shirts. Most of their hair looked as though they'd cut it themselves while drunk.

Squeezing in a date with Marijana
before Mileena shows up

As I walked towards the city centre, faces whitened and the atmosphere improved. Downtown Nis was pretty nice, with a wide pedestrian boulevard for its high street and many attractive old buildings. There was even a small castle tucked behind a grand fortified wall. It was cold and wet with barely a soul on the streets. Not a place to daygame.

Marijana had told her father about my visit, and he'd insisted I give them the address of my apartment so that they could go round and check it out, whether for my benefit or hers, I didn't know. What I did know was that I'd placed myself into a structurally vulnerable position by coming all this way to her home territory and requiring little investment from her. I was gambling that my gut instinct was correct, that she'd already fallen for me and would fuck at some point over the three nights I had in town.

Nis high street

I checked in and settled myself down with a Dennis Wheatley paperback for a couple of hours until Marijana finished her family obligations and came around. We ate in a glorious local restaurant, my steak and potatoes being among the best I'd ever had. Afterwards we sat in a nice café, then she came up to my room but wouldn't fuck. It was a pleasant evening and went exactly according to expectations. Marijana knew I was here for three days so she'd probably priced-in the need to refuse me the first evening, that would consolidate her self-image as not being too easy and free her up to fuck the next day.

The next day, she invited herself over around lunchtime when I'd barely gotten out of bed. Her mood was bright and breezy. She showed me a fantastic basement bar. We sat back sipping coffee in a padded leather booth, chatting and looking around, feeling so tranquil. It was exactly the life I wanted to live. Civilisation remains intact in Serbia. Masculine men and feminine women were everywhere. Of the ten girls I could see in the cafe, the top seven would have shone like stars in a London nightclub putting all the local trollops to shame. They weren't merely hot, they were Full Audrey. Well, physically they were probably more Full Sophia Loren but RSG had fallen into calling classy girls Audrey after Jimmy's predilection. Each wore an air of sophistication with posture and gestures to match. I was entranced. Afterwards, we ate a late lunch and broke for a few hours so she could run some family errands. Marijana came around in the evening, and we went out for dinner again.

As confident as I was of the eventual lay, she'd clearly crossed the sexual Rubicon, I just didn't know if it would happen fast enough to get it done that holiday. She came back into my apartment easily. I put some music on and we did some playful dancing before I picked her up over my shoulder, spinning her as she screeched to be let down. *Big-time arousal.* I tossed her down onto the sofa, climbed on her and made out. She immediately began grinding her crotch into me. That was the big signal it was on *right now*. I pulled her belt off without resistance, undressed her, carried her to the bed in the same room, and fucked her.

It was good sex, but immediately afterwards as we lay in bed, her forebrain fired up, and she began doubting herself. She conversation veered madly like a drunk driver on black ice with two shredded tires, careening this way and that out of control. Poor girl. Deep down, I could sense her satisfaction and liberation, but she desperately needed comfort after acting so far out of character. I stroked her hair and pulled her into me. As she nuzzled up against me, her clothes strewn across my apartment floor, I ruminated on how not only was she a chaste girl who just moments ago had doubled her lifetime cock-count, but also that she was of quite astonishing quality. She wasn't merely hot, but elegant, talented, womanly, and intelligent - the type of girl last seen in England circa-1960. I'd gotten another Full Audrey. I most definitely wanted to keep her around.

On my final day in Nis, Marijana came round to the apartment at lunchtime, and I took her directly to the bed and fucked her again. We went out for a walk and she showed me the castle. They'd built a delightful small cafe into the castle walls, probably a converted stables or store room from the days when the castle was employed in actual defence. I sat back with my glass of Johnnie Walker Black Label and a fat Cuban cigar, Marijana leaning into me.

"This is the life," I said aloud. "Whiskey, castles, and a cigar."
"And with a pretty girl?"
"Yes, and with a pretty girl. Living the dream."

How I always wanted to be

She was still trying to integrate her wild weekend (by her standards) into her identity, so it was no surprise she took umbrage at such an innocuous statement. "Oh, I could be any pretty girl, couldn't I?" she complained.

She knew there was no future in our relationship, but she yearned for the adventure and wider horizons that I represented. I left town early the next morning, feeling like a cowboy riding off into the sunset. I met up with Milena again in Belgrade and fucked her again then took a flight back to London. Marijana and I continued to talk on Facebook, but she soon engineered a pointless squabble to give herself an excuse to dump me. I wasn't happy about losing such a good girl, but it was an entirely predictable damage control effort on her part so I didn't resent her for it.

I was next in Belgrade in August 2013 and met Marijana for coffee as she was fortuitously in town. I was strictly friend-zoned but enjoyed the pleasant chat nonetheless. I spent six weeks in Belgrade in spring of 2014, and by now she was frequently there due to work. We met up for an hour in Studentski Park, and I could tell that she was horny.

"I haven't had sex since you were in Nis," she admitted. That was almost a year and a half earlier. Some girls really don't put out easily! I pulled her into my apartment right next to the park and fucked her. She lay in bed stroking my face. "Can you teach me how to have casual sex without feeling terrible afterwards?" she asked.

"No. It's not good for you to become that type of girl," I assured her.

I explained the differences between men and women's hard-wiring for casual sex and that she shouldn't go against her natural inclinations lest it degrade her ability to pair bond and find the quality man she wanted to marry.

"I'm an outlier," I explained. "You really don't want to become more like me."

"I think I just won't have much sex in my life," she moaned.

We met again that trip, but she was on her period. The final time I saw her (at the time of writing) was in September 2015. We had a drink in the cafe outside my apartment and then fucked in my apartment. It was her first sex since the last time I'd nailed her.

"You really need to get a boyfriend," I advised. "It's fine for me to release your sexual tension when I'm in town, but that's not a long-term solution." At twenty-six, time was on her side but if a few more years passed, her situation might yet become desperate.

The type of Game you do determines the type of girls you get. Daygame begins with the widest of nets – literally any girl walking anywhere. The lack of any pre-open filter means it's tremendously inefficient in terms of opens-to-closes. It's also tremendously stressful because you're stone cold sober and have to show intent early. However, the big positive is that without it, classy girls like Marijana are unlikely to enter into your orbit. I'd been very lucky indeed to not just find a girl like her in a nightclub but manage to make her interested in me in such an environment.

Three of my last four closes had been tall, young, leggy Serbian girls each with grace, class, and one prior sexual partner. I had arrived. Surely, I'd stepped up to a higher level of game and life. Four years into The Game, and I was now banging exactly the girls I dreamt of.

Surely nothing could go wrong now...

EPILOGUE

"It didn't make sense that I'd be here, in Château Hampstead. I mean, these guys were hard-core PUAs, but there I was. At that point I wasn't worried. Besides, it was fun. I got to make like I was notorious."

It was early 2013, and I lay in bed with Dovile. She'd still visit me from Lithuania, and it felt so comforting to have her around. We drifted off into sleep. What seemed like moments later, we were rudely awoken by The Stone Roses blasting out of studio speakers next door. I muttered darkly and checked my phone – 4 am. Fuck! Jimmy was obviously drunk and angry. Dovile put the pillow over her head and tried to block out the noise.

"Wake up!" he shouted, banging on my door. These were maybe the first words he'd spoken to me since Sarajevo the previous summer. "Wake up, you Geordie bastard."

I recognised Drunk Jimmy in the speech pattern and vocal tones. He'd obviously been out drinking, come home steaming, and gotten a bee in his bonnet about something. I remembered his stories about getting drunk in Newcastle and starting fights in bars for no reason. *Oh fucking hell, here we go*, I thought, *he's gotten fighty and decided to have it out with me*.

I'm not one to run from confrontation, and the six months of Cold War had exhausted me. I got out of bed, slipped on my pyjamas, and did a quick mental inventory of Jimmy's fighting style that I'd figured out watching him spar Lee a year earlier. I had to watch out for a long right hand over the top and perhaps a headbutt, though being five inches shorter than him the latter seemed unfeasible.

I opened the door a crack, keeping my foot firmly wedged behind it so he couldn't burst in and attack. Perhaps he'd drunk himself up into a state where he wanted to fight. For all I knew, he might have had a hammer in his hand.

My sleepy mind was blowing everything out of proportion. I'd only been awake twenty seconds so I wasn't thinking straight, it was the same sleepy mood that makes you think your dressing gown is a werewolf at the foot of your bed. To my surprise, Jimmy was standing a few feet back in the corridor, well out of punching range. He didn't look at all angry. As my brain finally woke up, I realised I'd gotten rather carried away in future-projecting conflict scenarios.

"I want to talk to you," he announced.

"Okay, let's go to your room because Dovile is in here" I replied.

RSG on the road

The familiar adrenalin rush of impending conflict bubbled through my bloodstream, and I loved it. We went in, he sat down on the bed, and I waited.

"This can't go on," he said. "We were great friends. I hate losing my good friends."

Jesus, that was a surprise! I'd never seen him so conciliatory. He didn't actually apologise (and to this day insists *I* abandoned *him* in

Sarajevo) but he was making a genuine effort to repair the burned bridge. I stood there nodding, my high alert status dissipating. Jimmy continued to tangle himself up in his own frame as he talked but the underlying message was clear. He wanted to go back to being friends and was willing to make the first move. I felt exactly the same way, but my own frame had prevented me from breaking the deadlock.

I felt relieved and silently thanked him for making the first move. There'd been bad behaviour on both sides, but it was now all water under the bridge. It may be that something had broken irretrievably but I agreed to give it a try. We shook hands and as I walked to the door he slumped over on his bed and fell into a drunken stupor.

Commaraderie with RSG

I showed myself out.

Things remained tense, but at least now we were speaking. It would take another two years of tentative contact, mostly on WhatsApp, before we'd both shaken off our various personal upheavals and gotten back into a groove. By then I was living in Newcastle, and he was alternating between Manchester and Zagreb. A few times earlier we'd had aborted meet-up attempts where logistics didn't quite work out. It was like trying to get a hot girl onto a Day 2.

"I'm surprised," John told me the day after our drunken ceasefire agreement. "We all knew Jimmy was having a meltdown, but there was the bigger, more permanent problem: that your frames are simply incompatible."

"I don't push my frame out. I'm the immovable object, not the irresistible force," I protested.

"Yeah, right," he sneered. "You're like a fucking woodpecker chipping away. All through 2012 you were getting progressively more full of yourself, and I think Jimmy instinctively wanted to get away from the toxic cloud."

That sounded harsh. I'm a good guy.

"Look, what is it that you do to everyone in the house? What's your position here?" he asked. I'd have liked to have replied "leader and inspiration," but I sensed he wasn't leaning in that direction.

John had folded his arms, staring at me. He had all the tell-tale facial ticks and body language that he was about to launch into a grand exposition of BodiThought. I pushed out a deep breath, relaxing like a boxer about to absorb a body shot.

"Everyone here is a compensatory narcissist," he said, meaning we were all former codependents who had used Game to switch into a kind of synthetic narcissist clothing. "There are only three exceptions. Lee is nice but dim. Mick is a normie with a hint of snide. And then there's you, a genuine bona-fide (full blown) natural narcissist."

"No, I'm not," I protested.

"Denial! Denial is the primary coping strategy of the narcissist!" he exclaimed, like a prosecutor waving a signed confession in front of a jury. He was greatly enjoying this, taking time to sip his green tea and savour the moment before continuing.

"So what is your role in the house? You are the Emperor Narcissist, you turn all of us fake narcissists back into co-dependents."

All I heard was *Emperor*. That sounded cool.

"You think Emperor sounds cool, don't you?" he said quickly. Fuck, he'd baited that trap. "That's pure grandiosity. Pure *narcissistic* grandiosity. Look, it's simple. We all have our frame wobbles, and when the world scares us we come up to you and let your unshakeable frame reassure us that the world does have meaning and that we can comprehend it. I do that, and Steve does that, coming to your room for help. It's a codependent relationship where you rebuild our frames when we're down and in return we feed you narcissistic supply"

"We were talking about Jimmy, not me. I don't see how this is relevant."

"Can't you see? Can't you SEE????" he almost shouted. "Tony disappeared into his room rutting fat slags off OK Cupid because his frame can't hold off yours. Johnny hides in his room watching US drama shows on his projector and reading Ayn Rand for the same reason. Jimmy is no fool, he instinctively realised your frame was corroding his so he pulled the ripcord and got the fuck out."

"You make it sound like I'm the reason *Rock Solid Game* fell apart," I retorted. He just looked at me, silently, then sipped his green tea. A man can convince anyone he's somebody else, but not himself.

I felt like he was painting me as Keyser Soze from my favourite movie, *The Usual Suspects*. The whole plot revolves around Verbal Gint, a nervous cripple played brilliantly by Kevin Spacey, being interviewed by police investigating a mass murder on an oil tanker. They are trying to show him that he was duped by his "best friend" who was really underground legend and criminal bogeyman Keyser Soze. The big reveal is that it's actually *Gint himself* who is Soze, architect of it all. Soze is just play-acting the role of Gint because a moment of carelessness got him arrested and he must avoid identification until his associates can secure his release.

My mind swirled and a new realisation began to dawn on me. For four years I believed I'd been making progress on my game journey, particularly in straightening out the kinks in my social skills and confronting my personal demons head on. I'd wrenched myself out of a lifestyle that didn't suit me, that of a corporate drone earning a high salary but remaining part of the herd. I'd *unplugged from the matrix*, working hard to become an International Man of Mystery. I'd devoured all manner of Game and self-improvement material to understand psychology and social dynamics. I'd read and travelled widely, like a renaissance man should. I'd even gone to therapy sessions precisely in order identify and resolve deeply buried issues.

I'd conscientiously flipped every stone in my quest to become a more balanced and more attractive man. Evidence was mounting that I'd been successful, too; the foreign adventures, the cool friends, and the hotter girls. I'd recognised myself slipping towards the Dark Side of game and pulled out of the nosedive, reassessing my motivations and changing my style.

I'd reached my goals. Game had *delivered*. I'd achieved so much I could probably even write a book about it some day. Here I was standing at the summit of Mount Awesome feeling very pleased with myself..... but John had hit a nerve I didn't even know was exposed.

And time marches on

Something didn't feel right.

My success felt fragile. Ephemeral. While I'd certainly come on in leaps and bounds, I'd deluded myself as to the scope of my achievement and the degree to which I'd improved my character. I was still difficult, manipulative, and ruthlessly self-interested. I didn't want to be. Clearly, I wasn't done with the Game.

Self-awareness had surfaced for a brief moment. After that my guess is I'd not hear from it ever again. The greatest trick your ego ever pulls is convincing you it doesn't exists. And like that – *poof!* – it is gone.

Continue your Player's Journey with Nick Krauser's other resources!

The Model

Everything you need to know about street pick-up is packed into these cutting-edge textbooks. Each volume is written to match your own progress in learning the art form. *Daygame Nitro* introduces the basics of street pick-up and inner game in a simple, easy-to-follow guide. *Daygame Mastery* breaks apart the model into minute detail to help you fine-tune your method. *Daygame Infinite* unlocks your potential with extensive vibe and calibration advice.

 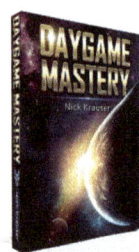 

The Journey

Dive deep into the Player's lifestyle with the most detailed and most insightful Game memoir ever written. Four massive volumes take you through every stage from zero to hero as Nick tells you his story. Higher level knowledge seeps out of every page. Live the life!

   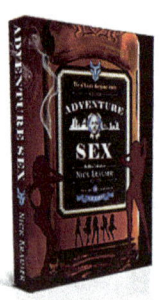

The Demonstration

It's one thing to understand the theory but another to watch, on video, how to run street game and master dating. *Daygame Overkill* provides a play-by-play breakdown of Nick's infield videos, showing you how to get Adventure Sex. *Black Book* explains the dating model in detail, and *Womanizers Bible* provides high-level theory on the Player's World.

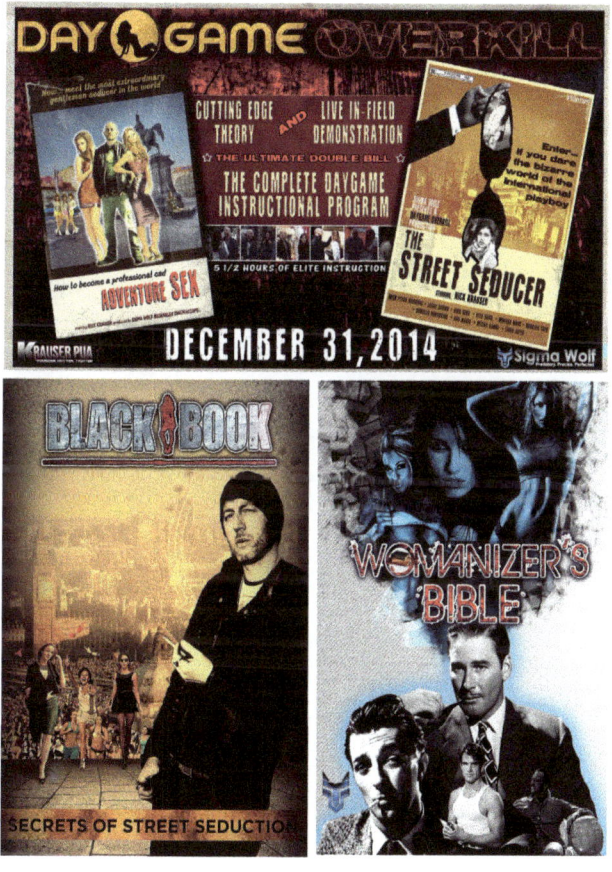

Check out sigmawolf.com and daygameoverkill.com to access these amazing resources.

www.ingramcontent.com/pod-product-compliance
Ingram Content Group UK Ltd.
Pitfield, Milton Keynes, MK11 3LW, UK
UKHW021347270725
7089UKWH00024B/388